Accounting for Colleges
and Universities

1970

BATON ROUGE

LOUISIANA STATE UNIVERSITY PRESS

Accounting for Colleges and Universities

REVISED EDITION

CLARENCE SCHEPS

AND

E. E. DAVIDSON

Preface

A GOOD ACCOUNTING system is a prime requisite of sound finance, which is an inseparable part of every business enterprise. Granting that the purpose of the educational institution is instruction, research, and public service—and not profit making—finance in all of its aspects is as important in the college and university as in the commercial organization. In the educational institution, therefore, the existence of an adequate system of accounts is essential if the fullest benefits are to be realized from the educational program of the institution.

This book is concerned with the problems of accounting in the college and university and sets forth techniques for their proper handling. The scope of the book encompasses every aspect of accounting and business practice. The "accounting system" is treated in a broad sense, including not only the fundamental techniques of record keeping and entry making but also a complete discussion of budgeting, purchasing, supply and equipment inventories, cost accounting, and financial reporting.

This volume is a revised edition of *Accounting for Colleges and Universities* by Scheps, published by the Louisiana State University Press in 1949. Its publication under the coauthorship of Scheps and Davidson is timely because the book is based on the latest revision of *College and University Business Administration*, which was published and copyrighted by the American Council on Education in

1968. The authors have made every effort to follow in minute detail the principles of accounting and financial reporting as set forth in *College and University Business Administration*. The authors use similar account titles, and in general track the terminology, definitions, and techniques which appear in that volume. In a sense this book can be viewed as a companion volume to the council's publication because it illustrates by actual entries, ledger accounts, journals and registers, forms and documents that which is only described in principle in the latter volume.

As stated previously, the material in this edition is based largely on the recommendations appearing in *College and University Business Administration*. The authors deeply appreciate the generous permission granted by the American Council on Education to use material from that publication without having to acknowledge each portion of the material so used. They are fully aware of the increased value of their publication by reason of such permission.

The authors also realize their indebtedness to the pioneering books in the field of college and university accounting and finance. They owe much to Lloyd Morey's *University and College Accounting*, E. V. Miles's *Manual of Teachers College Accounting*, and G. A. Mills's *Accounting Manual for Colleges*. John Dale Russell's book, *The Finance of Higher Education*, was of great value as a reference source in the field of college and university finance. *College & University Business* magazine published by McGraw-Hill, Inc., has been a useful source of reference.

The revision of the book was greatly assisted and expedited by the valuable editorial assistance supplied by George E. Van Dyke, who edited the 1968 version of *College and University Business Administration*.

Appreciation is expressed also to the following who read and commented on specific chapters: Tulane University—Felix C. Byxbe, Jesse B. Morgan, Lawrence J. Guichard, Samuel V. Cresap; University of Oklahoma—David A. Willard, Edwin E. Glover, Jack E. Coke, R. Dean McGlamery; University of Mississippi—John W. Savage, Doyle L. Russell, Robert S. Shaw, Jesse Tutor.

Much credit is due to Gilbert L. Lee, Jr., University of Chicago, for his careful reading of the entire manuscript and his helpful suggestions, most of which are incorporated in the text.

The authors wish to express their special gratitude and appreciation to the Esso Education Foundation for making available a grant which has permitted them to obtain research and editorial assistance and has made available the travel funds necessary to enable the authors to work together in revising this edition. The production of the volume would have been greatly delayed and handicapped without this generous contribution on the part of the Esso Education Foundation.

CLARENCE SCHEPS
Tulane University
New Orleans, Louisiana
August, 1969

E. E. DAVIDSON
Oklahoma State University
Stillwater, Oklahoma
August, 1969

Contents

Charts

Forms

Accounting for Colleges
and Universities

CHAPTER I

General Principles of College
and University Accounting and Finance

ACCOUNTING IS THE means through which financial data necessary to the efficient administration of colleges and universities are recorded, classified, and reported to institutional officers, controlling bodies, and the general public. The accounting system of an educational institution must meet the requirements of that institution. The forms and documents employed in the recording of financial data depend upon and vary because of a number of factors. The size of the institution, the nature of its control, the amount and sources of its revenues, the number and types of auxiliary enterprises which it operates are a few of the considerations which determine the appropriate form of its system of financial records. Regardless of the possible diversity of technical details, however, there are certain well-defined and accepted principles of college accounting and finance. The accounting and fiscal system for any institution, large or small, privately or publicly supported, independent or church related, should be based on these principles.

Principles of institutional accounting and finance reflect codification of theories and practices developed as the result of evolution over a long period of time. Prior to 1920 very little literature on the subject of college accounting was published. In the decade 1920–1930 a developing interest in governmental and institutional accounting spread to colleges and universities. The first authoritative book on the subject, *College and University Finance*, written by

Trevor Arnett, was published by the General Education Board in 1922. Although the book includes a chapter on accounting, this work is concerned primarily with the financing of endowed institutions. The first modern study of accounting for educational institutions, *University and College Accounting*, by Lloyd Morey, appeared in 1930 and since that date many studies on college and university financial reporting have been published. In the early 1930's Morey was the chairman of a national committee to develop standard reports for institutions of higher education. The final report of the committee appeared in 1935 under the title *Financial Reports for Colleges and Universities* and for more than a decade served as the principal source of reference for accounting and reporting principles for institutions of higher education. Following the publication of the committee report in 1935 and with the assistance of the General Education Board, the American Council on Education established the Financial Advisory Service, the purpose of which was to provide help, information, and advice for colleges and universities in financial and business administration.

The forerunner of this present volume, *Accounting for Colleges and Universities*, by Clarence Scheps, appeared in 1949. In 1952 a national committee of business officers and certified public accountants brought out a volume on accounting principles, known as *College and University Business Administration*, Volume I. In 1955 a companion volume dealing primarily with college and university business administration was published by the American Council on Education. In 1968 a third national committee, under the chairmanship of Clarence Scheps, produced a revision of *College and University Business Administration*—this time a single volume which dealt with both accounting principles and with college and university business administration. Chapter 14 of that volume, entitled "Principles and Procedures of Accounting and Financial Reporting," will become the standard reference for colleges and universities and will be widely followed. Much of the material in chapter 1 of this present volume is based on chapter 14 of the 1968 edition of *College and University Business Administration*.

Before enumerating and discussing the basic principles of accounting and financial reporting, as enunciated by the National

Committee, principles related to college and university business practices are grouped and discussed. Not all of these principles are related directly to the accounting office because they cover all the diverse functions of the office or group of offices usually referred to in college administration as the Business Office.

First, those principles which are concerned with the organization and responsibility of the business office and the chief business officer:

1. The business and financial functions of the college should be centralized in a single business officer responsible to the president.

2. The chief business officer should be appointed by the governing board upon the nomination of the president. The selection of this officer is an important factor in the effective business management of the institution because of the numerous and varied responsibilities centered in the business office. He should be qualified through experience to handle the business affairs of the institution and qualified by temperament to deal with the diverse and frequently unique personalities of the campus and business world with whom he must associate. In addition to holding at least a bachelor's degree, he should have what is often termed an "educational philosophy." Finally, he must realize fully that the purpose of his office is to serve the college and to help in the furtherance of its educational program.

3. The more important functions which should be centralized in the business office include (a) assistance in the preparation and the control of the budget, (b) collection and custody of all institutional funds, (c) handling the funds and properties belonging to endowments, (d) establishment and operation of a proper system of accounting and financial reporting, (e) supervision over the operation and maintenance of the physical plant, (f) supervision over the purchasing of supplies and the control over inventories, (g) financial supervision over auxiliary enterprises, (h) supervision over the financial aspects of student organizations and loan funds, and (i) participation in the long-range planning program for the entire institution.

Second, those principles which are concerned with the institutional budget:

1. An annual budget should be prepared covering all operations and all funds. The budget should be a carefully devised financial plan of operations for a given period of time, usually a year. The governing board should establish principles concerning the method of budget making as well as the routine of budget adjustments. In connection with the latter point, it is emphasized that every budget should either carry a contingency reserve or should leave unappropriated a portion of expected revenues which can be allocated by the chief executive or the board as unanticipated needs arise.

2. The budget not only must be carefully prepared but also must be carefully controlled. This control can best be achieved by incorporating the budget into the accounting records. Budget control should be as rigid as practicable, seeking to prevent serious overexpenditures in individual budgets. Budget reports of both revenues and expenditures should be made available at regular intervals, usually a month, to the governing board, institutional officers, and those responsible for individual budgets, which clearly disclose actual operations as compared with budget estimates.

Third, those principles which are concerned with the function of purchasing and stores control:

1. Responsibility for all institutional purchasing should be centralized in the business office. If the size of the institution justifies it, a separate office of purchasing, headed by a purchasing agent, may be created. Centralized purchasing is desirable for at least four principal reasons:

(a) It effects economies through quantity buying and through elimination of duplicate effort.

(b) Through the plan of requisitions, it makes possible a system of budgetary control.

(c) It facilitates in a great measure the receipt, the entry, and the auditing of invoices and other documents relating to expenditures.

(d) It releases faculty members from a time-consuming responsibility.

2. A logical adjunct of the purchasing function is the control over storerooms. Even in small colleges, substantial economies can be effected through quantity purchases of standard supplies used throughout the campus. The purchasing office, or other division of

the business office, should be responsible for the maintenance of an adequate inventory in the central storerooms.

3. Another subdivision of the purchasing function is the control over the physical property of the institution. In order to purchase intelligently, as well as for other reasons, a perpetual inventory of all movable equipment should be maintained by the business office and made readily available to the purchasing agent.

Fourth, those principles which are concerned with the operation of the physical plant:

1. There should exist centralized management of the operation and maintenance of the physical plant in all its phases. Preferably, the immediate responsibility for maintenance of plant should be vested in a superintendent or director of physical plant. This officer should be responsible directly to the chief business officer and should supervise all phases of the operation and maintenance of the physical plant.

2. Closely allied with plant operation and maintenance is the keeping of adequate cost records for the physical plant. The accounting system should be so devised that, with the cooperation of the operation and maintenance department, a distinction can be made between the cost of operating and maintaining that part of plant devoted to educational and general purposes and that part devoted to auxiliary enterprises. In addition, a record of the cost of operation and maintenance of buildings or other units should be provided as an integral part of the accounting system.

Fifth, those principles which are concerned with the postaudit:

As in every other type of organization, the accounts and records of an educational institution should be audited by competent independent accountants at least once a year. There are at least four purposes of the independent postaudit—verification of the accuracy of the financial records, verification of the integrity of the employees of the institution, expert advice on accounting methods and business practices, and verification of financial statements. The institution has an obligation to the state or to its benefactors and, accordingly, should make a periodical accounting of the funds entrusted to it. The best method of making such an accounting is through the independent audit. In the case of publicly supported institutions, these audits frequently are conducted by an auditing agency of the state. In such cases the audits should conform to the generally accepted principles of institutional auditing.

Sixth, those principles which are concerned with the relationship of the business office to student organizations and student loan funds:

1. The finances of student organizations and activities should be subject to the supervision of the business office. The usual examples of such student organizations are student body associations, student annuals, and student newspapers. The accounts and records of those organizations which are supervised should be made a part of the regular accounting system. All money collected by them should be deposited in the business office. Disbursements should be made by college checks against these funds. In cases where the organizations have a faculty advisor, all vouchers should be approved by that official.

2. The management of student loan funds should be predicated on principles of sound business practices and should be handled in such a manner as to insure adequate protection of the funds. Transactions involving interest and loans should be accounted for in the regular accounting system, and the business officer should be responsible for the ultimate collection of all loans. Although frequently the responsibility for making student loans vests in an officer outside the business office, there should be participation by the business officer in policies governing the awarding of such financial assistance.

Seventh, those principles which are concerned with the accounting for endowment and similar funds:

There should exist a suitable organization for the administration of endowment funds under the jurisdiction of the business office. The terms of each endowment gift should be adhered to and the accounts should be maintained in a way that will provide an adequate distinction between the income and principal of each fund. The business office should provide the governing board at frequent intervals with complete information regarding the status of the funds and the makeup of the investment portfolio. Responsibility with regard to the various aspects of the administration of endowments should be clearly outlined by the governing board. There should be special requirements with respect to the custody and the safeguarding of endowment securities and other investments. Responsibility for the investment program should be vested in the governing board. The audit of endowment funds should be thorough and complete.

BASIC PRINCIPLES AND STANDARD PROCEDURES
OF FINANCIAL REPORTING

College and University Business Administration, published in 1968, enumerates twenty-two basic principles relating to accounting and financial reporting. The chapters which follow herein, describing in detail the forms and procedures used in college and university accounting, are based on these principles. Terminology used throughout this volume, as well as the general classification of accounts, is based on *College and University Business Administration*.

To meet the requirements of financial accounting and reporting for colleges and universities the following basic principles are enumerated in chapter 14 of *College and University Business Administration:*

1. *The accounts should be classified in balanced fund groups in the books of account and in the financial reports.*

The obligations of a college or university are so varied and the use of its resources are so restricted that it is desirable to subdivide its monies into funds. Each fund has its own resources and obligations and is in every sense a separate accounting entity. According to *College and University Business Administration*, a fund is "an accounting entity established for the purpose of carrying on specific activities or attaining certain objectives in accordance with special regulations, or limitations." [1] The fund groups recommended are the Current Funds (Unrestricted and Restricted), Loan Funds, Endowment and Similar Funds, Annuity and Life Income Funds,

[1] American Council on Education, *College and University Business Administration* (Washington, 1968), 279.

Plant Funds (Unexpended and Investment in Plant), and Agency Funds.

2. *All financial transactions should be recorded and reported by fund group.*

The transactions, including receipts and disbursements, should be recorded in the appropriate fund groups and should not be intermingled. The Balance Sheet prepared at the end of the fiscal period provides for a disclosure of the assets, liabilities, and fund balances of each separately balanced fund group. Changes in fund balances from one fiscal period to another should be reflected in the Statement of Changes in Fund Balances.

3. *The Current Funds group consists of funds available for current operations, including those for restricted as well as those for unrestricted purposes.*

Balances of unrestricted and restricted funds should appear separately in the Current Funds group, even though the assets of the fund groups may be combined. Unrestricted current funds are those funds which are available for all purposes of the institution, subject only to the discretion of the governing board. Restricted current funds are those funds which, while available for current operating purposes, are subject to limitations or restrictions placed upon them by individuals or agencies outside the institution. If an institution elects to report unrestricted gifts in the statement of fund balances, the unallocated portion of such gifts should appear as a separate subdivision of current fund balances.

4. *The Loan Funds group consists of funds which are loanable to students, faculty, and staff.*

Loan funds, classified by source and purpose, constitute a separate fund group in the accounts and reports. Examples of different kinds of loan funds include appropriations from governmental bodies, gifts, grants, and bequests designated by donors to be used for student loans, some of which may be refundable under certain conditions, and funds which are otherwise unrestricted but which have been designated to be used as loan funds by the governing board.

Funds, the principal of which is to be invested with only the income available for loans, are classified as Endowment Funds and should be included in that fund group. The income from such funds should be transferred to the Loan Funds group and expended therefrom.

5. *The Endowment and Similar Funds group includes those funds whose principal is nonexpendable as of the date of reporting and is invested, or is available for investment, for the purpose of producing income.*

Three types of funds are included in this group:

(a) *Endowment funds* are funds the principal of which donors have stipulated must be maintained inviolate and in perpetuity with only the income from the investment of the funds available for expenditure.

(b) *Term endowment funds* are funds which may be released from the status of endowment upon the happening of a particular event or the passage of a stated period of time, as specified by the donors.

(c) *Quasi-endowment funds*, or funds functioning as endowment, are those funds which the governing board rather than a donor has determined, at least for the time being, are to be retained and invested as though they were endowment funds.

6. *Funds held in trust by others should not be reported as belonging to an institution.*

Such funds are not actually in the possession nor under the control of the college or university and, therefore, should not be reported as assets of the institution. However, where such funds are material in amount they should be indicated by footnote or other reference in the financial reports. Income from such funds is recorded in the Statement of Current Funds Revenues, Expenditures, and Transfers. The income is included under Endowment Income if the fund was established under an irrevocable trust. If the fund was established under a revocable trust, the income should be reported as a gift.

7. *The Annuity and Life Income Funds group includes those*

funds acquired by an institution subject to annuity contracts, living trust agreements, or gifts and bequests reserving life income to one or more beneficiaries.

Since Annuity and Life Income Funds have different characteristics and obligations, their transactions should be reported separately in the financial statements. Earnings from the investment of these funds should be reported in the Statement of Changes in Fund Balances—Annuity and Life Income Funds.

8. *The Plant Funds group consists of funds to be used for the construction, rehabilitation, and acquisition of physical properties for institutional purposes; funds already expended for plant properties; funds set aside for the renewal and replacement thereof; and funds accumulated for the retirement of indebtedness thereon.*

Properties belonging to endowment funds should be reported in the Endowment Funds group. Plant assets, including land, buildings, improvements other than buildings, and equipment, should be carried in the accounts at cost if purchased or constructed and at appraised values in the cases of gifts.

9. *The necessity for providing for renewals and replacements of the physical plant facilities and other real properties of an institution depends upon the class of property under consideration and the financial program of the institution.*

In the case of properties used for educational and auxiliary enterprises purposes, depreciation accounting as used in commercial organizations does not apply. However, if an institution wishes to do so, current funds revenues may be set aside for the renewal, replacement, or expansion of educational or auxiliary plant facilities. In such cases, cash or other liquid assets should be transferred from the Current Funds group to the unexpended plant funds section of the Balance Sheet. Current revenues so allocated should be reported in the Statement of Current Funds Revenues, Expenditures, and Transfers as transfers to Plant Funds. In order to protect the integrity of endowment funds principal, normal depreciation accounting concepts should be followed in accounting for the operations of real properties, except land, belonging to endowment and similar funds.

10. *The Agency Funds group consists of funds in the custody of the institution but not belonging to it.*

Funds of this nature include those belonging to student organizations, faculty committees, or other groups in the institution. Receipts and disbursements of such funds do not constitute current fund revenues and expenditures and are not included in current fund operating statements.

11. *Interfund borrowings of a temporary nature should be reported as assets of the fund group making the advances and as liabilities of the fund groups receiving the advances.*

The purpose of this principle is to insure that loans or advances made between fund groups are properly disclosed in the financial statements. In the fund group making the advance, the transaction is recorded as an asset; in the fund group receiving the advance, the transaction is recorded as a liability.

12. *All funds restricted by the donor or granting agency at the time of receipt with regard to the purpose for which they may be expended should be recorded as additions to the fund balances of the appropriate fund group.*

The purpose of this principle is to insure that the institution uses the resources in accordance with conditions imposed by a donor or a grantor outside the institution. Funds which otherwise are unrestricted as to use but upon which a governing board has placed restrictions are not restricted funds in the sense intended by this principle.

13. *Unrestricted current funds, exclusive of unrestricted gifts and bequests, regardless of source, must be reported as revenues in total in the year received or accrued, in the Statement of Current Funds Revenues, Expenditures, and Transfers.*

The principal sources of unrestricted revenues are tuition and fees, unrestricted endowment income, governmental appropriations for operations, indirect cost allowances, income from temporary investments of current funds, sales and services of educational departments, and the income of auxiliary enterprises.

14. *All unrestricted gifts and bequests must be reported initially in the year in which received in one statement, either the Statement of Current Funds Revenues, Expenditures, and Transfers, or the Statement of Changes in Fund Balances—Unrestricted Current Funds. The method employed must be used consistently from year to year.*

A major effect of this principle is to permit an option in the handling of unrestricted gifts and bequests. The institution may apply to the support of current operations all unrestricted gifts and bequests in the year in which received, or may hold unrestricted gifts and bequests for subsequent application or designation. The financial report should reflect in a single statement the total received during the year from unrestricted gifts and bequests and should clearly disclose how these resources were applied during the fiscal period. If an institution elects to apply unrestricted gifts and bequests to the support of current operations in the year in which received, all such receipts should be reported as current fund revenues in the Statement of Current Funds Revenues, Expenditures, and Transfers under the caption, Gifts.

If an institution elects to hold unrestricted gifts and bequests for later application—either to current operations or to plant, loan, or endowment purposes—the receipt of all unrestricted gifts and bequests must be reported in the Statement of Changes in Fund Balances—Unrestricted Current Funds—Gifts. As such receipts are applied to current operations, they must appear as unrestricted revenues in the Statement of Current Funds Revenues, Expenditures, and Transfers under the caption, Gifts Applied.

It is emphasized that *all* unrestricted gifts and bequests must be reported by one method or the other; it is improper to report a portion of such receipts in one manner and the balance in the other. It is emphasized also that the method employed must be followed consistently from year to year.

15. *Restricted current funds must be reported as revenues only to the extent expended during the year.*

Restricted current funds represent resources received for restricted operating purposes, the related expenditures of which may be extended beyond the fiscal year in which received. Such items constitute current revenues only to the extent the money is expended in the current fiscal year in accordance with the terms of the gift or donation.

16. *Transfers and allocations of unrestricted current funds must be reported in the Statement of Changes in Fund Balances—Unrestricted Current Funds, with the limited exception specified below.*

A governing board may assign unrestricted funds to fund groups other than current funds and may modify or reverse such designations at a later time. Also, unrestricted current funds may be set aside by the governing board for operating purposes in future fiscal years. The specific exception referred to in the principle occurs when it is the intention of a governing board that a portion of unrestricted revenues of the current fiscal year is to be transferred to another fund group. Such transfer may be reported as a deduction in the transfers section of the Statement of Current Funds Revenues, Expenditures, and Transfers.

17. *Earnings from endowment funds investments should be reported as income from such funds only to the extent that they are distributed to endowment income accounts.*

If endowment funds are separately invested, the earnings from the investment should be recorded in appropriate income accounts for the various funds and reported in full as income in the year received.

If endowment funds are pooled for investment management purposes, the earnings from the investments should be distributed to the income accounts of the participating funds in accordance with the method in which the investment pool is operated. The so-called market-value base of distribution is recommended, in which funds participate on the basis of the number of shares held by each fund.

It is recognized that some institutions use income stabilization reserves for the purpose of insuring regularity and consistency of the amount of endowment income from year to year. The method of establishing such reserves and of providing additions to them will also influence the distribution of endowment funds income.

A detailed discussion of the establishment and operation of investment pools and of the distribution of income from such pools is presented in chapter 10.

18. *The accounting system should be maintained and financial reports presented on the accrual basis.*

This principle signifies that current funds revenues should be reported when they become due, irrespective of the receipt of cash. Likewise, expenditures should include charges for material received and services rendered, even though disbursements are made in a later fiscal period. Materiality of a particular item may indicate that it is unnecessary to accrue a revenue or prorate an expenditure.

19. *Revenues and expenditures of auxiliary enterprises should be shown separately from other institutional operations.*

The revenues and expenditures of auxiliary enterprises should be reported separately from educational and general revenues and expenditures in the Statement of Current Funds Revenues, Expenditures, and Transfers.

20. *Budgets covering all operations of the institution should be prepared and adopted each fiscal year.*

The annual operating budget includes all current funds revenues and expenditures irrespective of source of revenues and purpose of expenditure. There should be an effective budget control system appropriate to the needs of the institution. Budgets for organized research projects, miscellaneous sponsored programs, and physical plant projects should also be prepared and adopted.

21. *Provision should be made for internal control and audit. In addition, there should be an annual audit by independent accountants.*

This principle emphasizes that there should be provision for adequate internal control through appropriate organization, assignment of duties and internal auditing procedures, and that there should be an annual audit by independent accountants.

22. *A comprehensive financial report should be prepared for submission annually to the chief executive officer of the institution and to the governing board.*

The institution's annual report should include at least a Balance Sheet, a Statement of Changes in Fund Balances, and a Statement of Current Funds Revenues, Expenditures, and Transfers. Other schedules and exhibits may be included, depending upon the wishes of the institution and the needs of those to whom the financial reports are addressed.

CHAPTER II

Development, Organization, and Personnel of the Business Office

In any consideration of accounting systems, the organization and the personnel of the business office must receive attention. The administrative organization of the business office is directly related to the accounting system. Without an adequate organization and a competent staff, no accounting system will perform satisfactorily.

Development of the Business Office

The business office as an independent administrative unit is a relatively recent development in the American college. Early American colleges were of small size and simple structure, and business matters were administered in part by their governing boards, and in part by the academic and executive branches of the college. Each faculty member or department head did the purchasing for his own division or department, sometimes from his "share" of the institutional funds. Account keeping was performed in a similarly unbusinesslike manner. As college enrollments multiplied, as institutional revenues increased, as auxiliary enterprises grew in size and importance, and as the academic and research structure of the institution became more complicated, business administration emerged as a distinct and separate function.

Today there is universal agreement that the business office is an important major unit in the administration of a college or university. Virtually every institution, however small, has an officer with the usual responsibilities of the chief business officer. This acceptance of the business office as an essential and integral part of college organization is predicated on two facts. The first is that the complicated and increasingly diverse activities of the modern educational institution make it essential that its financial affairs be administered by specialists. When it is realized that, in addition to a complicated academic structure involving large numbers of research projects and teaching programs, most institutions operate bookstores, dining halls, residence halls, college unions, printing shops, parking garages, photographic studios (to name some of the auxiliary enterprises generally found on campuses), the need for specialized business management is obvious.

The second factor contributing to the acceptance of the business office as an essential part of the administrative organization of educational institutions is the recognized conviction that the faculty and the president of the institution should perform only academic and administrative duties, leaving business and financial affairs to individuals especially trained in this field. This conviction is founded not only on the fact that academic officials usually lack the training and aptitude for handling complex financial matters but also on the assumption that these persons should not have to divert their energies and abilities from instruction and research.

Place of the Business Office in the Organization Chart of the College

As regards the location of the business office in the administrative framework of the college, two general types of organization are found—the unitary type and the multiple type (illustrated in Chart 2.1). In the unitary type, the president receives his authority by delegation from the governing board and in turn delegates certain administrative functions to the other officers of the institution, including the business officer. In this form of organization the president is solely responsible to the governing board. In the multiple type of organization the president and other administrative officers each receive a delegation of authority from the governing board and operate in more or less parallel spheres of authority. For example, the president is held responsible for academic and general policies, the business officer for fiscal and accounting matters.

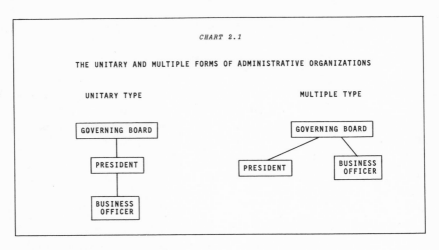

The unitary organization is by far the prevailing type among colleges and universities today and is the one which has proven to be administratively sound. Its chief advantage is that it allows complete centralization of authority in the president and makes the business function subordinate to the educational function. The weakness of the unitary type of organization may be that the business officer is subordinate to the president and, therefore, has no direct contact with the governing board. In actual practice, however, the business officer is directed by the president to work closely with those committees of the governing board which involve responsibilities in the business area—the building committee, the budget committee, the finance committee, and the like. Despite possible and theoretical weaknesses of the unitary type of organization, it is the one recommended by virtually every authority in educational administration and organization.

There is a possibility of a modified type of unitary organization which is illustrated in Chart 2.2. This arrangement makes the business officer responsible to the president in an administrative sense, but in an auditing and reporting capacity responsible directly to the governing board. It endows the business officer with that element of independence essential to any auditing agency.

Chart 2.3 illustrates the functional division of the college into four primary activities—that is, instruction and research, business

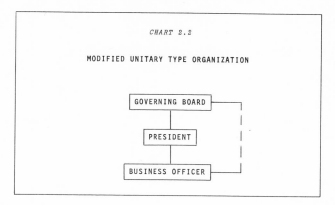

CHART 2.2

MODIFIED UNITARY TYPE ORGANIZATION

and finance, student affairs, and institutional development, the latter including public relations and fund raising. These are coordinate divisions, and, through their directors, each is responsible directly to the chief executive of the institution.

In 1968 *College & University Business* magazine (p. 74) published a "composite organizational chart" based on a study of 35 public universities with enrollments of 10,000 to 20,000. The general principles illustrated are applicable also to smaller colleges as well as to private institutions. The composite organizational structure is reproduced as Chart 2.4.

Functions of the Business Office

Business functions usually assigned to the business office include:

Budgets—assistance in preparation, administration, and control
Accounting
Internal auditing
Collection and custody of institutional funds
Preparation of reports
Purchasing and control of stores
Property control
Management of invested funds
Supervision of auxiliary enterprises
Supervision of operation and maintenance of physical plant, including planning and architectural services
Administration of nonacademic personnel program
Fiscal supervision over student organizations and loan funds

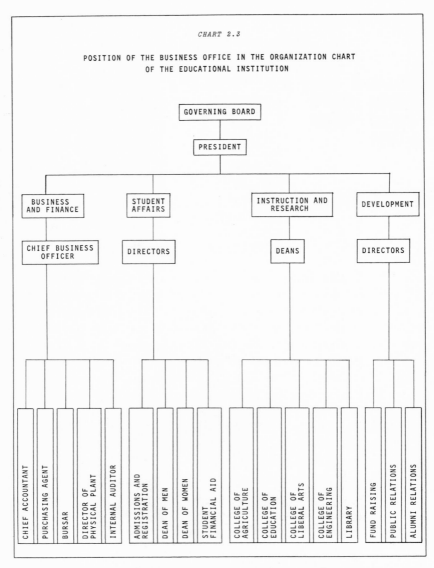

CHART 2.3

POSITION OF THE BUSINESS OFFICE IN THE ORGANIZATION CHART
OF THE EDUCATIONAL INSTITUTION

The business office has a dual responsibility with respect to the budget. It assists in its preparation and participates in the control of the budget after it has been adopted by the governing board. Moreover, the business officer is given the further responsibility of

CHART 2.4

COMPOSITE ORGANIZATIONAL CHART

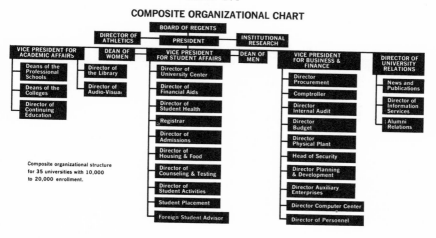

Composite organizational structure
for 35 universities with 10,000
to 20,000 enrollment.

advising the president in regard to requests for changes in the operating budget. In the preparation of the budget, the chief business officer usually acts as a financial advisor to the president. Armed with the financial history of the institution and with appropriate unit cost studies and analyses, the business officer is in an advantageous position to assist in preparing the budget. The president frequently depends on the advice and counsel of the chief academic officer, such as the dean of the college or the academic vice-president, working closely with the chief business officer to aid in this important task. The task of accumulating the data and of checking and typing the estimates also falls to the business officer and his staff. After the budget is submitted to and approved by the governing board, it must be controlled in order that the institution may function according to plan. A frequent method of budgetary control is to incorporate the budget into the accounting records. In the small college, however, and in a large university with sophisticated machine methods, budgetary control may be effected in other ways. Although the primary responsibility for adherence to the approved budget should rest with the budget head, the accounting office must assume the final authority in insuring that actual operations are in reasonable conformity with the financial plan as approved by the governing board.

As to the other functions of the business office, accounting and purchasing activities are important responsibilities. All records and methods of record keeping are prescribed and supervised by the buiness office. Although certain detailed accounting records, such as auxiliary enterprises, may be maintained in operating departments, the central business office must retain control over and responsibility for these subsidiary accounting arrangements.

Internal auditing and control are by-products of the accounting function, growing in importance as the institution grows. The business office as custodian of institutional funds must maintain a continuous review of all activities of the institution relating to the collection and disbursement of funds. The preparation of reports to the governing board and to the president and the compilation of financial information are other functions related to accounting. In addition, the fiscal system ordinarily calls for periodic budget reports to assist those responsible for the administration of individual budgets.

Central purchasing by the business office is an important function of that office and is a necessary supplement to the accounting system. The concept of centralized procurement does not preclude the active participation of academic and other departments in the purchasing process nor the delegation of some details of purchasing to agencies outside the business office. It simply means that the ultimate responsibility for all institutional procurement rests with the business office. The control and management of storerooms are closely allied to the purchasing function, as are also the control and management of movable property.

An important function sometimes assigned to the business office is that of the management of endowment and similar funds belonging to the institution. The extent and degree of business office responsibility for the management of invested funds depends upon the procedural arrangements at a given institution. Frequently, the primary responsibility for managing the investment of endowment funds is retained by the governing board or delegated to one of its committees. In other cases, this responsibility may be delegated to the chief business officer of the institution, with the board or a committee of the board acting on matters of broad investment policy. Regardless, however, of the variety of responsibilities with respect to the handling of endowment funds, the business office usually is called upon to maintain endowment funds records. It must also perform such auditing functions as will assure the safety of the assets of those funds and the use of the funds and income in accordance with any restrictions imposed by donors.

In most institutions the fiscal supervision over auxiliary enterprises such as bookstores, residence halls, dining halls, and laundries is considered to be a function of the business office. The degree of supervision and the extent to which the business office is responsible for the management of these activities varies among institutions.

The administration of the physical plant is another important responsibility of the business office. The immediate responsibility rests in a director of physical plant or a superintendent of buildings and grounds who is under the direction of the chief business officer. This business office function includes responsibility for physical plant planning and architectural services.

In most institutions the responsibilities of the business office include the administration of the personnel program involving the nonteaching staff. The immediate responsibility is assigned to a director of personnel who is responsible to the chief business officer.

An important function of the business office which is sometimes neglected is that of exercising supervision over the financial aspects of student organizations and loan funds. Such activities include student publications and student cooperatives. Fraternities and sororities are usually, but not always, excluded from this category.

Internal Organization of the Business Office

The internal organization of the business office has a direct bearing on the adequacy of the operation of the accounting system. An accounting system however scientific does not operate itself. Accounting personnel however competent and well trained cannot operate at peak efficiency without carefully planned internal organization which clearly fixes responsibilities, eliminates duplications, and avoids vacuums in the operations of the business office. Internal audit and control is an important adjunct of the properly organized business office.

The internal organization of the business office varies among institutions, being determined by the size of the institution, available budgets, personal attributes and abilities of the officers, and many other factors. Most college business officers are charged with nearly all the functions referred to above. But whether all of these activities are performed by one official in one office or several officers in several offices, depends upon the characteristics of the institution in question. Some of the factors which influence the organization of the business office and the size of its staff include the number of students enrolled, the number of faculty members, the amount of annual revenues and expenditures, the degree of centralization of business functions, the amount of endowment, the plan for management of invested funds, the extent of research grants and contracts, the volume of auxiliary activities, general policies regarding the supervision of the financial aspects of student activities, and the relationship of the institution to the community.

It is not practicable to consider all variations in the organizational plans of college business offices. However, the charts which follow attempt to illustrate some of the more typical organizations found in institutions ranging from the small liberal arts college to the large university. It is emphasized that the charts are presented only for purposes of illustration and that in practice the organiza-

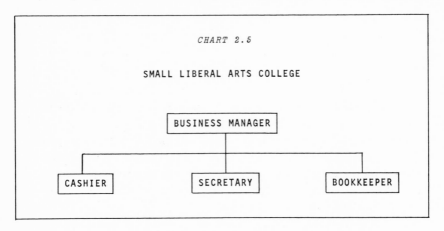

CHART 2.5

SMALL LIBERAL ARTS COLLEGE

BUSINESS MANAGER

CASHIER   SECRETARY   BOOKKEEPER

tion of business offices will vary, even among institutions of the same size, with respect to enrollment and total budget.

Chart 2.5 illustrates the business office of a small college having a fairly simple organization. Within this organization, a functional division of responsibilities is possible, one employee acting as a check on another.

In Chart 2.6 the chief business officer, the accountant, and the bursar essentially constitute the business office. The chief business officer assumes the functions of purchasing, assistance in budget preparation, fiscal management of the auxiliary enterprises, and supervision over the physical plant. The accountant is responsible for the accounts, the reports, and internal checks and auditing, while the bursar assumes the cashier function. This form of organization, with or without modification, is adaptable with equal advantage to a college smaller or larger than the one illustrated.

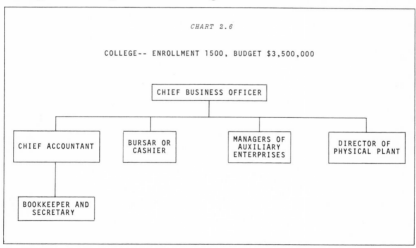

CHART 2.6

COLLEGE-- ENROLLMENT 1500, BUDGET $3,500,000

CHIEF BUSINESS OFFICER

CHIEF ACCOUNTANT | BURSAR OR CASHIER | MANAGERS OF AUXILIARY ENTERPRISES | DIRECTOR OF PHYSICAL PLANT

BOOKKEEPER AND SECRETARY

The organization illustrated in Chart 2.7 is an expansion of the organization shown in Chart 2.6.

Charts 2.8 and 2.9 illustrate a more complicated organization of a large state institution, with certain groupings of functions which become possible as the institution grows in size and complexity.

Title of the Chief Business Officer

No particular title is suggested for the chief business officer

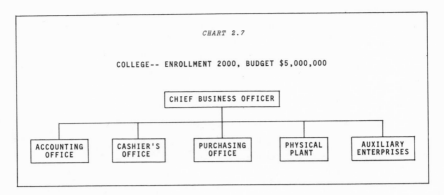

CHART 2.7

COLLEGE-- ENROLLMENT 2000, BUDGET $5,000,000

CHIEF BUSINESS OFFICER

ACCOUNTING OFFICE — CASHIER'S OFFICE — PURCHASING OFFICE — PHYSICAL PLANT — AUXILIARY ENTERPRISES

because there is no uniformity in this respect. In previous years such titles as bursar, financial secretary, auditor, and treasurer frequently were used to designate the chief business officer. Today, two titles are used more often than any others—Business Manager and Comptroller. Many chief business officers are being given a vice-presidential title, such as Vice-President for Business and Finance, Financial Vice-President, Vice-President—Business Affairs.

Qualifications of the Chief Business Officer

It is appropriate to consider the qualifications of the chief business officer of an educational institution. He should be equipped with appropriate experience and education. Although commercial business experience is valuable, he should understand the essential differences between the problems faced in a college or university and in business. A study by the American Council on Education summarizes the principal qualifications needed by a college business officer as follows:

In addition to special training, a position of responsibility in college and university business management calls for certain personal qualities. Among these, honesty and integrity are, of course, first. In close succession follow the qualities of tact, ability to cooperate, congeniality, and business judgment. There must then be added the essential qualities of untiring industry, initiative, and resourcefulness. An institutional business officer has contacts with a wide variety of persons. He is in contact with the members of the academic organization, with boards of trustees made up chiefly of business and professional men, with business concerns, students, and alumni. If he is in a public

CHART 2.8

ORGANIZATION CHART*

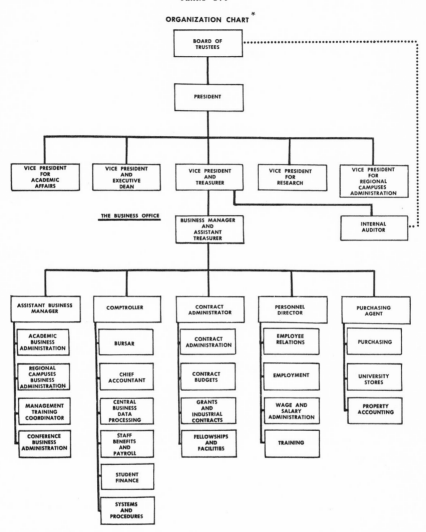

* Reproduced with the permission of Purdue University, Lafayette, Indiana.

institution he must have contact with members of the state legislature and with state and federal officers. A wide variety of problems and personalities present themselves in rapid succession.[1]

[1] American Council on Education Studies, *Training for College and University Business Administration, Series III, Financial Advisory Service,* Vol. I, No. 7, April, 1937, P. 10.

```
                              CHART 2.9


                      ORGANIZATIONAL STRUCTURE*

To carry out its responsibilities, the Business Office is functionally organized,
under the Business Manager, into five major operating areas headed by:  the
Assistant Business Manager, the Comptroller, the Contract Administrator, the
Director of Personnel Administration, and the Purchasing Agent.

The ASSISTANT BUSINESS MANAGER is responsible for the following departments:
The Director of Academic Business Administrators supervises Business Administra-
tors who serve as financial assistants to the Deans and are located in the major
schools of the University.  Business Administrators are assisted by Business
Representatives assigned as financial assistants to specific academic Department
Heads.
The Management Training Coordinator recruits and trains new administrative staff
and assists in the development of the total management staff of the Business
Office.
The Director of Regional Campus Business Administrators is responsible for the
Regional Campus business functions.  He is assisted by Business Administrators
and their staff located at each of the four Regional Campuses.
The Business Administrator for Conferences and Continuation Services assists in
the preparation of budgets for conferences on the main campus and registers and
collects fees from participants.

The COMPTROLLER is responsible for the following departments:
The Bursar is responsible for the assessment and collection of all student fees,
rents, and other monies on the main campus and serves as the University cashier.
Central Business Data Processing provides computer services, including systems,
programming, and operation, for all business operations.
The Chief Accountant's Office develops and maintains all accounting systems and
budgetary controls, accounts for all University expenditures and prepares finan-
cial reports, makes short-term investments and manages endowment funds, and ana-
lyzes financial data for management.
Staff Benefits and Payroll Office prepares all pay checks and administers all
insurance and retirement programs, including the counseling of staff members on
their benefits, the development of new benefits and reporting to the Federal
Government.
The Student Finance Office provides financial counseling and auditing for Uni-
versity sponsored student organizations and the disbursement and collection of
student loans including repayment counseling.
Systems and Procedures designs all business and related systems and procedures
for the University.

The CONTRACT ADMINISTRATOR is responsible for assisting in negotiations, ap-
proval of budget proposals, maintenance of controls and records, and preparation
of billings for sponsored research programs.

The DIRECTOR OF PERSONNEL ADMINISTRATION is responsible for recruitment, screen-
ing, reference of applicants, training programs, employee relations, wage and
salary administration, monitoring employment practices and the maintenance of
records for Clerical and Service staff.

The PURCHASING AGENT is responsible for the procurement of all materials, equip-
ment, supplies and contractual services for the University, and the operation of
University Stores.

The INTERNAL AUDITOR, who is administratively responsible to the Vice President
and Treasurer, is responsible for auditing all financial operations of the
University.
```

* Reproduced with the permission of Purdue University, Lafayette, Indiana.

College and University Business Administration states that the magnitude of business and financial responsibilities "in the administration of budgets and the programs they support require superior professional training, experience, management skills, and personal qualifications." The volume goes on to say that included in the qualifications of the chief business officer should be "one or more degrees from accredited institutions, along with either special educational training or practical experience as a junior officer in the business administration of an educational institution [and that] business officers should have a demonstrable understanding of the general aspects of educational philosophy and of the functions which their offices must perform. They must administer the fiscal and financial programs in such a way as to support the aims and objectives of their institutions, while at the same time maintaining fiscal integrity and economy." [2]

2 *College and University Business Administration,* 11–12.

CHAPTER III

Purchasing and Central Stores

COLLEGES AND UNIVERSITIES require a wide variety of materials, supplies, equipment, and services in their day-to-day operations, involving the expenditure of large sums of the institutions' money. Many of these items are unique and complex, and their procurement entails special problems. Long ago private business learned that purchasing could be done efficiently only by specialists; today, college and university administrators generally agree that institutional procurement, also, can be done best by those having specialized training and experience.

Centralized Purchasing. Regardless of the size of an institution, and whether the purchasing function is the full-time responsibility of a specialist or the part-time duty of some other official, the procurement operations in a college or university should be centralized within the institutional business organization.

The chief advantage in a system of centralized purchasing is economy in buying. A trained purchasing agent is able to find the most appropriate commodities at the lowest prices because he is constantly in touch with markets and sources of supply. Open competition by means of bids or other methods helps obtain goods at lower prices, and a centralized purchasing office provides the best means of performing the tasks necessary in requesting, verifying, and comparing bids. A centralized procurement organization, with its associated central storerooms, reduces costly overstocking of items, duplication of commodities, and failure to have essential items available when needed. By developing commodity specifications and enforcing these standards through centralized buying, it is possible to eliminate, or at least greatly reduce, unnecessarily wide ranges in size, color, material, and quality for the same items.

Second, centralized purchasing provides a uniform system of financial control. When purchasing is decentralized, budgetary control is difficult. Unless all purchases originate in a single office in conformity with standard procedures and unless approved requisitions precede the issuance of orders, budgetary control through the accounting system is practically impossible. In addition, the controls established through centralized purchasing make possible the systematic receipt and inspection of goods and the orderly handling, auditing, and recording of documents related to the procurement of commodities, and the payment of invoices.

In the third place, centralized purchasing releases faculty members from tedious and time-consuming tasks which are not part of their primary functions in the institution. Academic personnel are employed to instruct and carry out research. Seeking sources of supply, negotiating with vendors, bargaining with salesmen, studying market conditions, supervising the receipt and inspection of deliveries, tracing invoices, and other similar tasks in the procurement process consume time and energy. When responsibility for all phases of procurement is placed in the purchasing department, faculty members are free to perform their functions of teaching and research.

Finally, centralized purchasing, by fixing responsibility for buying in one department, makes possible an audit control over institutional expenditures for materials, supplies, equipment, and services which is impossible when purchasing is decentralized.

Centralized Purchasing Procedures. Under centralized purchasing, a single official in the business organization of a college or university is held responsible for all institutional procurement. However, this officer, usually known as a purchasing agent or director of purchasing, is not completely independent of other officers and departments of the institution; he is not at liberty to purchase what and when he pleases. A proper procurement program requires first of all a statement, notification, or other form of request to the purchasing department of the requirements of those who use materials, supplies, equipment, and services. This is done on a requisition form. Usually, the head of the using department has the authority to initiate requisitions for items to be charged to his departmental budget allocations, although in some instances the additional approval of a dean or director may be required.

Although the purchasing agent may have specialized training and experience in institutional procurement, he should always seek the advice and suggestions of the users when he is buying technical, specialized, and scientific laboratory equipment and supplies. Nevertheless, the performance of all the tasks related to the procurement of these items is the responsibility of the purchasing agent and the staff in his department.

The procurement of some items in an educational institution may be handled advantageously outside the routine of centralized purchasing. Examples are the day-to-day food requirements of dining halls, cafeterias, and food service departments, merchandise for resale in the student stores, and library books and periodicals.

In the area of food services, bids on a number of standard items may be obtained by the purchasing agent in cooperation with the dietician or director of the food service. A standing order may then be issued to the supplier whose bid was accepted, calling for the delivery of a commodity, at the bid price, as needed during a specified period of time. Authority is delegated to the director of the food services to purchase up to the amount of the standing order without further approval of the purchasing agent. The purchase of bread illustrates the procedure. Fresh bread is needed daily; it would be highly impractical to issue, process, and encumber individual orders for each day's purchases. Instead, bids are obtained from several bakeries, specifications calling for the delivery of bread at the agreed upon price, for a stated period of time, perhaps a month. One purchase order is issued for the estimated monthly cost of bread deliveries and goes through the regular channels of encumbrances in the accounting office. To obtain daily deliveries of bread in the quantities needed, the food service manager or his representative places an order each day by telephone, or otherwise, without further approval of the purchasing department or the issuance of formal documents. Through this procedure the purchasing department maintains control over purchases in the food service department and the accounting office maintains control over the food service budget with a minimum of routine work, especially on the part of the food service personnel.

Another example of delegating the purchasing function is in the buying of library books and periodicals. Little "shopping around" can be done in this area; consequently, the librarian is authorized to purchase these items. One advantage of this procedure is that it eliminates writing requisitions, which serve no good purpose in this case, and typing by the purchasing office of long lists of books and magazines, which lists are of use only in the library.

Another exception to centralized purchasing may be made in the case of the student store, in that the manager of that unit is given discretionary authority to buy merchandise which is to be resold in the store.

A procedure which offers certain practical advantages in institutional procurement, although it is not entirely an exception to the centralized purchasing concept, is the issuance of monthly standing orders for certain types of recurring purchases, usually small in amount, such as automobile and truck repairs. Instead of issuing individual orders for tire repairs and minor motor adjustments, a standing order for an estimated sum is issued to a local garage at the beginning of the month. Whenever possible, specific unit prices should be quoted in such orders. For example, in this instance the standing order could provide for "Labor, at $5.00 per hour," and "Parts at List Price, less 25%." Depending on the volume of business contemplated, these prices could be arrived at through competitive bids or by telephone quotation, negotiated by the purchasing department. The maintenance department is authorized then to obtain the services needed by direct contact with the garage. This procedure not only reduces the total number of orders issued but also the number of confirming orders required.

To be workable, any system of centralized purchasing must provide for emergency situations. The purchasing agent should prepare, and the chief business officer should promulgate, rules and regulations concerning emergency orders, and every effort should be made to guard against their abuse. Unregulated emergency orders may nullify budgetary control as well as other advantages of centralized purchasing. In cases of an emergency, the purchase should be reported to the purchasing department as soon as possible, so that a confirming requisition can be prepared and processed through the accounting office and a confirming purchase order can be issued.

Obviously, centralized purchasing does not mean that every item of materials, supplies, equipment, and service must be bought coldly and shrewdly on the basis of only a departmental requisition, without consulting the requisitioner. Centralized purchasing means the systematic centralization of responsibility over all institutional purchases, as well as a uniform and systematic method of channeling forms and documents involved in the procurement process. Effective purchasing, like other functions of the business office, is not an end in itself, but instead is an additional way of serving the institution in the execution of its educational program.

Purchasing Relations to the State and Community. In some states a centralized procurement organization performs the purchasing function for all institutions and agencies in the state. This arrangement has some advantages, and many state-controlled colleges and universities may be bound by law to place all purchases through the state organization. Some disadvantages exist, however. The plan does not necessarily enable institutions to eliminate positions or reduce numbers of employees in their own business offices because of the necessity to prepare special specifications, to perform the task of encumbrance accounting, follow-up orders, receiving procedures, and to see to other functions which cannot be performed by the state office. Often, delays in deliveries to the using institutions are caused by having to place orders through a distantly removed state office. Savings in prices are not always experienced through state purchasing, and frequently higher prices actually are paid. Frequently, there is a tendency for the purchasing function and organizations at the state level to become involved in politics.

Some of these objections can be overcome if state-controlled colleges and universities are permitted the option of placing orders either through the state purchasing system or directly with suppliers. For certain types of commodities having standard character-istics, institutions can profit by savings resulting from quantity purchasing on a state-wide basis. A contract for a standard item, such as paper towels, may be awarded by the state purchasing office with all institutions participating on a voluntary basis. The ques-tion of whether or not an institution should participate in purchas-ing procedures established for all state agencies and institutions must be answered with reference to the laws of the state and prac-tices and procedures of the state purchasing system.

Sometimes educational institutions are under pressure to pur-chase goods and services from local sources. The argument is ad-vanced that because the taxes or gifts of local businesses help to support the colleges or universities, they are obligated to spend their funds in the local community. It is more important to remember that educational institutions have a stronger obligation to spend their funds as wisely as possible, whether this means purchasing locally or from other marketing areas. It is suggested that an institu-tion can answer the argument, at least in part, by pointing out its total financial impact on the community through such things as the amount of salaries and wages paid to staff and faculty, most of which is spent locally, and the purchasing power for goods and services from local merchants brought to the community by students. If all other factors in the procurement procedure are equal, i.e., price, quality, and service, it might well be in the best interest of an insti-tution to buy from local sources. In any event, decisions to buy lo-cally rather than from other areas should not be made solely by the one responsible for the purchasing function. Such decisions, espe-cially if they involve the possibility of paying higher prices, should be made at the top level of administration and should be based on all the facts involved in the situation.

Purchasing Procedures. Procedures in a centralized purchasing system involve the following steps: (1) notification to the purchas-ing department by means of requisitions of the needs of using de-partments; (2) selection of, and negotiation with, suppliers; (3) issuance of purchase orders; (4) receipt of goods or services; (5) approval of invoices; (6) operation, supervision, and control of a system of storerooms on campus.

Issuance of Requisitions. The first step in purchasing is the issuance, by the head of the department needing the items, of a requisition addressed to the purchasing agent. Four types of requisitions may be used by an institution: the advance requisition, the purchase

FORM 3.1

BLANK COLLEGE
PURCHASE REQUISITION

To: The Purchasing Department   Date_____ Order No._____

Required Delivery Date_____

Name and Address of Vendor(s) Suggested

Department_____

Deliver To_____
(Bldg.)   (Room)

To Be Used For_____

Do Not Fill In

Promise Date_____ Ship Via_____

Cash Terms_____

F.O.B. Terms_____

Quantity	Please Give Full Description and Complete Specifications. Attach Written Quotations If Such Were Received.	Estimated Unit Price	Actual Unit Price	Total

College Policy: The Purchasing Agent Is Vested With The Sole Authority to Order Materials And Contract For Services. The College Will Honor No Obligation Except On A Previously Issued And Duly Authorized Purchase Order.

Departmental
and Object Code_____

Approved
If Necessary_____
President or Business Mgr.

Requested By_____

Approved_____
Purchasing Agent

Approved By_____
Dean or Administrative Head

Bid File Number_____

requisition, the stores requisition, and the work requisition.

The advance requisition is used in notifying the purchasing department of the estimated requirements for various commodities and services over a given period of time, such as a month, a quarter, or a semester. The purchasing agent thus is able to plan his buying in advance so that savings may be effected through consolidated, quantity purchases. Also, the purchasing agent is given the opportunity of taking advantage of fortuitous situations in buying certain supplies and commodities.

The purchase requisition (Form 3.1) is used for day-to-day needs. The stores requisition, illustrated and explained later in this chapter, is used when the desired items can be obtained from a storeroom on campus. The work requisition is used for requests involving maintenance and repair work to be performed by the appropriate shop or workers in the physical plant department of the institution. In most instances, the purchase requisition can be used in lieu of a work requisition.

Although variations exist among institutions in regard to the details of requisition procedures, the following points are usually found applicable to all educational institutions. Requisitions should be prepared in several copies, preferably by typewriter. One copy is retained by the using department, the other copies being forwarded to the purchasing department and other offices and departments, depending on the system. Distribution of copies is simplified if they are in different colors. Usually full instructions on the purchasing procedures of an institution are included in a Manual of Business Procedures, if such a publication is prepared. In the absence of such a manual, instructions on the preparation and use of requisitions should be printed on the reverse side of the form.

Following is an illustration of a set of instructions:

DIRECTIONS FOR DRAWING PURCHASE REQUISITIONS

(Use store requisition, Form 3.13, for materials and supplies located in institutional storerooms, office supply stores, dining hall stores, and physical plant stores.)

   I. GENERAL—Prepare requisitions on typewriter in triplicate and retain one copy. Send the other copies to the office of the purchasing agent. The latter copies must be signed by the department head and approved by the dean of your college.

II. CONTENT—Use the purchase requisition for all requests of materials, supplies (other than from stores), and service. Use this form, also, when requesting stamps from the college post office. Whenever possible include on a given requisition only items that can be ordered from one vendor.

III. SPECIFICATIONS—See that complete and accurate specifications are given for every item requested. Failure to do this will cause delay in filling the request.

IV. ESTIMATED COST—So far as possible, estimated cost of each item should be shown. A department, however, should not go to any particular trouble or expense to obtain estimates. The purchasing agent, upon request, will be glad to assist a department in securing prices.

V. AVAILABILITY OF FUNDS—No requisition should be submitted unless the funds are available. It is the duty of the department head to keep up with his own budget, and to assist in this process the accounting office will provide each department head with a budget statement at the beginning of each month.

VI. DEPARTMENTAL AND OBJECT CODE—All requisitions must be coded in the space headed Departmental and Object Code. Since the accounting department determines from this code the departmental budget to be charged, it is very important that the coding be done accurately. There are two parts to the code: the departmental, which indicates the department to be charged; and the object, which indicates the particular budget to be charged. Refer to the Chart of Accounts to determine the proper object code.

VII. PURCHASE ORDERS—The purchasing agent will issue all purchase orders. One copy of the order will be sent to the requisitioning department. Check each order carefully and notify the purchasing agent promptly of any errors or omissions.

VIII. RECEIVING PROCEDURE
a. Supplies—All orders of supplies, materials, and equipment will be delivered to the central receiving depot where they will be checked and compared with the original order. The receiving department will then deliver the order to the requisitioning department. The department head, or his authorized representative, must certify that the goods have been received in quantity and quality ordered, and that

an invoice based on such order is properly payable.
b. Service—All orders of service will be delivered direct to the requisitioning department. The department head will certify on a receiving report that the service has been rendered and that an invoice based on the order is properly payable. The order should be checked promptly by the requisitioning department, and the purchasing agent should be advised of any damage, improperly functioning equipment, shortages, etc.

The availability of funds must be determined and this should be done before a purchase order is written. Usually, the requisition, or a copy of it, goes through the accounting department for this determination, and this necessitates the recording of an estimated, or actual, cost of the items being requisitioned. As the using department normally has little or no knowledge of the cost, the requisition must first be sent to the purchasing department, where this information can be obtained and recorded on the form, and then sent to the accounting department for approval of funds. All this entails some time and may delay placing an order, but the step is essential if budgetary control is to function. Some institutions prepare the purchase order and then check for availability of funds.

If funds are not available, the requisition should be returned to the using department with an appropriate note. A question might be raised here as to the scope of authority of the accounting office in approving or disapproving requisitions. While it is true that department heads, with perhaps the approval of deans or directors, have the right to spend their allocated funds in accordance with the approved budget, nevertheless, it is the duty of the chief accountant to refuse to approve requisitions calling for illegal or obviously extravagant purchases. Rather than exercise veto power over requisitions, the accountant should refer questionable requisitions to the chief business officer or other appropriate administrative officer. Normally, requisitions are approved by the accounting office if funds are available in the specified accounts and budgets.

Obtaining Quotations and Selecting Vendors. The next steps in the procurement process are obtaining prices for the items requisitioned and selecting suppliers. For most large orders, written quotations should be obtained from at least three suppliers through the use of a request for quotation, illustrated in Form 3.2. This form should be printed on thin paper so that, by using carbon paper, a number of copies can be prepared at one typing, the only difference being in the name of the vendors. As a practical matter, and in the interest of conserving time, quotations often are obtained by telephone contacts. Care must be exercised, however, to prevent the development on the part of buyers of habits in patronizing certain suppliers to the exclusion of others. It is a good practice to have all quotations recorded on copies of the request for quotation form so that the purchasing department files will reflect the extent to which competition has been sought and obtained. In the case of purchases involving large sums of money, sealed bids should be required of suppliers.

The statutes of many states provide that state-controlled institutions must obtain bids on all orders in which the amount involved exceeds a specified sum. These laws may also specify that newspaper or other public advertisement must precede requests for bids; also, that the lowest bidder must be awarded the order, regardless of his ability to provide service, his reliability for delivery, and even the quality of his product.

Issuance of Purchase Orders. After quotations are obtained and suppliers are selected, purchase orders are then prepared and issued. Practices among colleges and universities differ in regard to the form, content, and number of copies of purchase orders and the uses to which the copies are put. Variations depend on the procedures for delivery on campus and the system of accounting and financial control, for example. The use of printing computers and other types of electronic equipment, also, will cause differences among institutions in the preparation and use of copies of purchase orders. It is generally agreed, however, that several copies of the purchase order should be prepared when the order is first typed in the purchasing department. Regardless of these variations, nevertheless, purchase orders should be prenumbered, and procedures for the issuance, use, and accounting of purchase order forms should be subject to the same audit and control as other business and finan-

FORM 3.2

```
Office of
Purchasing Agent          BLANK COLLEGE

              R E Q U E S T   F O R   Q U O T A T I O N
                     (This is not an Order)
TO:                                          Date_____

                        Please submit your quotations on such
                        items in the following list as you are
                        able to furnish.  Quotations must be in
                        this office by _____

                                 BLANK COLLEGE

   ┌──────────────────────────────┐   _____
   │ INQUIRY NUMBER               │       Purchasing Agent
   └──────────────────────────────┘
```

INSTRUCTIONS

Our specifications must be strictly adhered to or full particulars given regarding proposed substitutes.
Submit quotation on this form. Address to PURCHASING AGENT, BLANK COLLEGE.
It is requested that all items be quoted F.O.B. Blank College. All quotations will be so considered unless otherwise specified.
Our terms are 2% 10 days--Net 30 days unless otherwise specified.
The right is reserved to accept or reject all or any part of quotations submitted.
The right is reserved to cancel orders unless shipping date is maintained.

Quantity	Unit	Items and Specifications	Unit Price	Total Price

BLANK COLLEGE   Date_____

We propose to furnish above items at prices listed opposite each, and guarantee that if order is placed with us, we will furnish these goods or services in accordance with your specifications shown above unless otherwise indicated.

By_____

TERMS_____   Firm_____

F.O.B._____ BLANK COLLEGE   Street_____

Shipment will be made within _____ days
after receipt of order.   City_____ State_____ Zip___

cial documents and forms, such as prenumbered checks.

Following is a suggested list of copies of purchase order forms and the methods in which they are used:

COPY NUMBER	RECIPIENT AND USE

Original . . . . To supplier

2 . . . . To accounting department, for encumbrance recording

3 . . . . To purchasing department, for vendor file

4 . . . . To receiving depot, to be used in reporting receipt of materials. If there is no central receiving department, this copy is sent to requesting department to be used in reporting receipt of material.

5 . . . . To requesting department, for its permanent file

6 . . . . To purchasing department, for purchase order numerical file

Receipt of Goods and Approval of Invoices. The next steps in the procurement procedure are the receipt of materials ordered and the processing of vendors' invoices. Variations in these procedures will be found among institutions because of many factors, chief of which is the method of receiving materials. In some institutions all materials are delivered to a central receiving depot; in others, materials are delivered directly to the requisitioning department.

Central receiving has several advantages. It facilitates delivery to the institution by establishing and making known to suppliers a single point of delivery on the campus, thus obviating the problem often faced by delivery personnel of locating various departments and offices scattered over a wide campus. A central delivery depot can be staffed by trained and experienced personnel, so that it can be expected that packages, crates, boxes, and other containers will always be carefully, quickly, and efficiently examined and that the condition of materials upon arrival can be expertly noted. By comparing the goods delivered with the purchase order, verification can be made of the accuracy of shipment as far as quantity and general description are concerned. Deviations in these respects from the purchase order can be noted in the presence of the personnel of the carrier and reported promptly to the purchasing department.

The central receiving personnel probably will not be able to determine damage to technical and scientific equipment, especially if

FORM 3.3

```
┌──────────────────────────────────────────────────────────────────────────────────┐
│              BLANK COLLEGE                          ORDER NO.                       │
│         P U R C H A S E     O R D E R                                              │
│                                                                                    │
│                                                     Show this order number         │
│                                                     on invoices, packages,         │
│  Date_____            and shipping papers.           │
│                                                                                    │
│  ┌                              ┐    Promised Shipping Date                        │
│                                      _____                      │
│                                                                                    │
│                                      Cash Terms_____                    │
│                                      F.O.B. Terms_____                    │
│  └                              ┘    Ship Via_____    Requisition     │
│                                                                        No.         │
│  Please Ship, Subject to the Conditions Below, the Following Materials             │
├──────┬──────────┬─────────────────────────────┬─────────┬─────────┬───────────────┤
│ Item │ Quantity │     D e s c r i p t i o n   │  Unit   │  Total  │               │
│ No.  │          │                             │  Price  │  Price  │               │
├──────┼──────────┼─────────────────────────────┼─────────┼─────────┤    Code       │
│      │          │                             │         │         │     or        │
│      │          │                             │         │         │   Fund No.    │
│      │          │                             │         │         │               │
│      │          │                             │         │         │───────────────│
│      │          │                             │         │         │  Est. Cost    │
│      │          │                             │         │         │               │
│      │          │                             │         │         │   Partial     │
│      │          │                             │         │         │ Liquidations  │
├──────┴──────────┴─────────────────────────────┴─────────┴─────────┤               │
│  ADDRESS AND MAIL INVOICES IN DUPLICATE TO OFFICE OF THE COMPTROLLER               │
│                                                                                    │
│  SHIP AS FOLLOWS:                                                                  │
│                                   BLANK COLLEGE                                     │
│   BLANK COLLEGE                                                                    │
│   Receiving Department-ORDER NO.   By_____                     │
│                                          Purchasing Agent                          │
│  ACKNOWLEDGEMENT:  Acknowledge receipt of this order and advise when and           │
│                    from what point shipment will be made.                          │
│  SUBSTITUTIONS:  Substitutions or price increases will not be accepted             │
│                  without prior written approval of the Purchasing Agent.           │
│  INVOICES:  Address and mail invoices in duplicate to Office of the                │
│             Comptroller.  Show purchase order number.  Do not include              │
│             state or federal taxes.  Purchaser will furnish tax exemp-             │
│             tion certificate upon request.  Discount period to be cal-             │
│             culated from date invoice or material is received,                     │
│             whichever is later.                                                    │
│  CANCELLATIONS:  Blank College reserves the right to cancel all or any             │
│                  part of this order not shipped in accordance with terms           │
│                  and conditions stated above or on vendor's quotation.             │
│  CORRESPONDENCE:  Address all correspondence concerning this order to              │
│                   the Purchasing Dept. & refer to Order No.                        │
└──────────────────────────────────────────────────────────────────────────────────┘
```

it is internal. This means that department heads still must examine deliveries promptly, even from a central receiving depot, and report any problems to the purchasing department.

The central receiving procedure is as follows. All supplies and materials, with the exception of food supplies, merchandise for re-

FORM 3.4

PURCHASE ORDER
(Lower Portion)

PARTIAL DELIVERIES				APPROVED:	Liq.
Voucher No.	Amount	Voucher No.	Amount		
FOR ACCOUNTING OFFICE - 2				Purchasing Agent	

FORM 3.5

PURCHASE ORDER
(Lower Portion)

FUNDS AVAILABLE

Chief Accountant

FOR PURCHASING DEPARTMENT - 3

FORM 3.6

PURCHASE ORDER
(Lower Portion)

I certify that the above articles have been carefully serviced and rendered and that an invoice based on above is properly payable.

Date _____ Head of Department

I certify that the above articles have been carefully checked for quantity and quality. Any shortages or exceptions have been noted.

Date _____ Receiving Clerk

FOR RECEIVING DEPARTMENT - 4

FORM 3.7

PURCHASE ORDER
(Lower Portion)

This is a copy of the order placed from your requisition. In case of error, please notify Purchasing Department at once.

FOR REQUISITIONING DEPARTMENT - 5

FORM 3.8

PURCHASE ORDER
(Lower Portion)

FOR PURCHASING DEPARTMENT - 6

FORM 3.9

	BLANK COLLEGE		
	RECEIVING REPORT	NO.	

Received From:

For Account Of:

Order Reference_____

Date Received_____

Shipped Via_____

B/L or Express
Receipt No._____

Quantity	Description	Weight

Code	I certify the above material received:

Receiving Department   Requisitioning Department   Date

sale, and heavy equipment, are delivered to the central receiving depot, where they are examined and checked by the receiving personnel. If it is possible to check an order without unloading it from the vendor's truck, this is done. After checking, the vendor then delivers the order to the proper department. In most cases, however, it will be necessary to transship the goods by the institution's trucks. The receiving department personnel fills out a receiving report (Form 3.9) for the items received. The receiving report is then signed and delivered to the requesting department. When goods are delivered to the department, a second certification is placed on the receiving report by the department head or his authorized representative. The receiving report is then sent to the accounting office with a copy to the purchasing department, where it serves as evidence of the proper receipt of the goods. In case of partial deliveries, a partial delivery receiving report follows the same channels to the accounting office with a copy to the purchasing department.

Frequently, the central receiving depot is responsible for the payment of freight and express bills and may be assigned a petty cash fund from which to pay such items. In the case of orders for services, such as repairs and printing, the delivery is made directly to the requesting department, and the head of the department is responsible for forwarding the receiving report to the accounting office.

In regard to invoices, either of two plans may be followed. In one plan, a uniform invoice form prepared by the institution is sent with the purchase order to suppliers. One condition of the purchase agreement is that the vendor will bill the institution on this standard invoice. A system of this kind is difficult to establish among suppliers but it has many advantages. It replaces vendors' invoices which vary widely in size, shape, content, and color. The institutional invoice results in uniformity as to signatures, approvals, account numbers, codes, and other pertinent information needed in paying and accounting for invoices.

In the second plan, vendors submit bills to institutions on their own invoice forms. Under this plan, it is necessary for the institution to prepare a remittance voucher form. Such a form sets forth the necessary information about the purchase and the payment being made in a uniform and standard manner. The remittance voucher (Form 3.10) is prepared in at least four copies.

Files and Records. The maintenance of complete and accurate files and records in the purchasing department is an integral part of the procurement system. As purchase orders are issued, they are in numerical sequence and one copy should be filed in the purchasing

FORM 3.10

BLANK COLLEGE

R E M I T T A N C E   V O U C H E R

Department

Date_____

TO:

Cash Terms

F.O.B. Terms

Invoice Date	Vendor's Invoice Number	Receiving Report Number	Purchase Order Number	Invoice Price	Less Discount	Net Price

Charge	Amount

Invoice Checked_____

Prices and Terms Correct_____

Receiving Report Correct_____

Code and Department
  Charges Correct_____

Voucher Audited by:

_____

Date_____

For Library and Food Services Orders Only

I hereby certify that the above materials
have been received or services rendered
and that the voucher is properly payable:

Signed_____
      Director of Libraries (or)
      Director of Food Services
Date_____

Voucher No.

Check No.

department by the purchase order number. A second copy is filed in a vendor file in alphabetical order; another copy is maintained in a suspense file in date-order number sequence and serves as a basis of following up on purchases for which receiving reports have not been received after a period of time, such as two weeks. The follow-up process for unfilled orders and partial shipments continues until the order is complete or outstanding items have been cancelled. Completed orders are filed by departments according to departmental account numbers. Since the purchase order number appears on all copies of the form, cross-reference between all files in the purchasing department is maintained.

The filing system for purchase requisitions, receiving reports, and remittance advices is as follows. As requisitions are received in the purchasing department they are entered in a purchase requisition register (Form 3.11) which shows the date received, department requesting the materials, number and amount of requisition, and name of proposed vendor. The register also shows the location of the requisition if it is necessary to send it out of the purchasing department for any reason. The requisition then serves as a basis for the preparation of the necessary bid or quotation request. Should it be necessary to receive formal bids, the bid document is filed with the requisition in an open file and held until the bid opening date. When quotations or bids are received and a supplier has been selected, the purchase order is prepared and copies are distributed and filed in the manner previously described.

When the receiving report and remittance advice are received, the purchase order file can be closed on this particular transaction. The complete file consists of copies of the purchase requisition, the purchase order, the quotation document, the receiving report, and the remittance advice.

Advanced Order-Processing System. Requisition and purchasing procedures can be streamlined by implementing a small order, or verbal order, procedure. The extent to which this system is utilized will vary among institutions because of the size, location relative to market, and purchasing philosophy of each institution. Under this procedure, the requisition form is modified to include additional data and is prepared in the required number of copies to meet the needs of accounting and receiving procedures. No formal written purchase order is sent to vendors; rather, the purchasing department assigns a purchase order number to each transaction and transmits the required information to the vendor by telephone. This

FORM 3.11

BLANK COLLEGE				
P U R C H A S E R E Q U I S I T I O N R E G I S T E R				
Date	Proposed Vendor	Requesting Department	Purchase Req. No.	Amount

procedure saves mailing and typing costs and reduces processing time.

Storerooms and Stores Control. The supervision of storerooms and the control of stores inventories are important functions of a college or university procurement system. In most institutions, standard commodities used by many departments can be purchased economically in large quantities and placed in storerooms for future use. A system of storerooms has definite advantages. First, it makes possible quantity buying with the resulting economies. Second, it makes available for immediate use many items which otherwise would have to be purchased through the usual procedure of requisition, bid, purchase, and delivery from a supplier who usually is at some distance from the campus. Third, the system reduces the amount of clerical and paper work involved in purchasing by reducing the number of formal purchase orders written and issued.

The type and number of storerooms vary among colleges and universities with the size of the institution, proximity to local sources of supply, and other factors; but laboratory stores, physical plant or general stores, and office supply stores are found in nearly all institutions. Medical stores, food stores, and athletic stores are other types of stores frequently found in universities.

Laboratory storerooms should serve all the teaching fields offering laboratory work—botany, biology, chemistry, geology, geography, life sciences, metallurgy, physics, and zoology. By combining the needs of many laboratories the amount of supplies needed is sufficiently large to enable an institution to realize economies through quantity buying. A general storeroom in which general operating and maintenance supplies and materials are kept is necessary even in small colleges. An office supply storeroom is necessary also, since all offices on the campus use stationery and paper supplies, pens, pencils, ink, and other office materials. The office supply storeroom may be operated in connection with the student store or the general storeroom, as is done frequently in smaller institutions, or it may be operated by the purchasing department as a separate storeroom.

Inventory Control Over Storerooms. Supplies and materials in the various storerooms on a campus have a sizable monetary value and should be controlled and checked as carefully as cash. An adequate inventory accounting system requires (1) that all supplies received, on hand, and issued be accounted for both in quantity as well as in value; (2) that the inventory be controlled by general ledger accounts in the accounting department; and (3) that the inventory records and the general ledger accounts be verified periodically by physical count of the items in the storerooms.

Accounting control over inventories kept in storerooms is established through the use of a general ledger control account and subsidiary stores ledgers. The subsidiary stores ledgers consist of perpetual inventory cards for each type of commodity in the store and are maintained in the storerooms. A control account for each store is kept in the accounting office, and each storekeeper is held responsible for maintaining up-to-date, accurate, and complete inventory records. A type of perpetual inventory card is shown in Form 3.12. At any time after all entries are posted to these cards, the sum of the values on all cards should equal the balance of the inventory account in the general ledger. Discrepancies should be investigated and explained satisfactorily, and the accounting and inventory records should be reconciled.

Central Stores Procedures. The first step in establishing procedures and records for a campus storeroom is taking a physical inventory of commodities in each store and entering quantities, unit costs, and value balances on the perpetual inventory cards. If there are numerous items, a systematically arranged coded classification of commodities is useful. The code is arranged by commodity groups with subdivisions under each group, and inventory cards should be

FORM 3.12

BLANK COLLEGE

S T O R E S   L E D G E R

Stock Number

Article _____

Description _____

Unit _____
Minimum _____
Maximum _____

V e n d o r s

1		4	
2		5	
3		6	

Section	Shelf	Bin

ORDERS PLACED

Req.	Date	P.O.	Date	Quan.	Unit Price	Amount

RECEIPTS

Date	Rec. Rep.	Quan.	Amount

ISSUES

Date	Stores Order	Quan.	Unit Price	Amount

ON HAND

Quan.	Average Unit Cost	Amount

arranged in the same order. In many institutions, such coded classifications of items are prepared in many copies and distributed as catalogues, or commodity lists, to all departments on the campus.

The second step in the central stores procedures is ordering materials. Usually, responsibility is delegated to each storekeeper to maintain the stock of items in his store at reasonable levels. However, the purchasing agent, through consultations with department heads, should determine the items used widely by all departments and keep storekeepers informed so that as many as possible of the standard items can be well stocked in the stores on campus. When ordering materials for the inventories of stores, the regular purchase requisition should be used by storekeepers.

As goods are received at the storerooms, entries are made on the stores ledger, or inventory cards, in the columns under the heading Receipts. A copy of the purchase order usually is used as the posting medium for these entries. However, this plan has two disadvantages: first, the unit prices on the purchase orders often differ from the actual unit prices paid for the goods; second, transportation charges, which are additional costs of the goods in stores operations, are not on the purchase orders. To meet these difficulties, a copy of the remittance voucher is sent to the storekeepers and the actual costs of the goods are entered from this document.

New purchases should not be placed in storeroom bins and shelves and issued until the unit costs have been recorded. If it is necessary to issue new items before the inventory records are complete, the requisitions should be set aside and priced after the inventory records are posted.

The third step in the central stores procedure is issuing materials. The stores requisition, Form 3.13, is used for this purpose. It is prepared in triplicate by the using department and signed by the department head. One copy is retained in the department, the other two being presented to the store. Stores requisitions need not be approved by the accounting department for availability of funds but are certified only by department heads. This is a departure from strict budgetary control. Usually, the items requested from stores are needed immediately and one of the advantages of the central storeroom system is to provide prompt availability of commodities.

BLANK COLLEGE

No. _____

STORES ORDER

Date _____

Item Number	Quantity	Description	Price Unit	Price Total

Maintenance Order Number _____   Charge Code _____

Work Order Number _____   Department _____

Requested by _____

Received by _____

Delivered by _____

Date _____

Posted by _____

Date _____

Routing requisitions for all stores items through the regular encumbrance procedures is awkward, inconvenient, and time consuming. Budgetary safeguards can be established by placing maximum limits on stores requisitions. In addition, where necessary, the accounting department should notify storekeepers of those departments whose budget allocations for supplies and materials are nearing exhaustion.

Several methods are employed in pricing commodities issued from stores inventories. The two most commonly used in colleges and universities are the "first-in, first-out" and the "moving average" methods. Under the "first-in, first-out" method those units which are first bought and debited to the inventory record are is-

FORM 3.14

BLANK COLLEGE

INTERDEPARTMENTAL   INVOICE

Date_____

Credit Department of_____
                        Rendering Service or Furnishing Material

Charge Department of_____
                        Receiving Service or Material

Description	Amount

Charge: Account	Amount		Credit: Account	Amount
		POSTED CHARGE_____		
Services or Materials Received:		POSTED CREDIT_____	Services Rendered or Materials Delivered:	
		APPROVED_____ Chief Accountant		
Head of Department			Head of Department	
FOR ACCOUNTING OFFICE			Voucher No.	

sued first, so that in valuing the issues on a given requisition, the unit price of the earliest purchase is used until all articles of that purchase have been issued. Then the unit price of the next purchase is used, and so on. The method is illustrated as follows:

Total stock consist of 300 units purchased as follows:

100 units @ $1.10
200 units @ $1.05

Subsequently 120 units are issued. The value of this requisition is computed as follows:

100 units @ $1.10 $110.00
 20 units @ $1.05   21.00
120 units $131.00

Under the "moving average" method a new unit price is calculated at the time of each purchase. All issues are valued at this unit price until another purchase is made, then a new unit price is computed. Following is an illustration of this method:

On hand, July 1	100 units @ $.50	$ 50.00
Received, July 15	100 units @ $.75	75.00
	200 units	$125.00
Average unit price	$.625	
Purchased, July 17	100 units @ $.80	80.00
	300 units	$205.00
Average unit price	$.683	
Issued, July 20	100 units @ $.683	68.30
Balance	200	$136.70

The stores requisition is the basis for posting the perpetual inventory records, and appropriate entries are shown in the column headed Issues on Form 3.12. At regular intervals, the storekeeper classifies the stores requisitions by departments to be charged and summarizes these charges on the interdepartmental invoice, Form 3.14. This invoice, prepared in several copies, is used as follows:

1. One copy, to which is attached one copy of the stores requisi-

tions which bears the signature of the department head, is sent to the accounting department and forms the basis for charging the budget of the using department and crediting the inventory control account.

2. One copy, to which is attached the other copy of the departmental requisition, is retained in the storeroom files.

3. One copy is sent to the head of the using department so that he is informed of all stores transactions affecting his budget.

4. One copy is sent to the purchasing agent so that he will be informed as to the items that are moving out of the storerooms.

Variations in these forms and procedures are to be found among colleges and universities depending on the factors mentioned above in relation to the form, content, and use of other purchasing department forms.

The final step in centralized stores procedures is taking a physical inventory periodically, to check the accuracy of the accounting records and to reconcile the subsidiary stores ledgers with the controlling accounts in the general ledger. Some institutions check parts of the inventory as time permits, rather than taking a complete physical inventory once or twice a year.

Accounting Entries for Storeroom Purchases and Issues. The accounting entries in connection with the operation of an inventory system for storerooms are as follows:

1. Entry to set up stores inventory at the inception of a stores system, assuming goods already on hand (journal voucher):
   Stores Inventory (separate account for each storeroom)
      Reserve for Stores Inventory.
2. Entry to record the purchase of goods for inventory (voucher register):
   Stores Inventory
      Vouchers Payable.
3. Entry to record issues from stores (interdepartmental transfer journal):
   Expenditures Control (charge individual accounts in allocation ledger from invoices)
      Stores Inventory.
4. Entry to adjust reserve for stores to agree with stores inventory at end of year (journal voucher):
   Reserve for Stores Inventory

Unrestricted Current Funds Balances
(Reverse this entry if stores inventory has increased during the year).

Purchasing Systems Using EDP Equipment. Many educational institutions have converted part or all of their purchasing and stores operations to data processing equipment. Some institutions have simply placed vendor payments on the EDP systems by punching data cards from the document which normally is prepared as a remittance advice. These cards serve as the basis of computer processing and are used to liquidate encumbrances, charge appropriate accounts, prepare checks in payment, and generate paper records for distribution to appropriate offices.

In order to make the most use of the computer equipment, the initial entry into the EDP system should be achieved when the purchase order is written. At this point, the entire purchase order (or selected details therefrom) can be prepared for entry into the EDP system as a by-product of typing the purchase order. Data cards punched as a by-product of typing the purchase order can be achieved on a typewriter-punch unit and may contain all necessary accounting information releative to the purchase. The initial inquiry to check for available funds and to encumber the appropriate budget accounts becomes a routine computer run. As inquiry is made, the account is encumbered and, if funds are available, the purchase order is released to the vendor as explained previously. Copies of the purchase order may be used as a receiving report, or separate receiving reports may be prepared.

Invoices are received in the accounting office where they are matched with purchase orders and receiving reports. Cards are punched from the invoice (or a prepared remittance advice), entry is made into the system to liquidate encumbrances, charge appropriate accounts, and prepare checks to vendors.

As a by-product of these runs, equipment inventories can be prepared so that all equipment can be tagged. By proper classification and coding of items purchased, it is also possible to obtain lists of supplies acquired. Further, the computer can be utilized to analyze bids to determine lowest and best bids and to print tabulations giving total dollars to be expended.

CHAPTER IV

Classification of Accounts

THE PRIMARY PURPOSE of an accounting system is to furnish financial information to the management and other interested parties. In colleges and universities, adequate financial information is necessary for the efficient execution of educational, research, and public service programs. The first step in the installation of an accounting system in educational institutions is to ascertain what information is needed.

Accounting Details Dependent on Many Factors. The information to be provided by the accounting system is conditioned by various factors. The size of the institution, the amount of its budget, and the type of its organization—whether publicly supported or privately endowed, whether a large university or a liberal arts college—are important considerations. Another significant factor is the attitude of administrative officials toward accounting and financial information. A good accounting system should primarily furnish only the information that is needed and used. If, for example, in preparing budgets and in operating the institution generally, the management desires to use cost analyses and other detailed financial data, the accounting system should be designed to collect this information. In short, the predisposition of the administration toward accounting and business and fiscal methods is an important factor in the development of an accounting system. The desirability of having the accounting system provide financial information comparable to that of other similar institutions is an additional conditioning factor. In publicly supported institutions, state laws, as well as the requirements of the state government, unfortunately may determine the kind of information required. Occasionally, the statutes and regulations prescribe a uniform system of accounts for all state agencies, including those devoted to higher education.

After considering all the diverse factors involved, both internal and external, and after ascertaining the exact nature of the information required, it is then necessary to determine what accounts will provide this information and subsequently to arrange these accounts into a logical and orderly system of classification.

It is not possible to prepare a chart of accounts applicable to all colleges and universities. However, *College and University Business Administration* was designed in part to provide basic principles and standards of accounting and financial reporting for institutions of higher education. Because an increasing number of institutions followed the recommendations of the predecessor volumes, it is expected that the updated principles appearing in the 1968 edition of *College and University Business Administration* also will find wide acceptance. Furthermore, because the production of comparable financial statistics is desirable and should be regarded as an important function of the accounting system, adherence to the uniform principles of classifications now recognized and followed by most educational institutions throughout the country will facilitate the production of comparable financial data.

Classification by Funds in the General Ledger. The classification of accounts appearing in *College and University Business Administration* is divided into three parts—general ledger accounts, current funds revenue accounts, and current funds expenditure accounts. The general ledger, being the nucleus of the accounting system, contains or controls all the accounts comprising the system. It receives entries, in summary or in detail, of all financial transactions of the institution. The financial statements are prepared from the general ledger and supporting ledgers. Because of the nature of institutional finance, the use of resources generally is subject to limitations, restrictions, and designations. One function of the accounting system is to insure compliance with these provisions. This is accomplished by dividing the general ledger into separate funds, each being a separate and independent financial entity composed of a group of self-balancing accounts.

College and University Business Administration recommends the following fund structure as applicable to the majority of colleges and universities:

1. Current funds
   a. Unrestricted
   b. Restricted
2. Loan funds
3. Endowment and similar funds
4. Annuity and life income funds
5. Plant funds
   a. Unexpended
   b. Investment in plant
6. Agency funds

Current funds are those funds available for ordinary operation and maintenance, as well as those restricted by donors or other outside agencies for specific operating purposes. In most institutions, current funds embrace the bulk of the financing of the institution. Unrestricted current funds are those which can be expended without restriction, except for the usual budgetary limitations. Restricted current funds are those which, although expendable for current purposes, are subject to provisions limiting the use of these funds. Common types of restricted funds are grants from federal or state governments and donations from private foundations, individuals, and industry for designated instructional purposes or specific research projects. Funds applicable to the operations of auxiliary enterprises, such as college bookstores and dining halls, may be reported separately as a third subdivision of current funds.

General ledger accounts for current funds are classified into asset, liability, reserve, and fund balances accounts. Many of these accounts are virtually the same as those used in commercial accounting: for example, Cash, Petty Cash, Temporary Investments, Accounts and Notes Receivable, Inventory, Prepaid Expenses, Notes Payable, Deferred Revenues, and Allowance for Doubtful Accounts. Accounts peculiar to institutional organizations are Due from

Other Funds, Due to Other Funds, Departmental Allocations, Unrealized Revenues, Encumbrances, Provision for Encumbrances, and Unallocated Revenues. Due to Other Funds and Due from Other Funds relate to current funds borrowed from or loaned to other fund groups, hence appear with contrabalances in the other fund groups affected. Departmental Allocations, Unrealized Revenues, Encumbrances, Unallocated Revenues, and Provision for Encumbrances are budgetary accounts appearing in the ledger only if transactions involving the budget are entered in the accounts. The Departmental Allocations account represents the total of all budget allocations to departments and is equal to the Unrealized Revenues account in those cases where total available current funds revenues are allocated to departmental budgets. If the total of such revenues is not allocated to budget units, but a portion is retained to be made available for expenditure at a later time during the fiscal year, the Unallocated Revenues account is used. Obligations in the form of orders and contracts against allocations are recorded in the Encumbrances and Provision for Encumbrances accounts. No fixed asset accounts as used in commercial accounting are recorded in the current funds group, even though equipment is purchased from these funds. In governmental and institutional accounting, fixed asset accounts are recorded in the plant funds group.

Loan Funds include all funds the principal of which may be loaned. The excess of income over expenses of these funds serves to increase loanable principal. Assets of loan funds include Cash, Temporary Investments, and Notes and Interest Receivable on Loans. These accounts are balanced on the credit side of the ledger by the Loan Funds Balances account representing the principal of loan funds. If there are a number of loan funds, only control accounts should be maintained in the general ledger, with detailed accounts being carried in a loan subsidiary ledger.

The Endowment and Similar Funds group includes those funds whose principal is nonexpendable as of the date of reporting and are invested, or are available for investment, for the purpose of producing income. Included in this group are three types of funds: Endowment Funds, Term Endowment Funds, and Quasi-endowment Funds (or Funds Functioning as Endowment).

An endowment fund is one in which a donor has stipulated, as a condition of his gift, that the principal is to be maintained inviolate and in perpetuity, and that only the income from the investments of the fund may be expended.

Term endowment funds are those which a donor, by terms of his gift, has provided may be expended or used in other ways upon the happening of a particular event or the passage of a stated period of time. Once the use of these funds is changed, the funds should be transferred to and reported in the appropriate fund group. Funds held in trust by outside trustees should not be recorded in the records but may be reported as footnotes in the balance sheet. The values used should be provided by the outside trustees and reported on a current basis.

Quasi-endowment funds are those funds which the governing board of an institution, rather than the donor or an outside agency, has determined are to be retained and invested. The term Funds Functioning as Endowment may also be used to identify such funds. A governing board may determine at any time in the future that such funds may be used in some other manner. They may be expended for any operating purpose, either designated or undesignated; they may be expended for plant purposes; or they may be used as loan funds. When this occurs, Quasi-endowment Funds should be transferred from the Endowment and Similar Funds group to the appropriate fund group as indicated by the new use to which the funds are to be put.

The usual asset accounts of the Endowment and Similar Funds group are Cash and Investments unless the funds are pooled for investment purposes, in which case the asset account would be Pooled Investments. The usual accounts on the credit side of the general ledger include Notes Payable and, if improved real properties is one type of investment, Mortgages Payable and Reserve for Depreciation. Accounts for the balances of the three types of funds—Endowment Funds Balances, Term Endowment Funds Balances, and Quasi-endowment Funds Balances—are also included here.

The Annuity and Life Income Funds group includes funds acquired by an institution subject to annuity contracts, living trust agreements, or gifts and bequests reserving life income to one or more beneficiaries. The asset accounts of these funds include Cash and Investments. The equity accounts include those for payables or other forms of indebtedness of the funds, an account for Undistributed Income, and fund balance accounts for Annuity Funds Balances and Life Income Funds Balances.

Plant Funds are divided into at least two balanced sections— Unexpended Plant Funds and Investment in Plant. The first section includes funds designated for or restricted to the construction, rehabilitation, and acquisition of physical plant. The second section includes funds already expended on fixed property and equipment.

The asset accounts of the Investment in Plant section include clude Cash and Temporary Investments, while the equity accounts include Accounts and Notes Payable, Mortgages Payable, and Unexpended Plant Fund Balances.

The asset accounts of the Investment in Plant section include Land, Buildings, Improvements Other Than Buildings, and Equipment. Construction in Progress may be included as an asset account if capitalization of such accounts during construction is desired. The liability accounts for this section include Notes Payable, Bonds Payable, Mortgages Payable, and Net Investment in Plant.

If desired, two additional balanced sections of Plant Funds may be used—Funds for Renewals and Replacements and Funds for Retirement of Indebtedness. The former represents cash or other assets designated for or restricted to the renewal and replacement of plant assets. The latter represents funds available for the retirement of indebtedness.

Agency Funds are those funds over which the institution exercises custodianship but which are not controlled or owned by it. Examples are student deposits, deposits of fraternities and other student or faculty organizations, and breakage deposits. Cash, Temporary Investments, and Agency Funds Balances are accounts typical of this group.

Relative to the classification of accounts in the general ledger, several points should be emphasized. Each fund group exists in complete independence of the other fund groups, being contained in a separate section of the general ledger. Each of these fund sections is balanced in itself. To illustrate this fund relationship, consider the entries required to record a loan from one fund group to another group—e.g., from Unrestricted Current Funds to Endowment Funds. In the lending fund group (Unrestricted Current Funds), the entry is a debit to Due from Endowment and Similar Funds and a credit to Cash; in the borrowing fund group (Endowment and Similar Funds), the entry is a debit to Cash and a credit to Due to Unrestricted Current Funds. Also, consider the entries required to record the purchase of equipment out of current funds. In Unrestricted Current Funds, the entry is a debit to Expenditures (supported by debits to individual departmental or office budgets), and a credit to Cash. In the Plant Funds group (Investment in Plant section), the entry is a debit to Equipment and a credit to the account for Net Investment in Plant.

In order to illustrate the classification of accounts by funds, a pro forma balance sheet is presented on pages 68–69.

Classification of Revenues and Expenditures. In regard to the classification of revenues and expenditure accounts, it is to be noted that these accounts reflect the current operations of an institution and relate only to Current Funds. The transactions of the other fund groups are additions to and deductions from the balances or principal of the funds and are reflected in the statements of changes in balances of the appropriate fund groups.

Classification of Revenues. In regard to the classification of current funds revenues, *College and University Business Administration* recommends a breakdown by sources of revenue and, in particular, a distinct separation of Educational and General Revenues, Student Aid, and Revenues from Auxiliary Enterprises. The volume defines current funds revenues as "all receipts and accruals of unrestricted current funds and of restricted and designated current funds expended during the current fiscal period." [1] Following is an outline of the recommended classification of revenues.

    I. Educational and General (including all revenues available for the educational program of the institution)
       A. Student Tuition and Fees
       B. Governmental Appropriations

[1] *College and University Business Administration,* 277.

    C. Endowment Income
    D. Gifts (or Gifts Applied)
    E. Sponsored Research
        1. Governmental
        2. Nongovernmental
    F. Other Separately Budgeted Research
    G. Other Sponsored Programs
        1. Governmental
        2. Nongovernmental
    H. Recovery of Indirect Costs—Sponsored Programs
    I. Sales and Services of Educational Departments
    J. Organized Activities Relating to Educational Departments
    K. Other Sources
  II. Student Aid (including funds to be used for fellowships, scholarships, grants-in-aid, and prizes and awards)
 III. Auxiliary enterprises (including those enterprises not directly related to the educational activities of the institution but existing for the purpose of serving the student body and faculty)

At the option of the institution, Student Aid may be merged with Educational and General, each category being subtotaled.

The extent to which each of the three categories of revenues is detailed in the accounting records depends upon conditions at, and the desire of, individual institutions. Some itemizing of the main divisions under Educational and General is usually desirable. Obviously, the revenue from each auxiliary enterprise should be reported separately. The accounting system can be made to provide the amount of detailed information desired by increasing or decreasing the number of accounts in the revenue chart.

Classification of Expenditures. College and University Business Administration recommends that expenditures be classified by function and by organization unit. A further classification by object is offered as an additional optional classification. Expenditures for Student Aid and for Auxiliary Enterprises should be distinctly separated from those for Educational and General functions. Classification by function is the grouping of expenditures according to the general end or purpose for which the funds were expended. The following list of functional classifications meets the requirements of most colleges and universities:

FORM 4.1

BLANK COLLEGE

B A L A N C E   S H E E T
At End of Fiscal Year

ASSETS

I. CURRENT FUNDS
A. Unrestricted:
   Cash
   Accounts Receivable
   Less: Allowance for Doubtful Accounts
   Inventories

      Total Unrestricted
         Current Funds $_____

B. Restricted:
   Cash
   Due from Agency Funds
   Total Restricted Current Funds $_____
      TOTAL CURRENT FUNDS   _____

II. LOAN FUNDS
   Cash
   Notes Receivable
   Interest Receivable
   Due from Unrestricted Current Funds
      TOTAL LOAN FUNDS $_____

III. ENDOWMENT AND SIMILAR FUNDS
   Cash
   Investments, at cost

   TOTAL ENDOWMENT AND SIMILAR FUNDS $_____

LIABILITIES AND FUND BALANCES

I. CURRENT FUNDS
A. Unrestricted:
   Accounts Payable
   Due to Other Funds
   Agency Funds
   Loan Funds
   Deferred Revenues
   Provision for Encumbrances
   Unrestricted Current Funds Balances
      Total Unrestricted Funds
         Balances $_____

B. Restricted:
   Restricted Current Funds Balances
      Total Restricted Current Funds $_____
         TOTAL CURRENT FUNDS

II. LOAN FUNDS
   Loan Funds Balances

      TOTAL LOAN FUNDS $_____

III. ENDOWMENT AND SIMILAR FUNDS
   Endowment Funds Balances:
   Endowment Funds
   Term Endowment Funds
   Quasi-Endowment Funds

   TOTAL ENDOWMENT AND SIMILAR FUNDS $_____

BLAIR COLLEGE

B A L A N C E   S H E E T
At End of Fiscal Year
(Continued)

ASSETS

IV. ANNUITY AND LIFE INCOME FUNDS
Cash
Investments, at cost
TOTAL ANNUITY AND LIFE INCOME FUNDS $‗‗

V. PLANT FUNDS
A. Unexpended:
Cash
Temporary Investments, at cost
Accounts Receivable
Total Unexpended Plant Funds $‗‗
B. Renewals and Replacements:
Cash
Accounts Receivable
Temporary Investments, at cost
Total Renewals and Replacements Funds $‗‗
C. Retirement of Indebtedness:
Cash
Temporary Investments, at cost
Total Retirement of Indebtedness Funds $‗‗
D. Investments in Plant:
Land
Buildings
Improvements Other than Buildings
Equipment
Total Invested in Plant Funds $‗‗
TOTAL PLANT FUNDS $‗‗

VI. AGENCY FUNDS
Cash
Due from Unrestricted Current Funds
TOTAL AGENCY FUNDS $‗‗

LIABILITIES AND FUND BALANCES

IV. ANNUITY AND LIFE INCOME FUNDS
Annuity Funds Balances
TOTAL ANNUITY AND LIFE INCOME FUNDS $‗‗

V. PLANT FUNDS
A. Unexpended
Accounts Payable
Unexpended Plant Funds Balances
Total Unexpended Plant Funds $‗‗
B. Renewals and Replacements:
Renewals and Replacement Funds Balances
Total Renewals and Replacements Funds $‗‗
C. Retirement of Indebtedness:
Retirement of Indebtedness Funds Balances
Total Retirement of Indebtedness Funds $‗‗
D. Investments in Plant:
Bonds Payable
Net Investment in Plant:
From Governmental Appropriations
From Gifts
From Current Funds
Total Invested in Plant Funds $‗‗
TOTAL PLANT FUNDS $‗‗

VI. AGENCY FUNDS
Due to Restricted Current Funds
Agency Funds Balances
TOTAL AGENCY FUNDS $‗‗

I. Educational and General
   A. Instruction and Departmental Research
   B. Organized Activities Relating to Educational Departments
   C. Sponsored Research
   D. Other Separately Budgeted Research
   E. Other Sponsored Programs
   F. Extension and Public Service
   G. Libraries
   H. Student Services
   I. Operation and Maintenance of Physical Plant
   J. General Administration
   K. Staff Benefits
   L. General Institutional Expenses
II. Student Aid
III. Auxiliary Enterprises

At the option of the institution, Student Aid may be merged with Educational and General, each category being subtotaled.

The grouping by function is simply a logical arrangement of the accounts for purposes of financial statements and to facilitate uniformity among institutions. Obviously, more detailed information is required. Actually, individual accounts bearing the captions shown above would not be set up in the books of account; but accounts should be set up to the extent needed and grouped according to the functions shown, to provide the desired amount of detailed information regarding the expenditures of an institution.

Classification of expenditures by organization unit is the primary classification for recording detailed expenditures. An organization unit is a department, office, or subdivision of either which comprises a distinct administrative unit, such as the president's office, business office, and the various departments of instruction. The budget, like the accounts, should be set up by organization units and funds should be allocated to these various units.

The object classification is a method of classifying expenditures according to that which is received in return for the expenditures; for example, personal services, supplies and expense, and equipment. Although the budget is established by organization units, frequently it is broken down further into objects and allocated on this basis to organization units. Thus, the budget for the vice-president's office may be subdivided into salaries, wages, supplies and expense, and equipment; the funds so allocated must be expended in this manner. The object breakdown may be carried further by subdividing supplies and expense, for instance, into office supplies, instructional supplies, travel, etc. This classification process may be carried still further by breaking down office supplies and instructional supplies into more detailed categories. However, the advantages derived from the use of detailed classifications must be balanced against the increased cost of obtaining the information.

The following chart summarizes the classification of expenditures and indicates the subdivision of expenditure accounts:

I. Educational and General (General Function)

  A. General Administration (Specific Function)

    1. Office of the Vice-President for Academic Affairs (Organization Unit)

      a. Salaries (General Object)
      b. Wages (General Object)
      c. Supplies and Expense (General Object)

        (1) Office Supplies (Specific Object)
        (2) Telephone (Specific Object)
        (3) Travel (Specific Object)

      d. Equipment (General Object)
        (1) Desks (Specific Object)
        (2) Filing Cabinets (Specific Object)

Thus, an expenditure by the vice-president's office for office supplies, as an example, is classified first by organization unit, then by general object, and finally by specific object. For statement purposes, the vice-president's office is classified as to specific function under General Administration and as to general function under Educational and General. From the point of view of the actual accounts, the general objects—salaries, wages, supplies and expense, and equipment—would be account titles. In small institutions, one account for the vice-president's office might be sufficient, with a further analysis of expenditures made possible through the use of codes.

Transfers from Current Funds. Transfers from current funds are reported in the transfer section of the Statement of Current Funds Revenues, Expenditures, and Transfers. *College and University Business Administration* defines transfers as "the identification of the authorization by a governing board of a specific change in the use of funds, and the moving of the assets, liabilities, and balances from one fund group to another." [2] Examples are transfers from current funds to student loan funds, to quasi-endowment funds, and to plant funds for additions to plant assets, for debt service or for renewal and replacement of plant assets.

Chart of Accounts. A chart of accounts, based on the principles enumerated above and suitable for a college or university, is presented below and serves as a basis for the accounting system explained in the following chapters. Because the use of codes or symbols is customary in college accounting, a suggested code of accounts is presented with the chart. This chart probably contains more detailed accounts than would be needed by most institutions, particularly smaller colleges, and is intended to be illustrative of the possibilities for proper classification of data. Institutions must adapt the chart and coding system to their own needs and requirements.

The chart of accounts comprises five sections. The first section is a summary of account code numbers. The second section presents a chart of general ledger accounts. The third section presents a chart of expenditure accounts classified by function and organization unit. This classification applies to the allocations ledger. The fourth section presents a chart of revenue accounts, hence applies to the revenues ledger. The fifth section presents a chart of expenditure accounts classified by general object and also by detailed object.

The same chart of accounts is readily adaptable to electronic data processing systems; however, a different coding system may be required. This coding system is discussed in detail in chapter 8, "Data Processing Systems."

2 *Ibid.*, 282.

CHART OF ACCOUNTS

GENERAL LEDGER—CURRENT FUNDS—UNRESTRICTED

Asset Accounts

Number	Title
1001	Cash—General Account
1002	Cash—Salary Payroll Account
1003	Cash—Wage Payroll Account
1004	Petty Cash
1005	Bank Transfers
1006	Cash Over and Short
1011	Due from Other Funds
1015	Accounts Receivable—Student (Control)
1016	Accounts Receivable—Others (Control)
1020	Notes Receivable
1023	State Appropriations Receivable
1031	Inventories
1035	Physical Plant Stores
1041	Work in Process
1051	Prepaid Expenses and Deferred Charges
1061	Expenditures (Control)
1062	Restricted Expenditures (Control)
1063	Transfers to Other Funds (Control)
1071	Encumbrances
1081	Temporary Investments
1091	Unrealized Revenues

CHART OF ACCOUNTS

GENERAL LEDGER—CURRENT FUNDS—UNRESTRICTED

Liability and Fund Balance Accounts

Number	Title
1201	Vouchers Payable
1211	Due to Other Funds
1221	Notes Payable
1231	Employee Life Insurance Deductions
1232	State Teachers' Retirement System Deductions
1233	Withholding Tax Deductions
1234	Social Security Deductions
1241	Deferred Revenues
1251	Revenues (Control)
1252	Restricted Revenues (Control)

1261	Departmental Allocations (Control)
1271	Provision for Encumbrances—Current Year (Control)
1272	Provision for Encumbrances—Prior Year (Control)
1275	Allowance for Doubtful Accounts
1301	Unallocated Revenues
1351	Unrestricted Current Funds Balances

CHART OF ACCOUNTS

GENERAL LEDGER—CURRENT FUNDS—RESTRICTED

Asset Accounts

Number	Title
1501	Cash—First National Bank
1511	Due from Other Funds
1521	Accounts Receivable
1581	Temporary Investments

Liability and Fund Balance Accounts

1701	Vouchers Payable
1711	Due to Other Funds
1721	Provision for Endowment Income Stabilization
1851	Restricted Current Funds Balances (Control)

CHART OF ACCOUNTS

GENERAL LEDGER—LOAN FUNDS

Asset Accounts

Number	Title
2001	Cash—Second National Bank
2011	Due from Other Funds
2022	Notes Receivable (Control)
2031	Interest Receivable
2081	Temporary Investments

Liability and Fund Balance Accounts

2201	Vouchers Payable
2211	Due to Other Funds
2215	Allowance for Doubtful Loans
2241	National Defense Student Loan Funds—Repayable to Government
2242	National Defense Student Loan Funds—Institutional Share
2251	Loan Funds Balances (Control)

CHART OF ACCOUNTS

GENERAL LEDGER—ENDOWMENT AND SIMILAR FUNDS

Asset Accounts

Number	Title
3001	Cash—First State Bank
3011	Due from Other Funds
3051	Investments—Securities (Control)
3052	Investments—Real Estate (Control)
3111	Unamortized Premiums on Bonds

Liability and Fund Balance Accounts

Number	Title
3201	Vouchers Payable
3211	Due to Other Funds
3221	Reserve for Depreciation on Real Estate
3224	Mortgages Payable
3231	Reserve for Accumulation of Bond Discounts
3241	Undistributed Pool Income
3242	Income (Control)
3301	Net Adjusted Gains and Losses
3351	Endowment Funds Balances (Control, if number of such funds is large)
3352	Term Endowment Funds Balances (Control, if number of such funds is large)
3353	Quasi-endowment Funds Balances (Control, if number of such funds is large)

CHART OF ACCOUNTS

GENERAL LEDGER—ANNUITY AND LIFE INCOME FUNDS

Asset Accounts

Number	Title
4001	Cash—Second State Bank
4011	Due from Other Funds
4051	Investments—Securities (Control)
4052	Investments—Real Estate (Control)

Liability and Fund Balance Accounts

Number	Title
4201	Vouchers Payable
4211	Due to Other Funds
4301	Undistributed Income—Annuity Funds (Control)
4302	Undistributed Income—Life Income Funds (Control)
4401	Net Adjusted Gains and Losses
4551	Annuity Funds Balances (Control)
4651	Life Income Funds Balances (Control)

CHART OF ACCOUNTS

GENERAL LEDGER—UNEXPENDED PLANT FUNDS

Asset Accounts

Number	Title
5001	Cash—Third State Bank
5005	State Appropriations Receivable
5011	Due from Other Funds
5081	Temporary Investments
5091	Construction in Progress
5095	Encumbrances (Optional)

Liability and Fund Balance Accounts

5101	Vouchers Payable
5111	Due to Other Funds
5120	Provision for Encumbrances (Optional)
5123	Bonds Payable
5151	Unexpended Plant Funds Balances (Control, if more than one such fund)

CHART OF ACCOUNTS

GENERAL LEDGER—FUNDS FOR RENEWALS AND REPLACEMENTS

Asset Accounts

Number	Title
5201	Cash—First National Bank
5211	Due from Other Funds
5215	Accounts, or Notes, Receivable
5271	Assets of Funds on Deposit With Others

Liability and Fund Balance Accounts

5301	Vouchers Payable
5311	Due to Other Funds
5341	Balance of Funds on Deposit With Others
5351	Renewal and Replacement Funds Balances (Control)

GENERAL LEDGER—FUNDS FOR RETIREMENT OF INDEBTEDNESS

Asset Accounts

Number	Title
5401	Cash—Second National Bank
5402	Cash—Trustee Account
5411	Due from Other Funds
5481	Temporary Investments

Liability and Fund Balance Accounts

5501	Vouchers Payable
5511	Due to Other Funds
5541	Balance of Funds in Trustee Account
5551	Retirement of Indebtedness Funds Balances (Control)

CHART OF ACCOUNTS

GENERAL LEDGER—INVESTMENT IN PLANT

Asset Accounts

Number	*Title*
5605	Land (Control)
5606	Buildings (Control)
5607	Improvements Other Than Buildings (Control)
5608	Equipment (Control)
5611	Due from Other Funds
5691	Construction in Progress

Liability and Fund Balance Accounts

5701	Vouchers Payable
5711	Due to Other Funds
5722	Notes Payable
5723	Bonds Payable
5724	Mortgages Payable
5751	Net Investment in Plant

GENERAL LEDGER—AGENCY FUNDS

Asset Accounts

Number	*Title*
6001	Cash—Third National Bank
6011	Due from Other Funds
6081	Temporary Investments

Liability and Fund Balance Accounts

6201	Vouchers Payable
6211	Due to Other Funds
6251	Agency Funds Balances (Control)

EXPENDITURE ACCOUNTS
(Classified by Function and Organization Unit)

I. EDUCATIONAL AND GENERAL
   A. Instruction and Departmental Research
      College of Liberal Arts

1	Office of the Dean
2	Aerospace Studies
3	Art
4	
5	Biology
6	Chemistry
7	Classics
8	
9	
10	English
11	History
12	Home Economics
13	
14	Mathematics
15	Military Science
16	Modern Languages
17	Music
18	
19	
20	Naval Science
21	Philosophy
22	Physics
23	Psychology
24	
25	Sociology and Anthropology
26	Speech and Theater
27	
28	
29	

College of Business and Government

31	Office of the Dean
32	Accounting
33	Economics and Business Administration
34	Journalism
35	Business Education and Office Administration
36	Political Science

College of Education

41	Office of the Dean
42	Health, Physical Education, and Recreation
43	Library Science
44	Reading Clinic

College of Engineering

51	Office of the Dean
52	Chemical Engineering

53 Civil Engineering
54 Geology and Geological Engineering
55 Mechanical Engineering
56 Electrical Engineering
57 Seismological Observatory

School of Law
61 Office of the Dean
62 Law Extension
63 Legal Institute for Agriculture and Resource Development

School of Pharmacy
71 Office of the Dean

Graduate School
81 Office of the Dean
82 City Planning

Summer Session
91 Office of the Director
92 University
93 School of Law

Other Instructional Expenses
95
96

B. Organized Activities Relating to Educational Departments
101 Computer Center
102 Home Economics Cafeteria
103 Farm

C. Sponsored Research
111 Federal (Accounts for individual projects are further identified by contract or agreement number.)
131 Other Sponsors (Individual accounts identified appropriately)

D. Other Separately Budgeted Research
151 Bureau of Business and Economic Research
152 Bureau of Education Research
153 Engineering Experiment Station
154 Institute of Urban Research
155 Bureau of Governmental Research
156 Bureau of School Services

E. Other Sponsored Programs
161 Training Grants and Contracts (Individual accounts for grants and contracts, identified by numbers)
171 Instructional Institutes

F. Extension and Public Services
181 Office of the Director

182   Extension Classes and Testing Service
183   Conferences, Institutes, and Short Courses
184   Program Planning and Library Service
185   Educational Film Production
186   Correspondence Study

G. Libraries
201   General Library
202   Law Library
203   Pharmacy Library

H. Student Services
301   Dean, Division of Student Personnel
302   Dean of Women's Office
303   Registrar's Office
304   Student Counselling Center
305   Religious Life
306   Placement Office
307   Student Financial Aid Office
308   Student Activities
309   Health Services

I. Operation and Maintenance of Physical Plant
321   Administration
322   Janitorial Services
323   Maintenance of Buildings
324   Furniture and Equipment Repair
325   Operation of Grounds
326   Maintenance of Streets and Drives
327   General Trucking
328   Planning and Construction
329   Fire Protection
331   Utilities
332   Electrical and Mechanical Services
333   Property Insurance
334   Other Maintenance, Renovations, and Alterations of Physical Plant

J. General Administration
351   Office of the President
352   Office of the Executive Vice-President
353   Office of the Vice-President for Academic Affairs
354   Business Manager
355   Accounting Office
356   Bursar
357   Internal Auditor
358   Purchasing
359

K. Staff Benefits
    371   Employers Contribution to Retirement System
    372   Social Security
    373   Group Insurance
    374   Health, Medical, and Surgical Insurance
    375   Workmen's Compensation Insurance

L. General Institutional Expense
    381   Alumni Activities
    382   Nonacademic Personnel
    383   University Development
    384   Mail Service
    385   Catalogues, Bulletins, and Directories
    386   Commencement
    387   Convocations, Conferences, and Institutes
    388   Official Entertainment
    389
    390   Memberships in Organizations (Institution)
    391   Telephone and Telegraph (Unless charged to operating budgets)
    392   Travel (Unless charged to operating budgets)
    393
    398   Provision for Doubtful Accounts
    399   Other General Institutional Expense

II. STUDENT AID
    401   Scholarships and Fellowships
    402   Prizes and Awards

III. AUXILIARY ENTERPRISES
    451   Bookstore
    461   Cafeteria
    471   Residence Halls—Single
    472   Residence Halls—Married
    481   Intercollegiate Athletics
    491   College Union
    495   Airport

REVENUE ACCOUNTS
(Classified by Source of Revenues)

I. EDUCATIONAL AND GENERAL
  A. Student Tuition and Fees
    501   Resident Tuition
    502   Nonresident Tuition
    503   Late Registration Fee

    504 Course Change Fee
    505 Deferred Test and Examination Fee
    506 Advanced Standing Examination Fee
    507 Music Fee
    508 Diploma Fee
    509 Thesis Fee
    510 Summer Session
    511 University Extension
B. Governmental Appropriations
    601 State Appropriations—General Support
    602 Research Institute of Pharmaceutical Sciences
C. Endowment Income
    611 Unrestricted
    612 Restricted
D. Gifts (or Gifts Applied)
    621 Gifts (or Gifts Applied)
E. Sponsored Research
    631 Federal Government—Grants
    632 Federal Government—Contracts
    633 Foundations
    634 Business and Industry
F. Other Separately Budgeted Research
    641 University Funds
    642 Other Sources
G. Other Sponsored Programs
    651 Governmental—Training Grants and Contracts
    652 Governmental—Instructional Institutes
    653 Nongovernmental—Training Grants
H. Recovery of Indirect Costs—Sponsored Programs
    661 Federal
    662 Nonfederal
I. Sales and Services of Educational Departments
    701 Engineering Testing
    702 Home Economics
J. Organized Activities Relating to Educational Departments
    721 Computer Center
    722 Home Economics Cafeteria
    723 Farm
K. Other Sources
    731 Library Fines
    732 Interest and Capital Gains on Temporary Investments of Current Funds
    733 Transcripts

734   University News Service
735   Swimming Pool
736   Sale of Surplus Equipment
737   Educational Allowance Reimbursement

II. STUDENT AID
     901   Gifts
     902   Endowment Income

III. AUXILIARY ENTERPRISES
     951   Bookstore—Sale of Books
     952   Bookstore—Sale of Supplies
     953   Bookstore—Miscellaneous Sales
     961   Cafeteria
     971   Residence Halls—Single
     972   Residence Halls—Married
     981   Intercollegiate Athletics—Student Fees
     982   Intercollegiate Athletics—Gate Receipts
     983   Intercollegiate Athletics—Game Guarantees
     984   Intercollegiate Athletics—Miscellaneous
     991   College Union
     995   Airport

OBJECT CLASSIFICATION OF EXPENDITURES

010   SALARIES

011   Salaries—Teaching
012   Salaries—Other Professional
013   Salaries—Nonprofessional

020   WAGES

021   Wages—Graduate Teaching
022   Wages—Other Graduate
023   Wages—Other Professional
024   Wages—Nonprofessional
025   Wages—Undergraduate Students

030   SUPPLIES AND EXPENSE

031   Instructional Supplies
032   Office Supplies
033   Janitorial, Cleaning, and Laundry Supplies
034   Printing, Binding, and Reproducing
035   Repairing and Servicing to Equipment
036   Postage and Freight

037   Telephone and Telegraph (Unless charged to General Institutional Expense)

038   Travel (Unless charged to General Institutional Expense)

040   EQUIPMENT

041   Scientific Equipment
042   Office Machines and Equipment
043   Furniture and Furnishings
044   Physical Plant Machines and Tools
045   Motor Vehicles
046   Books
047   Livestock

NAME OF SUBSIDIARY LEDGER—BY FUNDS	NAME OF CONTROL ACCOUNT IN GENERAL LEDGER	DESCRIPTION
I. Current Funds		
A. Unrestricted		
1. Accounts Receivable	Accounts Receivable	Includes an account for each debtor. Total of detail accounts equals control account.
2. Allocations	Expenditures Departmental Allocations	Includes accounts with each organization unit listed in chart of accounts, Section II. Totals of different columns in subsidiary agree with respective control accounts in general ledger.
3. Revenues	Revenues Unrealized Revenues	Includes accounts with each type of revenue. Totals of different columns agree with respective control accounts in general ledger.
B. Restricted		
1. Restricted Funds	Restricted Funds Balances	Includes an account with each restricted fund. Total of balances of restricted funds equals control account.
II. Loan Funds		
1. Notes and Interest	Notes Receivable Interest Receivable	Includes an account with each person to whom a loan has been made. Account is subdivided to show amount due on principal and inter-

NAME OF SUBSIDIARY LEDGER—BY FUNDS	NAME OF CONTROL ACCOUNT IN GENERAL LEDGER	DESCRIPTION
		est. Totals of columns agree with respective control accounts.
2. Loan Funds	Loan Funds Balances	Includes an account with each separate loan fund. Total of all funds agrees with control account.

III. *Endowment and Similar Funds*

1. Investments	Investments	Includes an account with each security or parcel of real estate. Total of all accounts in subsidiary ledger agrees with control accounts.
2. Endowment Funds Term Endowment Funds Quasi-endowment Funds	Endowment Funds Balances Term Endowment Funds Balances Quasi-endowment Funds Balances	Includes an account with each separate endowment fund. Total of individual funds agrees with control account.

IV. *Annuity and Life Income Funds*

1. Annuity and Life Income Funds	Annuity and Life Income Funds Balances	Includes an account with each separate annuity and life income fund. Total of individual funds agrees with control account.

V. *Plant Funds*

A. Unexpended Plant Funds

1. Unexpended Plant Funds	Unexpended Plant Funds Balances	Includes an account with each fund in the unexpended plant funds group. Total of all funds equals control account.

B. Renewals and Replacement Funds

1. Renewals and Replacement Funds	Renewals and Replacement Funds Balances	Includes an account with each fund in the renewals and replacement fund group. Total of all funds equals control account.

NAME OF SUBSIDIARY LEDGER—BY FUNDS	NAME OF CONTROL ACCOUNT IN GENERAL LEDGER	DESCRIPTION
C. Retirement of Indebtedness 1. Retirement of Indebtedness Funds	Retirement of Indebtedness Funds Balances	Includes an account with each fund in the retirement of indebtedness funds group. Total of all funds equals control account.
D. Investment in Plant 1. Plant	Land Buildings Improvements Other Than Buildings Equipment	Includes accounts with each type of plant asset. The ledger is subdivided to provide details under each of the four control accounts.
VI. *Agency Funds* 1. Deposit	Agency Funds Balances	Includes an account with each student or organization having funds on deposit with the college. Total of funds on deposit equals control account.

CHAPTER V

Preparation and Control
of the Current Funds Budget

THE EVER-EXPANDING programs and needs of educational institutions create financial problems and pressures of a magnitude experienced in few other organizations. The dollars for financing these programs and needs are usually limited. Because demands on institutional resources normally exceed such resources, some workable plan of coordinating demands and revenues is essential. The document designed to accomplish this objective in colleges and universities is the institutional budget. A budget should be formulated covering all current funds activities of the institution, including auxiliary enterprises, sponsored research, and other institutional programs. The current funds budget is discussed in this chapter.

Definition and Functions of the Budget.[1] The budget is defined as "a statement of the proposed expenditures for a fixed period, or for a specific project, or program, and the proposed means of financing the expenditures."[2] It is, furthermore, an authorization, after approval by the governing board, to incur the expenditures and to collect the revenues. In the business world the budget formulates a program of sales, production, and finance which assures management that a plan is being followed which will insure an approxi-

[1] The term "budget" in institutional finance generally refers to the budget of current funds. Although the operations of other funds may be covered by some type of working plan or budget, it is in the Current Funds group that the budget assumes the most importance.
[2] *College and University Business Administration,* 276.

mately known profit. In the field of education, the budget serves other purposes. It is both an instrument of control and limitation and a comprehensive financial plan for efficient and serviceable operation.

From the negative point of view, the budget places limitations on the administration of the institution and its subdivisions. This purpose of the budget is illustrated in the state institution, which is financed largely through the contributions of the taxpayers. The taxpayers vest the authority of control in a board of laymen, variously known as supervisors, trustees, or governors. This board meets infrequently and its members give but little of their time to the actual administration of the institution. In order, then, that the governing board may exercise its prerogatives—that is, to guide the institution and to determine its policies—it is necessary that a financial plan be formulated in advance outlining the operations of the institution for a given period of time. The governing board thus extends its control over the institution by means of this plan or budget, which places limitations on the president's powers of control and supervision over the detailed expenditures of funds for the various divisions of the college. In like manner, the budget enables the president of the institution to extend his control over the detailed operation of the institution.

One purpose of the budget is to insure that the institution does not obligate itself in a given period of time in excess of resources available during such period. This applies to private as well as state supported colleges and universities. In privately controlled schools, overspending results in the impairment of capital funds of the institution, or even in bankruptcy. In publicly supported institutions, overspending results in legal complications. The budgets of most state institutions are approved by the legislature and a state budget agency, hence, cannot be legally exceeded.

Too often these negative purposes are regarded as the sole function of the budget. The budget has greater significance as a positive, constructive device. The purposes of the educational institution are education, research, and public service. The activities of the institution, which in the aggregate promote these purposes, must be financed. The budget embodies the educational program in terms of dollars. It coordinates not only needs and finances but also the various interests which coexist in the college. It is the financial plan through which the various activities of the institution are carried on most efficiently. Moreover, the budget typifies the working of the democratic process. The budget as adopted is not the product of the president's desires, the desires of the business office, or the desires of a segment of the faculty. Instead, it tends to meet the requirements of the faculty, president, deans, business officers, and students. The budget is a chart and plan without which a college cannot function satisfactorily.

Relationship of the Budget to the Institutional Organization and Accounting System. The budget is related both to the functional organization of the institution and its accounting system and must be devised in conformity with the organization chart of the college or university. In most institutions, the nucleus of the budget is the department—either the instructional department, the administrative unit, or the organized division, such as the bookstore, dining hall, or athletic department. The head of each organization unit prepares and is guided by a budget. Logically, the head of a department must also be the head of a budget unit. Although one person may be required to administer two or more budgets, two department heads should not administer a single budget. The budgets for general expenses, covering such activities as commencement, conferences, convocations, and social activities, are usually placed under the jurisdiction of a faculty member whose field of interest is akin to the purpose of that budget in question. Frequently committees are appointed to prepare and execute budgets of a general nature. Budgets for expenses incurred in connection with finances, such as pension contributions, group insurance, and sinking fund contributions, are usually prepared and supervised by the chief business officer.

Because the accounts conform to the lines of the college organization, the budget should conform to the chart of accounts. Referring to the suggested chart of expenditure accounts presented in chapter 4, one finds one or more accounts each for expenses of the president's office, the business office, the department of art, the operation and maintenance department, the bookstore, and so on. The budget not only follows the accounting system, it is reflected also in the periodic financial statements.

It is sometimes said that two budgets are involved in the operation of state colleges and universities—the legislative budget and the internal or operating budget. The legislative budget, as its name implies, is a request for funds submitted to the legislature, whereas the operating budget is the financial plan based on the legislative appropriation. The budget for the legislature is a summary of the detailed budget which is designed for and later serves as a basis for the preparation of the operating budget. Of course, if the legislature fails to appropriate as much as is requested, the detailed budget must be adjusted accordingly before being implemented.

The appropriation made by the legislature may be in either a lump sum or in detail. On the one hand, a lump appropriation means that a certain sum of money is made available to be spent at the discretion of the institution. On the other hand, a detailed appropriation binds the institution to conform to each item of its budget. Between these extremes are many possibilities. For example, many legislatures appropriate one sum for ordinary operating expenses and a separate sum for capital outlay, allowing the institution to exercise discretion in the expenditure of funds from each appropriation. There exists a tendency on the part of state legislatures to appropriate a lump sum for ordinary operating expenses, but to make "line item" appropriations for equipment, special repairs, and building projects.

However the legislative appropriation is made, the internal allocations in the operating budget of the institution are detailed under major classes of expenditures. Some institutions subdivide departmental budgets into such categories as salaries, wages, supplies and expense, and equipment. Others employ a threefold division, i.e., personal services, supplies and expense, and equipment. Note that any important item of expense can be elevated into the position of a coordinate budget. For example, this is done in case of traveling expenses, where the institution desires to exercise a specific control over this type of expense. In many colleges, particularly the small ones, only one allocation is made to each department. The account for this department, through the use of codes, is maintained in such a manner that it may be analyzed periodically in order to obtain details of expenditures.

Preparation of the Budget. There are two broad phases in the preparation of the budget: (1) the estimation of expenditures, and (2) the estimation of revenues. Theoretically, in institutional finance, the estimate of expenditures, representing needs, precedes the estimate of revenues. In practice, however, as resources usually are limited, this procedure seldom is followed. Instead, an attempt is made to relate, or balance, necessary expenditures and expected revenues simultaneously. Although the determination of needs is the paramount consideration in the preparation of the budget, it is necessary at the same time to estimate the expected revenues. In the state institution, the predominant sources of revenues are appropriations by the state legislature, funds for sponsored programs, student fees, sales of organized activities relating to instruction, and auxiliary enterprises. Revenues from the last three sources may be estimated in advance with a reasonable degree of accuracy, but estimating the amount the legislature will appropriate presents difficulties. Usually the institution estimates as carefully as possible the revenues that are more or less under its control, then forecasts the appropriation obtainable from the legislature. In some states, funds are dedicated to the college by constitutional provision, so that the total revenue can be estimated with greater accuracy. In preparing estimates of revenue from student fees and from sales made by auxiliary enterprises and organized activities, statistics of past enrollment, the number of scholarships to be offered, as well as business and financial conditions, are considered. As regards legislative appropriations, the political situation may be a factor. Many states maintain budgetary departments which correlate needs of the various state agencies with anticipated revenues before budgets are presented to the legislature. Under such conditions the state institution secures aid from the budget department in estimating legislative appropriations. The major sources of revenue accruing to the privately controlled institution include student fees, earnings from endowment investments, gifts and grants from private sources, funds for sponsored programs, and sales of auxiliary enterprises. The private institution normally does not receive financial assistance from the state legislature; otherwise, the problems of estimating revenue are similar to those of the public organization.

In preparing estimates of revenue, the business office plays the major role, particularly in estimating student fees, income from endowments, state appropriations, and federal grants and contracts. To assist in estimating revenue from auxiliary enterprises and miscellaneous sources, the manager or director of each enterprise submits a formal estimate.

Some institutions, after estimating revenues as accurately as possible, issue a tentative allotment to each department head. This allotment is not final but is used to initiate the budget process and to prevent departmental requests from greatly exceeding available resources. After issuing tentative allotments, department heads are given an opportunity to justify requested changes in them. Throughout all steps of budget preparation, a definite calendar should be followed. This calendar should call for the completion of the budget well before the end of the fiscal year but should afford sufficient time at each stage of the process, to allow for needed deliberation.

After the issuance and revision of tentative allotments, the budgetary process is as follows:

Step one: Budget request forms, described later in this chapter, are sent out by the president to deans and department heads (with a letter setting forth guidelines).

Step two: Formal requests are obtained from heads of departments or other organizational units after they have been developed, with the advice and cooperation of their respective faculties.

Step three: The deans of colleges and directors of other organizational units are called upon to approve the requests of the departments of their respective colleges or divisions. In small colleges, the deans and department heads may work together in preparing the budget requests so that steps one and two tend to merge.

Step four: The business office consolidates all budget requests and prepares a tentative or preliminary budget for guidance of the president in making revisions.

Step five: The president and his representatives study the departmental requests and begin their revision in view of needs and available resources. The chief business officer provides statistics and unit cost studies to assist at this stage of the budgetary process. A committee consisting of the president, business officer, deans, and representatives of the faculty may be established to review the budget. In such review, each department head should be given opportunity to present reasons for the adoption of his own budget. If departmental requests exceed available or anticipated resources of the college, the paring process begins. This process may consist of: elimination of new projects of services; reduction of increases in existing services; reduction of expenses in connection with a planned expansion of enrollment; elimination of increases over last year's budget.

In paring the budget, there is a tendency to conform too closely to past expenditures. If a given department has been uneconomical in the past, basing the budget entirely on past performance encourages future excesses. Throughout the budgetary process intelligent consideration should be given to new trends and new developments—in short, to future needs as well as to past performance. Program budgeting, discussed later in this chapter, assists in an intelligent review of needs.

Step six: The final step in the budgetary process is approval of the budget by the president and, in turn, its submission by the chief executive to the governing board for final approval.

Unallocated Revenues, or Contingent Reserves. As fully explained later in this chapter, the budget as adopted must be controlled rigidly. The easiest way to disparage the budget and to limit its usefulness in institutional administration is to permit departmental budgets to be overspent. This practice thwarts the financial plan, however laboriously worked out. On the other hand, any budget, however carefully prepared, will have to be revised in some respects to meet contingencies arising during the year. Thus, in a well-prepared budget, provision is made for reasonable changes. The required elasticity is accomplished by including a contingency reserve in the budget. This reserve may be created by leaving unallocated some institutional revenue. The reserve is ordinarily placed under the control of the president of the institution and becomes effective only after the department head requesting the change obtains written approval (See Form 5.9).

Budget Forms. Uniformity of procedure is of prime importance in preparing the budget. For this reason, definite rules and instructions, together with necessary forms, should be provided for those who engage in the budgetary process. These forms include:

FORM 5.1

BLANK COLLEGE B U D G E T R E Q U E S T S 1968-1969	Chemical Engineering Department	Code
	LETTER OF EXPLANATION	

Use this form for any necessary explanation of Budget Requests, including reasons for any increase or unusual items. (If necessary, use more than one sheet--------please do not use plain paper.)

Budget Item	E x p l a n a t i o n	*Do not use this space*
SALARIES	Department Position No. 7 - New position, Assistant Professor. The justification for a new position in Chemical Engineering was set forth in a memorandum to the Dean of the College of Engineering of October 7. Points developed included the need to keep teaching loads at a reasonable level, the need to provide increased manpower to handle the growing graduate program, the need to devote more effort to research, the need to provide increased staff flexibility, the need to engage in more public relations activity and professional activity. Because of steadily rising demands for qualified engineering personnel, it is expected that a salary of $12,000 will be required to attract the type of teacher-researcher desired.	
WAGES	New staff position W-2 - Clerk Stenographer. The steady increase of office work during the past two years necessitates the addition of a Clerk-Stenographer (half-time) to be shared with Civil Engineering (half-time). Only the availability of two, part-time Work Study students during the past year has permitted the office work to be taken care of without the serious overloading of the present secretary. The requested increase in graduate assistantship stipends is required to meet the national competition.	
SUPPLIES AND EXPENSE	The increase requested is a simple reflection of the increased cost of supplies and services and the demand for more instructional supplies as the number of graduate students increases.	
EQUIPMENT	The amount requested, $2,300, will provide for one item of equipment which has been scheduled for addition to the laboratory (Unit Operations) for the past three years. Additional equipment is actually needed, but it is anticipated that some of this equipment can be procured in connection with the equipping of the addition to Carrier Hall to be built as Phase IV of the Science Center.	

Department Chairman

FORM 5.2

BLANK COLLEGE B U D G E T R E Q U E S T S 1968-1969				Chemical Engineering Department			Code
S a l a r i e s							
Dept. Pos. No. (1)	NAME Title of Position (2)	No. of Mos. (3)	Present Salary Rate (4)	Increase Decrease* Requested (5)	Recommended By Dept Chairman (6)	Approved By Dean (7)	Approved By President (8)
1.	FRANK A. SMITH Associate Dean of the School of Engineering and Professor of Chemical Engineering	12	$14,000	$3,000		$17,000	$17,000
2.	RUSSELL E. BAKER Professor and Radiation Safety Officer	9	11,000	2,500	13,500	13,500	13,500
3.	BILL E. CARTER Professor	9	11,000	2,500	13,500	13,500	13,500
4.	J. ROGER JOHNSON Professor of Chemistry and Chemical Engineering (part-time) (See Chemistry Dept.)	9	-0-	-0-	-0-	-0-	-0-
5.	JAMES JONES Associate Professor	9	11,500	1,250	12,750	12,750	12,750
6.	TED MILES, JR. Assistant Professor and Research Engineer (Paid by Engr. Experiment Station)	9	7,500 (2,500) (10,000)	750 (250) (1,000)	8,250 (2,750) (11,000)	8,250 (2,750) (11,000)	8,250 (2,750) (11,000)
7.	_____		New	12,000	12,000	12,000	Disapproved
	TOTAL SALARIES _____ ➤ (List Totals on Last Page Only)				$77,000	$77,000	$77,000
Prepared and Approved By							
Dept. Chairman		Division Head			Checked By		
Dean		President			Entered On Budget	Business Manager	

1. Letter of Explanation (Form 5.1)—This form, being the letter of transmittal from the department head to the president, is primarily used to justify any unusual budgetary requests and to state reasons for any increases. It also may be used to suggest improve-

ments in the department or to explain its future plans and objectives.

2. Salaries (Form 5.2)—All salaried positions with required explanatory details are listed on this form. In addition to the entries

FORM 5.3

<table>
<tr><td colspan="2" rowspan="2">BLANK COLLEGE
B U D G E T   R E Q U E S T S
1968-1969</td><td colspan="5"></td><td rowspan="2"></td></tr>
<tr><td colspan="5">Chemical Engineering
Department</td><td>Code</td></tr>
<tr><td colspan="8">W a g e s</td></tr>
<tr><td>Dept.
Pos.
No.
(1)</td><td>NAME
Title of Position
(2)</td><td>No.
of
Mos.
(3)</td><td>Present
Wage
Rate
(4)</td><td>Increase
Decrease*
Requested
(5)</td><td>Recommended
By Dept.
Chairman
(6)</td><td>Approved
By
Dean
(7)</td><td>Approved
By
President
(8)</td></tr>
<tr><td colspan="8">LIST SEPARATELY EACH POSITION ON REGULAR MONTHLY WAGE STATUS</td></tr>
<tr><td>W-1</td><td>MRS. DORA H. McHENRY
Secretary
(Paid by Civil Eng.)</td><td>12</td><td>$ 1,620
(1,620)
(3,240)</td><td>$ 90
(90)
(180)</td><td>$ 1,710
(1,710)
(3,420)</td><td>$ 1,710
(1,710)
(3,420)</td><td>$ 1,710
(1,710)
(3,420)</td></tr>
<tr><td>W-2</td><td>Clerk-Stenographer
(Paid by Civil Eng.)</td><td>12</td><td>New</td><td>1,350
(1,350)
(2,700)</td><td>1,350
(1,350)
(2,700)</td><td>1,350
(1,350)
(2,700)</td><td>Out</td></tr>
<tr><td>197</td><td>Graduate Assistant</td><td>9</td><td>2,400</td><td>100</td><td>2,500</td><td>2,500</td><td>2,500</td></tr>
<tr><td>198</td><td>Graduate Assistant</td><td>9</td><td>2,400</td><td>100</td><td>2,500</td><td>2,500</td><td>2,500</td></tr>
<tr><td>199</td><td>Laboratory Assistant</td><td>9</td><td>1,800</td><td>700</td><td>2,500</td><td>2,500</td><td>2,500</td></tr>
<tr><td colspan="8">TOTAL ANNUAL REQUIREMENT--MONTHLY WAGE POSITIONS ——▶</td></tr>
<tr><td colspan="5">DETAIL OF MISCELLANEOUS WAGE REQUIREMENTS
500 hours at $1.25 per hour for student wages.</td><td>625</td><td>625</td><td>625</td></tr>
<tr><td colspan="5">TOTAL WAGES
(List Totals on Last Page Only)</td><td>$11,185</td><td>$11,185</td><td>$9,735</td></tr>
<tr><td colspan="8">Prepared and Approved By</td></tr>
<tr><td>Dept.
Chairman</td><td></td><td colspan="2">Division
Head</td><td></td><td colspan="2">Checked
By</td><td></td></tr>
<tr><td>Dean</td><td></td><td colspan="2">President</td><td></td><td colspan="2">Entered
On
Budget</td><td>Business Manager</td></tr>
</table>

shown in the illustration, Form 5.2 might include persons on part-time, persons transferred from one position to another, promotions, and persons on leave. To achieve the greatest possible uniformity in

FORM 5.4

		Budget For 1967-1968 (3)	Increase Or Decrease* (4)	Requested By Dept. Chairman (5)	Approved By Dean (6)	Approved By President (7)
	BLANK COLLEGE					
	B U D G E T R E Q U E S T S 1968-1969			Chemical Engineering Department		Code
	S u p p l i e s a n d E x p e n s e					
Object Code (1)	Items (2)	Budget For 1967-1968 (3)	Increase Or Decrease* (4)	Requested By Dept. Chairman (5)	Approved By Dean (6)	Approved By President (7)
201	Building and Electrical Supplies					
202	Food Supplies					
204	Fuel, other than motor vehicle					
205	Instructional Supplies	$1,700	$1,050	$2,750	$2,750	
206	Janitorial, Laundry, Cleaning Supplies					
207	Motor Vehicle Supplies					
209	Office Supplies	300	100	400	400	
217	Power Plant Supplies					
218	Dues and Subscriptions	50	–0–	50	50	
219	Heat, Light, Power, and Water					
220	Insurance and Bond Premiums					
221	Postage and Freight on Commodities	100	–0–	100	100	
222	Printing and Binding and Reproducing	100	100	200	200	
223	Repairing and Servicing Property	450	350	800	800	
225	Telephone and Telegraph	380	320	700	700	
226	Travel	1,100	–0–	1,100	1,100	
227	Contractual Services					
230	Fees for Professional Services					
231	Advertising					
232	Health Service Supplies					
	TOTALS	$4,180	$1,920	$6,100	$6,100	$4,100

Prepared and Approved By				
Dept. Chairman		Division Head	Checked By	
Dean		President	Entered On Budget	Business Manager

personnel service requests, a model form, meeting all possible requirements, should be sent to each department head.

3. Wages (Form 5.3)—All permanent wage employees should be listed by name. Positions to be filled should be set up where needed. Miscellaneous wage funds should be included for casual labor.

4. Supplies and expense (Form 5.4)—Each department head is required to list on this form the items needed for his department. Only the important requirements with respect to supplies and expense need be itemized.

5. Equipment (Form 5.5)—As regards equipment, the department head lists separately each item requested. The equipment budget frequently is controlled in detail; that is, the expenditure of funds for equipment must follow the detailed items of the budget. Devi-

FORM 5.5

BLANK COLLEGE BUDGET REQUESTS 1968-1969	Chemical Engineering Department		Code
Equipment			
Items (1)	Requested By Dept. Chairman (2)	Approved By Dean (3)	Approved By President (4)
Five-Stage, Liquid-liquid Denver Extraction Unit (new apparatus to fill major gap in stage-wise laboratory apparatus)	$2,300	$2,300	$2,300
TOTALS	$2,300	$2,300	$2,300

Please list all equipment in detail using estimated cost where actual cost is not known.
If additional sheets are required use Detail Sheet (Form 2) and summarize above.

Prepared and Approved By					
Dept. Chairman		Division Head		Checked By	
Dean		President		Entered On Budget	Business Manager

BLANK COLLEGE B U D G E T R E Q U E S T S 1968-1969		Chemical Engineering Department		Code

Summary of Departmental Requests and Approved Budget

Budget	Budget For 1967-1968	Increase or Decrease* Requested	Requested By Dept. Chairman	Approved By Dean	Approved By President
Salaries	$55,000	$10,000	$65,000	$65,000	$65,000
Wages	9,000	735	9,735	9,735	9,735
Supplies and Expense	4,180	680*	4,100	4,100	4,100
Equipment	1,000	1,300	2,300	2,300	2,300
TOTALS	$69,180	$11,355	$81,135	$81,135	$81,135

Comments:

Prepared and Approved By

Dept. Chairman		Division Head		Checked By		
Dean		President		Entered On Budget		Business Manager

ESTIMATED REVENUES	BLANK COLLEGE B U D G E T R E Q U E S T S 1968-1969	College or Division Auxiliary Enterprises

Department Bookstore

Code No. 65	Sheet No. 5

Items	Budget Estimated Revenue 1967-1968	Estimated Revenue 1968-1969	Increase or Decrease* Over 1967-1968
Sale of Textbooks	$200,000	$240,000	$ 40,000
Sale of Supplies	20,000	30,000	10,000
Sale of Wearing Apparel	19,000	20,000	1,000
TOTAL REVENUE	$239,000	$290,000	$ 51,000

ations are allowed only upon properly approved requests.

6. Departmental summary (Form 5.6)—This form summarizes requests for salaries, wages, supplies and expense, and equipment.

7. Estimated Revenues (Form 5.7)—The head of each department or division which produces any revenue submits revenue estimates on Form 5.7. Revenues that do not pertain to a particular division, such as that from state appropriations or endowments, are estimated on this form by the chief business officer.

FORM 5.8

BLANK COLLEGE B U D G E T S U M M A R Y 1968-1969			
	Estimated 1967-1968	Approved 1968-1969	Inc. or Dec. Over 1967-1968
REVENUES			
Educational and General			
Student Tuition and Fees			
Governmental Appropriations			
Endowment Income			
Gifts			
Sponsored Research			
Other Separately Budgeted Research			
Other Sponsored Programs			
Recovery of Indirect Costs			
Sales and Services of Educational Departments			
Organized Activities Related to Instruction			
Other Sources			
Total Educational and General			
Student Aid			
Auxiliary Enterprises			
TOTAL REVENUES			
EXPENDITURES			
Educational and General			
Instruction and Departmental Research			
Organized Activities Relating to Educational Departments			
Sponsored Research			
Other Separately Budgeted Research			
Other Sponsored Programs			
Extension and Public Service			
Libraries			
Student Services			
Operation and Maintenance of Physical Plant			
General Administration			
Staff Benefits			
General Institutional Expense			
Total Educational and General			
Student Aid			
Auxiliary Enterprises			
TOTAL EXPENDITURES			

8. Budget Summary (Form 5.8)—After all requests from departments have been collected and estimates of revenue prepared, they are accumulated and summarized on Form 5.8. This summary is supported by detailed revenue estimates and expenditure budgets.

At least four copies of the complete budget documents are necessary for internal operating purposes. These copies go to the president, the chief business officer, the auditor, and the chief academic officer, respectively. Usually for presentation to the governing board, a special summary is prepared in which only personal services are itemized. With regard to the budget submitted to the state legislature, in some states the budgetary forms are prescribed. Usually these forms require summarized information for the institution as a whole and can be prepared easily from the detailed operating budget.

Budgets of Self-Supporting Activities and Enterprises. Generally, all current revenues and expenditures should be included in the current funds budget. Operations of all departments, including those producing revenues sufficient to finance themselves, should be controlled by the institutional budget. In cases where the department is wholly self-supporting, such as a cafeteria, dining hall, or bookstore, estimates of revenue and proposed expenditures may be incorporated in the budget with the understanding that the entire revenue from such enterprise is available for expenditure by that enterprise. If operations result in increased revenues, the expenditure budget should be increased by an amount sufficient to finance the enhanced operations. In other words, the budget for self-supporting departments should be flexible and should be expanded or contracted in proportion to actual operations. Some institutions handle self-supporting activities in a revolving or working-capital fund, not a part of or controlled by the current funds budget. This procedure is satisfactory, provided the self-supporting enterprise is considered part of the regular operations of the institution. If the financing of auxiliary or self-supporting activities in a revolving fund fosters or encourages the notion of separate ownership, then such a plan is not satisfactory. In the event certain activities are financed through a revolving fund, for statement purposes the expenditures and revenues of such activities should be combined with the expenditures and revenues of other current funds.

Control of the Budget. The budget, having been prepared, reviewed, and approved by the president, the governing board, and the legislature or state budgeting agency, is placed in operation. There are two phases of control exercised over budgets of educational institutions.

The first, pertaining only to the state institution, is external control exercised by some agency of the state. Ordinarily this agency is interested in ascertaining that the total budgetary appropriation is not exceeded. In some states such control is exercised through the medium of the postaudit, normally conducted by the state auditing agency. The control may be of a continuous nature, being exercised by a state budgetary department through the use of work programs and a system of periodic allotments. Under this plan, the institution submits a work program broken down into periods—frequently quarters—and requests that funds be allotted to it on this basis. In approving these requests, the state budgeting department issues allotments authorizing the institution to expend a stipulated amount for the period in question. The purpose of this system is to enable the state to correlate expenditures with revenues continuously throughout the fiscal year. The privately controlled institution is not concerned with this type of budgetary control. In a few states, control is by line item.

Second, and more important from the accounting point of view, is the internal control over the detailed operating budget exercised by the institution itself. If the budget is to have meaning, and if the wishes of the governing board relative to the budget are to be carried out, the accounting system must provide for budgetary control. Institutions usually exercise this control by recording the budget in the accounting records, so that the progress of each budget is reviewed constantly. Through a system of requisitions and encumbering of purchase orders which are entered as a charge against the appropriate budget, strict budgetary control is effected. In small institutions, budgetary control may be predicated on files on outstanding purchase orders and a system of periodic reports on the progress of the departmental budgets. However, regardless of the size of the institution, two factors are of fundamental importance to budgetary control; first, centralized purchasing, and, second, a requisitioning system under which the accounting office approves all requisitions (or purchase orders) prior to the issuance of purchase orders.

An outline of the steps necessary to obtain complete budgetary control over expenditures follows:

1. The budget is recorded in detail in the accounting records.

2. Personnel services are controlled through personnel action forms which are set up by the accounting office only if funds are available. Likewise, no wage payroll voucher is processed if funds are not available.

3. All purchasing is done by the business office upon the requisition of the department head.

4. Prior to the issuance of the purchase order, the accounting office approves the requisition or the purchase order relative to the availability of funds.

5. When issued, the purchase order is entered as a charge or encumbrance against the appropriate departmental budget, thus effecting a reduction of the available balance.

6. The accounting office prepares monthly statements for each budgetary unit, showing the exact status of its budget.

7. Adjustments of budgets for unanticipated needs are formally approved and entered in the accounts.

Budgetary control should also be related to revenues. Obviously, the expenditure budget can be executed fully only if all estimated resources are realized. If, for example, the enrollment unexpectedly declines, resulting in decreased revenues, it will be necessary to adjust budget allotments accordingly, unless new sources of revenue are found. If it is possible to relate decreased revenue to a particular department, for example, if bookstore sales are less than estimated, it may be possible to reduce the bookstore budget of expenditures correspondingly, without affecting other budgetary units. Budget adjustments may be made on a request for budget revision, Form 5.9.

Recording the Budget in the Records. As soon as the accounting department receives an approved copy of the budget, entry is made on a journal voucher (Form 5.10) to record the unrealized revenues and the allocations to departments:

FORM 5.9

BLANK COLLEGE

R E Q U E S T   F O R   B U D G E T   R E V I S I O N

Date _____

Account	Chemical Engineering Name of Unit | Code No. Present Budget	Revisions Requested		Revised Budget
		Increases	Decreases	
Salaries				
Wages				
Supplies and Expense	$4,100.00	$600.00	-0-	$4,700.00
Equipment				
TOTAL	$4,100.00	$600.00	-0-	$4,700.00

(The above section may be detached and used for continuation sheets where necessary.)
Explain fully the reasons for this request for revisions in the above budget.
Attach extra sheets if necessary.

    The budget was reduced to $4,100 from our actual budget of $4,180 for 1967-68. We cannot operate the full year without additional funds. This request will provide new funds for instructional supplies only.

Salary or Wage Rates Approved   _____
(where required)   Director of Personnel

Requested by   Recommended Means of Financing Request:

_____
   (Department Chairman or
    Administrative Head)   Charge
                                          Increase to:Unallocated Revenues $ 600.00
Approval Recommended
                                          Credit
                *   Decrease to:_____ $_____
_____
           Dean
                                          _____
Approval Recommended   Business Manager
                                          Approved
_____   Date_____ _____
      Division Head   President

FORM 5.10

BLANK COLLEGE
JOURNAL VOUCHER

Year 19__-19__

No._____

Date_____

	Account Number	Subsidiary		General Ledger	
		Debit	Credit	Debit	Credit

Explanation:_____

Prepared By:_____ Approved:_____

FORM 5.11

BLANK COLLEGE
REVENUES LEDGER

Account Bookstore

Account No._____

Sheet No.____1____

Date	Description	Voucher Number	Unrealized Revenues		Revenues Realized		Unrealized Balance
			Amount	Total To Date	Amount	Total To Date	
7-1-8	Set Up Budget	JV 1	$290,000	$290,000			$290,000
7-5-8	Cash Receipts	CV 1		290,000	$4,000	$4,000	286,000
7-6-8	Interdepartmental Sales	JV 2			1,000	5,000	285,000

Unrealized Revenues	$10,000,000	
Departmental Allocations		$9,900,000
Unallocated Revenues		100,000

To record the budget as approved by the governing board June 1, 19___.

Entries in subsidiary accounts:

IN REVENUES LEDGER (See Form 5.11)

Debit individual revenue accounts, for example:	
Resident Tuition	$2,000,000
Nonresident Tuition	50,000
Bookstore (From Budget Form 5.7)	
Textbooks	240,000
Supplies	30,000
Wearing Apparel	20,000
Dining Halls (From Budget Form 5.7)	
Sales	600,000

IN ALLOCATIONS LEDGER (See Forms 5.13, 5.14, 5.15, & 5.16)

Credit individual departmental budget accounts, for example:	
Chemical Engineering (From Budget Form 5.6)	
Salaries	65,000
Wages	9,735
Supplies and Expense	4,100
Equipment	2,300
Electrical Engineering (From Budget Form 5.6)	
Salaries	80,000
Wages	12,000
Supplies and Expense	4,000
Equipment	3,000

The above entry indicates that the total estimate of revenues is $10,000,000 and that $9,900,000 is allocated to the various organization units. The balance of $100,000 remaining in the Unallocated Revenues account constitutes a budgetary contingency reserve. The general ledger account Unrealized Revenues controls the detailed estimates in the revenues ledger. Similarly, the Departmental Allocations account in the general ledger controls the individual allocations accounts in the allocations ledger. As revenue is actually realized, credits are made to the Current Funds Revenues Control account in the general ledger. Charges against departmental allocations are recorded as debits to the Expenditures Control account.

Form 5.11 illustrates one of the subsidiary revenue accounts appearing in the revenues ledger. The budget is recorded as a debit in the Unrealized Revenues column of this account. Subsequently, as revenues are realized, the amount collected or accrued is entered in the Revenues Realized column. The balance, at any time, represents the amount of revenue yet to be realized from that particular source. In some institutions there may be a requirement to identify separately interdepartmental transactions. In such cases, separate columns can be used in the revenues ledger to record cash transactions and interdepartmental transactions.

Forms 5.12, 5.13, 5.14, and 5.15 illustrate how the detailed allocation accounts are recorded in the allocations ledger. Following the outline of the budget, separate ledger sheets are set up for salaries, wages, supplies and expense, and equipment for each department or other organization unit. The amount budgeted for each respective allocation is entered as a credit in the Allocations column. As requisitions are approved for the department (chemical engineering in the illustration) and orders are issued, the amounts of such orders are entered in the Orders Placed column. This results in a decrease in the Unencumbered or Free Balance of that particular budget. Subsequently, when the materials are received and the actual amount of the expenditure is determined, the encumbered order is liquidated by entering a credit in the Orders Paid column and a debit in the Expenditures column. The Free Balance is adjusted automatically for any difference between the amount of the order and the actual cost of materials. At any time, after all vouchers have been posted, the available balance in any budget can be ascertained readily. This procedure assists in the approving of requisitions—a step in budgetary control. The illustration of this process refers to the supplies and expense budget, but it applies to all other budgets except that for salaries and wages. As the number of employees and the amounts of their pay are known in advance, it is not absolutely necessary to encumber salaries or wages. However, some

FORM 5.12

BLANK COLLEGE

ALLOCATIONS LEDGER

Division: College of Engineering

Department: Chemical Engineering

Budget: Salaries

Sheet No. _____

Orders Placed, Paid, or Cancelled	Order Number	Date	Name or Description	Voucher Number	Object Code	Amount Paid	Allocation	Balance
		7- 1-	Set Up Budget	JV 1	100		65,000 00cr	65,000 00cr

FORM 5.13

BLANK COLLEGE

ALLOCATIONS LEDGER

Division: College of Engineering

Department: Chemical Engineering

Budget: Wages

Sheet No. _____

Orders Placed, Paid, or Cancelled	Order Number	Date	Name or Description	Voucher Number	Object Code	Amount Paid	Allocation	Balance
		7- 1-	Set Up Budget	JV 1	200		9,735 00	9,735 00

FORM 5.14

BLANK COLLEGE

ALLOCATIONS LEDGER

Division: College of Engineering

Department: Chemical Engineering

Budget: Supplies and Expense

Sheet No. ___

Orders Placed, Paid, or Cancelled	Order Number	Date	Name or Description	Voucher Number	Object Code	Amount Paid	Allocation	Balance
		7- 1-	Set Up Budget	JV 1	300		4,100 00cr	4,100 00cr
100 00	79240	7-20-	Brown Electronics		300			4,000 00cr
100 00cr	79240	8- 1-	Brown Electronics	784	300	100 00		4,000 00cr

FORM 5.15

BLANK COLLEGE

ALLOCATIONS LEDGER

Division: College of Engineering

Department: Chemical Engineering

Budget: Equipment

Sheet No. ___

Orders Placed, Paid, or Cancelled	Order Number	Date	Name or Description	Voucher Number	Object Code	Amount Paid	Allocation	Balance
		7- 1-	Set Up Budget	JV 1	400		2,300 00cr	2,300 00cr

colleges follow the practice of encumbering the salaries and wages budgets at the beginning of the year and liquidating for each payroll. Methods of payroll control are discussed in chapter 6.

The importance of rendering budget reports to the department heads has been explained. One way to obtain this report is to design the allocations ledger so that a duplicate sheet is provided by inserting a carbon between two identical ledger sheets. Thus, the budget statement becomes a by-product of posting, obtained without additional work. Moreover, providing the department head with an exact duplicate of the formal ledger sheet assists the business office in the discovery of errors and differences. Computerized and tabulating systems easily produce duplicate copies for budget heads. In a hand-posted system, a summarized monthly report, showing the condition of each budget, takes the place of the duplicate ledger sheet.

Revising the Budget. There are at least four methods of effecting budget revisions: (1) increasing both revenue estimates and departmental allocations (2) decreasing revenue estimates and departmental allocations; (3) increasing one allocation and decreasing another; (4) transferring credits from the contingent reserve or unallocated revenues account to a departmental budget. The entries to record each of these types of changes are as follows:

1. Increased revenues from bookstore sales to increase the bookstore allocation for supplies and expense:

Unrealized Revenues
    Departmental Allocations

In the revenues ledger, debit Bookstore Revenues (estimated) account. In the allocations ledger, credit the Bookstore Supplies and Expense account in the Allocations column.

2. Decreased revenues from registration fees absorbed by decreasing the supplies and expense budget of the accounting office.

Departmental Allocations
    Unrealized Revenues

In the revenues ledger, decrease the budget estimate originally set up for registration fees. In the allocations ledger, reduce the supplies and expense budget of the accounting office by a debit in the Allocations column.

3. The supplies and expense budget of the department of chemistry is increased. This increase is offset by a decrease in the equipment budget of the department of history.

    Departmental Allocations
        Departmental Allocations

In the allocations ledger, the appropriate budgets of the two departments are increased and decreased, respectively.

4. An increase in the salaries budget of the registrar's office is financed by a transfer from unallocated revenues.

    Unallocated Revenues
        Departmental Allocations

In the allocations ledger, the salaries budget of the registrar's office is increased.

Closing Budgetary Accounts. The final phase of the budgetary process relates to the closing entries required at the end of the year and the disposition of unused allocations in particular departments. For convenience and clarity in describing closing entries, the following example is presented.

Original revenues estimate	$10,000,000
Actual revenue realized	9,900,000
Original budget allocations	8,000,000
Subsequent budget allocations	1,900,000
Actual expenditures	8,900,000
Encumbrances at end of year	800,000

Using the above figures, an incomplete trial balance of the general ledger is prepared as follows:

	Debit	*Credit*
Departmental Allocations		$ 9,900,000
Unrealized Revenues	$10,000,000	

Unallocated Revenues		$100,000
Revenues		9,900,000
Expenditures	$8,900,000	
Encumbrances	800,000	
Provision for Encumbrances		800,000

The following closing entries are made on journal vouchers:

1.	Departmental Allocations	$ 9,900,000	
	Unallocated Revenues	100,000	
	Unrealized Revenues		$10,000,000

To close budgetary accounts for revenues and expenditures into Unrealized Revenues.

2.	Revenues	$ 9,900,000	
	Expenditures		$ 8,900,000
	Encumbrances		800,000
	Unrestricted Current Funds Balances		200,000

To close nominal accounts for actual cash revenues, expenditures and encumbrances into Unrestricted Current Funds Balances.

In the above illustrations, transactions for the year produced an increase in the unallocated balances of unrestricted current funds of $200,000. This balance may be used to finance expenditures in the succeeding year or, in the publicly supported institution, it may have to be turned back to the state treasurer as an unexpended appropriation.

Referring to the illustration, observe that while $9,900,000 was allocated to various departmental budgets, only $9,700,000 (Expenditures plus Encumbrances) was actually expended. This means that there are free balances in the allocations ledger totalling $200,000.

There are several methods of handling unused departmental balances. In some public institutions, as has been stated, the unallocated balance reverts to the state. In such cases, Unrestricted Current Funds Balances is debited and Cash is credited to record the refund. If the balance can be retained, there are three possible methods available to the institution. First, all free departmental balances can be lapsed at the end of the year and closed into Unrestricted Current Funds Balances. This is the procedure assumed in the above illustration. Entry two is supported by debits to detail accounts of those departments having free balances. Second, the departments may be allowed to retain their unspent balances. If such is the case, it can best be handled by closing all accounts, as outlined, but allocating in the new budget the current balance of $200,000 to those departments which had unexpended balances. Third, unexpended departmental balances can be closed into Unrestricted Current Funds Balances but earmarked for general institutional purposes or for the particular departments from which they were requested.

Although a difference of opinion seems to exist as to the preferred method of disposing of unused departmental allocations, most accountants feel inclined toward the first plan discussed above—that is, the lapsing of all balances into a general unallocated balances account. Any reservations of balances in the name of departments endow those departments with a strong sense of ownership; hence, accumulated unallocated balances may be difficult to obtain for institutional purposes if emergencies should arise.

With respect to the revenues ledger, since detail estimates were $100,000 greater than actual revenues realized, it is necessary to close the detail accounts which have balances. In actual practice it is seldom possible to estimate exactly the amount of revenue from each source; hence, at the end of the year some revenue accounts are overrealized and other accounts are underrealized. In the illustration the net underrealization of revenue is $100,000.

Program Budgeting. Currently under consideration by a number of colleges and universities is a system of financial planning called program budgeting. Program budgeting—or planning-programming-budgeting-systems—has been in use by the United States Department of Defense since 1961, and since 1965 efforts have been under way to extend the system to other federal departments and federal agencies. This system, generally referred to as P.P.B.S., or program budgeting, focuses on the most effective use of available resources to meet predetermined goals and objectives.

P.P.B.S. is designed for long-range planning and budgeting, and as such, is generally developed to cover five- or ten-year periods. Institutional programs are the central factor in program budgeting, rather than the organization unit, as in the traditional budget system. The program budget attempts to establish and clarify the relationships between the goals or objectives, the resultant programs and activities derived from the goals, the economic impact of the proposed programs, and expression of costs in financial terms in a long-range budget. It also contributes to the decision-making process by providing analyses of alternative program decisions in terms of anticipated costs and expected benefits.

It might be well to mention at this point that the program budgeting concept may in certain instances make extensive use of computers and computer technology. However, it does not necessarily attempt to computerize the decision-making process, although it makes use of quantitative analytical methods.

In relating program budgeting to colleges and universities, it is essential to develop the basic concept of the system. The institution's goals or objectives are usually set out in institutional documents and in many instances will be clearly defined. For example, the goals may be expressed in general terms, such as instruction, research, and extension and public service. Such statements of goals do not provide the specific objectives of the institution which would permit programs to be formulated and evaluated. Goals or objectives of the institution therefore must be defined in terms of "program categories" which have identifiable end-products. For example, because one of the major goals of the institution is instruction, then the end-product, "program categories," becomes the degree programs in the respective fields, i.e., BBA degree in accounting. "Program categories" then must be further subdivided into "program subcategories." The program subcategories may then require further subdivision into "program elements." This kind of program structure may be made clear by the following partial outline:

I. INSTRUCTION (Institutional Goal)

    A. Instruction Leading to Degree(s)
       1. Bachelors Degree (Program Category)

a. Instruction Department A (Program Subcategory)
    (1) Personnel Costs ⎫
    (2) Supplies and Maintenance ⎬ Program Elements
b. Instruction Department B ⎭
    (1) Personnel Costs
    (2) Supplies and Maintenance
c. Etc.

The following comparison of the conventional budget format with the program budget format may assist in explaining the program budgeting concept.

In conventional budget making, the concern essentially is with the added cost of continuing the same functions, operations or programs, expansion of these functions, or the addition of new ones. It is generally assumed that the expenditure base from which the budget-making process begins is correct. Program budgeting, on the other hand, makes no such assumption but sets out the programs and applies analytical tools to measure the cost-benefit/cost-effectiveness before alternative decisions are made.

Williams presents a tabulation which further compares program budgeting with traditional or fiduciary budgeting. [3]

FORM 5.16[4]

Conventional Budget Format

Budgetary Unit_____			
Item	1964/1965 Appropriations	1965/1966 Increase or Decrease	1965/1966 Estimated Total Budget
I. Salary & Wages			
A. Academic			
B. Nonacademic			
II. Nonsalary Items			
A. Supplies & Expense			
B. Equipment			

[3] *Ibid.*, 15.

[4] Harry Williams, *Planning for Effective Resource Allocation* (American Council on Education, 1966), 8.

FORM 5.16 CONT.

Program Budget Format

Budetary Unit _____ (core department) _____

Item	64/65	65/66	66/67	67/68	68/69	Change over Program Period
FACULTY						
T/R Ratio [a]						
T/S Ratio [b]						
SCH-Int. [c]						
SCH-Ext. [d]						
SCH-Ug. [e]						
SCH-G. [f]						
COSTS-Oper.						
Faculty						
SCH-Ug.						
SCH-G.						
COSTS-Invest.						
Faculty						
Student						
SUPPORT						
Staff						
Supplies						
Equipment						
Space—Faculty						
Space—Support Staff						

[a] Teaching/Research ratio in faculty.
[b] Faculty/Student ratio in program element.
[c] Student Class Hours—students internal to this element.
[d] Student Class Hours—students external to this element.
[e] Student Class Hours—undergraduate.
[f] Student Class Hours—graduate.

THE FOCUS OF PROGRAM AND FIDUCIARY BUDGET:

PROGRAM BUDGETING	FIDUCIARY BUDGETING
Alternating ways to achieve university goals and objectives	Sources of funds
Major programs in teaching and research	Constraints on receipt and expenditure of funds
Resource requirements explicitly related to each program and subprogram	Aggregates of expenditures on Administration Teaching and Research Maintenance Student Services

"True" cost of major programs and program elements	Legal and administrative
Marginal and opportunity costs	Accounting for funds
Long time periods	Average cost ratios
Level of activities "Produced"	Short time periods
	Purely fiscal matters

Program budgeting cuts across conventional departmental lines and measures the performance of a program in terms of output. In this manner, program elements which are possible substitutes for others may be given full consideration; thus, program budgeting introduces a degree of competition designed to achieve greater effectiveness. Effectiveness may be considered as a measure of the extent to which a general program accomplishes its objectives and is related to benefits which may be thought of as the utility to be derived from a given program. This is the cost-benefit/cost-effectiveness approach as employed in program budgeting.

The next major objective of program budgeting is the aspect of control. Essentially, this involves the determination of how well a new program is being implemented. This process differs little from present institutional practices in many areas of budget making, since traditionally there has been follow-up on new programs to be certain that implementation follows the plan.

The final objective of program budgeting involves data and information. The system, if properly set up, will produce certain data that were not previously in evidence. These data will enable the institution to make decisions in terms of the total program rather than on a departmental basis. This is possible because the programs relate to the end-product(s) rather than to the administrative organization or function of the institution.

In summary, the important features of program budgeting are as follows:

1. The time-frame for budgeting is extended from the usual one-year period to a minimum of five years and may be extended to a longer period.

2. The purpose of program budgeting is planning. Thus, it becomes essential to examine the cost and benefit implications of alternative courses of action for the future. The program budget shows existing programs extended over time and the effects of decisions already made.

3. The full cost of programs and program alternatives must be calculated if correct decisions are to be made. Certain support programs must be allocated to academic programs to determine full cost. It may be necessary to construct a cost model in order to be able to review the interrelationship of resources and costs.

4. Program budgeting is dynamic, aiming at a continuous management process.

Although program budgeting as considered above would require a reconstructing of the present function-departmental-object systems in use in colleges and universities, it is possible to construct computer systems that would permit one to convert the present systems to the equivalent program budgeting. One might refer to such a system as a "crosswalk" or "bridge." While such a "crosswalk" is not presently available, neither is the full-blown framework and supporting details for a well-developed P.P.B.S. The future will bring both and fair evaluations of P.P.B.S. can then be made. In the meantime, the program budget philosophy can be used as a tool to improve the efficiency and management of institutional programs while continuing to use the present accounting system to collect expenditure data.

CHAPTER VI

Accounting for Current Funds
—Expenditures and Disbursements

IN THIS CHAPTER, the routine accounting procedures employed in the recording and posting of expenditures of current funds are explained and the records and documents used are illustrated. Although the discussion pertains to current funds, it is emphasized that the accounting routines for all funds are welded into one integrated system, hence, some of the forms and records may be used in funds other than current. The system is described from the point of view of both unrestricted current and restricted current funds.

The ledgers used in recording expenditures of current funds are the general ledger (Form 6.1) and the allocations ledger (Forms 5.12, 5.13, 5.14, and 5.15). As explained in an earlier chapter, the general ledger contains control accounts and receives, in summary or in detail, entries representing all financial transactions. It is posted monthly from the journals. In larger institutions, because of the volume of transactions, postings may go directly to general ledger accounts, obviating the need for some or all original entry journals. Subsidiary to, and controlled by, the general ledger is the allocations ledger, which contains ledger accounts for each department listed in the budget. (See Chart of Accounts, chapter 4, for complete list of allocations ledger accounts.) As already explained, the allocation or allotment to each department may be divided into four parts—salaries, wages, supplies and expense, and equipment—with a ledger account for each part of the allocation. To facilitate proving the accuracy of postings to the various suballocations and to localize errors, there are four subcontrol accounts over the allocations ledger, one each for salaries, wages, supplies and expense, and equipment.[1] The sum of the various columns of these four subcontrol accounts, after all entries are posted, equals the control

FORM 6.1

			Debits		Credits		
Date	Description	Reference	Amount	Total To Date	Amount	Total To Date	Balance

BLANK COLLEGE — GENERAL LEDGER — Account Title — Account Number____ — Sheet Number____

accounts in the general ledger (Expenditures, Encumbrances, and Departmental Allocations).[2] At least monthly, each group of suballocation accounts in the allocations ledger is balanced against its respective subcontrol account and, in turn, the total of the subcontrol is checked against the general ledger controls.

Use of Mechanical Accounting Equipment. Colleges and universities, like other organizations handling a large volume of financial transactions, are realizing more and more the advantages of mechanical accounting devices. Most modern installations of college and university accounting systems make use of one or more accounting machines. It is not to be understood, however, that every institutional business office, irrespective of its volume of business, needs

[1] This procedure is a routine which may not be applicable or desirable in some systems. It is merely suggested as an assisting device in setting up the allocations ledger. Obviously, a single general ledger control account would be sufficient, and a number of institutions use only one.

[2] Expenditures controls the "Amount Paid" column of the allocations ledger; Encumbrances controls the "orders placed, paid or cancelled" (balance at end of posting period is the amount of orders outstanding), and Departmental Allocations controls the "Allocation" column.

mechanical equipment. Moreover, it is not to be implied that in cases where mechanical equipment should be used, such equipment can be used to advantage in all operations of the accounting system. Individual colleges have their peculiar needs. Different types of accounting machinery are constructed to meet varying situations. Before mechanical equipment is installed, an intelligent survey should be made to ascertain, first, whether machines should be installed, and, second, what types of machines would be most efficient and appropriate for the various kinds of accounting work to be performed.

There are many advantages to be derived from using mechanical accounting devices. Of great value is the accuracy which results from the use of machines. Not only is the legibility of the records enhanced, but the machine itself is equipped with various devices to prevent the occurrence of errors or to provide automatic methods of discovery should errors be made. Also, mechanical equipment lends itself well to the assembly-line process of accounting. By reducing most accounting procedures to a routine, fewer highly trained accountants are needed in the business office. The work can be performed satisfactorily at a lower cost with the assistance of accounting machines. Finally, the ability of accounting machines to make multiple copies brings about a tremendous saving of time and effort. Such statements as budgetary reports to department heads can be produced as a part of the ledger posting process. Journals can be produced as a by-product of writing checks or posting ledgers. All payroll documents, including checks, check registers, and earnings records, can be produced simultaneously in one operation.

Some of the more important accounting functions that accounting machines perform include: (1) maintenance of budgetary control records; (2) preparation of vouchers and voucher register; (3) writing of checks and check register for payment to vendors; (4) writing of payroll checks, payroll register, and earnings records; (5) keeping of investment records; (6) posting of accounts receivables; (7) keeping of revenue and general ledger records; and (8) reports to departments. Many of the functions listed above will be described fully in this chapter.

There are several types of accounting machines on the market. A number of companies manufacture several types of machines which are particularly adaptable to certain kinds of operations. Each institution will want to investigate the market before making a decision as to what type best fits its needs.

Use of Electronic Data Processing Equipment. Institutions of higher education, like business and commercial organizations, are realizing more and more the advantages of electronic data processing systems. Not only are many large institutions converting their accounting systems to computers but plans are being made to institute total information systems in the future. The number of accounting and administrative procedures that can be programmed into an EDP system is almost limitless. The result is greater accuracy and speed, and for large institutions, substantial savings in labor costs. Oftentimes, an institution may not have the volume of paperwork to justify the use of EDP equipment. In such instances, an intelligent survey should be made to ascertain if some other type of mechanical equipment should not be used. See chapter 8 for a detailed discussion of the data processing systems.

Procedure in Machine Posting. Because many college and university business offices use mechanical accounting equipment, the authors at this point will outline the procedure in machine posting.[3] The first step in posting documents, such as purchase orders, invoices, payrolls, and interdepartmental invoices, to the allocations ledger is to accumulate a number of like documents into a batch or group. This group, known as a "run," is sent to the machine operator with a prelist or proof total, so that the correctness of the posting may be determined immediately after the batch is posted. A convenient procedure is to face the whole with a posting proof sheet (Form 6.2). Since four subcontrols are maintained in the allocations ledger, it is desirable to segregate the documents according to these subdivisions, with a predetermined total for each division, as illustrated in Form 6.2. Within each subdivision, the documents are arranged in the order of the accounts in the allocations ledger. The operator posts the documents by divisions and obtains an automatic

---

[3] The routines described here can be applied, with some adaptation, to a handwritten accounting system.

machine total for each division. This result is checked by an employee other than the machine operator against the predetermined total on the posting proof sheet, and, if the two totals agree, the accuracy of the operation is proved. The posting proof sheet serves also as the medium of posting to the four subcontrol accounts.

FORM 6.2

BLANK COLLEGE			
POSTING PROOF SHEET			
		No. 1	
		Date 7/1/69	
		Item	Total
DEBIT			
Expenditures--Total			17,000
Salaries		6,300	
Wages		3,000	
Supplies and Expense		7,300	
Equipment		400	
CREDIT			
Orders Liquidated			8,000
Supplies and Expense		7,550	
Equipment		450	
DOCUMENTS AND NUMBERS			
Debits			
Invoice vouchers 1 through 25			
Credits			
Purchase orders 1 through 20			
Prepared by:	Posted O.K.		
	Operator		

Original Journals. In describing the original journals used in accounting for expenditures, it is assumed that a separate set of journals is employed for each group of funds. Thus, current funds expenditures are recorded in voucher and check registers especially devised for that group. Disbursements of other funds—plant, endowment, loan, and agency—are recorded in separate sets of the same type journals. This method is not the only one employed in college accounting systems. Frequently, one series of journals is used to account for the expenditures or disbursements of all funds. In other words, all disbursements, irrespective of the fund to which charged, are recorded in the same voucher and check register. In such systems, the charges are distributed to proper fund accounts either by means of special columns or by codes.

In the system herein described, the following journals are used in connection with the accounting for expenditures and disbursements:

1. The voucher register (Form 6.3) used to record all current funds vouchers other than payroll vouchers and interdepartmental transfer vouchers.

2. The check register (Form 6.4) used to record the issuance of all checks in payment of vouchers other than payroll vouchers.

3. The payroll check register (Form 6.16) used to record payroll checks for salaries and wages.

4. The orders placed and liquidated journal (Form 6.5) used to record the amount of orders placed and liquidated.

5. The interdepartmental transfer journal (Form 6.6) used to record interdepartmental invoices.

6. The general journal (Form 5.10, Chapter 5) used to record transactions which cannot be entered in any other journal. Such transactions include opening and closing entries, correction of errors, and budgetary adjustments. This journal usually consists of a series of individual journal vouchers.

The above journals, with the exception of the check registers, are standard columnar journal sheets, having appropriately printed column headings. The check registers result automatically from writing checks on the accounting machine.

In the following several sections, the accounting for expenditures of current funds is considered.

FORM 6.3

		Reference		Vouchers	Expendi-	Miscellaneous		
						BLANK COLLEGE		
						VOUCHER REGISTER		
Date	Payee	Voucher No.	Check No.	Payable	tures	L.F.	Account	Amount

FORM 6.4

BLANK COLLEGE

CHECK REGISTER

Posted By_____ Checked By_____ Sheet No._____

Check Number	Date	Voucher Number	Payee	Amount of Check	Reconcili- ation

FORM 6.5

BLANK COLLEGE

ORDERS PLACED AND LIQUIDATED JOURNAL

Date	Reference	Orders Placed	Orders Liquidated

Accounting For Orders and Invoices. Purchasing routine has been explained in chapter 3. An initial phase of purchasing is the routing of the requisition to the purchasing office in order to secure quotations and bids and the preparation of the purchase order. The purchase order, before released to the vendor, is audited both as to the availability of funds and as to extensions and codings. The audit

FORM 6.6

		Debits			Credits		
Date	Invoice No.	Expenditures	Stores	Revenues	Expenditures	Stores	Revenues

BLANK COLLEGE

INTERDEPARTMENTAL TRANSFER JOURNAL

is performed by the accounting office. The auditing of codes on the purchase order is important, inasmuch as this code indicates the account to be charged in the allocations ledger. The purchase order is checked as to availability of funds by reference to the Free Balance column in the proper account in the allocations ledger. If funds are available, one copy of the approved purchase order is sent back to the purchasing department authorizing release of the order to the vendor. The copy retained in the accounting office is placed in a departmental order file until the order is received. If funds are not available in the departmental allocations account, both copies of the purchase order are returned to the purchasing office with such notification.

Approved purchase orders are sorted as to code sequence and tabulated on a posting proof sheet. The batch of orders is then posted as encumbrances against the proper allocations accounts. The amount of each order is entered in the Orders Placed, Paid or Cancelled column of the allocations ledger, resulting in a decrease in the free or unencumbered balance of the account.

After details have been posted to the subsidiary ledger, the total amount of the orders placed, as shown by the posting proof sheet, is entered in the Orders Placed column of the orders placed and liquidated journal. At the end of the month, when this journal is summarized, the following entry is posted to the general ledger:

Encumbrances
    Provision for Encumbrances—Current Year

The individual orders are then filed by departments, awaiting delivery of the goods.

As explained in chapter 3, the receiving report, certifying that the goods have been properly received, is sent by the receiving clerk to the accounting department. When both the receiving report and the invoice have been received in the accounting office, these documents are matched with the purchase order. A copy of the requisition may also be provided by purchasing if necessary. The proper audit of the voucher includes a checking of extensions, additions, and codes, a comparison of the vendor's invoice with both the receiving report and the order, and a verification of all signatures and approvals. Under this procedure, duplicate payments are virtually impossible, since the voucher document consists of the purchase order and receiving report, in addition to the vendor's invoice. For a double payment to occur, it would be necessary to duplicate not only the vendor's invoice, but also the purchase order and the receiving report—an extremely unlikely series of duplications.

After the voucher is properly audited, it is sent to the voucher clerk to be numbered and entered in the voucher register. Invoices eligible for cash discount are paid early enough to take advantage of such discounts. At the end of the month, the summarized voucher register is posted to the general ledger as follows:

Expenditures
Miscellaneous Accounts (Itemized)
   Vouchers Payable

Having been audited and entered in the voucher register, the voucher is prepared for machine posting in the same manner as the purchase order—that is, it is grouped with other invoices, separated into classes of expenditures, and arranged by departments within each class. A posting proof sheet is prepared which shows the total charges to the subcontrol accounts and the credits to those accounts for the amount of orders liquidated. The entry in the allocations ledger is made by recording the amount of the purchase order in the Orders Placed, Paid or Cancelled column and the amount of the invoice in the Amount Paid column. The machine adds back to the free balance the amount of the purchase order credit, deducts from that balance the amount of the invoice, and automatically calculates and prints the new balance of the allocation. By means of object codes a detailed analysis of expenditures is possible.

In the case of partial deliveries, it is necessary to liquidate only that portion of the order which has been completed. This end is accomplished by subtracting, on the posting margin of the purchase order, the amount to be liquidated from the total amount of the order.

The machine posting of invoices may be facilitated by designing the purchase order and invoice voucher so that the machine operator is able, without having to turn several documents to get the information, to liquidate the amount of the purchase order and to charge the amount of the invoice. Referring to the illustration of the purchase order on page 45, observe that the right-hand margin of that document contains the amount of the encumbrance to be released and that the departmental code is indicated on the same line in the center of the order. All necessary posting information is furnished at a glance.

After the invoice has been posted to the detail account in the allocations ledger, the amount of orders liquidated is entered in the Orders Liquidated column of the orders placed and liquidated journal. At the end of the month, this column is posted in total to the general ledger as follows:

Provision for Encumbrances—Current Year
    Encumbrances

The balance of the Encumbrances account, after all entries have been posted at the end of the month, reflects the total orders outstanding and serves as a control over the sum of all open orders in the Orders Placed, Paid or Cancelled columns in the allocations ledger.

The final step in accounting for the invoice is the preparation of a check in payment thereof. Some institutions follow the practice of paying each invoice with a separate check as soon as it is audited. This plan is profitable, however, only in large organizations, being advantageous because it results in an even flow of routine clerical work. It has the disadvantage of reducing cash balances, thus providing less funds to invest in short-term securities. More practicable for the smaller college is the procedure of filing the audited invoices by vendors and drawing one check weekly or bimonthly covering all the invoices of a particular vendor. Of course, if an invoice affords a discount for prompt payment, a check should be drawn in time to obtain the discount. Form 6.7 illustrates the type of check

FORM 6.7

GENERAL FUND CHECK

			BLANK COLLEGE	No. 1
			GENERAL FUND	
Check Number	Date	Voucher Number	Pay to the Order Of	Amount
			BLANK COLLEGE	
To				
FIRST NATIONAL BANK				
BLANK, STATE			Chief Accountant	
50-309				
			Business Manager	

used in connection with the payment of invoices where a machine accounting system is in use. Entry in the check register (Form 6.4) is written simultaneously with the check. Many colleges use a voucher-check in which the voucher and the check are inseparable documents. At the end of the month, the check register is summarized and posted to the general ledger as follows:

Vouchers Payable
    Cash

The balance of the Vouchers Payable account represents the outstanding current obligations at the end of the month and controls the file of unpaid invoices.

In the state-supported institution, the above procedure for invoices and checks may have to be modified to conform with the state's fiscal procedure. The following are typical fiscal relationships existing between the state college and the state government:

1. The funds of all agencies, including those concerned with higher education, are deposited and kept in a state depository. The institution certifies vouchers to the state treasurer and state warrants are issued in payment.

2. The funds available to the institution are divided into two classes: (a) the state appropriation, which is kept and disbursed by the central government; and (b) fees and sales revenues, which are kept and disbursed locally by the institution.

3. The state maintains a central fiscal organization which not only purchases and writes checks for state institutions but also keeps many of the accounting records which otherwise would be kept by the institution. Invoices and payrolls are approved by the college and sent to a central state office, where checks are prepared and issued.

4. The college withdraws its appropriation in lump sum or in installments and does its own purchasing, disbursing, and accounting.

In concluding this discussion of accounting for orders and invoices, attention is directed to methods of handling orders outstanding at the end of the fiscal year. Generally, there are two methods followed by colleges and universities. In the first method, outstanding orders at the end of the year are considered as expenditures. Thus, in the closing entries both Expenditures and Encumbrances are closed into Unrestricted Current Funds Balances.

The Provision for Encumbrances—Current Year account is closed into Provision for Encumbrances—Prior Year and is carried forward into the new year. As invoices on the encumbered orders arrive in the new period, they are charged against this account. At the same time, those departmental budgets which have orders outstanding remain open and, as invoices come in, charges are made against these encumbered budgets. Separate allocations ledger accounts are maintained for expenditures chargeable against encumbered allocations of the previous period and expenditures chargeable against current budgets. At the end of the period, or at such time as all encumbrances have been fully liquidated, any balance remaining is closed into Unrestricted Current Funds Balances. In some institutions, an excess of the invoice price over the order price (amount of encumbrance) is charged against the new budget of the department involved. The entries in journal form, to illustrate the above method of handling purchase orders outstanding at the end of the fiscal year, are as follows:

1. Entry to close expenditures and encumbrances at end of fiscal year:

> Unrestricted Current Funds Balances
> Encumbrances
> Expenditures

In the allocations ledger, individual accounts are debited for amount of free and unencumbered balance. Carry forward amount of unpaid orders outstanding.

2. Entry to close out Provision for Encumbrances—Current Year:

> Provision for Encumbrances—Current Year
> Provision for Encumbrances—Prior Year

No entry required in the allocations ledger.

3. Entry to record liquidation in current year of orders encumbered in previous year:

> Provision for Encumbrances—Prior Year
> Vouchers Payable

In the allocations ledger, debit individual accounts (previous year).

4. Entry to close the Provision for Encumbrances—Prior Year:

> Provision for Encumbrances—Prior Year
> Unrestricted Current Funds Balances (if actual expenditures are less than amount provided for encumbrances)

In the method just described, financial statements prepared at the end of the year include outstanding encumbrances as well as actual expenditures.

A second method of handling encumbrances at the end of the

year involves the carrying forward to the new allocations the accounts of sufficient balances to cover outstanding purchase orders.
The old allocation accounts are closed out completely. Financial
statements are based upon expenditures without inclusion of outstanding encumbrances. As invoices on the encumbered orders are
received in the current year, they are charged against current budgets in the same manner as current expenditures. The entries, in
journal form, to illustrate, are as follows:

1. Entry to close departmental allocations at end of fiscal year:

Unrestricted Current Funds Balances
    Expenditures

In the allocations ledger, close out all accounts completely.

2. Entry to set up provision for balances carried forward to cover
   encumbrances:

Unrestricted Current Funds Balances
    Provision for Balances Carried Forward to Cover Encumbrances

Encumbrances and Provision for Encumbrances are carried forward into the new year and are used to account for current orders.

At the beginning of the new fiscal year, the current departmental
budgets are increased by the amount of the balances carried forward
to cover encumbrances as illustrated below:

Provision for Balances Carried Forward to Cover Encumbrances
    Departmental Allocations

In the allocations ledger, credit individual accounts. Invoices on
encumbered orders are charged to current budgets in the usual manner by debiting Expenditures and crediting Vouchers Payable.

Accounting for Payrolls. Three general types of payrolls are used
in colleges and universities: (1) salary payrolls for instructional, administrative, and clerical personnel; (2) wage payrolls for laborers
who work by the hour; and (3) payrolls for student labor. Many institutions have incorporated student and wage payrolls into one, as
both are paid on an hourly basis.

The first step in accounting for the above types of payrolls is the determination of the personnel to be paid. There are several sources from which the authorized record of personnel may be compiled. Salaried employees are usually listed by name in the annual budget, being approved by the governing board. In addition, usually some form of annual employment contract is issued by the president, a copy of which is received in the payroll office. Labor personnel ordinarily do not appear by name in the annual budget, and contracts are not issued to this class of employees. For such personnel, the establishment of the payroll is predicated upon written advices of employment from the various employing departments or from a central employment or personnel office. Generally, student employment is handled through a student employment office or is maintained as a separate and distinct function of the central personnel office. From these various sources, the institutional payroll, or roster, is compiled, taking the form of a roster card (Form 6.8) for each employee. These roster cards serve as a perpetual record, because once they are set up, they require adjustment only when there is a change in the status of an individual employee. The student labor section of the file may consist of work cards, supplied at the beginning of each semester by the student employment office.

From the roster cards, an earnings record (Form 6.9 or Form 6.16) is prepared for each employee. This record serves several important

FORM 6.8

BLANK COLLEGE			
R O S T E R C A R D			
Name_____			
Address_____			
_____ Phone_____			
Date	Title	Department	Salary

FORM 6.9

BLANK COLLEGE

EARNINGS RECORD

Name

Social Security No.

Title

Withholding Exemptions

Dept. Code   Position Number

Department

	Department	Code	Monthly Amount
Split			
Salary			
Detail			

Gross Pay $

Salary Rate   Per

Effective Date

Annuity Amount

Adjusted Contract Amt.

Monthly Group Life

Monthly Blue Cross

Monthly Income Protection

F.I.T. Specified Amt.

Remarks

Retirement Member   FICA Member

Period Ending	Gross Pay	Add Emol.	Adj. Gross	FIT	FICA	State Retire.	Group Life	Blue Cross	Income Protect. Insur.	Emol.	Misc. Ded. Amount	Misc. Ded. Code	Net Pay
Jul													
Aug													
Sep													
Oct													
Nov													
Dec													
Jan													
Feb													
Mar													
Apr													
May													
Jun													
Jul													
Aug													

Budget Amount

	Encumbrance		Liquidation	
	Date	Amount	Date	Amount
Increase				
Decrease				

purposes. It is used as the voucher or payroll in case of salaried employees, no other document being required to initiate the salary payroll check. For all employees, it provides an accumulated record of earnings for use in reporting to the federal and state governments for purposes of income taxes and social security. It is a valuable source of information in preparing the budget. It serves as a check on duplicate salary payments because an individual record is set up for properly authorized employees only. It calls attention to changes in earnings from the prior period, thus assisting the auditor in ascertaining whether salary increases are authorized. Finally, because it records all deductions made from the employee's salary, it serves as a valuable aid in checking and verifying deduction accounts. Under a machine accounting system, the earnings record is written at the same time as the salary check, hence is produced with little additional effort. Under an electronic data processing system, earnings record information would be generated as a by-product of running the payroll, and a hard copy printout would be available for review.

One problem that arises in connection with the establishment of the salary payroll is that of split salaries, where an employee teaches or works in more than one department. In such cases, the salary of the employee must be allocated or split between the two or more organization units involved. If the employee is a faculty member, his salary may be divided in proportion to the number of credit hours or other measurement of effort he devotes to teaching and/or research in each department. In the case of nonteaching personnel, the allocation is based on the relative amount of time devoted to each department. If costs are to be collected accurately, the allocation must be changed when the duties of the employee change. Ordinarily, the accounting office can determine the allocation at the start of each year by reference to the approved budget.

Although the establishment of the official payroll is an important beginning in payroll procedure, equally important is a well-defined channel through which the accounting department receives prompt notice of the addition of new employees, changes of status, and terminations. This end may be accomplished through the use of the request for personnel action form (Form 6.10). In many state institutions, the employment of certain clerical and wage personnel is regulated through a state civil service system. In such cases, it may be necessary to establish a procedure for obtaining from the state civil service department a written certification for all additions or changes to the payroll.

BLANK COLLEGE   FORM 6.10   REQUEST FOR PERSONNEL ACTION

The use of time records and reports as required by wage and hour laws is widespread in colleges and universities. The application of minimum wage legislation to colleges and universities has forced uniformity in hours of employment, wage rates at the lower levels, and overtime pay. Many institutions have well-developed sick leave, vacation, retirement, and sabbatical leave plans. Good business practice demands that the institution establish rules and regulations to be applied uniformly throughout the college and administered through the business office.

In all colleges and universities, time reports are now required for all employees who are covered by the Fair Labor Standards Act as amended in 1966.

A well-organized accounting system should include a procedure under which time reports, kept in each department and covering nonexempt employees (under the Fair Labor Standards Act as amended in 1966), are submitted to the accounting office in support of the payroll voucher and salary check. A type of report commonly used is the attendance report (Form 6.11). If this kind of time report is used, it may be made to serve as support for a payroll voucher and as an independent time report. A leave and vacation card (Form 6.12) is a necessary part of the payroll records.

In colleges and universities, the usual procedure is to prepare payroll vouchers for nonsalaried or labor personnel only, the earnings record serving as an individual voucher in the case of salaried employees. Form 6.13 is suitable for use as a wage payroll voucher for all employees and student labor. Labor payrolls are prepared in duplicate by the head of the organization unit and submitted to the accounting office. An important part of the payroll procedure for labor is the establishment of definite dates for submission of payrolls and the drawing of payroll checks. A good plan is to close the payroll period several days before checks are to be issued. This procedure affords the accounting office time to make the necessary audit of the payroll vouchers and to prepare checks. An example of payroll dates for a bimonthly labor payroll follows:[4]

[4] Because the Fair Labor Standards Act requires that covered employees be paid overtime for time worked in excess of forty hours per week after February, 1969, a number of institutions find it convenient to pay these employees every two weeks. Some institutions have placed all covered employees on an hourly basis and all exempt employees on a salary basis.

FORM 6.11

BLANK COLLEGE

ATTENDANCE REPORT

Date (Month and Year) _____

Department _____

Name	1	2	3	4	5	6	7	8	9	10	11	12	13	14	15	16	17	18	19	20	21	22	23	24	25	26	27	28	29	30	31	Deductions

Code:
X = Worked
A = Sick Leave, No Deduction
B = Vacation
C = Absent Without Leave, Deduction
D = Holiday

Signed: _____

_____
Department Head

_____
Employee

FORM 6.12

BLANK COLLEGE											
L E A V E A N D V A C A T I O N R E C O R D											
Name_____ Department_____											
Address_____											
Year:				Year:				Year:			
Code	From	To	Total Time	Code	From	To	Total Time	Code	From	To	Total Time

Code: A = Sick Leave With Pay
        B = Vacation
        C = Leave Without Pay
        D = Other

First Period—From the first through the fifteenth—

    Payroll vouchers due in the accounting office on the sixteenth and payroll checks ready for distribution on the twenty-first.

Second Period—From the sixteenth through the last day of the month—

    Payroll vouchers due in the accounting office on the first and payroll checks ready for distribution on the sixth.

If the number of employees on all payrolls is considerable, it may be advisable to stagger the payroll dates—that is, arrange for each of the different types of payrolls to fall due on a different date, so that the work of auditing payrolls and writing checks is fairly evenly distributed through the month. Staggering of payrolls is particularly important under a machine accounting system in which one machine is required to write all records in addition to writing payroll and other checks.

The recommended procedure in distributing payroll checks is to issue them to department heads to be distributed by them to the individual employees of their particular department. All undistributed checks should be returned promptly to the accounting office.

FORM 6.13

BLANK COLLEGE

W A G E   P A Y R O L L   V O U C H E R

Department_____

For Period Beginning_____, 19___ Through _____, 19___

Payroll No.	Check No.	Name	Pay Basis	Time	Rate	Gross Amount	With-holding Tax	Social Security Tax	State Retire-ment	Blue Cross	Net Amount

Charge		Pay Basis	Certification and Approval		
Account	Amount	1 Hour	I certify that the services for which payment is requested have been rendered.		Department Head
		2 Day			
		3 Week			
		4 Month	Approved for payment_____		
		5 Special	For the Chief Accountant		
Auditor_____		Rates Verified	Computed by	Checked by	Wage Voucher No.

This method is preferable to that under which each individual employee calls in person at the business office for his check. However, it is a good practice for a representative of the accounting office to be present occasionally when checks are distributed to workers, as a partial safeguard against padded payrolls. If a student employment office is maintained, students are usually required to call at that office for their checks. Some institutions may find it convenient to send payroll checks to the respective banks for deposit to the employees' accounts.

After an audit of the payroll vouchers, in the case of laborers, and of the earnings records, in the case of salaried personnel, the payroll checks are written by machine. Because more information is needed on the payroll check than on the general check and because bank reconciling and postauditing are facilitated, it is customary to use separate payroll bank accounts and a separate series of payroll checks. Different colors of paper may be used for the wage and salary checks, respectively. A payroll check is illustrated in Form 6.17. The entries in journal form required to effect a transfer of funds from the general bank account to the payroll bank account are as follows:

1. On bank transfer voucher (Form 6.14) and entered in voucher register:
   Bank Transfers
      Vouchers Payable

2. In the check register (general bank account):
   Vouchers Payable
      General Bank Account

3. In cash receipts journal (check is routed through the cashier as with all other receipts):
   Payroll Bank Account
      Bank Transfers

One advantage of the mechanical method of payroll check writing is that the payroll check register, the earnings record, and the payroll check are written simultaneously in a single operation. This operation is accomplished through the use of carbon paper inserted between the documents. The relationship between these records is illustrated on page 143.

The final steps in the payroll process are the distribution and posting of the payroll to the proper allocations ledger accounts and the entries made at the end of the month in the general ledger. The method of posting payroll vouchers to the detail departmental accounts has been explained. Since salary payrolls are based solely on the earnings records, there are no individual vouchers from which to post. Therefore, a salary distribution sheet (Form 6.18) is prepared from the payroll check register and used as the basis for posting the departmental salaries and wages accounts in the allocations ledger. The general ledger entries for all cash payrolls come from a monthly summary of the payroll check register. This summary is illustrated in the following journal entry:

FORM 6.14

BLANK COLLEGE

Voucher No._____

BANK TRANSFER AND REIMBURSEMENT
VOUCHER

Date_____

Issue check in the amount of $_____ payable to _____

on _____ Bank, _____ Fund,

for purpose of _____

_____

DEBIT	General Ledger		Subsidiary
	Account	Amount	Account
CREDIT			

Prepared By_____

Approved_____
         Chief Accountant

Entered Voucher Register_____

Posted Allocations Ledger_____

Paid by Check Number_____

FORM 6.15

BLANK COLLEGE

PAYROLL CHECK REGISTER

Sheet No. _____

Posted By _____   Checked By _____

Pay Period	Gross Earnings	Date	Deductions — Group Ins.	Tchr. Ret.	Accts. Rec.	With-holding Tax	Misc.	Code	Check No.	Net Earnings	Date	Pay Period Ending	Pay to the Order of	Amount of Check	Reconciliation
Jan.	100.00	1/31/69	2.00	4.00					1	94.00	1/31/69	Jan.	John Doe	94.00	

FORM 6.16

EARNINGS RECORD

Year _____
Salary – Reg. _____   Name _____
Basis _____
Salary – S.S. _____   Dept. _____
P.I.K. _____
Charge: _____

Pay Period	Gross Earnings	Date	Deductions — Group Ins.	Tchr. Ret.	Accts. Rec.	With-holding Tax	Misc.	Teachers Ret.	Deductions — Group Ins.	Other	Code	Check No.	Net Earnings
Jan.	100.00	1/31/69	2.00	4.00								1	94.00

FORM 6.17

EMPLOYEE'S STATEMENT OF EARNINGS

Pay Period	Gross Earnings	Date	Deductions — Group Ins.	Tchr. Ret.	Accts. Rec.	With-holding Tax	Misc.	Code	Check No.	Net Earnings
Jan.	100.00	1/31/69	2.00	4.00					1	94.00

Please Detach This Statement Before Depositing This Check

SALARY PAYROLL ACCOUNT
BLANK COLLEGE

Date	Pay Period Ending	Pay to the Order of	Amount
1/31/69	Jan.	John Doe	94.00

BLANK COLLEGE

To: Second National Bank
Blank, State
56–501

_____ President
_____ Business Manager

Expenditures (for total amount of payroll):

Due to Acme Life Insurance Company (for deductions from salaries for group life insurance)

Due to State Teachers' Retirement System (for deductions from salaries for the retirement system)

Withholding Tax Deductions—Federal (for income tax deductions)

Withholding Tax Deductions—State (for income tax deductions)

F.I.C.A. Deductions (for Social Security deductions)

Second National Bank—Salary Payroll account (for net amount of salary payroll)

Third National Bank—Wage Payroll account (for net amount of wage payroll)

Accounting for Traveling Expenses. The regulations of many institutions relative to travel by employees on institutional business include the provision that a travel request or authorization must be submitted and approved before each trip. In case of employees who travel constantly or seasonally, then monthly or even annual travel requests are used. The use of a travel authorization (Form 6.19) has three advantages. First, it serves the same function as the purchase requisition in a system of budgetary control. Second, it gives the business office an opportunity to learn about anticipated trips before such trips are made. Third, it assists the accounting office in the auditing of expense vouchers, in that it prevents disagreements (after the trip has been made) as to what items are to be reimbursed. Fourth, it safeguards against duplicate payments of expense vouchers.

Upon completion of a trip, the individual making the trip submits a travel expense voucher (Form 6.20 and reverse). One of the regulations covering travel vouchers is that the voucher must be typewritten on a special form so that the preparation of a new voucher document is unnecessary. Some colleges encumber the travel requests. In such cases, it is necessary to liquidate the amount of the request at the time of entering the expense voucher.

The travel expense voucher follows the same channels as do the other vouchers. It is audited, entered in the voucher register, posted to the allocations ledger, and paid.

Accounting for Petty Cash. One requirement of a voucher system, such as is assumed here, is that all disbursements be made by check.

FORM 6.18

Code	Budget Unit	Object	Amount

BLANK COLLEGE

MONTHLY   SALARIES   DISTRIBUTION

No._____

Date_____

Code	Budget Unit	Object	Amount
351	President	012	
		013	
354	Business Manager	012	
		013	
355	Accounting Office	012	
		013	
358	Purchasing	012	
		013	
451	Bookstore	013	
461	Cafeteria	013	
471	Residence Halls - Single	012	
		013	
491	College Union	012	
		013	
495	Airport	012	
		013	
	TOTAL		

Under such a system, it is necessary to have on hand cash from which to pay small bills. The generally accepted method of doing this is through the use of the imprest petty cash fund. Under the imprest system, a fixed sum is established as a petty cash fund. The exact amount of the fund depends on the specific requirements of the department in question. A voucher is prepared and a check is drawn payable to the individual designated as custodian of the

FORM 6.19

```
                           BLANK COLLEGE
                 T R A V E L    A U T H O R I Z A T I O N
Submit One Set
Per Individual
                            Date_____        _____
                                                        Travel
                                                        Request
To:  Business Manager, Blank College                    Number

From:_____ Title_____
       In compliance with college regulations and state laws
permission is respectfully requested for authorization to attend
the following convention, association, or meeting.      _____
                                                        Code

_____  _____
Name of Convention, Association, or Meeting   Place of Meeting


_____         _____
        Date of Meeting                       Mode of
                                              Transportation    _____
  PURPOSE OF CONVENTION, ASSOCIATION, OR MEETING:               Est.
                                                                Cost
```

This space for use by Accounting Office

```
_____        _____
    Departmental Code                Signature
ESTIMATED COST:                     APPROVED:

Transportation_____   1._____
                              Department Chairman        Date

Meals and Lodging_____  2._____
                              Dean or Administrative Head  Date

Other_____  3._____
                              President (if necessary)   Date
                                    Subject to
                                Availability of funds

Total_____   _____
                              Funds Available - Accounting  Date
White Copy for Accounting
Blue Copy for Auditor
Yellow Copy for President
Green Copy for Department Chairman    See back of pink copy for
Pink copy for Individual              University Travel Policy
```

fund. The entry in the voucher register to record the establishment of the fund is a debit to Petty Cash (with a corresponding entry to a subsidiary account) and a credit to Vouchers Payable.

FORM 6.20
(front)

Standard Form No. 223E Form Prescribed By State Auditor April 1964	VOUCHER FOR REIMBURSEMENT OF EXPENSES INCIDENT TO OFFICIAL TRAVEL

BLANK COLLEGE _____ Dr.
(Department)

To_____

Address_____

_____
(Official Duty)
_____

For mileage for privately owned motor vehicle used by me for transportation, and/or lieu allowance, and for reimbursement for subsistence (meals and lodging) and other expenses paid by me in the discharge of official duty

from _____19___ to_____19___, as per itemized statement within.

Amount Claimed			Amount Due (as per office verification)		
For	Dollars	Cents	For	Dollars	Cents
Subsistence					
Travel					
Other					
Total			Amount Verified: Correct For		

Subject to any differences determined by verification, I certify that the above amount claimed by me for travel expenses for the period indicated is true and just in all respects, and that payment for any part thereof has not been received.

Approved for Payment:_____ Payee_____
(Department Chairman)

_____ Title___Business Manager___ Verified By_____

ACCOUNTING CLASSIFICATION

The Above Claim Is Requested To Be Charged To:			The Above Claim Is Verified For Charge To:		
Department	Code	Amount	Department	Code	Amount
Travel Authorization			Travel Authorization		
No._____			No._____		

The check is cashed by the payee (custodian of the fund) and disbursed in accordance with specific regulations. When cash is disbursed, a receipt or voucher (Form 6.21) is obtained from the payee.

FORM 6.20
(back)

STATEMENT OF TRAVELING EXPENSES INCURRED BY_____

From_____19___ to_____19___

| Date | Points of Travel | | Motor Vehicle | | Air or Rail Fare | Date | Items | Amount |
	From	To	Miles	Mileage Amount				
Total Amounts (carry to page 1)						Total (carry to page 1)		

Statement of Cost of Meals and Lodging							State Place and Purpose of Visit

Date	Break-fast	Lunch	Dinner	Hotel Room	Daily Total	Place Where Expense Incurred	
							Complete the following if travel was out of state and by automobile:
							Meeting commenced at _____ _M
							on _____ and terminated
							(date)
							at _____ _M on _____
							(date)
Total							Accompanied by:
Total Subsistence (carry to page 1)							_____
							_____

Note: Receipts for amounts paid for lodging and other expenses, other than for meals, must accompany this voucher.

At definite intervals, or whenever necessary, a check is drawn payable to the custodian to reimburse the petty cash fund to its original amount. A petty cash reimbursement voucher (Form 6.22) is used

FORM 6.21

BLANK COLLEGE
BUSINESS OFFICE

P E T T Y   C A S H   V O U C H E R

Paid To_____ $_____

For_____

_____

Approved   Received Payment

_____   _____

Accounts to be Charged   _____ _____

_____ _____

to support the reimbursing check. The entry in the voucher register to record the reimbursement voucher is a debit to Expenditures or Revenues (for refunds of revenues) and a credit to Vouchers Payable. The allocations ledger accounts are charged from the individual petty cash vouchers, which are permanently attached to the

FORM 6.22

BLANK COLLEGE   Voucher No._____

P E T T Y   C A S H   R E I M B U R S E M E N T
V O U C H E R

Date_____

Date	Paid To	Explanation	Amount

Pay To:_____ $_____
Signed   (Custodian of Fund)

Charge Accounts: Entered:

_____ $_____   _____ $_____

_____ $_____   _____ $_____   Allocations Ledger

_____ $_____   _____ $_____

_____ $_____   _____ $_____   Revenue Ledger

General Ledger

Approved for Reimbursement _____
Auditor

reimbursement voucher. If expenditures made from petty cash are chargeable to funds other than current funds, petty cash is reimbursed by separate checks on the proper funds. Where numerous petty cash funds are needed, a single large working cash fund might be established from which small petty cash funds and expense advances could be set up.

Care must be taken to safeguard the petty cash fund. It is sometimes necessary to advance sums of cash to various auxiliary enterprises for making change and to the receiving clerk for paying small freight and express bills. In such cases, audits should be made of these funds from time to time. Since petty cash is misused easily, the amount of the fund should be small and its use should be restricted to specific types and amounts of expenses.

Accounting for Interdepartmental Transactions. Interdepartmental transactions are a peculiar characteristic of college and university accounting. Transactions of this kind are of a noncash nature, yet have an important effect on the accurate determination of costs and operating results. At least three types of transactions fall within this category: (1) sales by auxiliary enterprises and organized activities to other institutional departments, (2) sales and services of the maintenance department, and (3) miscellaneous sales or transfers between departments. These types of interdepartmental transactions differ and each is treated differently in the accounting records.

The first type, sales to a department by an auxiliary enterprise (such as a bookstore) or by an organized activity (such as a dairy), must be recorded for two reasons. First, the selling agency is judged by its profit and loss statement; hence, it must receive credit for all its sales. Second, the buying department has expended some of the funds allotted to it in the budget, and so it must be charged with the cost of the purchase. Many interdepartmental transactions of this type occur. For example, the bookstore sells office supplies to nearly every department; the farm sells produce to the dining hall; and the dairy sells raw milk to the creamery, which, in turn, sells milk to the dining halls. In journal form, the entry to record interdepartmental transactions of this type is as follows:

Expenditures (in the Allocations Ledger, debit the account of the purchasing department)
Revenues (in the Revenues Ledger, credit the account of the selling department)

If there is a requirement that interdepartmental expenditures and revenues be kept separate from so-called "cash" expenditures and revenues, appropriate adjustments would have to be made in the accounts to reflect the distinction between the two types of transactions.

The second type of interdepartmental transaction arises from the sales and services of the maintenance department which renders service to both the academic and administrative departments and to the auxiliary enterprises. The former departments are not charged with ordinary upkeep and maintenance but are billed only when the maintenance department serves them in an unusual manner, for example, by construction of a cabinet or filing case. On the other hand, auxiliary enterprises must be assessed for all overhead costs occasioned by the existence of the enterprise on the campus, for example, repairs to equipment, trucking services, utilities, and janitorial services. The following entry, in journal form, illustrates a transaction in which service rendered by the maintenance department is charged to some other department:

Expenditures (in the Allocations Ledger, charge budget of the department receiving the service)
Expenditures (in the Allocations Ledger, credit appropriate maintenance account)

The third type of interdepartmental transaction arises out of incidental transfers between instructional departments; for example, the department of art "buys" some supplies from the department of history. The entry to record this transfer is as follows:

Expenditures (charge supplies and expense budget of the art department)
Expenditures (credit supplies and expense budget of the history department)

All interdepartmental transactions originate on interdepartmental invoices (Form 3.14) which are made out in triplicate by the selling department and approved by the department receiving the service or supply. The accounting department, the selling department, and the receiving department receive a copy of the invoice. The accounting department's copy of the interdepartmental invoice is numbered and entered in the interdepartmental transfer journal. The detail charges and credits are posted directly from the invoices; the general ledger is posted from a monthly summary of the interdepartmental transfer journal.

Analysis of Expenditures. The primary accounts for expenditures are set up for purposes of budgetary control and therefore are broken down no further than the budget classes of expenditures—that is, salaries, wages, supplies and expense, and equipment. It is essential, however, that the accounting system furnish more detailed information within each general object class. Thus, for each entry in the Amount Paid column of the allocations ledger a code number is placed in the Object Code column, designating the specific object of the expenditure. At the end of the month, these codes are analyzed and the detailed information desired is accumulated. One method of accumulating this information is by means of a columnar analysis sheet. Another method makes use of unit tickets or cards. The advantage of the second plan lies in the ease of handling and filing the unit tickets, as compared with manipulating the bulky columnar analysis sheets, and also in the fact that it makes possible a greater division of labor. These tickets (Form 6.23) may be spread in a binder so that a comparative analysis is readily made available for all previous months. If an EDP or a tabulating machine system is being used, the analysis of expenditures is produced electronically.

Accounting for Expenditures of Restricted Current Funds. Restricted current funds are those funds which are expendable for operating purposes but which are restricted by an outside agency or person as to use, as distinguished from unrestricted current funds, which are available for any current purpose. A fund is not to be classified as restricted whose use is subject to the control of the governing board of the institution. Since restricted current funds

FORM 6.23

Expenditures for Month	Object Classification		Expenditures to Date
	BLANK COLLEGE		
	ANALYSIS OF EXPENDITURES		
	Department_____		
	010	Salaries	
	011	Teaching Salaries	
	012	Other Professional Salaries	
	013	Nonprofessional Salaries	
	010	Total	
	020	Wages	
	021	Graduate Teaching Wages	
	022	Other Graduate Wages	
	023	Other Professional Wages	
	024	Nonprofessional Wages	
	025	Undergraduate Student Wages	
	020	Total	
	030	Supplies and Expense	
	031	Instructional Supplies	
	040	Equipment	
	041	Scientific Equipment	
	042	Office Machines and Equipment	
	043	Furniture and Furnishings	
	044	Machines and Tools	
	045	Motor Vehicles	
	046	Books	
	047	Livestock	
	040	Total	
		Grand Total	

are expendable for current purposes, the expenditures and revenues of these funds may be combined with those of unrestricted current funds in financial statements. Common types of restricted current funds are gifts for scholarships and fellowships or for the purchase of books or equipment; grants from foundations, industries, individuals, and governmental bodies for research projects and other sponsored programs; and income from investments of endowment funds restricted by donors as to use. Another type of restricted fund found in publicly supported institutions results from the fiscal system in effect in some states. Some state laws require that all revenues with the exception of revenues from specified student activities, such as student publications, be turned over to the state treasury. The Restricted Current Funds group may be used to account for the funds which are retained.

There are several methods of accounting for the expenditures of restricted current funds. Three of these methods will be explained and illustrated. In the first method, restricted funds are made a part of the regular unrestricted current funds budget and separate accounts are included for them in the allocations ledger. The routine of requisitioning, purchasing, and invoicing is identical with the routine for regular unrestricted current funds transactions. As restricted current funds are received, however, they are taken into the Restricted Current Funds group as credits to the proper balance accounts. Periodically, usually each month, the Unrestricted Current Funds group is reimbursed by the Restricted Current Funds group for expenditures made on its behalf during that period, this reimbursement being credited to Revenues. The amount of the reimbursement is determined by reference to those allocation ledgers accounts designated as restricted. Revenue taken in from restricted current funds, according to *College and University Business Administration,* is limited to the amount actually expended from restricted funds during the year. Receipts of the Restricted Current Funds group not expended are reflected in the accounts and on the balance sheet as part of Restricted Current Funds balances.

Journal entries, illustrating this method of accounting for the transactions of restricted current funds, are given below:

1. To record receipt of funds, expendable for current purposes, but subject to designated restrictions:

    a. IN RESTRICTED CURRENT FUNDS:
       Cash
         Restricted Current Funds Balances

In subsidiary Restricted Current Funds Ledger, credit individual accounts.

b. In Unrestricted Current Funds:
No entry required.

2. To record expenditures chargeable to restricted current funds:

a. In Restricted Current Funds:
No entry required.

b. In Unrestricted Current Funds:
Restricted Expenditures (control)
Vouchers Payable
In subsidiary Allocations Ledger, charge proper account (designated as restricted current funds) .

3. To record monthly reimbursement from restricted to unrestricted current funds:

a. In Restricted Current Funds:
Restricted Current Funds Balances
Cash
In subsidiary Restricted Current Funds Ledger, charge proper accounts.

b. In Unrestricted Current Funds:
Cash
Restricted Revenues (control)
In Revenues Ledger, credit appropriate revenues accounts.

There are several advantages in this method of handling restricted funds. First, the handling of restricted funds expenditures along with those of the unrestricted current funds results in a smoother accounting routine. Second, this method fits in with a system of budgets and budgetary control, and in addition, obviates the necessity of preparing two budgets, one for unrestricted current and another for restricted current expenditures. Third, it makes unnecessary any merging of expenditures for purposes of financial statements, as all current funds expenditures can be determined from the allocation ledger without consolidating the unrestricted accounts with the restricted accounts.

A second method, closely related to the one just described, is used in many institutions. The unrestricted current funds budget includes restricted revenues and expenditures, and the Departmental Allocations and Unrealized Revenues accounts include estimates of these funds. All transactions involving restricted funds are recorded entirely within the Restricted Current Funds group. At the end of each month, expenditures and revenues of restricted current funds are brought into the unrestricted current funds section of the general ledger. Revenues, as in the first method, are limited to the amount of restricted current funds expended. The following entries, in journal form, illustrate the second method of handling restricted current funds transactions:

1. To record receipt of funds, expendable for current purposes, but subject to designated restrictions:

> IN RESTRICTED CURRENT FUNDS:
>   Cash
>   Restricted Current Funds Balances
> In subsidiary Restricted Current Funds Ledger, credit individual accounts.

2. To record expenditures of restricted current funds:

> IN RESTRICTED CURRENT FUNDS:
>   Restricted Current Funds Balances
>   Cash
> In subsidiary Restricted Current Funds Ledger, charge proper accounts.

3. To transfer to unrestricted current funds, the revenues and expenditures of restricted current funds:

> a. IN UNRESTRICTED CURRENT FUNDS:
>   Expenditures
>   Revenues
> In Allocations Ledger, debit individual accounts. In Revenues Ledger, credit individual accounts.
> b. IN RESTRICTED CURRENT FUNDS:
>   No entry required.

A third method of handling restricted current funds is to record all transactions involving such funds entirely within the Restricted Current Funds group. This method necessitates the use of practically all of the original journals explained above, as well as a subsidiary expenditure ledger for individual restricted accounts. Each entry in the detail ledger is coded with the standard object code number, and at the end of the year the expenditures of the Restricted Current Funds group are merged with those of the Unrestricted Current Funds group. In like manner, revenues of restricted current funds are consolidated with unrestricted current funds revenues.

Accrual Accounting. In connection with the accounting systems of colleges and universities, it is suggested that current funds revenues be reported as these revenues become due, and expenditures should include charges for materials received and services rendered, even though these items may not have been paid. Thus, colleges and universities should follow the accrual method of accounting for revenues and expenditures, as is presently practiced by commercial concerns.

Good judgment must be exercised in determining whether or not minor items of revenues and expenditures are to be accrued. If the items are not material in nature, it is expected that such items would not be accrued. Those items which should be accrued are material in amount, so that the financial statements will properly reflect the actual revenues and expenditures of the institution. Accrual accounting methods should be applied to all funds of the institution.

CHAPTER VII

Accounting for Current Funds
—Revenues and Receipts

THE LEDGERS USED in accounting for revenues are the general ledger and the subsidiary revenues ledger. The account Revenues in the general ledger represents the total revenues realized to date and controls the detailed revenue accounts in the revenues ledger. The account Unrealized Revenues is a budgetary account,[1] indicating the total estimated revenue for the period. It remains unchanged during the year, unless the revenue budget is revised. Postings to the general ledger for revenues and other cash receipts are made from the cash receipts journal, and postings to the revenues ledger are made directly from the daily cash receipts records. At least once a month, the detailed accounts in the revenues ledger are reconciled with the control accounts in the general ledger.

Relationship Between Fiscal Systems of State and Institution. Before discussing the accounting procedure for revenues, consideration must be given to the fiscal relationship existing between institution and state because the form of this relationship is an important factor in determining how the publicly supported institution must account for its revenues. From the point of view of the handling of revenues, state fiscal systems fall into four major groups. First, in some states, publicly supported institutions are permitted

---

1 Some accountants consider the Unrealized Revenues account as both a budgetary and a proprietary account. Budget estimates of revenues are debited to this account while realized revenues are credited.

to retain all receipts from student fees and sales of auxiliary enterprises and to receive an additional appropriation from the state for the balance of their needs. Second, in some states, institutions remit all receipts to the state treasury, receiving credits for their receipts against which warrants may be drawn. Third, in some states, institutions turn over all receipts to the state, receiving an appropriation from the legislature to cover their entire budgets. Fourth, in some states, institutions retain certain specified funds, such as revenues from student activities, but remit all other receipts to the state treasury.

The first plan, which is the one employed in many of the states and which applies to all privately controlled institutions, serves as the basis for the present discussion. The second plan differs but slightly from the first in that receipts are deposited in the state treasury instead of a college depository. Under this plan, accounting procedure for revenue requires that a receivable account (such as Funds in State Treasury) be charged with receipts instead of a bank account. Under the third plan, whereby institutions remit all receipts to the treasury and receive all monies through state appropriations, colleges have only that revenue which is received from the state through legislative appropriation. Therefore, as receipts from student fees and other institutional revenues are accrued or collected, they are credited, not to a revenue, but to a liability account, since they represent debts to the state treasurer. When this plan is followed, however, it is recommended that a detailed revenue ledger be kept to accumulate statistical information relative to sources of receipts and to control these receipts from a budgetary point of view. Although these receipts are not retained, they must be budgeted and collected on behalf of the state treasury. Under this plan, as receipts are collected from various sources, they are credited to Revenues Due to State and are posted in the usual manner to detailed revenue accounts. As payments of these collections are made to the treasurer, an account, Remittances of Revenue to State, is charged. The account Revenues Due to State remains open until the end of the year, and thus serves as a control over the detailed ledger, which is regarded as a memorandum or statistical ledger. Under the fourth plan, whereby institutions retain only specified funds, such funds should be retained as restricted funds and accounted for as such.

Some accounting problems arising in connection with revenues and cash receipts are segregated and considered below:

Accounting for Revenues from Registration. The procedure described below is suggested in connection with registration. It assumes a centralized registration plan in which a large area, such as a gymnasium, auditorium, or library, is set up and equipped each term or semester for the registration process. Faculty advisors, representatives of the registrar, business officer, deans of students, and other administrative officers are stationed in the area, and all students are required to carry out and complete their registration in that area. The payment of fees, or making suitable arrangements with the representative of the business office for their payment, is considered a part of the registration procedure.

1. Upon entering the registration room, the student receives a complete registration packet, or folder, containing personal information cards, subject and course cards, and other forms to be filled in.

2. The student meets with his faculty advisors, determines his course of study, and fills out the registration materials contained in the packet.

3. The student goes to the dean of men (or women) or director of student housing, where his registration packet is stamped "dormitory" or "nondormitory."

4. The student goes to the registrar's station, where all fees and charges are assessed. If the student intends to live in a dormitory, his assessment includes dormitory charges for the semester. Fee assessments are made on prenumbered assessment slips (Form 7.1). These slips are made in triplicate, the assessor keeping one copy and giving the original and the second copies to the student.

5. A "checker" verifies the footings and calculations on the student's assessment slip. At this point, the student indicates his intentions as to the complete or partial payment of his fees and other charges. If prepared to pay in full, he takes step 7. If, however, he can pay only part of his fees, he takes step 6.

6. The student arranges with the chief business officer or other

official of the business office to pay his fees in deferred installments. If the deferment is granted, the student receives a written approval, then takes step 7.

7. At the business office station, the student presents to a cashier both copies of his assessment slips, along with his registration packet. He then either pays the amount indicated or presents the written permission to extend the time of payment. The cashier indicates on the assessment slips the amount paid or charged (if any), and stamps Paid on both copies of the assessment slip. One copy of the assessment slip is retained by the cashier. The other goes to the student as a receipt.

8. As a final step, the entire registration packet is taken up when the student presents the stamped receipt. In view of the fact that the student cannot leave the registration area without paying his fees and cannot officially complete his registration until his stamped registration packet is taken up, there is little possibility that a student will be officially registered without having paid or made provision for his fees.

Note that in the above procedure all assessments of fees and charges are made by representatives of the registrar's office and that the sole function of the business office is to collect the fees. This procedure, generally followed in colleges and universities, has much to commend it. The registrar's office is more familiar with courses of study and laboratory fees and, therefore, greater accuracy of assessment results. Similarly, the business office, by restricting its activities to collections, can proceed much faster and with less possibility of error. Since the registrar retains a duplicate copy of all assessment slips, this method provides an excellent means of internal check on the income from registration by separating the duties of assessing and collecting fees. It also serves as a check on the cashiers, who handle considerable sums of money during the short period of registration.

There are many variations of the registration procedures just described. Decentralized registration systems and the use of mechanical devices, such as the computer or tabulating machinery, result in different methods of handling registration materials. Preregistration, which a growing number of institutions follow, may

162 ACCOUNTING FOR COLLEGES AND UNIVERSITIES

FORM 7.1

```
┌──────────────────────────────────────────────────────────────────────┐
│                        BLANK COLLEGE              No. 0001             │
│            A S S E S S M E N T    F E E    S L I P                     │
│                                                                        │
│  Name_____   Date_____           │
│  Identification No.                                                    │
├──────────────────────────────────────────────────────┬────────────────┤
│                      C h a r g e s                     │     Amount     │
├──────────────────────────────────────────────────────┼────────────────┤
│     Resident Tuition                                   │                │
│     Nonresident Tuition                                │                │
│     Late Registration Fees                             │                │
│     Course Change Fee,                                 │                │
│     Deferred Test and Examination Fee                  │                │
│     Advanced Standing Examination Fee                  │                │
│     Music Fee                                          │                │
│     Diploma Fee                                        │                │
│     Thesis Fee                                         │                │
│     Residence Hall                                     │                │
│     Student Activity                                   │                │
│     Summer Session                                     │                │
│     University Extension                               │                │
│        Miscellaneous:                                  │                │
│            Accounts Receivable--Students               │                │
│     Net Cash Paid                                      │                │
├──────────────────────────────┬─────────────────────────────────────────┤
│  Official Cashier's Stamp     │                                         │
│                               │      _____        │
│                               │                Assessor                 │
└───────────────────────────────┴─────────────────────────────────────────┘
```

eliminate some or all the steps just described. Prebilling permits the student to pay by mail or over an extended period and changes to some extent the procedures on registration day.

As regards the accounting entries for registration income, the total amount collected at the end of each registration day is receipted in the usual manner and credited to Undistributed Revenues. Although some institutions distribute their receipts as a part of the registration process, it is generally not practicable to attempt to distribute the receipts among the various revenue accounts until some time after the registration period. However, as soon as possible after registration, a detailed distribution of the registration income should be made by the accounting office. The use of mechanical equipment simplifies the distribution procedure greatly. In a manual system, columnar working pads can be used, the columns being headed: Name of Student, Assessment Slip Number, Total Fees, Exemptions (for scholarships), Accounts Receivable, Cash Paid, Resident Tuition, Nonresident Tuition, and so on (a column being provided for each source of revenue). As the assessment slips are distributed on the worksheet, the mathematical correctness of each assessment is verified. From the columnar worksheet distribution, after checking and balancing, the following journal entry is prepared:

Accounts Receivable—Students (Debit individual detailed accounts in Accounts Receivable Ledger.)
Expenditures (The scholarship exemptions are charged as expenditures against the student aid budget.)
Undistributed Revenues
    Revenues (Credit individual revenue accounts in the Revenues Ledger.)
    Due to Other Funds (For money collected during registration on behalf of other funds—such as student loan funds.)

The last phase of the registration process, as it concerns the business office, is the additional auditing of the assessment slips. The first step in the audit is to account for each assessment slip by number. If an assessment slip is spoiled during the process of registration, the assessor voids the slip and sends it to the accounting office. Thus, it is revealed that a missing slip is the result of either the failure of a student to complete his registration or the withholding of a receipt by a cashier to cover a fraud. In addition to accounting for the assessment slips by number, a further verification is accomplished by comparing the slips in the accounting office with the records in the registrar's office.

Another phase of the auditing process consists of the verification of certain types of registration income. For example, the business office must make a reasonable effort to check further the assessment or nonassessment of the nonresident tuition. Laboratory fees should be verified by obtaining from instructors lists of students attending each laboratory class, but these lists cannot be obtained until several weeks after school has begun. Dormitory and dining hall revenues should be verified from lists or registers provided by the dormitory and dining hall managers, respectively. All fee exemptions, such as those for academic and athletic scholarships, should be verified (from some independent source).

After the registration period is over, late fees should be assessed by the registrar's office. A supplementary charge slip (Form 7.2) is used for this purpose. This form is prepared in duplicate by the registrar, who retains one copy. The other copy is presented to the cashier by the student when he pays his fees. The student, in turn, receives a cashier's receipt which he takes back to the registrar's office to complete the process. Examples of supplementary fees are diploma fees, transcripts, and special examination fees. In general, cash should not be collected in the registrar's office, but fees should be assessed only in that office by representatives of the registrar.

FORM 7.2

```
                                                                    No. 1
                        BLANK COLLEGE
                         Business Office

          S U P P L E M E N T A R Y    C H A R G E    S L I P

                                              Date_____

   Charge:_____      $_____
   For_____

   Accounts To Be Credited:
   _____
                                        Signed_____
   _____

```

Forms 7.3 and 7.4 are used in connection with student and other accounts receivable. Deferred assessments or sales on accounts are charged to individual accounts in the accounts receivable ledger (Form 7.3). The statement of account (Form 7.4) can be produced as a by-product of posting the individual account and necessitates no additional preparation. The sum of the individual accounts in the accounts receivable ledger must always balance with the Accounts Receivable control account in the general ledger.

FORM 7.3

```
┌─────────────────────────────────────────────────────────────────────┐
│                        BLANK COLLEGE                                  │
│                        Business Office                                │
│              A C C O U N T S    R E C E I V A B L E                   │
│                                                                       │
│     Name_____  Month_____      │
│                                                                       │
│     Address_____      │
├──────┬─────────────────────┬───────────┬─────────┬─────────┬─────────┤
│ Date │     Description     │ Reference │ Charges │ Credits │ Balance │
├──────┼─────────────────────┼───────────┼─────────┼─────────┼─────────┤
│      │                     │           │         │         │         │
│      │                     │           │         │         │         │
│      │                     │           │         │         │         │
└──────┴─────────────────────┴───────────┴─────────┴─────────┴─────────┘
```

Accounting for Daily Receipts. The usual sources of daily receipts are sales of auxiliary enterprises, collections of accounts receivable, receipt of state appropriations and federal grants, revenues from endowment investments, private gifts and grants, and collection of miscellaneous fees, such as diploma and transcript. The receipts of auxiliary enterprises, such as the college bookstore and cafeteria, are deposited daily with the cashier, with cash register tapes, sales tickets, and any other original documents supporting the cash. A small envelope prepared by the auxiliary enterprise, such as the one illustrated in Form 7.5, serves as a daily report and is also a convenient method of filing the sales tickets and other documents.

FORM 7.4

```
┌─────────────────────────────────────────────────────────────────────┐
│                        BLANK COLLEGE                                  │
│                        Business Office                                │
│              S T A T E M E N T   O F   A C C O U N T                  │
│                                                                       │
│     Name_____  Month of_____       │
│                                                                       │
│     Address_____                                  │
│            _____                                  │
│          Detach here and return top portion with remittance          │
├──────┬─────────────────────┬───────────┬─────────┬─────────┬─────────┤
│ Date │     Description     │ Reference │ Charges │ Credits │ Balance │
├──────┼─────────────────────┼───────────┼─────────┼─────────┼─────────┤
│      │                     │           │         │         │         │
│      │                     │           │         │         │         │
│      │                     │           │         │         │         │
└──────┴─────────────────────┴───────────┴─────────┴─────────┴─────────┘
```

FORM 7.5
(Envelope)

```
                              BLANK COLLEGE
              D A I L Y   C A S H   R E C E I P T S   R E P O R T

              _____
                             Name of Unit

                                       Date_____

CHARGE
  Cash_____

  Cash Short or Over_____

                                             Total

CREDIT
  Sales_____

  Cash over and Short_____

                                             Total



        Place in this envelope all evidence concerning the receipts, including cash
   register tapes, coupons, and sales tickets.


   Signed_____
                        Manager of Unit


   Received and Checked_____
                                 Cashier
```

The collection of accounts receivable does not give rise to any particular accounting problem; neither does the receipt of state appropriations, endowment income, or miscellaneous revenues. The primary points to emphasize in connection with the account-

FORM 7.6

```
┌─────────────────────────────────────────────────────────────────┐
│                         BLANK COLLEGE                    No. 1    │
│                        Business Office                            │
│                   C A S H    R E C E I P T                        │
│                                          Date_____  │
│  Received                                                         │
│  From_____  $_____  │
│                                                                   │
├──────────────────────────────────────────────┬────────┬──────────┤
│        C r e d i t    A c c o u n t           │  No.   │  Amount  │
├──────────────────────────────────────────────┼────────┼──────────┤
│                                                │        │          │
│                                                │        │          │
│                                                │        │          │
├──────────────────────────────────────────────┴────────┴──────────┤
│                   Signed_____              │
│                                      Cashier                      │
└─────────────────────────────────────────────────────────────────┘
```

ing for receipts are, first, that all receipts, regardless of source or amount, should be received by the college cashier, and, second, that the receipts of each day should be deposited intact in the bank. Form 7.6 is a type of cash receipt. This form is prepared in duplicate.

At the end of the day, the cashier prepares three different reports—the daily cash report (Form 7.7), the distribution of revenue (Form 7.8), and the cash receipts voucher (Form 7.9). The daily cash report, in which the composition of the cash is analyzed, assists the auditor in verifying the day's receipts. The distribution of revenue form is a convenient method of posting to the detailed revenues ledger and is prepared from the cash receipts. An alternative method of posting the revenues ledger is to post from the individual receipts. The first method is preferable, however, in that posting from a summary considerably reduces the amount of detail posting necessary. After the cashier balances the cash received for the day with the cash receipts, the daily cash receipts voucher (printed envelope) is prepared. This voucher is then audited by some employee of the accounting division other than the cashier, and is entered in the cash receipts journal (Form 7.10). At the end of the month, the cash receipts journal is summarized to provide a posting source to the general ledger. Since the receipts of all funds are entered in the cash receipts journal, the summary is divided into balanced fund groups. Following is an illustration of the monthly posting summary for the cash receipts journal:

1. UNRESTRICTED CURRENT FUNDS
   First National Bank—General Account
   Second National Bank—Salary Payroll Account
   Third National Bank—Wage Payroll Account
   Cash Over and Short
       Revenues
       Accounts Receivable—Students
       Accounts Receivable—Others
       Due to Other Funds
       Cash Over and Short
       Expenditures
       Due from Other Funds
       Bank Transfers

2. RESTRICTED CURRENT FUNDS
   First National Bank—Restricted Funds
       Restricted Funds Balances

3. LOAN FUNDS
   First National Bank—Loan Funds
       Notes and Interest Receivable
       Income
       Loan Funds Balances

4. AGENCY FUNDS
   Third National Bank—Agency Funds
       Agency Funds Balances

Accounting for Refunds. Usually the cashier is required to handle two types of refunds—refunds of expenditures and refunds of revenues. Refunds of expenditures, resulting from overpayments made by the institution, are entered on the cash receipts as a credit to Expenditures (with the individual departmental allocation indicated). On the cash receipts voucher, the total of such refunds is credited to Expenditures and is posted to the general ledger through the monthly summary. The proper subsidiary accounts in the allocations ledger are credited directly from the cash receipts.

Refunds of revenues, such as registration fees, board payments,

FORM 7.7

```
+-----------------------------------------------------------------------+
|                          BLANK COLLEGE                                |
|              D A I L Y   C A S H   R E P O R T                        |
|                                                                       |
|                         Date_____                |
|                         Rec._____Through_____             |
+-----------------------------------+-------+--------+--------+         |
|              I t e m s            | No.   | Amount | Total  |         |
+-----------------------------------+-------+--------+--------+         |
| Checks (attach adding machine tape)                                   |
|                                                                       |
| Currency-------------------------- $20                                |
|    "     --------------------------  10                               |
|    "     --------------------------   5                               |
|    "     --------------------------   1                               |
|                                               xxx                     |
| Coins----------------------------- $ 1.00                             |
|    "     --------------------------  .50                              |
|    "     --------------------------  .25                              |
|    "     --------------------------  .10                              |
|    "     --------------------------  .05                              |
|    "     --------------------------  .01                              |
|                                               xxx                     |
| Other (itemize)                                                       |
|                                                                       |
|                                               xxx                     |
| Total Cash in Drawer--------------------------  xxx                   |
| Add:  Cash Items------------------------------  xxx                   |
| Deduct: Advances for Change-------------------  xxx                   |
| Cash Short or Over----------------------------  xxx                   |
| Total Per Cash Receipts-----------------------  xxx                   |
|                                                                       |
| Correct_____   Signed_____                     |
|           Auditor                       Cashier                       |
+-----------------------------------------------------------------------+
```

and dormitory charges are made by the cashier out of petty cash or in the accounting office by check. One important regulation concerning refunds of revenues is that such refunds should always be initi-

FORM 7.8

BLANK COLLEGE		
REVENUES DISTRIBUTION SHEET		
Date_____		
C.R.V. No._____		

Acct. No.	Account Name	Amount
500	Student Fees:	
501	Resident Tuition	
502	Nonresident Tuition	
503	Course Change Fee	
504	Advanced Standing Exam Fee	
505	Diploma	
700	Other Sources:	
731	Library Fines	
732	Int. on Temp. Investments	
733	Transcripts	
734	News Service	
735	Swimming Pool	
	Total for Day	

ated by some office or department other than the business office. In other words, if a student is entitled to receive a refund of registration fees, the registrar's office should issue a refund order (Form 7.11), which authorizes the cashier or accounting office to make the refund to the student. The refund order also may be used in case of a student's withdrawal from the dormitory or dining hall during a semester. In such cases, it should be issued by the Dean of Men (or Women) or by the manager of the dining hall or dormitory. The refund order is prepared in duplicate, the originating office keeping a copy. The refund order serves as a permanent support to the petty cash voucher or other expenditure document. The detail revenues accounts affected are debited either directly from the expenditure vouchers or from a summary prepared at the end of the month.

Accounting for Unrestricted Gifts and Bequests. According to *College and University Business Administration,* "all unrestricted gifts and bequests must be reported initially in the year in which re-

FORM 7.9

BLANK COLLEGE				No. 0001	
C A S H R E C E I P T S V O U C H E R					

Date_____

General Funds	Acct. No.	Amount	Other Funds	Acct. No	Amount

Debits:
  Cash - First Nat. - Gen.
  Cash - Second Nat. - Sal.
  Cash - Third Nat. - Wage
  Cash - Over and Short
Other:
	1001
	1002
	1003
	1006
			Debits:
			  Cash - F.N.B. -
			    Restricted
			  Cash - S.N.B. - Loan
			  Cash - F.N.B. -
			    Endowment
			  Cash - S.N.B. - Annuity
			  Cash - T.N.B. -
			    Unexpended Plant Funds
			  Cash - F.N.B. - R & R
			  Cash - T.N.B. - R of Ind.
			  Cash - F.N.B. - Agency
			
			Other:
				
				1501
				2001
				
				3001
				4001
				
				5001
				5201
				5401
				6001	

Total Debits			Total Debits		

Credits:
  Bank Transfers
  Accounts Receivable -
    Students
  Accounts Receivable -
    Other
  Expenditures
  Revenues
  Cash - Over and Short
Other
	1005
	
	1015
	
	1016
	1061
	1251
	1006
			Credits:
			  Restricted Current
			    Funds Balances
			  Loan Funds Balances
			  Endowment Fund
			    Balances
			  Unexpended Plant Fund
			    Balances
			  R & R Plant Fund Bal.
			  Agency Fund Balances
			
			Other:
				
				1851
				2251
				
				3251
				
				5151
				5351
				6251	

Total Credits			Total Credits		

POSTED	

Accounts Receivable
  Students_____ Other_____
  Revenue Ledger_____
  Expenditure Ledger_____
  Cash Receipts Journal_____
  Student Deposits_____
  Other_____
	Prepared By_____
	                            (Cashier)
	Approved By_____
	                            (Auditor)
	Receipt No._____through No._____

ceived in one statement, either the Statement of Current Funds Revenues, Expenditures, and Transfers, or the Statement of Changes in Fund Balances—Unrestricted Current Funds. Whichever method

FORM 7.10
(Left Side)

BLANK COLLEGE
C A S H   R E C E I P T S   J O U R N A L
DEBITS

Date	Cash Receipts Voucher No.	General Funds			Restricted Funds	Loan Funds	Endowment Funds	Agency Funds	Other	
		General	Payroll	Wage					Account	Amount

FORM 7.10
(Right Side)

BLANK COLLEGE
C A S H   R E C E I P T S   J O U R N A L

Unrestricted Current Funds				Restricted Funds		Loan Funds		Agency Funds		Other		
Reserves	Accounts Receivable	Miscellaneous		Account	Amount	Account	Amount	Account	Amount	Fund	Account	Amount
		Account	Amount									

FORM 7.11

BLANK COLLEGE   No. 1
Business Office

R E F U N D   O R D E R

Date_____

Refund:_____ $_____

For_____

_____

Accounts To Be Charged

_____

_____   Signed_____

is employed must be used consistently from year to year." [2] Thus the institution has an option in the recording and reporting of unrestricted gifts and bequests. Following is an illustration of the accounting involved in each of the alternative methods.

[2] *College and University Business Administration,* 150.

Assume that in the current fiscal year $500,000 is received from donors, representing unrestricted gifts and bequests. Of this amount, by action of the trustees, $250,000 is to be used to finance current operations, $50,000 for an addition to plant, and $200,000 as a fund functioning as endowment.

1. The institution records all gifts received as revenues in the year in which received:

   a. To record receipt of gift:
   In Unrestricted Current Funds:

Cash	500,000	
Revenues		500,000

   In the Revenues Ledger, credit the revenue account Gifts.

   b. To record transfers to other funds:
   In Unrestricted Current Funds:

Transfers to Unexpended Plant Funds	50,000	
Transfers to Endowment and Similar Funds	200,000	
Cash		250,000

   (If there are a number of transfers during the year, subsidiary accounts should be maintained.)
   Entries reflecting receipt of the transfers would be made respectively in the Plant Funds and the Endowment and Similar Funds groups.

2. The institution reports all gifts received in the Statement of Changes in Fund Balances—Unrestricted Current Funds—Gifts.

   a. To record receipt of gift:
   In Unrestricted Current Funds:

Cash	500,000	
Unrestricted Current Funds Balances—Gifts		500,000

   b. To record application of portion of the gift to current operations:
   In Unrestricted Current Funds:

Unrestricted Current Funds Balances—Gifts	250,000	
Revenues		250,000

In the Revenues Ledger credit the revenues account Gifts Applied.

c. To record transfers to other funds:
   In Unrestricted Current Funds:

Unrestricted Current Funds Balances—Gifts	250,000	
Cash		250,000

Entries reflecting receipt of the transfers would be made respectively in the Plant Funds and Endowment and Similar Funds groups.

Thus, in either of the foregoing methods, the financial report will reflect in a single statement the total amounts received during the year from unrestricted gifts and bequests and the disposition of those gifts. In the first method illustrated, all transactions involving unrestricted gifts were disclosed in the Statement of Current Funds Revenues, Expenditures, and Transfers. In the second method, in which the institution elected to hold unrestricted gifts and bequests for later application, unrestricted gifts and their disposition were disclosed in the Statement of Changes in Fund Balances—Unrestricted Current Funds—Gifts. If the trustees had decided to retain a portion of the unrestricted gifts for application in a subsequent fiscal year, the unapplied portion would be reflected in the account Unrestricted Current Funds Balances—Gifts and would be disclosed on the balance sheet.

Receipts of Funds Other Than Current Funds. As explained, the receipts of all funds are accounted for through the same channels, are evidenced by the same documents (the cash receipt and the cash receipts voucher) and are posted from the same journal (the cash receipts journal). In the case of those fund balances which are supported by subsidiary ledgers, the detail information is posted to these ledgers from the cash receipt. A detailed explanation of accounting for funds other than current is given in chapters 10, 11, and 12.

CHAPTER VIII

Data Processing Systems

A DECISION TO install an electronic data processing system (EDP system) in a college or university entails the expenditure of substantial sums of money. In addition to the cost of renting or purchasing the computer and the required peripheral equipment, there are commitments for staff, space, site preparation, furniture, equipment, and operating supplies. For these reasons, careful consideration should be given to a number of factors before the decision is reached.

It should first be ascertained that EDP equipment is actually needed, that its acquisition and operation will contribute to improved administration of the institution, and that the outlays of moneys and added costs will be justified by more complete financial records and reports than are being produced by present equipment and procedures. An extensive exploration should be made of all the possible uses of the computer and related equipment to determine its application to teaching and research, as well as to administrative purposes, including, for example, student records, budget preparation, accounting and financial reporting, payroll operations in all aspects, gifts and financial promotion programs, and personnel records, reports, and analyses. An accurate determination should be made of the cost of the initial installation and of the annual expenditures for rentals, salaries and wages, and other expenses associated with an EDP system. Finally, the decision as to make, style, and quantity of equipment should be made with great care in the light of these and other factors.

A computer installation generally requires major changes in the accounting system. The exact nature of these modifications, how long it will take to achieve them, and what kinds of results may be expected after the EDP equipment is installed are points of special concern to the college and university business officer and should be determined in advance.

The purposes of this chapter are (1) to discuss the feasibility study which should be made prior to the installation of an EDP system, (2) to analyze the kind of organization required for the EDP center, (3) to examine the preinstallation planning required before the change to a computer system is made, and (4) to examine modifications to be made to the accounting and financial reporting systems in order to utilize the computer efficiently.

The Feasibility Study. In order to resolve the major problems which an institution faces in converting a conventional accounting system to an electronic data processing system, it is considered essential that a feasibility study be conducted in depth.

The basic objective of this study should be to determine the economic desirability and technical feasibility of placing business, administrative, research, and teaching functions on a computer or computers. Specifically, the study should cover the following areas: (1) the business and administrative systems to be placed on the computer, (2) the economic implications of changing to computer systems, (3) the computer time required for both scientific and non-scientific applications, (4) the length of time required to convert the systems initially selected for change, (5) the qualifications and number of staff required to design the new system and perform the conversion, (6) the proper layout of physical facilities, (7) the selection of appropriate equipment, and (8) the organizational structure for the electronic data processing center and the number of persons required to operate it.

Few educational institutions will find it possible to conduct such feasibility studies without the help of outside consultants.

Organizational Structure of the EDP Center. EDP installations may be organized along two different lines. One approach is to establish a centralized EDP center to handle all institutional data processing. An alternate possibility is to establish two EDP centers: one for teaching and research and the other for administrative purposes, i.e., accounting, financial reporting, admissions, registration, development, student records, financial aid, and other noninstructional and nonresearch activities. The first organization described would be under the direction of the chief academic officer. Under the second type of organization one EDP center would function as an adjunct to teaching and research activities and would be directly responsible to the chief academic officer. The other EDP center would be established for administrative record keeping and computation and would be under the jurisdiction of the chief business officer.

There are several major problems inherent in the operation of a single, centralized computer center. (1) Because the authority for processing all data is centralized in one office, established lines of authority may be disrupted. (2) The establishment of schedules of work may present problems. All users prefer prime time as opposed to less desirable time, such as the night shift. Moreover, it is possible that a major user might suffer because of lack of access to the computer at the time most desirable to him. (3) A single EDP center necessitates the transporting of materials from operating offices to the center, thus creating additional possibilities of loss or misplacement of important data, basic documents, and programs. While these problems are valid at the present time, new developments in computer technology may remove them from concern in the future. If a centralized center is established, its equipment should have sufficient speed and memory capacity to provide virtually instantaneous service to most users.

It should be pointed out that with the centralized system there will be an increase in peripheral units, necessitating increases in equipment costs. Moreover, because of the greater sophistication demanded of a highly centralized computer center, a more technically oriented staff will be required. The added equipment and more highly skilled staff will be required to support instructional and research needs rather than those related to administrative applications.

Preinstallation Planning. Once the decision to install electronic data processing equipment has been made, a detailed plan for the installation must be prepared. This preinstallation planning is vital to a smooth and successful system and encompasses the following major areas: (1) determining the initial applications to be placed on the equipment; (2) establishing a time schedule; (3) establishing the organization; (4) defining the problems, programming, and testing procedures for each application; (5) planning the conversion to the computer; (6) determining the equipment requirements and delivery dates; (7) training the staff of the center; and (8) planning the installation of equipment. The foregoing steps can be handled adequately only if a high-level administrative officer is assigned full responsibility for preinstallation phases.

The initial accounting applications normally would include those related to accounts receivable, accounts payable, payroll, general ledger, budget preparation and control, cash receipts, and check writing. Other accounting-related applications readily adaptable to computer operations include gift records, student loans and other institutional financial aid programs, personnel records, and inventory systems.

Preinstallation activities require the establishment of target dates for each major phase of the program. A number of forms have been developed for the guidance of administrative officials responsible for the installation of data processing systems. One such form is that suggested by the International Business Machines Corporation (Form 8.1).[1]

As soon as the preinstallation planning has been completed, the next and most important part of the installation is that of establishing a competent organization to implement the installation, to manage the conversion, and finally, to operate the center. In the final analysis, the success of the EDP center depends to a large extent on the quality of the training, knowledge, and skill of the personnel who will operate it. The competence of the director of the center is of utmost importance.

The first step in the process of converting to EDP accounting pro-

[1] International Business Machines Corporation, *Planning for an IBM Data Processing System* (New York, 1961), 6.

IBM_____DATA PROCESSING SYSTEM PREINSTALLATION SCHEDULE

	DELIVERY DATE			DATE PREINSTALLATION SCHEDULE ESTABLISHED	SYSTEM NO.

	EST. LEAD TIME FOR COMPLETION PRIOR TO DELIVERY (NO. OF MO.)	STARTING DATES		COMPLETION DATES	
		ESTIMATED	ACTUAL	TARGET	ACTUAL
1. ESTABLISHMENT OF ORGANIZATION					
INCLUDES:					
A. APPOINTMENT OF DATA PROCESSING MANAGER B. SELECTION OF PLANNING AND PROGRAMMING STAFF					
2. INITIAL EDUCATIONAL PROGRAM					
INCLUDING:					
A. EXECUTIVE SEMINAR B. PROGRAMMING CLASS FOR DATA PROCESSING MANAGER AND PROGRAMMING STAFF					
3. GENERAL SYSTEMS DESIGN					
IN PLANNING FOR THIS PHASE CONSIDERATION MUST BE GIVEN TO MANY REQUIREMENTS INCLUDING THE PERTINENT ITEMS INDICATED BELOW.					
A. ESTABLISHMENT OF PREINSTALLATION SCHEDULE OF EVENTS. (BAR CHARTS) B. APPLICATION DEFINITION BASED PRINCIPALLY ON THE FOLLOWING ITEMS:					
1. REVIEW OF SOURCE DOCUMENTS 2. ANALYSIS OF FILE REQUIREMENTS 3. DETERMINATION OF REPORT REQUIREMENTS 4. ESTABLISHMENT OF DUE-IN AND DUE-OUT SCHEDULES 5. DEFINITION OF PROCEDURES WITH REGARD TO WORK FLOW 6. DEFINITION OF ORGANIZATIONAL CHANGES REQUIRED 7. DETERMINATION OF REQUIREMENTS FOR OPERATING PERSONNEL					
C. GENERAL FLOW-CHARTS D. BLOCK DIAGRAMS E. ALL BASIC CHANGES TO EXISTING SYSTEM DETERMINED AND AGREED TO AND A PLAN IN OPERATION TO EFFECT THEM					
4. REVIEW OF PHYSICAL INSTALLATION PLANS					
THIS MUST BE ACCOMPLISHED IN A MEETING WITH THE IBM SALES ENGINEERING REPRESENTATIVE, AND MUST CONSIDER THE FOLLOWING MAJOR ITEMS:					
A. SPACE B. POWER C. AIR CONDITIONING D. ROOM CONSTRUCTION E. CABLE REQUIREMENTS					
5. DETAILED SYSTEM DESIGN					
IN ESTABLISHING THE SCHEDULE FOR THIS ITEM CONSIDERATION SHOULD BE GIVEN TO THE FOLLOWING PERTINENT SUBJECTS:					
A. DETAILED FLOW CHARTS B. DETAILED BLOCK DIAGRAM OF MAJOR APPLICATION C. CODING BEGUN D. DETERMINATION OF DETAILED EQUIPMENT SPECIFICATIONS E. REVIEW OF SAVINGS AND COST ANALYSIS F. REVIEW OF DETAILED PREINSTALLATION SCHEDULE OF EVENTS (CODING TESTING ROOM CONSTRUCTION. ETC.)					
6. FIRST TEST SESSION COMPLETED					
7. ESTABLISHMENT OF CONVERSION PROCEDURES					
CONSIDERATION TO BE GIVEN TO:					
A. TIME SCHEDULE B. EQUIPMENT REQUIREMENTS C. PERSONNEL REQUIREMENTS D. PROCEDURES AND CONTROLS					
8. ESTABLISHMENT OF FIRM DELIVERY DATE METHOD OF DELIVERY, SPECIAL HANDLING REQUIREMENTS					
9. MACHINE ROOM LAYOUT AND CABLE ORDER APPROVED					
10. SELECTION AND TRAINING OF OPERATING PERSONNEL					
A. CONSOLE OPERATORS B. TAPE HANDLERS AND EQUIPMENT OPERATORS C. LIBRARIAN D. OTHERS					
11. CONVERSION AND MAJOR APPLICATION PROGRAMS TESTED AND READY FOR VOLUME OR PARALLEL PILOT RUNS					

cedures is to design the new system. At this stage, the flow of work charts and formats for accomplishing each particular program must be established. Once the system is designed, the programmer can convert design steps into a machine-readable language which will permit the computer to accept the written program and produce results from input data taken from cards or tapes. Proper design is critical to the success of an EDP operation; a highly skilled staff at this point will help assure the success of the installation.

The preparation of programs should begin well in advance of the actual computer installation so that most applications can be programmed, tested, and "debugged" prior to the arrival of the computer and related equipment. The actual conversion to the new system will require several weeks. It is generally considered desirable to run parallel operations on both the old and new systems for approximately thirty to sixty days.

Manufacturers of equipment usually are acquainted with the needs of institutions of comparable size and function and can give advice on a specific list of equipment. A survey of comparable institutions, including discussions with persons knowledgeable about equipment capabilities in those institutions, will help insure that equipment of proper size and capacity is selected. Factors to consider include a determination that the equipment has the capacity and speed necessary to meet assumed needs and that it is compatible, without reprogramming, with higher speed and larger capacity machines that may be needed in the future. Another method of selecting equipment is to employ a consulting firm to survey the needs of the institution and to give advice on the equipment list.

The education and training of staff is not a major problem in most institutions, because operators and keypunch personnel can be trained in a short time. With the advent of more sophisticated large-scale computer systems, the position of the operator is important. The director and systems personnel, or programmers, must be carefully selected. Frequently, personnel are selected from within the institution and trained in systems analysis and computer techniques.

The physical installation for the modern computer does not require extensive air conditioning or heat control and may be accomplished by the modification of space to meet the electrical requirements of the equipment. In most cases, the computer manufacturer furnishes these requirements, and the physical plant department of the institution modifies the space so that the installation can be made without difficulty. In general, the following physical requirements must be met: (1) year-round cooling, (2) humidity control, (3) supply of cold water needed for cooling units on certain types of equipment.

Accounting and Financial Reporting. The balance of the chapter is devoted to a discussion of the accounting and financial reporting applications involved in the EDP system.

The Chart of Accounts. The conversion from a conventional accounting and fiscal system to an EDP system usually requires changes in coding in the chart of accounts. In some cases, modifications in the chart itself may be necessary, although a college or university having a satisfactory chart of accounts as described in this volume probably will find it necessary to change only the code numbers as it converts to an EDP system. The code numbers in the chart of accounts are the key to an efficient accounting system on electronic data processing equipment. Each digit in the code must be significant in order to avoid needless punching of extra digits. Superfluous digits take up space, cause extra punching, use up computer memory, and waste both time and machine capacity. It is highly desirable to create an accounting code that is sufficiently flexible to allow for expansion but at the same time avoids the use of digits which have no significance. If an institution has a well-organized chart of accounts, complete reorganization is not required; it is necessary only to modify the account code numbers.

Coding System for EDP. The use of an EDP system requires the assignment of account numbers in a coded arrangement so that budgetary and accounting transactions can be recorded and reported in a variety of classifications. Each digit or group of digits in the code number should identify the account as to fund, type of transaction, and budget unit. The EDP system thus is provided with a means of sorting the accounts into any of these classifications for summary financial reports.

The system illustrated here consists of a code comprising ten digits for the basic number, followed by three digits representing

object codes. The total of thirteen digits is divided into six groups
(XX-X-X-X-XXXXX-XXX). The first two digits identify the fund
group to which the account belongs. The third digit provides the
fiscal year designation. The fourth digit is a ledger designation,
while the fifth digit designates the campus or branch. The next five
digits are as follows: two for function, one for college or division,
and the last two for budget accounts. The illustration which follows
is presented to show how these digits might be assigned.

(A)	(B)	(C)	(D)	(E)	(F)
XX –	X –	X –	X –	XXXXX –	XXX

(A) XX   *Fund Designation*
                     00   Unassigned
                     01   Unrestricted Current
                     02   Restricted Current
                     10   Loan
                     20   Endowment
                     21   Term Endowment
                     22   Quasi-endowment
                     30   Annuity and Life Income
                     40   Unexpended Plant
                     41   Renewals and Replacements
                     42   Retirement of Indebtedness
                     43   Investment in Plant

(B) X   *Fiscal Year Designation*
                     0   Fiscal Year 1969–1970
                     1   Fiscal Year 1970–1971
                     2   Fiscal Year 1971–1972
                     3   Fiscal Year 1972–1973
                     4   Fiscal Year 1973–1974
                     5   Fiscal Year 1974–1975
                     6   Fiscal Year 1975–1976
                     7   Fiscal Year 1976–1977
                     8   Fiscal Year 1977–1978
                     9   Fiscal Year 1978–1979

(C) X   *Ledger Designation*
                     0   Unassigned
                     1   General Ledger
                     2   Revenues Ledger
                     3   Allocations Ledger
                     Others as needed

(D) X   *Campus or Branch Designation*
                     0   Unassigned
                     1   General University
                     2   Branch #1
                     3   Branch #2
                     4   Veterinary Medicine
                     5   Agricultural Experiment Station
                     6   Cooperative Extension
                     Others as needed

(E) XX X XX
      1   2   3
            (1) XX *Function Designation*
                     00   Unassigned
                     10   Revenues—Student Tuition and Fees
                     11   Revenues—Governmental
                                     Appropriations
                     12   Revenues—Gifts (or Gifts Applied)
                     13   Revenues—Sponsored Research
                     14   Revenues—Other Separately
                                     Budgeted Research
                     15   Revenues—Other Sponsored
                                     Programs
                     16   Revenues—Recovery of Indirect
                                     Costs
                     17   Revenues—Sales and Services of
                                     Educational Departments
                     18   Revenues—Organized Activities
                                     Related to Educational
                                     Departments
                     19   Revenues—Other Sources
                     30   Expenditures—Instruction and
                                     Departmental Research
                     40   Expenditures—Organized Activities
                                     Related to Educational
                                     Departments
                     50   Expenditures—Sponsored Research
                     52   Expenditures—Other Separately
                                     Budgeted Research
                     54   Expenditures—Other Sponsored
                                     Programs
                     60   Expenditures—Extension and Public
                                     Service
                     62   Expenditures—Libraries

64	Expenditures—Student Services
70	Expenditures—Operation and Maintenance of Physical Plant
80	Expenditures—General Administration
90	Expenditures—Staff Benefits
95	Expenditures—General Institutional Expenses

(2) X   *College or Division*

0	Unassigned
1	Agriculture
2	Arts and Sciences
3	Business
4	Education
5	Engineering
6	Home Economics
7	Technical Institute
8	Graduate
9	Unassigned

(3) XX   *Budget Accounts*

00	Unassigned
01	Dean's Office
02	Biochemistry
03	Agricultural Economics
04	Agricultural Education
05	Agricultural Engineering
06	Agronomy
07	Animal Sciences
08	Other Departments

(4) XXX *Object Code* (can be further detailed, as desired)

000–199	Salaries
200–399	Wages
400–699	Supplies and Expense
700–899	Equipment

To illustrate the use of the coding system, wages paid by the university in 1969–1970 for the College of Business, Dean's Office, would be coded as follows: 01-0-3-1-30301-200. The first two digits indicate that the transaction involves the unrestricted current funds group. The next digit, 0, designates the fiscal year 1969–1970. Digit 3 indicates that the allocations ledger is involved. The Campus or

Branch code, 1, is the General University as distinguished from branches or other campuses. The next two digits, 30, classify the expenditure as Instruction and Departmental Research. The College of Business is digit 3, followed by the account number 01, designating the Dean's Office. The last three digits, 200, identify the object of expenditure as wages.

Budget Preparation. Budget preparation can be successfully adapted to an electronic data processing system. The first step in automating the budget is to punch data cards, using the coding system as described above, for each item of revenue and expenditure involved in the current year's operation. This provides a starting point for the preparation of estimates for the budget of the succeeding year.

After preparation of data cards punched from revenue and expenditure estimates for the current year, the desired number of printouts is produced by the computer. Listings of revenue estimates are sent to the chief business officer to be used in the preparation of the revenue portion of the budget for the new year. The sections involving expenditures are sent to the budget heads so that they may indicate employees' salary rates requested for the new year, new wage rates, requests for new salary and wage positions, additional amounts required for supplies and expense and equipment, and appropriate justifications for each increase. Subsequent to consideration and approval of departmental requests, data cards are again prepared reflecting the new figures for each budget account.

When the budget has finally been approved by the president and the governing board, a final, revised computer run is made in order to produce the official budget for the year for appropriate distribution. In the process of running the budget, other statistical data and/or calculations can be produced which may prove helpful in budgetary formulation. For example, one or more of the following items of information can be produced: tenure reports; personnel statistical reports, prepayroll analysis; personnel master records; and salary averages by ranks, colleges, and departments.

Budget revisions to increase or decrease departmental appropriations should be handled in the same manner as approval of the original budget document. The approved budget revision forms become the source documents for the preparation of punched cards used to reflect changes in revenue and expenditure accounts. Personnel status forms are the source documents from which data cards are punched to reflect changes in personnel.

Monthly budget statements are produced for salaries, wages, supplies and expense, and equipment on which are shown allocations, encumbrances, expenditures, and unexpended allocations balances. These statements are prepared as the budget is updated each month from transactions previously punched into cards or tapes. As the transactions deck or tape is processed against the budget ledger deck of cards or tapes, all records are updated. Most EDP systems provide for the transfer of information to tape or disc, thereby speeding up the updating process.

Budget Control, Expenditures, and Disbursements. After the budget has been approved, control of expenditures must be exercised by the business office to prevent the overexpenditure of departmental allocations. In chapter 5, budgetary control principles were presented which apply to most institutional accounting systems regardless of the equipment used; that is, manual, bookkeeping machine, punched card, or EDP systems. Briefly, the budget control system suggested is based on centralized purchasing and the encumbering of budget allocations with the estimated cost of materials, supplies, and equipment to be procured on approved purchase orders. The encumbrance system can be automated through the preparation of data cards and, subsequently, magnetic tape, to which information is transferred directly from the purchase orders. When materials are received and invoices obtained from vendors, data cards are punched from remittance advices to remove the encumbrance and simultaneously charge the expenditure to the budget allocation, updating the unexpended balance in the budget document and accounting records. These same cards may also be used in preparing checks in payment to vendors.

The Payroll System. Payrolls normally are divided into the two major categories of salaries and wages. Salary payrolls are placed on the computer through the use of salary budget sheets which provide complete details as to name and rank of each authorized individual to be paid, number of months to be paid during the fiscal period, rate of compensation, amount of salary, and accounts to be charged. The salary budget tape (or disc pack) showing all pertinent information, such as name, rank, salary, and deductions information, is used to prepare the check for each individual listed on the salary payroll.

Wage payrolls also require a master tape setting forth pertinent details about each individual. In order to complete the payroll for wage personnel, it is necessary to ascertain the number of hours each employee has worked during the payroll period. Payrolls of the previous period, provided by the computer, produce all the information required for the new payroll except the number of hours or days worked. The computer printouts are forwarded to the appropriate departments so that the number of days or hours worked can be inserted by the department head. The names of persons who may have left the employ of the institution are deleted and names of new employees are added. Any changes in hourly or daily wage rates also are noted. After certifying that the work for which pay is requested has been performed, the printouts are returned to the payroll office. The data are then sent to the computer center for processing and for the issuance of wage checks.

As a by-product of producing the salary and wage payrolls, several subsidiary records are automatically available from computer records. For example, totals-to-date for earnings, federal and state income tax withholdings, Social Security (FICA) taxes, and cumulative information relative to group life insurance and other insurance payments, retirement payments, and other deductions may be compiled as a result of computer processing. It is possible also to update the budget document to reflect salary and wage expenditures as well as unexpended salary and wage balances.

Other Fund Groups. EDP equipment and systems are readily adaptable to accounting and reporting the financial transactions of fund groups other than current funds and should be utilized in these areas to the fullest extent.

In the Endowment and Similar Funds group, EDP systems are effective in recording investments, comparing market and book values of securities, and providing comparative and evaluative data on the growth of endowment funds and earnings from their investments. Amortization of premiums and discounts on bond transactions can be handled to advantage through the use of the computer.

Loan funds have increased considerably in recent years because of the vast expansion of federal and state funds available for loans to students. The computer can be of great assistance in the collection of student loans by preparing statements both for the institution and for students, indicating due dates, amounts of periodic payments, amounts of interest due, and other pertinent data about the loans.

The operations and transactions of the various subgroups of Plant Funds can be computerized with great effectiveness, especially those relating to building and construction projects. Reports of costs, comparisons of costs with estimates or budgets, and construction progress reports are examples of periodic reports on new buildings that can be prepared and updated expeditiously through the use of EDP equipment and systems.

Agency funds, especially those involving student bank or deposit accounts, can be computerized to advantage.

Financial Reporting. The computer can be used to prepare interim reports as well as the annual financial report. The annual report, at least in preliminary form, may be produced as a by-product of recording transactions in the departmental allocations accounts and in the accounts for the other fund groups.

CHAPTER IX

Accounting for Current Funds
—Illustration

IN THE PRECEDING chapters there has been presented a complete discussion of the various phases of the accounting system as it pertains to current or operating funds. In chapter 3 the routine of purchasing and stores control was discussed. In chapter 4 a complete chart of accounts, including general ledger, revenues and expenditures, was presented. Chapter 5 dealt with the preparation and control of the current funds budget, while chapters 6 and 7 were concerned with routine bookkeeping and accounting procedures for the expenditures and revenues of current funds. In order to amplify and supplement the explanatory material covered in the foregoing chapters, a complete illustration of accounting for current funds is presented in this chapter. Transactions are presented in general journal form with explanations regarding the purpose of the entry and the journal or register in which the entries are recorded. To present a complete picture, the current funds section of the balance sheet at the beginning of a period is given. Then, transactions involving typical operations are entered in journal form and are posted to illustrative general ledger accounts. A balance sheet before closing entries are made is presented. Finally, closing entries are entered and posted, and a Balance Sheet and a Statement of Changes in Fund Balances at the end of the period are prepared. The illustration treats separately the two groups of current funds—that is, Unrestricted Current and Restricted Current Funds.

ACCOUNTING FOR CURRENT FUNDS

A. Balance Sheet at Beginning of Period

BLANK COLLEGE
BALANCE SHEET
(Beginning of Period)

ASSETS		LIABILITIES AND FUND BALANCES	
CURRENT FUNDS:		CURRENT FUNDS:	
Unrestricted:		Unrestricted:	
Cash	$ 86,000	Accounts Payable	$ 12,000
Temporary investments, at cost	100,000	Provision for encumbrances-- prior year	132,000
Accounts receivable--students, less allowance for doubtful accounts of $4,000	5,000	Deferred revenues	90,000
		Fund balances	55,200
Accounts receivable--other, less allowance for doubtful accounts of $2,000	1,000		
Inventories, at cost	90,000		
Prepaid insurance	7,200		
Total Unrestricted Current Funds	$289,200	Total Unrestricted Current Funds	$289,200

B. Recording of Typical Transactions

	GENERAL LEDGER		SUBSIDIARY LEDGER	
	Dr.	Cr.	Dr.	Cr.
1. Entry to record the unrestricted current funds budget (Journal Voucher):				
Unrealized Revenues	3,710,000			
Departmental Allocations		3,486,000		
Unallocated Revenues		224,000		
In Revenue Ledger (posted from budget):				
Resident Tuition			216,000	
Nonresident Tuition			30,000	
State Appropriations			1,800,000	
Dining Halls			660,000	
All Other Revenue Accounts			1,004,000	
			3,710,000	
In Allocations Ledger (posted from budget):				
President's Office:				
Salaries				55,000
Wages				5,000
Supplies and Expense				22,200
Equipment				6,000
Art Department:				
Salaries				76,400
Wages				4,000
Supplies and Expense				2,250
Equipment				600
All Other Allocations Accounts				3,314,550
				3,486,000
2. Entry to record the issuance of purchase orders (Orders Placed and Liquidated Journal, in summary):				
Encumbrances	330,000			
Provision, for Encumbrances-- Current Year		330,000		
In Allocations Ledger (Purchase Orders):				
Departmental Allocations Accounts				330,000

	GENERAL LEDGER		SUBSIDIARY LEDGER	
	Dr.	Cr.	Dr.	Cr.
3. Entries to record payment of invoices covered by purchase orders:				
a. To liquidate encumbrances (Orders Placed and Liquidated Journal, in summary):				
Provision for Encumbrances-- Current Year	325,000			
Encumbrances		325,000		
In Allocations Ledger (Purchase Orders):				
Departmental Allocations Accounts				325,000
b. To charge expenditures (Voucher Register, in summary):				
Expenditures	315,000			
Vouchers Payable		315,000		
In Allocations Ledger (Invoices):				
Departmental Allocations Accounts			315,000	
4. Entry to record issuance of checks (Check Register):				
Vouchers Payable	314,400			
Cash		314,400		
5. Entries to record transfer from general to payroll bank account:				
a. In Voucher Register:				
Bank Transfers	140,000			
Vouchers Payable		140,000		
b. In Check Register:				
Vouchers Payable	140,000			
Cash		140,000		
c. In Cash Receipts Journal:				
Salary Payroll Bank Account	140,000			
Bank Transfers		140,000		
6. Entry to record payroll (Payroll Register):				
Expenditures	189,600			
Due to Teacher Retirement System		9,600		
Withholding Tax Deductions		30,000		
Social Security Deductions		10,000		
Salary Payroll Bank Account		140,000		
In Allocations Ledger (Payroll Distribution):				
Departmental Allocations Accounts			189,600	
7. Entry to establish Petty Cash Fund (Voucher Register):				
a. Petty Cash	6,000			
Vouchers Payable		6,000		
b. Vouchers Payable	6,000			
Cash		6,000		
In Petty Cash Subsidiary Ledger (Voucher Register):				
Custodian of Fund			6,000	
8. Entry to replenish Petty Cash-- $3,600 expended (Voucher Register):				
Expenditures	3,600			
Vouchers Payable		3,600		

	GENERAL LEDGER		SUBSIDIARY LEDGER	
	Dr.	Cr.	Dr.	Cr.
In Allocations Ledger (Petty Cash Vouchers):				
Departmental Allocations Accounts			3,600	
9. Entry to record payment of invoices applicable to orders issued in previous fiscal year (Voucher Register):				
Provision for Encumbrances--Prior Year	108,000			
Vouchers Payable		108,000		
In Allocations Ledger (Prior Year):				
Departmental Allocations Accounts			108,000	
10. Entry to close outstanding encumbrances of prior year since all orders have been paid (Journal Voucher):				
Provision for Encumbrances--Prior Year	24,000			
Unrestricted Current Funds Balances		24,000		
11. Entry to record purchase of materials for storeroom (Voucher Register):				
Stores Inventory	192,000			
Vouchers Payable		192,000		
12. Entry to record issuance of materials to departments (Interdepartmental Transfer Journal):				
Expenditures	186,000			
Stores Inventory		186,000		
In Allocations Ledger (Interdepartmental Invoices):				
Departmental Allocations Accounts			186,000	
13. Entry to record sale of materials to outside agency (Cash Receipts Journal):				
Cash	600			
Stores Inventory		600		
14. Entry to record issuance of materials to Plant Funds (Interdepartmental Invoice):				
Due from Unexpended Plant Funds	3,000			
Stores Inventory		3,000		
(In Unexpended Plant Funds, debit Unexpended Plant Funds Balances and credit Due to Unrestricted Current Funds.)				
15. Entry to adjust stores inventory at book value to physical inventory (Journal Voucher):				
Unrestricted Current Funds Balances	600			
Stores Inventory		600		
16. Entry to record sales of supplies by bookstore to departments (Interdepartmental Transfer Journal):				
Expenditures	90,000			
Revenues		90,000		
In Allocations Ledger (Interdepartmental Invoices):				
Departmental Allocations Accounts			90,000	

	GENERAL LEDGER		SUBSIDIARY LEDGER	
	Dr.	Cr.	Dr.	Cr.
In Revenues Ledger (Interdepartmental Invoices):				
Bookstore--Sales				90,000
17. Entry to record collection of student tuition and fees (Cash Receipts Journal):				
Cash	240,000			
Revenues		240,000		
In Revenues Ledger (Summary of Registration Revenues):				
Revenues Accounts				240,000
18. Entry to record issuance of student loans (Voucher and Check Registers):				
a. Due from Loan Funds	12,000			
Vouchers Payable		12,000		
b. Vouchers Payable	12,000			
Cash		12,000		
(In Loan Funds group, debit Notes Receivable and credit Due to Unrestricted Current Funds.)				
19. Entry to record collection of student loans (Cash Receipts Journal):				
Cash	6,000			
Due from Loan Funds		6,000		
(In Loan Funds group, debit Due to Unrestricted Current Funds and credit Notes Receivable.)				
20. Entry to record charging student fees based on promissory notes (Journal Voucher):				
Accounts Receivable--Students	12,000			
Revenues		12,000		
In Accounts Receivable Ledger (Registration Slips):				
Individual Student Accounts			12,000	
In Revenues Ledger (Summary of Registration Slips):				
Revenues Accounts				12,000
21. Entry to record collection of fees previously charged (Cash Receipts Journal):				
Cash	9,000			
Accounts Receivable--Students		9,000		
In Accounts Receivable Ledger (Cash Receipts):				
Individual Student Accounts				9,000
22. Entry to record increase in allowance for doubtful accounts (Journal Voucher):				
Expenditures	1,800			
Allowance for Doubtful Accounts		1,800		
In Allocations Ledger (Journal Voucher):				
Departmental Allocations Accounts-- Provision for Doubtful Accounts			1,800	

	GENERAL LEDGER		SUBSIDIARY LEDGER	
	Dr.	Cr.	Dr.	Cr.
23. Entry to record charging off student accounts receivable as uncollectible (Journal Voucher):				
Allowance for Doubtful Accounts	300			
Accounts Receivable--Students		300		
In Accounts Receivable Ledger (Journal Voucher):				
Individual Student Accounts				300
24. Entries to record receipt of students accounts receivable previously written off as uncollectible (Journal Voucher and Cash Receipts Journal):				
a. Accounts Receivable--Students	120			
Allowance for Doubtful Accounts		120		
In Accounts Receivable Ledger (Journal Voucher):				
Individual Student Accounts			120	
b. Cash	120			
Accounts Receivable--Students		120		
In Accounts Receivable Ledger (Cash Receipts Journal):				
Individual Student Accounts				120
25. Entry to record collection of sales of auxiliary enterprises (Cash Receipts Journal):				
Cash	1,283,600			
Revenues		1,283,600		
In Revenues Ledger (Cash Receipts):				
Revenues Accounts				1,283,600
26. Entries to record transfers to Plant Funds for plant additions (Voucher Register and Check Register):				
a. Transfers to Unexpended Plant Funds	60,000			
Vouchers Payable		60,000		
b. Vouchers Payable	60,000			
Cash		60,000		
(In Unexpended Plant Funds group, debit Cash and credit Unexpended Plant Funds Balances.)				
27. Entry to record purchases of equipment for departments (Voucher Register):				
Expenditures	60,000			
Vouchers Payable		60,000		
In Allocations Ledger (Invoices):				
Departmental Allocations Accounts			60,000	
(In the Investment in Plant Section of Plant Funds debit Equipment and credit Net Investment in Plant.)				
28. Entry to record allocation to renewal and replacement reserve for property of auxiliary enterprises (Voucher Register and Check Register):				
a. Expenditures	6,000			
Vouchers Payable		6,000		

	GENERAL LEDGER		SUBSIDIARY LEDGER	
	Dr.	Cr.	Dr.	Cr.
b. Vouchers Payable	6,000			
Cash		6,000		
In Allocations Ledger (Voucher Register):				
Departmental Allocations Accounts			6,000	
(In the Funds for Renewals and Replacements group, debit Cash and credit Renewals and Replacements Funds Balances.)				
29. Entry to record refund of expenditures (Cash Receipts Journal):				
Cash	6,000			
Expenditures		6,000		
In Allocations Ledger (Cash Receipts):				
Departmental Allocations Accounts				6,000
30. Entry to record refund of revenues (Voucher Register and Check Register):				
a. Revenues	1,200			
Vouchers Payable		1,200		
b. Vouchers Payable	1,200			
Cash		1,200		
In Revenues Ledger (Invoices):				
Revenues Accounts			1,200	
31. Entry to record sales of used equipment originally purchased out of current funds at a cost of $3,000 (Cash Receipts Journal):				
Cash	600			
Revenues		600		
In Revenues Ledger (Cash Receipts):				
Revenues Account--Sale of Surplus Property				600
(In Plant Funds group--investment in plant section--debit Net Investment in Plant and credit Equipment $3,000.)				
32. Entry to record collection of revenues applicable to subsequent accounting period (Cash Receipts Journal):				
Cash	60,000			
Deferred Revenues		60,000		
33. Entry to transfer Deferred Revenues to Revenues at beginning of accounting period (Journal Voucher):				
Deferred Revenues	60,000			
Revenues		60,000		
In Revenues Ledger (Journal Voucher):				
Revenues Accounts				60,000
34. Entries to record payment of Restricted Current Funds expenditures from Unrestricted Current Funds (Voucher Register and Check Register):				
a. Restricted Expenditures	110,000			
Vouchers Payable		110,000		
b. Vouchers Payable	110,000			
Cash		110,000		

	GENERAL LEDGER		SUBSIDIARY LEDGER	
	Dr.	Cr.	Dr.	Cr.
In Allocations Ledger:				
Restricted Allocations Accounts			110,000	
35. Entry to record receipt of reimbursement from Restricted Current Funds to cover expenditures made from Unrestricted Current Funds during period (Cash Receipts Journal):				
Cash	110,000			
Restricted Revenues		110,000		
In Revenues Ledger (Cash Receipts):				
Revenues Accounts				110,000
(In Restricted Current Funds, debit Restricted Current Funds Balances and credit Cash.)				
36. Entry to record receipt of state appropriation (Cash Receipts Journal):				
Cash	1,500,000			
Revenues		1,500,000		
In Revenues Ledger (Cash Receipts):				
Revenues Accounts				1,500,000
37. Entry to record sundry expenditures chargeable against departmental budgets (Voucher Register):				
Expenditures	2,470,800			
Vouchers Payable		2,470,800		
In Allocations Ledger (Vouchers):				
Departmental Allocations Accounts			2,470,800	
38. Entry to record issuance of checks in payment of audited vouchers (Check Register):				
Vouchers Payable	2,300,000			
Cash		2,300,000		
39. Entry to record insurance expired during period (Journal Voucher):				
Expenditures	1,800			
Prepaid Insurance		1,800		
In Allocations Ledger (Journal Voucher):				
Departmental Allocations Account-- Property Insurance				1,800
40. Entry to record approval of voucher covering payment of withholding tax deductions and social security taxes to federal government (Voucher Register):				
a. Expenditures	10,000			
Withholding Tax Deductions	30,000			
Social Security Deductions	10,000			
Vouchers Payable		50,000		
b. Vouchers Payable	50,000			
Cash		50,000		
In Allocations Ledger (Vouchers):				
Departmental Allocations Account-- Employer's Contribution to Social Security			10,000	

	GENERAL LEDGER		SUBSIDIARY LEDGER	
	Dr.	Cr.	Dr.	Cr.
41. Entry to record purchase of temporary investments (Voucher Register and Check Register):				
a. Temporary Investments (Cost)	60,000			
Vouchers Payable		60,000		
b. Vouchers Payable	60,000			
Cash		60,000		
In Investment Ledger (Vouchers):				
Investment Accounts			60,000	
42. Entry to record purchase of temporary investments through Trust Department of bank--bank account charged by debit advices (Journal Voucher):				
Temporary Investments (Cost)	60,000			
Cash		60,000		
43. Entry to record sale of temporary investments costing $18,000 for $19,200 (Cash Receipts Journal):				
Cash	19,200			
Temporary Investments		18,000		
Revenues		1,200		
In Investment Ledger (Cash Receipts):				
Investment Accounts				18,000
In Revenues Ledger (Cash Receipts):				
Revenues Account--Interest and Capital Gains on Temporary Investments				1,200
44. Entry to record sale of temporary investments costing $6,000 for $4,800 (Cash Receipts Journal):				
Cash	4,800			
Revenues	1,200			
Temporary Investments		6,000		
In Revenues Ledger (Cash Receipts):				
Revenues Accounts--Interest and Capital Gains on Temporary Investments			1,200	
In Investment Ledger (Cash Receipts):				
Investment Accounts				6,000
45. Entries to record adjustments to budget (Journal Voucher):				
a. Increase in revenues estimates allocated to departments:				
Unrealized Revenues	6,000			
Departmental Allocations		6,000		
In Revenues Ledger (Journal Voucher):				
Revenues Accounts			6,000	
In Allocations Ledger (Journal Voucher):				
Departmental Allocations Accounts				6,000
b. Increase in one department, decrease in another:				

	GENERAL LEDGER		SUBSIDIARY LEDGER	
	Dr.	Cr.	Dr.	Cr.
Departmental Allocations	30,000			
Departmental Allocations		30,000		
In Allocations Ledger:				
Departmental Allocations Accounts			30,000	30,000
c. Increase in departmental budget financed by transfer from contingency reserves:				
Unallocated Revenues	60,000			
Departmental Allocations		60,000		
In Allocations Ledger:				
Departmental Allocations Accounts				60,000
46. Entry to record unpaid portion of state appropriation (Journal Voucher):				
State Appropriation Receivable	300,000			
Revenues		300,000		
In Revenues Ledger (Journal Voucher):				
Revenues Accounts				300,000
47. Entry to record receipt of gift from alumnus (Cash Receipts Journal):				
Cash	300			
Revenues		300		
In Revenues Ledger (Cash Receipts):				
Revenues Accounts--Gifts				300
48. Entry to record recovery of indirect costs--sponsored programs (Cash Receipts Journal):				
Cash	5,000			
Revenues		5,000		
In Revenues Ledger (Cash Receipts):				
Revenues Accounts				5,000
(In Restricted Current Funds, debit Restricted Current Funds Balances and credit Cash.)				
49. Entry to record transfer to plant funds of debt service on educational plant (Voucher Register and Check Register):				
a. Transfer to Funds for Retirement of Indebtedness	50,000			
Vouchers Payable		50,000		
b. Vouchers Payable	50,000			
Cash		50,000		
(In Plant Funds for Retirement of Indebtedness, debit Cash and credit Retirement of Indebtedness Funds Balances.)				
50. Entry to record transfer to Plant Funds for Retirement of Indebtedness for debt service on auxiliary enterprise plant (Voucher Register and Check Register):				
a. Expenditures	35,000			
Vouchers Payable		35,000		
b. Vouchers Payable	35,000			
Cash		35,000		

	GENERAL LEDGER		SUBSIDIARY LEDGER	
	Dr.	Cr.	Dr.	Cr.

(In Allocations Ledger, debit auxiliary
enterprises subsidiary accounts.)

(In Plant Funds for Retirement of
Indebtedness, debit Cash and credit
Retirement of Indebtedness Funds Balances.)

51. Entry to record transfer of unrestricted
income from Endowment to Unrestricted
Current Funds (Cash Receipts Journal):

Cash	20,000			
Revenues		20,000		

In Revenues Ledger (Cash Receipts):

Revenues Account--Endowment Income--Unrestricted				20,000

(In Endowment and Similar Funds, debit
Income-Control [or undistributed pool
income] and credit Cash.)

52. Entry to record closing of departmental
allocations and unrealized revenues
(Journal Vouchers):

Departmental Allocations	3,552,000			
Unallocated Revenues	164,000			
Unrealized Revenues		3,716,000		

53. Entry to record closing of expenditures,
revenues, and transfer accounts (Journal
Vouchers):

Revenues	3,510,300			
Restricted Revenues	110,000			
Transfers to Unexpended Plant Funds		60,000		
Transfers to Funds for Retirement of Indebtedness		50,000		
Expenditures		3,363,600		
Restricted Expenditures		110,000		
Encumbrances		5,000		
Unrestricted Current Funds Balances		31,700		

54. Entry to record collection of advances made
to other funds (Cash Receipts Journal):

Cash	9,000			
Due from Loan Funds		6,000		
Due from Unexpended Plant Funds		3,000		

C. General Ledger--Unrestricted Current Funds Section

Cash

	Beginning balance	86,000	Entry 4	Remittances	314,000
Entry 13	Sale of Stores	600	Entry 5b	Transfer to Payroll	
Entry 17	Collections	240,000		Account	140,000
Entry 19	Collections	6,000	Entry 7b	Petty Cash	6,000
Entry 21	Collections	9,000	Entry 18b	Student Loans Issued	12,000
Entry 24b	Collections	120	Entry 26b	Transfer to Plant Funds	60,000
Entry 25	Sales of Auxiliaries	1,283,600	Entry 28b	Remittances	6,000
Entry 29	Refund of Expenditures	6,000	Entry 30b	Remittances	1,200
Entry 31	Sale of Used Equipment	600	Entry 34b	Remittances	110,000
Entry 32	Deferred Revenues	60,000	Entry 38	Remittances	2,300,000
Entry 35	Reimbursement of		Entry 40b	Remittances	50,000
	Restricted		Entry 41b	Investments	60,000
	Expenditures	110,000	Entry 42	Investments	60,000
Entry 36	State Appropriation	1,500,000	Entry 49b	Transfer to Funds for	
Entry 43	Sale of Investments	19,200		Retirement of	
Entry 44	Sale of Investments	4,800		Indebtedness	50,000
Entry 47	Alumnus Gift	300	Entry 50b	Debt Service	35,000

(Cash, continued)

Entry 48	Recovery of Indirect Costs	5,000		
Entry 51	Endowment Income	20,000		
Entry 54	Due from Other Funds	9,000		
	(155,620)			

Salary Payroll Bank Account

Entry 5c	Transfer from General Account	140,000	Entry 6	Payroll Checks	140,000

Petty Cash

Entry 7a	Establish Fund	6,000	
	(6,000)		

Bank Transfers

Entry 5a	Transfer to Payroll Bank Account	140,000	Entry 5c	Payroll Bank Account	140,000

Accounts Receivable--Students

	Beginning balance	9,000	Entry 21	Collections	9,000
Entry 20	Student Fees	12,000	Entry 23	Accounts Written Off	300
Entry 24a	Reinstatement of Accounts Written Off	120	Entry 24b	Collections	120
	(11,700)				

Accounts Receivable--Other

	Beginning balance	3,000
	(3,000)	

State Appropriation Receivable

Entry 46	Unpaid Appropriation	300,000
	(300,000)	

Due from Loan Funds

Entry 18a	Student Loans Issued	12,000	Entry 19	Collections	6,000
		12,000	Entry 54	Repayment by Loan Funds	6,000
					12,000

Due from Unexpended Plant Funds

Entry 14	Issues to Plant Funds	3,000	Entry 54	Repayment by Unexpended Plant Funds	3,000

Stores Inventory

	Beginning balance	90,000	Entry 12	Issues to Departments	186,000
Entry 11	Purchases	192,000	Entry 13	Cash Sales	600
			Entry 14	Issues to Departments	3,000
	(91,800)		Entry 15	Adjustment to Physical Inventory	600

Temporary Investments

	Beginning balance	100,000	Entry 43	Sales	18,000
Entry 41a	Purchases	60,000	Entry 44	Sales	6,000
Entry 42	Purchases	60,000			
	(196,000)				

Prepaid Insurance

	Beginning balance	7,200	Entry 39	Expired Insurance	1,800
	(5,400)				

Transfers to Unexpended Plant Funds

Entry 26a	Plant Additions	60,000	Entry 53	Closing	60,000

Transfers to Funds for Retirement of Indebtedness

Entry 49a	Debt Service	50,000	Entry 53	Closing	50,000

Expenditures

Entry 3b	Invoices	315,000	Entry 29	Refund of Expenditures	6,000
Entry 6	Payroll	189,600	Entry 53	Closing	3,363,600
Entry 8	Petty Cash Expenditures	3,600			
Entry 12	Stores Issues	186,000			
Entry 16	Bookstores Sales to Departments	90,000			
Entry 22	Allowance for Doubtful Accounts	1,800			
Entry 27	Invoices	60,000			
Entry 28a	Replacement Reserve	6,000			
Entry 37	Invoices	2,470,800			
Entry 39	Expired Insurance	1,800			
Entry 40a	Social Security Taxes	10,000			
Entry 50a	Debt Service	35,000			
		3,369,600			3,369,600

Restricted Expenditures

Entry 34a	Invoices	110,000	Entry 53	Closing	110,000

Encumbrances

Entry 2	Orders Placed	330,000	Entry 3a	Orders Liquidated	325,000
			Entry 53	Closing	5,000
		330,000			330,000

Unrealized Revenues

Entry 1	Record Budget	3,710,000	Entry 52	Closing	3,716,000
Entry 45a	Budget Adjustments	6,000			
		3,716,000			3,716,000

Vouchers Payable

Entry 4	Checks Issued	314,400		Beginning balance	12,000
Entry 5b	Checks Issued	140,000	Entry 3b	Audited Vouchers	315,000
Entry 7b	Checks Issued	6,000	Entry 5a	Audited Vouchers	140,000
Entry 18b	Checks Issued	12,000	Entry 7a	Audited Vouchers	6,000
Entry 26b	Checks Issued	60,000	Entry 8	Audited Vouchers	3,600
Entry 28b	Checks Issued	6,000	Entry 9	Audited Vouchers	108,000
Entry 30b	Checks Issued	1,200	Entry 11	Audited Vouchers	192,000
Entry 34b	Checks Issued	110,000	Entry 18a	Audited Vouchers	12,000
Entry 38	Checks Issued	2,300,000	Entry 26a	Audited Vouchers	60,000
Entry 40b	Checks Issued	50,000	Entry 27	Audited Vouchers	60,000
Entry 41b	Checks Issued	60,000	Entry 28a	Audited Vouchers	6,000
Entry 49b	Checks Issued	50,000	Entry 30a	Audited Vouchers	1,200
Entry 50b	Checks Issued	35,000	Entry 34a	Audited Vouchers	110,000
			Entry 37	Audited Vouchers	2,470,800
			Entry 40a	Audited Vouchers	50,000
			Entry 41a	Audited Vouchers	60,000
			Entry 49a	Audited Vouchers	50,000
			Entry 50a	Audited Vouchers	35,000
				(547,000)	

Withholding Tax Deductions

Entry 40a	Remittance	30,000	Entry 6	Payroll Deductions	30,000

Social Security Deductions

Entry 40a	Remittance	10,000	Entry 6	Payroll Deductions	10,000

Due to Teacher Retirement System

		Entry 6	Payroll Deductions	9,600
			(9,600)

Deferred Revenues

Entry 33	Transfer to Revenues	60,000	Entry 32	Beginning balance	90,000
				Revenues Collected in Advance	60,000
				(90,000)	

Revenues

Entry 30a	Refund of Revenues	1,200	Entry 16	Bookstores Sales to Departments	90,000
Entry 44	Loss on Sale of Investments	1,200	Entry 17	Student Fees--Cash	240,000
Entry 53	Closing	3,510,300	Entry 20	Student Fees--Charge	12,000
			Entry 25	Sales of Auxiliaries	1,283,600
			Entry 31	Sales of Used Equipment	600
			Entry 33	Transfer Deferred Revenues	60,000
			Entry 36	State Appropriation	1,500,000
			Entry 43	Profit on Sale of Investments	1,200
			Entry 46	Unpaid State Appropriation	300,000
			Entry 47	Alumnus Gift	300
			Entry 48	Recovery of Indirect Costs	5,000
			Entry 51	Endowment Income	20,000
		3,512,700			3,512,700

Restricted Revenues

Entry 53	Closing	110,000	Entry 35	Reimbursement of Restricted Expenditures	110,000
		110,000			110,000

Departmental Allocations

Entry 45b	Budget Adjustment	30,000	Entry 1	Record Budget	3,486,000
Entry 52	Closing	3,552,000	Entry 45a	Budget Adjustments	6,000
			Entry 45b	Budget Adjustments	30,000
			Entry 45c	Budget Adjustments	60,000
		3,582,000			3,582,000

Provision for Encumbrances--Current Year

Entry 3a	Orders Liquidated	325,000	Entry 2	Orders Placed	330,000
				(5,000)	

Provision for Encumbrances--Prior Year

Entry 9	Orders Liquidated	108,000		Beginning balance	132,000
Entry 10	Close Encumbrances	24,000			
		132,000			132,000

Allowance for Doubtful Accounts--Students

Entry 23	Accounts Written Off	300		Beginning balance	4,000
			Entry 22	Increase Allowance	1,800
			Entry 24a	Reinstatement of Account Written Off	120
				(5,620)	

Allowance for Doubtful Accounts--Other

Beginning balance	2,000
(2,000)	

Unallocated Revenues

Entry 45c	Budget Adjustment	60,000	Entry 1	Record Budget	224,000
Entry 52	Closing	164,000			
		224,000			224,000

Unrestricted Current Funds Balances

Entry 15	Adjust book to physical inventory	600		Beginning balance	55,200
			Entry 10	Close Prior Year Encumbrances	24,000
			Entry 53	Closing	31,700
				(110,300)	

D. Balance Sheet Before Closing

BLANK COLLEGE

BALANCE SHEET
(Before Closing)

ASSETS

CURRENT FUNDS:

Unrestricted:

Cash		152,620
Investments, at cost (approximate market $225,000)		196,000
Accounts receivable: Students, less allowance for doubtful accounts of $5,620	6,080	
Other, less allowance for doubtful accounts $2,000	1,000	7,080
State appropriation receivable		300,000
Inventories, at cost		91,800
Prepaid insurance		5,400
Due from other funds: Loan funds	6,000	
Unexpended Plant Funds	3,000	9,000
Transfers to other funds: Unexpended Plant Funds	60,000	
Retirement of Indebtedness	50,000	110,000
Unrealized revenues	3,716,000	
Less: Realized revenues	3,621,300	95,700
Total Unrestricted Current Funds		967,600

LIABILITIES AND FUND BALANCES

CURRENT FUNDS:

Unrestricted:

Accounts payable		547,000
Due to Teacher Retirement System		9,600
Deferred revenues		90,000
Provision for Encumbrances-- Current Year		5,000
Departmental allocations	3,552,000	
Less: Expenditures 3,473,600		
Encumbrances 5,000	3,478,600	73,400
Unallocated revenues		164,000
Fund balances		78,600
Total Unrestricted Current Funds		927,600

E. Balance Sheet After Closing

BLANK COLLEGE
BALANCE SHEET
(After Closing)

ASSETS			LIABILITIES AND FUND BALANCES	
CURRENT FUNDS:			CURRENT FUNDS:	
Unrestricted:			Unrestricted:	
Cash		161,620	Accounts payable	547,000
Investments, at cost (approximate market $225,000)		196,000	Due to Teacher Retirement System	9,600
Accounts receivable:			Deferred revenues	90,000
Students, less allowance for doubtful accounts of $5,620	6,080		Provision for encumbrances-- Current Year	5,000
Other, less allowance for doubtful accounts of $2,000	1,000	7,080	Fund balances	110,300
State appropriation receivable		300,000		
Inventories, at cost		91,800		
Prepaid insurance		5,400		
Total Unrestricted Current Funds		761,900	Total Unrestricted Current Funds	761,900

F. Statement of Changes in Fund Balances

BLANK COLLEGE
STATEMENT OF CHANGES IN FUND BALANCES
UNRESTRICTED CURRENT FUNDS
FOR THE YEAR ENDED JUNE 30, 19__

	Total	Unallocated	Allocated
Balances, July 1, 19__	55,200	45,200	10,000
Additions:			
Excess of revenues over expenditures	141,700	141,700	
Release of prior year encumbrances	24,000	24,000	
	165,700	165,700	
Deductions:			
Adjustment of book to physical inventory	600	600	
Transfers to Unexpended Plant Funds	60,000	60,000	
Transfers to Funds for Retirement of Indebtedness	50,000	50,000	
	110,000	110,000	
Balances, June 30, 19__	110,300	110,300	10,000

ACCOUNTING FOR RESTRICTED CURRENT FUNDS

A. Balance Sheet at Beginning of Period

BLANK COLLEGE
BALANCE SHEET
(Beginning of Period)

ASSETS		LIABILITIES AND FUND BALANCES	
CURRENT FUNDS:		CURRENT FUNDS:	
Restricted:		Restricted:	
Cash	41,000	Accounts payable	6,000
Temporary investments, at cost	52,000	Provision for endowment income stabilization	4,000
Accounts receivable--principally agencies of the U.S. government	145,000	Fund balances	228,000
Total Restricted Current Funds	238,000	Total Restricted Current Funds	238,000

B. Recording of Typical Transactions

	GENERAL LEDGER		SUBSIDIARY LEDGER	
	Dr.	Cr.	Dr.	Cr.

1. Entry to record receipt of restricted donation for specific purpose (Cash Receipts Journal):

| Cash | 17,000 | | | |
| Restricted Current Funds Balances | | 17,000 | | |

In Restricted Current Funds Ledger (Cash Receipts):

| Individual fund accounts | | | | 17,000 |

(Expenditures chargeable against Restricted Current Funds may be recorded in Unrestricted Current Funds, the latter fund later to be reimbursed from Restricted Current Funds, or they may be accounted for in the operating accounts of the restricted funds. General ledger operating controls would be used in both Unrestricted and Restricted Current Funds.)

2. Entry to record recovery of indirect costs-- sponsored programs (Voucher Register and Check Register):

a. Restricted Current Funds Balances	45,000			
Vouchers Payable		45,000		
b. Vouchers Payable	45,000			
Cash		45,000		

(In Unrestricted Current Funds, debit Cash and credit Revenues.)

3. Entry to record reimbursement by Restricted Current Funds to Unrestricted Current Funds for expenditures made out of Unrestricted Current Funds (Voucher Register and Check Register):

a. Restricted Current Funds Balances	10,000			
Vouchers Payable		10,000		
b. Vouchers Payable	10,000			
Cash		10,000		

In Restricted Current Funds Ledger (Vouchers):

| Individual Restricted Fund Accounts | | | 10,000 | |

(In Unrestricted Current Funds, debit Cash and credit Restricted Revenues-- individual revenues accounts.)

4. Entry to increase provision for endowment income stabilization (Cash Receipts Journal):

| Cash | 10,000 | | | |
| Provision for endowment income stabilization | | 10,000 | | |

(In Endowment and Similar Funds, debit Income and credit Cash.)

5. Entry to record refund to grantor of restricted donation (Voucher Register and Check Register):

a. Restricted Current Funds Balances	500			
Vouchers Payable		500		
b. Vouchers Payable	500			
Cash		500		

	GENERAL LEDGER		SUBSIDIARY LEDGER	
	Dr.	Cr.	Dr.	Cr.

In Restricted Current Funds Ledger (Vouchers):

Individual Restricted Fund Accounts — — 500 —

C. General Ledger--Restricted Current Funds Section

Cash

		Dr.				Cr.
	Beginning balance	41,000	Entry	2b	Remittances	45,000
Entry 1	Receipt of Donation	17,000	Entry	3b	Remittances	10,000
Entry 4	Income Stabilization	10,000	Entry	5b	Remittances	500

(12,500)

Accounts Receivable

Beginning balance   145,000

(145,000)

Temporary Investments

Beginning balance   52,000

(52,000)

Vouchers Payable

Entry	2b	Checks Issued	45,000			Beginning balance	6,000
Entry	3b	Checks Issued	10,000	Entry	2a	Audited Vouchers	45,000
Entry	5b	Checks Issued	500	Entry	3a	Audited Vouchers	10,000
				Entry	5a	Audited Vouchers	500

(6,000)

Provision for Endowment Income Stabilization

			Beginning balance	4,000
	Entry 4	Income Received		10,000

(14,000)

Restricted Current Funds Balances

Entry	2a	Recovery of Indirect Costs	45,000	Entry 1	Beginning balance Donation	228,000 17,000
Entry	3a	Reimbursement to Unrestricted Current Funds	10,000			
Entry	5a	Refund to grantor	500		(189,500)	

D. Final Balance Sheet--Restricted Current Funds

BLANK COLLEGE

BALANCE SHEET
(End of Period)

ASSETS		LIABILITIES AND FUND BALANCES	
CURRENT FUNDS:		CURRENT FUNDS:	
Restricted:		Restricted:	
Cash	12,500	Accounts payable	6,000
Temporary investments, at cost (approximate market $55,000)	52,000	Provision for endowment income stabilization	14,000
Accounts receivable--principally agencies of the U.S. government	145,000	Fund balances	189,500
	209,500		209,500

E. Statement of Changes in Fund Balances

BLANK COLLEGE

STATEMENT OF CHANGES IN FUND BALANCES
RESTRICTED CURRENT FUNDS
FOR THE YEAR ENDED JUNE 30, 19___

	Total	Educational and General	Student Aid
Balances, July 1, 19___	228,000	205,000	23,000
Additions:			
Governmental appropriations	17,000	17,000	
	17,000	17,000	
Deductions:			
Expenditures	10,000	8,000	2,000
Indirect cost recoveries on sponsored programs transferred to Unrestricted Current Funds	45,000	45,000	
Refunds to grantors	500		500
Balances, June 30, 19___	189,500	169,000	20,500

CHAPTER X

Accounting for Endowment
and Similar Funds

ACCORDING TO STATISTICS compiled by the United States Office of Education for the year 1967, earnings from endowment and similar funds amounted to $454,000,000. The total amount of endowment funds at book value, not including funds subject to annuity agreements, was approximately $9,000,000,000. The importance of endowment funds in the college and university accounting system is evident from these statistics.

Definition of Endowment and Similar Funds. Principle 5, *College and University Business Administration*, states: "The Endowment and Similar Funds group includes those funds whose principal is nonexpendable as of the date of reporting and is invested, or is available for investment, for the purpose of producing income." [1]

Three types of funds are included in this group:

(a) *Endowment Funds* are those the principal of which donors have stipulated must remain inviolate and in perpetuity with only the income from the investment of the funds being available for expenditure. If the income can be used for general operating purposes, the funds are classed as unrestricted and the income is transferred to and accounted for in the Unrestricted Current Funds group. If the income is restricted by donors to designated uses, the funds are classed as restricted and the income is transferred to and

---

[1] *College and University Business Administration*, 144.

accounted for in the appropriate fund group to comply with the restrictions. Examples of restricted endowment funds are those the income of which is designated for the support of a particular instructional position or department, for maintenance and operation of certain buildings, for research projects, for scholarships or fellowships, and for loan funds. One institution classifies its restricted endowment funds in the following manner:

1. Professorships and Chairs
2. Library
3. Research
4. Fellowships and Scholarships
5. Prizes and Awards
6. Loans
7. Building Maintenance
8. Equipment
9. Lectures
10. Miscellaneous

The terms of an endowment fund may require that the income be added to the principal annually until a given amount has been accumulated. Then, the income may be used for designated purposes.

Occasionally, gifts for endowment purposes are not turned over directly to an institution but instead are placed by the donor in the hands of a trustee. The trustee invests the funds, turning over the income to the institution to be used in accordance with the terms of the gift. Since such funds are not actually in the possession nor under the control of the institution, they should not be reported as belonging to an institution. Where such funds are material in amount, they should be indicated by footnote or other reference in the financial reports, as Funds Held in Trust by Others.

(b) *Term endowment funds* are those which donors have stipulated may be released from the status of endowment upon the happening of a particular event or the passage of a stated period of time. Examples are (1) a gift which stipulates that a fund is to be held as endowment, the income to be used for the maintenance of a building, until the bonds used to finance the building are retired; or

(2) a gift for endowment purposes which stipulates that after twenty years the governing board may expend the principal at its discretion.

(c) *Quasi-endowment funds, or funds functioning as endowment,* are those which the governing board, rather than a donor, has determined, at least for the present, are to be retained and invested as though they were endowment funds.

The three types of funds should be reported in the Endowment and Similar Funds section of the Balance Sheet, with each group being reported separately in the equity section.

All gifts and bequests and other receipts of funds in this group, all transfers to and from the group, as well as all forms of principal reductions, should be reported in the Statement of Changes in Fund Balances—Endowment and Similar Funds.

Principles Governing Accounting and Reporting of Endowment Funds. From the point of view of college and university business officers, the more important considerations in handling endowment and other nonexpendable funds involve, first, an accurate and complete knowledge of all legal provisions pertaining to the funds, and, second, an accurate distinction between the income and principal of the funds. The business officer must be thoroughly familiar with the terms of each gift and bequest. He must be prepared to safeguard the investment of endowment funds and the disbursement of income therefrom according to the conditions imposed by the gift. The maintenance of an accurate distinction between principal and income is extremely important. His institution is entitled to the exact net income from its endowment funds—to give it more would encroach upon the principal of the funds, and to give it less would be unfair to the purposes to which the endowment funds are dedicated. Therefore, the accounts must always reflect an accurate and equitable separation of principal and income.

College and University Business Administration, chapter 14, lists the following principles governing the management, recording, and reporting of endowment and other similar funds.[2]

> (a) The total of each of the subgroups of funds should be identified separately in the accounts and in the equity section of the balance sheet.

[2] *Ibid.,* 145ff

(b) The funds may be classified further to show those for which the income is unrestricted in use and those for which the income is restricted by donors to specific uses.

(c) The funds in the Endowment and Similar Funds group may be pooled for effective investment management unless prohibited either by statute or by the terms of the instruments of gift. It is preferable not to merge assets of Annuity and Life Income Funds, unloaned balances of Loan Funds, and unexpended balances of Current, Plant, and Agency Funds groups with Endowment and Similar Funds in the investment pool.

(d) If the assets of the funds in this group are pooled for investment purposes, only one control account need be maintained to reflect book values for each class of investments in the pool. For report purposes, the assets may be shown together in appropriate classes of investments, whether or not the investments are pooled.

(e) The operation of an investment pool necessitates adopting procedures that will provide for the equitable distribution of income and the assignment of capital appreciation to all funds participating in the pool. The market-value method is preferable to the book-value method in the operation of investment pools.

(f) In the event other funds are admitted for investment purposes to the endowment pool, special attention must be given to the accounting arrangements for admittance to and withdrawal from the pool to preclude crediting such funds with investment income and realized, or unrealized, net gains properly attributable to the permanently invested funds.

(g) Pooled investment income should be distributed to the income accounts of the participating funds without consideration of the gain or loss account, in order to prevent dilution of the proper share of the various funds in the aggregate investment income of the pool.

(h) Realized gains and losses on investment transactions affect the principal of the invested funds either (1) by increasing or decreasing the individual fund balances or (2) by retaining as an undistributed accumulation the balances that are proportionately applicable to each fund. Such capital gains and losses are not operating revenues and expenditures, and should not be treated differently from the amounts representing the original fund balances. They are subject to the same restrictions and limitations on investment, expenditure, and disposition as the funds from which they arose. *In some instances, realized gains and losses may be attributable to income as a matter of law, for example, when such treatment is required by a specific instrument or gift.*

(i) Investments purchased for the funds in this group should be recorded in the accounts and reported at cost. Gifts of securities and other donated assets should be recorded and reported at their market value or at an expertly appraised value as of the date of the gift.

(j) The book value of investments should not be changed to reflect fluctuations in market prices. However, market values, based on appropriate periodic review of the investments, should be disclosed in the balance sheet by means of a footnote or other reference.

(k) In order to maintain unimpaired the principal of the funds in this group, provisions should be made for the depreciation of real properties which are the investment of funds in this group and for the amortization of premiums on securities purchases. Provision may also be made for the accumulation of discounts.

(l) Endowment and term endowment funds should not be invested in institutional property.

(m) Endowment and term endowment funds should not be advanced for the use of other funds or fund groups.

(n) The principal of endowment and term endowment funds must not be hypothecated, and their investments must not be pledged for any purpose.

The following accounts are used in accounting for Endowment and Similar Funds:

ASSETS

Cash
Due from Other Funds
Investments-Securities (Control)
Investments-Real Estate (Control)
Reserve for Depreciation on Real Estate
   (Credit Balance Account)
Unamortized Premiums on Bonds

LIABILITIES AND FUNDS BALANCES

Vouchers Payable
Due to Other Funds
Mortgages Payable
Income—Control
Undistributed Pool Income
Reserve for Accumulation of Bond Discounts
Net Adjusted Gains and Losses
Endowment Funds Balances
Term Endowment Funds Balances
Quasi-endowment Funds Balances
   (or Funds Functioning as Endowment Funds Balances)

Pledges of gifts for endowment funds normally are not recorded in the accounting records. They may be so recorded, however, if they represent legitimate, collectible obligations. If pledges are entered in the accounts, a Pledges Receivable account would be set up in the asset accounts, the amount of the pledges being credited to a temporary account such as Balance of Pledges Outstanding. As they are paid, the amounts would then be credited to the appropriate funds balances account with details in the subsidiary accounts for Endowment and Similar Funds.

Accounting for the Investments of Endowment Funds. Endowment funds may be invested in bonds, preferred and common stocks, debentures, mutual fund shares, notes, mortgages, real estate, leases, oil and gas royalties, and even in business ownership. Investments should be recorded at total cost, including commissions, taxes, and all other costs of acquisition. Gifts of investments should be valued at market values as of the day on which title to the investments is transferred to the college or university. For listed securities, an appropriate valuation is the average of the high and low prices for the day; for unlisted securities and for real estate investments, valuations should be established by competent appraisers.

Expenses in connection with investment supervision, advice, and counsel, and other expenses of endowment funds management may be charged against the income from the investments before the income is distributed to the appropriate funds, or may be shown as operating expenses of the institution, either as a separate item of General Institutional Expense or as part of the expenses of the treasurer's office, comptroller's office, or business office.

Realized gains and losses on the sale of investments are credited or charged to an account for Net Adjusted Gains and Losses. The balance in this account usually is carried forward from year to year, although it may be distributed periodically to the funds involved. If the realized gains and losses are distributed to funds participating in an investment pool, the same method of distribution should be used as is used in distributing the income from the pool to the participating funds, as described on pages 224–28.

For the majority of institutions, the accounting problems of endowment funds investments revolve around investments in bonds, stocks, mortgages, and real estate.

Accounting for Investments in Bonds. The more important accounting problems relating to bond investments include the handling of premiums and discounts, accrued interest, and profits and losses on the sale of these securities. Bonds generally are purchased at either a premium or a discount, seldom at par. If they are purchased at a premium, amortization of the premium is necessary in order to prevent a diminution of the principal of the funds for which the bonds were purchased. If purchased at a discount, the principal of the funds involved is not endangered, and for that reason most institutions do not amortize discounts. However, *College and University Business Administration* states, "Premiums should be amortized and discounts accumulated ratably at the time income is received." [3]

Premiums and discounts may be accounted for in either of two ways. They may be included in the recorded cost of the bonds at the time of purchase, or they may be shown separately from the cost of the securities. In the former method, the total cost of the bonds is recorded in the Investments-Securities (Control) account and in all subsidiary accounts for bond investments, and the sums representing the amortization of premiums and discounts are also recorded in these accounts. In the second method, the bond investments are recorded at par value in the Investments-Securities (Control) account; premiums are set up as deferred charges in an account for Unamortized Premiums on Bonds; and discounts are shown as deferred credits in an account for Reserve for Accumulation of Bond Discounts.

There are three methods of amortizing premiums, each of which is used by educational institutions. The first is the straight-line method, in which the premiums are written off over the life of the bonds in equal amounts at each interest date. The second, generally referred to as the scientific or actuarial method, involves the use of interest tables and is based on an amortization schedule. The amount of amortization at any interest date is represented by the difference between the nominal interest income (par value of the bonds times the contractual interest rate) and the actual or ef-

3 *Ibid.,* 210.

fective interest income (par value of the bonds plus the unamortized premium times the yield rate of interest). The third method is termed the "bonds outstanding method" and is used in amortizing the premiums on serial bonds, in which case the first two methods are inapplicable. Under this method, the amount of par value of bonds owned at each interest date over the life of the issue is determined. The proportion that the amount of par value bonds outstanding at each interest date bears to the total par value of bonds outstanding is applied to the premium and determines the amount of periodic amortization.

In each of the methods of amortization, premiums are completely written off by the time the bonds mature. In the event the bonds are sold before their maturity, the unamortized premiums are included in the value of the bonds when determining the gain or loss on the sales.

Amortization of premiums is accomplished through periodic, usually annual, charges against the income from the bonds. If the bonds are assets of an investment pool, the charge is to the Undistributed Pool Income account; if they are the investments of separately invested funds, the charge is to the Income-Control account. If premiums are recorded in the Unamortized Premiums on Bonds account, the credit for the amortization is to this account. If premiums are included as part of the cost of the bonds, the credit is to the Investments-Securities (Control) account and to the appropriate bond investment accounts in the subsidiary ledger. The following entries, all in the Endowment and Similar Funds accounts, illustrate the methods of recording amortization of premiums on bonds under various conditions:

1. Bonds are part of pooled investments, and premiums are recorded separately from the investment account:

Undistributed Pool Income
    Unamortized Premiums on Bonds

2. Bonds are part of pooled investments, and premiums are recorded as part of the cost of the bonds:

Undistributed Pool Income
  Investments-Securities (Control)

3. Bonds are investments of separately invested funds, and premiums are recorded separately from the investment account:

Income-Control
  Unamortized Premiums on Bonds

4. Bonds are investments of separately invested funds, and premiums are recorded as part of the cost of the bonds:

Income-Control
  Investments-Securities (Control)

The amortization of discounts involves annual charges against either the Reserve for Accumulation of Bond Discounts account or the Investments-Securities (Control) account (depending on the method used in accounting for the discounts), and credits to the income accounts of the funds involved. This procedure might call for the actual transfer of cash from the Endowment and Similar Funds group to another fund group; and this, conceivably, could necessitate the sale of investments or a disruption of the investment program. The following entries illustrate the accounting for amortization of discounts under various conditions, all entries being in the Endowment and Similar Funds accounts:

1. Bonds are part of pooled investments, and discounts are recorded separately from the investment account:

Reserve for Accumulation of Bond Discounts
  Undistributed Pool Income

2. Bonds are part of pooled investments, and discounts are recorded as part of the cost of the bonds:

Investments-Securities (Control)
  Undistributed Pool Income

3. Bonds are investments of separately invested funds, and discounts are recorded separately from the investment account:

Reserve for Accumulation of Bond Discounts
    Income-Control

4. Bonds are investments of separately invested funds, and discounts are recorded as part of the cost of the bonds:

Investments-Securities (Control)
    Income-Control

Bonds ordinarily are bought and sold between regular interest paying dates. Since bond indentures call for the paying of interest to bondholders only on stipulated dates, the problem arises of accounting for the interest accrued between the last date on which interest was paid and the date of purchase or sale. The end result in accounting for accrued interest is that the income of the fund group to which the income is dedicated is charged when bonds are purchased and is credited when they are sold. If the bonds are in an investment pool, accrued interest items are first recorded in the account for Undistributed Pool Income; if they are the investments of separately invested funds, accrued interest is first shown in the Income-Control account. The following entries, all in the Endowment and Similar Funds accounts, illustrate the handling of transactions involving accrued interest under various conditions:

1. Entry to record purchase of bonds plus accrued interest:

Investments-Securities (Control)
Undistributed Pool Income (if bonds are in the investment pool),
    or Income-Control (if bonds are for separately invested funds)
        Cash

2. Entry to record collection of income:

Cash
    Undistributed Pool Income (if bonds are in the investment

pool), or Income-Control (if bonds are for separately invested funds)

3. Entry to record sale of bonds plus accrued interest:

Cash
    Investments-Securities (Control)
    Undistributed Pool Income (if bonds are in the investment pool), or Income-Control (if bonds are for separately invested funds)

No entries for accrued interest are needed in other fund groups at the time of purchase or sale of bonds, because accrued interest items are reflected in the income accounts in the Endowment and Similar Funds group before the income is distributed to the other fund groups.

When bonds are sold before maturity, it is necessary to account for the gains or losses on the sale. Such gains or losses generally are credited or charged to the Net Adjusted Gains and Losses account, although they may be carried directly to the accounts for the principal or balances of the funds involved. The gain or loss is the difference between the book value of the bonds (par plus unamortized premiums, or less accumulated discounts) and the proceeds from the sale. The following entries, all in the Endowment and Similar Funds accounts, illustrate the handling of transactions involving the sale of bonds at a profit and at a loss:

1. Bonds sold at a profit:

Cash
    Investments-Securities (Control)
    Unamortized Premiums on Bonds (if bond premiums are recorded in this account)
    Net Adjusted Gains and Losses, for amount of gain (or, to principal or balance of the fund involved)

2. Bonds sold at a loss:

Cash
Net Adjusted Gains and Losses, for amount of gain (or, to principal or balance of fund involved)

Investments-Securities (Control)
Unamortized Premiums on Bonds (if bond premiums are recorded in this account)

Accounting for Investments in Stocks. Accounting for investments of endowment funds in stocks does not present serious problems. Stock purchases should be recorded in the accounts at cost, including brokerage fees, taxes, and other costs. Fluctuations in the market value should be ignored in the accounting records, although noted appropriately in financial reports.

Information relative to market value of securities is essential to the proper management of the portfolio. However, such data should be gathered in memorandum accounts and not reflected in basic accounting records.

Stocks may be held in an investment pool or may represent investments of specific endowment funds. A complete discussion of pooled investments appears later in this chapter.

Profits and losses on the sale of stock rights should be treated as additions to or deductions from the principal accounts involved. Stock dividends are not income and do not increase the value of the investment account. Such dividends should be recorded only as an increase in number of shares owned. If stock rights are sold, the chief problem presented is a determination of the profit or loss on the sale of the rights. Profit or loss on the sale of stock rights is the difference between the cost assigned to the rights and the proceeds from the sale of the rights. The cost of the rights is found by apportioning the cost of the old stock between the rights and the stock on the basis of the relative market value of each at date of issuance of rights. Assuming the rights of a stock are selling at $20, the cost of the old stock is $84, and the market value of the stock ex-rights is $100, the assigned cost of each right is $\frac{20}{120}$ x $84 or $14. The profit on the sale of one right is $6. The following entry should be made to record the sale of one right:

IN ENDOWMENT FUNDS:
Cash   20
   Investments-Securities (Control)   14
   Endowment Funds Balances   6

If an institution avails itself of the opportunity to purchase new shares through stock rights, the cost of the new shares should be charged to the investment account.

The following entries illustrate the accounting for various transactions in the endowment funds because of investments in stocks:

1. Entry to record purchase of stocks (recorded at cost):

   Investments-Securities (Control)
      Cash

2. Entry to record receipt of cash dividend:

   Cash
      Income-Control, or Undistributed Pool Income

3. Notification of receipt of stock dividend:

   No entry required, only notation in Investment Ledger increasing number of shares held.

4. Entry to record payment of fees to security consultant:

   Income-Control, or Undistributed Pool Income
      Cash

5. Entry to record sale of stocks at a profit:

   Cash
      Investments-Securities (Control)
      Net Adjusted Gains and Losses, or Endowment Funds Balances

6. Entry to record sale of stocks at a loss:

   Cash
   Net Adjusted Gains and Losses, or Endowment Funds Balances
      Investments-Securities (Control)

Accounting for Investments in Real Estate. The chief accounting problems in connection with the investment of endowment funds in real estate are: (1) valuation of real estate acquired; (2) accounting for income, expenses, and the net operating income from each property; and (3) depreciation. Real estate may be acquired by gift, by purchase, or by mortgage foreclosure. If acquired by gift, it should be recorded at market value, or if there is not a readily determinable market value, at fair appraisal value. Property acquired by purchase should be recorded at full cost, including commissions, brokerage fees, costs of appraisals, fees for examining and recording title, delinquent taxes, if any, and all costs necessary to put the property into revenue-producing condition.

Property acquired as a result of foreclosure of mortgages should be recorded at cost, as described above, including the unpaid balance of the mortgage, all expenses in connection with foreclosure, taxes and insurance unpaid at date of foreclosure, and extraordinary repairs. If foreclosed property is sold or if a deficiency judgment is obtained, the proceeds should be credited in full to the asset account for the mortgage. If the proceeds exceed the balance of the asset account, the net profit on the transaction should be credited to the endowment principal account or to Net Adjusted Gains and Losses. Any loss on the transaction should be charged in the same manner.

Institutional property constructed or purchased as an investment of quasi-endowment funds should be accounted for in the same manner as outside property.

All items of income and expense related to real estate investments should be reflected in the Income-Control account. The determination of net income on each parcel of real estate is best handled by establishing an account for each property in a subsidiary ledger to which expenses are charged and income is credited. The more usual expenses chargeable against income from real estate consist of management fees and commissions, taxes, expenses for repair and maintenance of the properties, and insurance. Any expenditures which add to the value of the investment, such as improvements and special assessments, should be charged to the investment account.

At the end of the year the net income from each real estate investment is transferred to the appropriate fund group. As a general rule, real estate investments are not included in investment pools and would be considered the investments of separately invested funds. If the endowment funds so invested are restricted, the net income is transferred to the Restricted Current Funds Balances (Control) account (and to the appropriate account in the subsidiary ledger) and is expended in accordance with the terms of the gift. If the endowment funds invested in real estate are unrestricted, the net income is transferred to the Revenues (Control) account in the Unrestricted Current Funds group and may be used for any operating purpose.

Following is an illustration of the accounting for income and expenses of endowment funds real estate:

1. Entry to record receipt of rental income:

   In ENDOWMENT FUNDS
   Cash
      Income-Control
   In the subsidiary ledger, credit the account set up to record income and expenses of each real estate investment involved.

2. Entry to record payment of expenses, such as taxes, insurance, and repairs:

   In ENDOWMENT FUNDS
   Income-Control
      Cash
   In the subsidiary ledger, debit the appropriate operating account for each real estate investment involved.

3. Entries to record transfer of net income to proper fund group:

   a. In ENDOWMENT FUNDS
      Income-Control
         Cash
   In subsidiary ledger debit individual operating accounts for all real estate investments involved.

   b. In UNRESTRICTED CURRENT FUNDS, if endowment fund is unrestricted:
      Cash
         Revenues (Control)
   In Revenues Ledger credit Unrestricted Endowment Income.

c. IN RESTRICTED CURRENT FUNDS, if endowment fund is restricted:
Cash
   Restricted Funds Balances
In Restricted Funds Ledger credit appropriate restricted funds balance account.

Depreciation on Real Estate. In order to protect the principal of an endowment fund which has been invested in real estate, suitable provision must be made for depreciation. Land, not being subject to loss in value through use, is not depreciable and therefore is not included in depreciation computations. Buildings and other structures, on the other hand, possess a limited income-producing life. Funds must be accumulated, therefore, out of income from the properties or from other current funds revenues to make up for reductions in the original value of this type of investment. This end is accomplished by means of periodic charges—depreciation expense—against the real estate operating accounts, and credits to the Reserve for Depreciation carried in the Endowment and Similar Funds group. Funds represented by the Reserve for Depreciation should be invested and the income received should be added to the reserve. Any acceptable method of depreciation may be used, but the straight-line method is the one most frequently employed in colleges and universities. The following entries illustrate the treatment of depreciation and the accumulation of the reserve for depreciation:

1. Entry to record depreciation:

IN ENDOWMENT FUNDS
Income-Control
   Reserve for Depreciation
In the subsidiary ledger debit the appropriate operating account for each real estate investment involved.

2. Entry to record investment of depreciation reserve:

IN ENDOWMENT FUNDS
Investments-Securities (Control)
   Cash

Investment Pools. Each endowment fund constitutes a separate, inviolate fund, the principal of which must be maintained separate and distinct from all other funds. Ordinarily, however, institutions are permitted to pool or group the cash and other assets belonging to various endowment funds in order to effect better management of the funds. This procedure is highly advantageous to the institution for two reasons. First, it permits greater diversification of investments with respect to geographical location, type of security, and type of enterprise, therefore affording greater safety than is possible when individual endowment funds are invested separately. Second, it permits greater flexibility in the investment program in that an institution can more easily find suitable investments in the units required than would be possible if the small amounts of uninvested cash of each fund had to be invested separately. Of course, if the terms of a particular endowment fund specify that it shall be invested separately, then pooling of the fund in question would not be possible. The principal accounts of funds participating in a pool should reflect the extent to which each endowment participates.

Income from pooled investments is recorded in the endowment funds group by crediting an account called Undistributed Pool Income. Periodically, the income reflected in this account should be distributed to the participating funds. For funds participating in the pool which are unrestricted, the income is transferred to the Unrestricted Current Funds group. For participating funds which are restricted, the income is transferred to the balance account in the appropriate fund group.

There are two principal methods of allocating income to participating funds. The preferred method is known as the "market-value" method; the other is known as the "book-value" method. Under the latter plan, income is allocated to participating funds on the basis of the balance in the principal of each fund. Balances may be those which exist at the time of distribution or may represent the average of the beginning and ending balances. In some instances, balances are based on monthly averaging. If a fund is added to or taken out of the pool, the basis of entry or exit is the book value of the fund. The book-value method is unfair to funds which entered the pool when asset values were relatively low, as compared with those which entered at a time when asset values were relatively high.

As stated previously, the market-value method is more equitable to participating funds and is the preferred method of allocating income to funds participating in an investment pool. Under this method, income "is distributed to the various funds on the basis of the assignment to each fund of a number of shares that is calculated on the market value of the assets of the pool at the time of entry of the fund in the pool." [4] When the pool is established, an arbitrary value is assigned to each participating share in the pool. For example, a fund of $50,000 might have 5,000 shares valued at $10 per share. After the establishment of the pool, assets are revalued periodically—weekly, monthly, or quarterly—and a new share value is determined by dividing the number of shares outstanding into the new asset values of the investments at market. Funds may be admitted to or withdrawn from the pool only on investment dates or, in the alternative, funds may enter or leave the pool at any time, shares being valued as of the latest valuation date.

To illustrate the operations of an investment pool, assume its establishment with shares valued arbitrarily at $10:

	Book Value	Market Value	No. of Shares	Unit Value
Fund A	$ 50,000	$ 50,000	5,000	$10
Fund B	25,000	25,000	2,500	10
	$ 75,000	$ 75,000	7,500	$10

Assume that Fund C is admitted to the pool six months later. At that time the unit share value is $12:

Fund A	$ 50,000		5,000	$12
Fund B	25,000		2,500	12
Total	75,000	90,000	7,500	12
Fund C	36,000	36,000	3,000	12
	$111,000	$126,000	10,500	$12

Assume that Fund B is withdrawn at the end of the year:

Fund A	$ 50,000		5,000	$13
Fund B	25,000		2,500	13
Fund C	36,000		3,000	13
	111,000	136,500	10,500	13
Fund B	(25,000)	(32,500)	(2,500)	13
Total	$ 86,000	$104,000	8,000	$13

4 *Ibid.*, 44.

In distributing income earned by the pool, total investment income is divided by total number of shares participating in the pool in order to determine the rate of income per share. Appropriate adjustment is made for shares held less than a full year. In the above illustration, assuming income to be $5,250 for the entire year, that figure divided by the number of shares (10,500) equals a rate per share of $0.50, and the distribution would be:

Fund A - 5,000 shares @ .50		2,500
Fund B - 2,500 shares @ .50		1,250
Fund C - 3,000 shares @ .50 (6 months)		750
Total		4,500

This leaves $750 to be distributed between Funds A and B in the ratio of their respective shareholdings (5,000 to 2,500 or two-thirds to A and one-third to B).

Thus, Fund A would receive a total of $3,000; Fund B, $1,500; and Fund C, $750.

If the book-value basis were used instead of the market-value basis and, assuming book value to be the mean of the beginning and ending balances, the distribution would be as follows:

	Book Value	Percent of Total	Income Distribution
Fund A	$50,000	53.8	$2,824
Fund B	25,000	26.9	1,412
Fund C ($36,000 for ½ year)	18,000	19.3	1,014
	$93,000	100.0%	$5,250

As stated previously, the book-value basis results in an inequitable distribution, favoring the most recently admitted fund, in this illustration Fund C.

An income stabilization reserve may be established to stabilize and regularize the amount available for annual use from the pooled investment income. The total amount of income reserved for this purpose should be reasonable, say, not more than one full year's income.

Either of two methods may be employed in creating the stabilization reserve. First, a portion of the total income may be retained and not allocated to participating funds before distribution of the pooled investment income to the several funds. It must be recognized, if this method is used, that the reserve belongs to all participating funds. It is essential, therefore, to maintain a record of the share each fund has in the reserve. Some of the funds are unrestricted; others may be restricted or may belong to fund groups other than Endowment and Similar Funds. Under this method, the income stabilization reserve is reflected in the restricted current funds section of the Balance Sheet.

Under the second method, the stabilization reserve is created entirely out of the income of unrestricted endowment funds, after the distribution from the pool is made. Under this plan, the stabilization reserve is reflected as part of the Unrestricted Current Funds Balances on the Balance Sheet.

Realized gains and losses on endowment funds investments are recorded in the account Net Adjusted Gains and Losses. The net amount in this account usually is accumulated from year to year, although it may be distributed annually to the participating funds. If an institution elects to distribute net gains and losses, it should be done by the method described above for distributing income. As stated previously, unrealized gains and losses are not reflected in the records.

The following entries illustrate accounting for pooled endowment funds:

1. Entry to record merger of several endowment funds into pool:

   IN ENDOWMENT FUNDS
   Only subsidiary entries needed, showing which endowment funds are being merged into the pool.

2. Entry to record receipt of income on pooled investments:

   IN ENDOWMENT FUNDS
   Cash
       Undistributed Pool Income

3. Entry to record creation of stabilization reserve out of total income from pooled investments:

    a. IN ENDOWMENT FUNDS
       Undistributed Pool Income
         Cash

    b. IN RESTRICTED CURRENT FUNDS
       Cash
         Provision for Endowment Income Stabilization

4. Entry to Record Distribution of Pooled Income:

    a. IN ENDOWMENT FUNDS
       Undistributed Pool Income
         Cash

    b. IN UNRESTRICTED CURRENT FUNDS—For income on Unrestricted
       Endowment Funds
       Cash
         Revenues

    c. IN RESTRICTED CURRENT OR OTHER FUNDS—For income on Re-
       stricted Endowment Funds
       Cash
         Appropriate Funds Balances

Subsidiary Ledger Records. The following subsidiary ledger records are used in accounting for the transactions of endowment and other nonexpendable funds:

1. Endowment Funds Ledger (Form 10.1). This ledger is used to record the principal of each endowment, life income, and annuity fund in possession of the institution which is separately invested. The ledger is subdivided to show balance of cash, unamortized premium or discount, and investments made, as well as the total principal of the fund. The sum of the fund principal columns in the subsidiary ledger should agree with the general ledger control account Endowment Funds Balances. Postings to the subsidiary ledger are made daily from original documents, such as cash receipts, invoice vouchers, and journal vouchers.

For pooled endowment funds, the endowment funds ledger would be subdivided only to record additions to, deductions from, and balances of principal.

2. Investment Ledger (Form 10.2). This ledger is used to record pertinent information pertaining to investments in bonds, stocks,

FORM 10.1

BLANK COLLEGE

E N D O W M E N T   F U N D S   L E D G E R

Name of Fund _____

Restrictions: As To Income _____
              As To Principal _____

Date	Reference	Explanation	Cash		Premiums and Discounts			Investments			Fund Principal
			Receipts	Disbursements	Acquired	Amortized	Balance	Acquired	Disposed of	Balance	

FORM 10.2
(front)

BLANK COLLEGE

I N V E S T M E N T   L E D G E R

Name of Investment _____

Class of Investment _____

         Fund Group _____
         Name of
         Endowment Fund _____

Date	Reference	Explanation	Principal			Premiums and Discounts on Investments or Reserve for Depreciation			Income		
			Debits	Credits	Balance	Debits	Credits	Balance	Debits	Credits	Balance

FORM 10.2
(back)

B O N D S

Date Purchased_____ Price_____

Date of Maturity_____ Callable_____

Interest: Rate_____% Amount_____ Date_____

Serial Numbers_____

Type of Bond_____ (Registered or Coupon)

Remarks:_____
_____
_____
_____

Date Sold_____ Price_____

N O T E S   A N D   M O R T G A G E S

Date of Loan_____ Maturity_____

Description of Property_____
_____
_____

Interest: Rate_____% Amount_____ Date_____

Remarks:_____
_____
_____

S T O C K S

Date Purchased_____ Price_____

Callable_____ Convertible_____

Dividend: Rate_____ Amount_____ Date_____

Type of Stock_____

No. of Shares_____ Par Value_____

Remarks:_____
_____
_____
_____

Date Sold_____ Price_____

R E A L   E S T A T E

Date of Acquisition_____ How Acquired_____

Price, If Purchased_____ Appraisal_____

Description of Property_____

Rental: Rate and When
        Collected_____

Depreciation: Rate_____ Amount_____

Remarks:_____
_____

Date Sold_____ Price_____

notes, mortgages, and real estate. The form is applicable also as a subsidiary ledger for temporary investments of all fund groups. The investment ledger should be subdivided into fund groups, with a subcontrol account over each group. The sum of the balances of the principal columns in each fund group should agree with the general ledger control account for investments of that group. In the case of Endowment and Similar Funds, there may be separate control accounts for pooled investments and for individual investments. If properly arranged, this ledger produces information not only by funds but also by types of investments. Entries in the investment ledger are made from original documents, such as cash receipts, invoices, and journal vouchers.

ILLUSTRATION

Following is an illustration of the accounting for Endowment and Similar Funds. It gives a beginning Balance Sheet, typical transactions during the fiscal year, a final Balance Sheet, and a Statement of Changes in Fund Balances. The entries involving premiums and discounts on bonds are based on the method of accounting in which bonds are recorded in the Investments-Securities (Control) account at par value, premiums are charged to the Unamortized Premiums on Bonds account, and discounts are credited to the Accumulation for Bond Discounts account. The discussions and illustrations on pages 238 and 240 describe the entries to be made if bonds were recorded at full cost value in the Investments-Securities (Control) account.

Annuity and Life Income Funds. Annuity and life income funds are funds acquired by an institution subject to agreements requiring payments to one or more designated beneficiaries during the life of those individuals. If the institution is obligated to pay a stipulated amount, the fund is classified as an annuity fund. If the institution binds itself to pay to the beneficiaries only the income earned by the assets of the fund, it is classified as a life income fund.

Upon the death of the beneficiary or at any other specified time, the principal of the annuity or life income fund becomes the property of the institution to be used in accordance with the terms of the agreement. Such funds may be unrestricted or restricted as to use.

Annuity and life income funds, like endowment funds, may be invested in securities or real estate and may, if agreements permit, be pooled with other annuity and life income funds for investment purposes. *College and University Business Administration* suggests, "It is preferable not to merge assets of Annuity and Life Income funds . . . with Endowment and Similar Funds in the investment pool." [5]

Separate accounts must be maintained for the receipts, disbursements, and balances of each fund in this group. Separate accounts also must be established for recording income belonging to each fund and for disbursements to annuitants and life income beneficiaries. Form 10.1 illustrated on page 229 is suitable for use in accounting for the transactions of annuity and life income funds which are separately invested. A ledger form showing additions, deductions, and balances may be used to account for the principal of annuity and life income funds the investments of which are pooled.

In the case of annuity funds, the excess or deficiency of investment income over payments to annuitants may either be credited or charged annually to the balance, or principal, of the fund involved or may be accumulated in a separate account until the annuity agreement terminates. At that time, the accumulation is credited or charged to the fund principal. If the principal is exhausted before the termination of the annuity agreement, one of the following procedures is recommended to meet future obligations: (a) set up a reserve fund from the residue of matured unrestricted annuities; (b) draw upon the principal of unrestricted annuity funds.

Realized gains and losses on investment transactions, if the funds are separately invested, should be credited or charged directly to the principal of the funds involved. If the assets are pooled for investment purposes, an account for Net Adjusted Gains and Losses should be used. If there is an unexpended balance in this account at the end of the period, it should be reported on the equity side on the Balance Sheet.

Distribution of income from investment pools, as well as distribution of net gains and losses to participating funds, should be made

[5] *College and University Business Administration*, 145.

in accordance with the market-value method previously explained in this chapter.

Annuity and Life Income Accounts. The following accounts are used in accounting for annuity and life income funds.

ASSETS

Cash
Due from Other Funds
Investments—Securities (Control)
Investments—Real Estate (Control)
Reserve for Depreciation (Credit Balance Account)

LIABILITY AND FUNDS BALANCES

Vouchers Payable
Due to Other Funds
Undistributed Income—Annuity Funds (Control)
Undistributed Income—Life Income Funds (Control)
Net Adjusted Gains and Losses
Annuity Funds Balances (Control)
Life Income Funds Balances (Control)

Receipts of income and disbursements to beneficiaries are recorded in the annuity and life income fund group as follows:

1. Entry to record receipt of earnings on investments:

Cash
    Undistributed Income

2. Entry to record payments to beneficiary:

Undistributed Income
    Cash

Notations as to the receipt of income and the disbursement to beneficiaries are made also in the subsidiary annuity and life income ledger.

Accounting for the investments of annuity and life income funds presents no different problems from those of endowment funds; hence, no further discussion of this subject is needed.

ILLUSTRATION

Following is an illustration of the accounting for endowment and similar funds and for annuity and life income funds. It gives a beginning Balance Sheet, typical transactions during the fiscal year, a final Balance Sheet, and a Statement of Changes in Fund Balances.

ACCOUNTING FOR ENDOWMENT AND SIMILAR FUNDS

A. Balance Sheet at Beginning of Period

BLANK COLLEGE

BALANCE SHEET
(Beginning of Period)

ASSETS		LIABILITIES AND FUND BALANCES	
ENDOWMENT AND SIMILAR FUNDS:		ENDOWMENT AND SIMILAR FUNDS:	
Cash	100,000	Mortgages Payable on Real Estate	15,000
Investments--Securities	1,500,000	Funds Balances:	
Investments--Real Estate (Less Reserve for Depreciation) (Funds held in Trust by Others-- $100,000)	250,000	Endowment Funds	1,525,000
		Term Endowment Funds	100,000
		Quasi-endowment Funds	175,000
		Net Adjusted Gains and Losses	35,000
Total Endowment and Similar Funds	1,850,000	Total Endowment and Similar Funds	1,850,000

B. Recording Typical Transactions--Endowment Funds

	GENERAL LEDGER		SUBSIDIARY LEDGER	
	Dr.	Cr.	Dr.	Cr.
1. Entry to record receipt of gift in cash for endowment purposes (Cash Receipts Journal):				
Cash	22,000			
Endowment Funds Balances		22,000		
In Endowment Funds Ledger (Cash Receipts Journal):				
Principal Account			22,000	
2. To note receipt of gift of $5,000 to be held in trust for institution:				
No entry required, only memorandum record in both the General Ledger and the Endowment Funds Subsidiary Ledger.				

	GENERAL LEDGER		SUBSIDIARY LEDGER	
	Dr.	Cr.	Dr.	Cr.
3. Entry to record receipt of gift of land for endowment purposes (Journal Voucher):				
Investments--Real Estate (at current market, or appraised, value)	10,000			
Endowment Funds Balances		10,000		
In Investment Ledger (Journal Voucher):				
Real Estate Account			10,000	
In Endowment Funds Ledger (Journal Voucher):				
Principal Account				10,000
4. Entry to record purchase of rental property as investment of a separately invested restricted endowment fund (Check Register):[5]				
Investments--Real Estate	8,000			
Cash		8,000		
In Investment Ledger (Invoice):				
Real Estate Account			8,000	
5. Entry to record purchase of four bonds, face value $4,000, at 102, plus accrued interest of $60 for the investment pool (Check Register):				
Investments--Securities	4,000			
Unamortized Premiums on Bonds	80			
Undistributed Pool Income	60			
Cash		4,140		
In Investment Ledger:				
Bond Account			4,080	
6. Entry to record purchase of three bonds, face value $3,000, at 102, plus accrued interest of $45 for a separately invested unrestricted endowment fund (Check Register):				
In Endowment Funds (Check Register):				
Investments--Securities	3,000			
Unamortized Premiums on Bonds	60			
Income-Control	45			
Cash		3,105		
In Investment Ledger (Invoice):				
Bond Account			3,060	
In Endowment Funds Ledger (Journal Voucher):				
Income Account for Fund Involved			45	
7. Entry to record purchase of two bonds, face value $2,000, at 102, plus accrued interest of $30 for a separately invested restricted endowment fund (Check Register):				
In Endowment Funds (Check Register):				
Investments--Securities	2,000			
Unamortized Premiums on Bonds	40			
Income-Control	30			
Cash		2,070		
In Investment Ledger (Invoice):				
Bond Account			2,040	

[5] Entries involving vouchers payable omitted for simplicity.

	GENERAL LEDGER		SUBSIDIARY LEDGER	
	Dr.	Cr.	Dr.	Cr.

In Endowment Funds Ledger (Journal Voucher):

Income Account for Fund Involved			30	

8. Entry to record purchase of five bonds, face value $5,000, at 98, plus accrued interest of $100 for the investment pool (Check Register):

Investments--Securities	5,000			
Undistributed Pool Income	100			
Cash		5,000		
Reserve for Accumulation of Bond Discounts		100		

In Investment Ledger (Invoice):

Bond Account			4,900	

If the bonds were purchased for a separately invested fund, the $100 of accrued interest would be debited to the Income-Control account, rather than to the Undistributed Pool Income account. Appropriate entries then would be made by journal voucher in the Endowment Funds Subsidiary Ledger by debiting the income account for the fund involved.

9. Entry to record purchase of stocks for the investment pool (Check Register):

Investments--Securities	60,000			
Cash		60,000		

In Investment Ledger (Invoice):

Common Stocks Account			40,000	
Preferred Stocks Account			20,000	

10. Entry to record receipt of income from pooled investments (Cash Receipts Journal):

Cash	60,000			
Undistributed Pool Income		60,000		

11. Entry to record receipt of income from investments of a separately invested endowment fund (Cash Receipts Journal):

Cash	5,000			
Income-Control		5,000		

In Endowment Funds Ledger (Cash Receipts Journal):

Income Account for Individual Fund Involved				5,000

12. Entry to record payment of expenses for management of investments in the investment pool (Check Register):

Undistributed Pool Income	3,000			
Cash		3,000		

13. Entry to record annual depreciation charge on rental property (investment of a separately invested restricted endowment fund (Journal Voucher):

Income-Control	1,000			
Reserve for Depreciation on Real Estate		1,000		

In Endowment Funds Ledger (Journal Voucher):

Income account for individual fund involved				1,000

	GENERAL LEDGER		SUBSIDIARY LEDGER	
	Dr.	Cr.	Dr.	Cr.
14. Entry to record amortization of premiums on bonds in the investment pool (Journal Voucher):				
Undistributed Pool Income	4			
Unamortized Premiums on Bonds		4		
In Investment Ledger (Journal Voucher):				
Bond Account				4
15. Entry to record amortization of premiums on bonds of separately invested endowment funds (Journal Voucher):				
Income-Control	6			
Unamortized Premiums on Bonds		6		
In Endowment Funds Ledger (Journal Voucher):				
Income account for individual funds involved			6	
In Investment Ledger (Journal Voucher):				
Bond Account				6
16. Entry to record amount added annually to Provision for Endowment Income Stabilization from investment pool (Journal Voucher):				
a. In Endowment Funds				
Undistributed Pool Income	2,000			
Cash		2,000		
b. In Restricted Current Funds				
Cash	2,000			
Restricted Current Funds Balances		2,000		
In Restricted Current Funds Ledger:				
Provision for Endowment Income Stabilization Account				2,000
17. Entry to record sale of two bonds from investment pool at 103, plus accrued interest of $20 (Cash Receipts Journal):				
Cash	2,080			
Investments--Securities		2,000		
Net Adjusted Gains and Losses		22		
Undistributed Pool Income		20		
Unamortized Premium on Bonds		38		
In Investment Ledger (Cash Receipts Journal):				
Bond Account				2,038
18. Entry to record distribution of net amount in Undistributed Pool Income to participating funds (Journal Voucher):				
a. In Endowment Funds				
Undistributed Pool Income	54,856			
Cash		54,856		
b. In Other Fund Groups				
Appropriate entries would be made in each fund group involved, debiting Cash and crediting Revenues, and Endowment Income-- Unrestricted (for unrestricted current funds), and the accounts for the balances or principal of other funds involved.				

| | GENERAL LEDGER | | SUBSIDIARY LEDGER | |
	Dr.	Cr.	Dr.	Cr.
19. Entry to record distribution of net income from investments of separately invested endowment funds (Journal Voucher):				
a. In Endowment Funds				
Income-Control	3,919			
Cash		3,919		
In Endowment Funds Ledger:				
Income accounts for each fund which is separately invested, and to which income has been credited as received, as in Entry 11, above.			3,919	
b. In Other Fund Groups				
Appropriate entries would be made in each fund group involved, as in (b) in Entry 18 above.				
20. Entry to record sale of common stocks costing $5,000, at a profit of $100 (Cash Receipts Journal):				
Cash	5,100			
Investments--Securities		5,000		
Net Adjusted Gains and Losses		100		
In Investments Ledger (Cash Receipts Journal):				
Common Stocks Account				5,000
21. Entry to record sale of preferred stocks costing $5,000, at a loss of $500 (Cash Receipts Journal):				
Cash	4,500			
Net Adjusted Gains and Losses	500			
Investments--Securities		5,000		
In Investment Ledger (Cash Receipts Journal):				
Preferred Stocks Account				5,000
22. Entry to record transfer of Unrestricted Current Funds for purpose of establishing a Quasi-endowment Fund (Cash Receipts Journal):				
Cash	5,000			
Quasi-endowment Funds Balances		5,000		
In Endowment Funds Ledger (Cash Receipts Journal):				
Principal Account				5,000
(In Unrestricted Current Funds, debit Transfers to Endowment Funds and credit Cash.)				
23. Entry to record transfer of Term Endowment which, by passage of time, had become free of restrictions, to Unexpended Plant Funds (Cash Receipts Journal):				
Term Endowment Funds Balances	20,000			
Cash		20,000		
In Endowment Funds Ledger:				
Principal Account			20,000	
(In Unexpended Plant Funds, debit Cash, credit Unexpended Plant Funds Balances.)				

C. General Ledger--Endowment Funds Section

Cash

	Beginning Balance	100,000	Entry 4	Purchase of Property	8,000
Entry 1	Gift received	22,000	Entry 5	Purchase of Bonds	4,140
Entry 10	Pool income	60,000	Entry 6	Purchase of Bonds	3,105
Entry 11	Income from separately		Entry 7	Purchase of Bonds	2,070
	invested funds	5,000	Entry 8	Purchase of Bonds	5,000
Entry 17	Sale of Bonds	2,080	Entry 9	Purchase of Stocks	60,000
Entry 20	Sale of Stocks	5,100	Entry 12	Investment management	
Entry 21	Sale of Stocks	4,500		expenses	3,000
Entry 22	Transfer from Current		Entry 16	Transfer to Restricted	
	Funds	5,000		Funds	2,000
			Entry 18	Transfer to Other Funds	54,856
			Entry 19	Transfer to Other Funds	3,919
	(37,590)		Entry 23	Transfer to Plant Funds	20,000

Investments--Securities

	Beginning Balance	1,500,000	Entry 17	Sale of Bonds	2,000
Entry 5	Bonds	4,000	Entry 20	Sale of Stocks	5,000
Entry 6	Bonds, separate	3,000	Entry 21	Sale of Stocks	5,000
Entry 7	Bonds, separate	2,000			
Entry 8	Bonds	5,000			
Entry 9	Stocks	60,000			
	(1,562,000)				

Investments--Real Estate

	Beginning Balance	275,000	
Entry 3	Gift	10,000	
Entry 4	Rental Property		
	purchased	8,000	
	(293,000)		

Mortgages Payable on Real Estate

	Beginning Balance	15,000

Reserve for Depreciation on Real Estate

		Beginning Balance	25,000
	Entry 13	Depreciation	1,000
		(26,000)	

Unamortized Premiums on Bonds

Entry 5	Purchase of Bonds	80	Entry 14	Amortization of Premiums	4
Entry 5	Purchase of Bonds	60	Entry 14	Amortization of Premiums	6
Entry 7	Purchase of Bonds	40	Entry 17	Sale of Bonds	38
	(132)				

Endowment Funds Balances

		Beginning Balance	1,525,000
	Entry 1	Gift	22,000
	Entry 3	Gift	10,000
		(1,557,000)	

Term Endowment Funds Balances

Entry 23 Transfer to Plant Funds 20,000	Beginning Balance	100,000
	(80,000)	

Quasi-endowment Funds Balances

	Beginning Balance	175,000
	Entry 22 Transfer from Current Funds	5,000
	(180,000)	

Net Adjusted Gains and Losses

Entry 21 Sale of Preferred Stocks 500	Beginning Balance	35,000
	Entry 17 Sale of Bonds	22
	Entry 20 Sale of Common Stocks	100
	(34,622)	

Undistributed Pool Income

Entry 5 Accrued Interest	60	Entry 10 Income	60,000
Entry 8 Accrued Interest	100	Entry 17 Accrued Interest on Sale	
Entry 12 Management Expenses	3,000	of Bonds	20
Entry 14 Amortization of Premiums	4		
Entry 16 Stabilization Reserve	2,000		
Entry 18 Distribution	54,856		
	60,020		60,020

Income--Control

Entry 6 Accrued Interest	45	Entry 11 Income on Separately	
Entry 7 Accrued Interest	30	Invested Fund	5,000
Entry 13 Depreciation on Rental			
Property	1,000		
Entry 15 Amortization of Premiums	6		
Entry 19 Distribution	3,919		
	5,000		5,000

Reserve for Accumulation--Bond Discounts

	Entry 8 Purchase of Bonds	100
	(100)	

D. Balance Sheet at End of Period

BLANK COLLEGE
BALANCE SHEET
(End of Period)

ASSETS		LIABILITIES AND FUND BALANCES	
ENDOWMENT AND SIMILAR FUNDS:		ENDOWMENT AND SIMILAR FUNDS:	
Cash	37,590	Mortgages Payable on Real Estate	15,000
Investments--Securities	1,562,000	Reserve for Accumulation of Bond Discounts	100
Investments--Real Estate (Less		Fund Balances:	
Reserve for Depreciation)	267,000	Endowment Funds	1,557,000
Unamortized Premiums	132	Term Endowment Funds	80,000
(Funds Held in Trust by		Quasi-endowment Funds	180,000
Others--$105,000)		Net Adjusted Gains and Losses	34,622
Total Endowment and Similar		Total Endowment and Similar	
Funds	1,866,722	Funds	1,866,722

E. Statement of Changes in Fund Balances
Endowment and Similar Funds
For the Year Ended 19__

	Total	Endowment Funds	Term Endowment Funds	Quasi-endowment Funds	Net Adjusted Gains And Losses
Balances, Beginning of Year	1,835,000	1,525,000	100,000	175,000	35,000
Additions:					
Gifts	32,000	32,000			
Transfers from Current Funds	5,000			5,000	
	37,000	32,000		5,000	
Deductions:					
Expiration of Term Endowment	20,000		20,000		
Net Losses on Sales of Securities	378				378
	20,378				
Balances, End of Year	1,851,622	1,557,000	80,000	180,000	34,622

ACCOUNTING FOR ANNUITY AND LIFE INCOME FUNDS

A. Balance Sheet at Beginning of Period

BLANK COLLEGE

BALANCE SHEET
(Beginning of Period)

ASSETS		LIABILITIES AND FUND BALANCES	
ANNUITY AND LIFE INCOME FUNDS:		ANNUITY AND LIFE INCOME FUNDS:	
Cash	5,000	Undistributed Income--Life Income Funds	2,000
Investments--Securities	100,000	Undistributed Income--Annuity Funds	1,000
		Annuity Funds Balances	25,000
		Life Income Funds Balances	77,000
Total Annuity and Life Income Funds	105,000	Total Annuity and Life Income Funds	105,000

B. Recording of Typical Transactions

	GENERAL LEDGER		SUBSIDIARY LEDGER	
	Dr.	Cr.	Dr.	Cr.
1. Entry to record receipt of $5,000 as gift subject to annuity agreement (Cash Receipts Journal):				
Cash	5,000			
Annuity Funds Balances		5,000		
In Annuity and Life Income Funds Ledger (Cash Receipts):				
Principal Account				5,000
2. Entry to record investment of annuity funds in securities:				
Investments--Securities	6,000			
Cash		6,000		
In Investment Ledger (Invoices):				
Securities Account			6,000	

	GENERAL LEDGER		SUBSIDIARY LEDGER	
	Dr.	Cr.	Dr.	Cr.
3. Entry to record receipt of life income fund (Cash Receipts Journal):				
Cash	10,000			
Life Income Funds Balances		10,000		
In Annuity and Life Income Funds Ledger (Cash Receipts):				
Principal Account				10,000
4. Entry to record receipt of income on investments of annuity funds (Cash Receipts Journal):				
Cash	1,250			
Undistributed Income--Annuity Funds		1,250		
5. Entry to record payment to beneficiaries of annuity funds (Check Register):				
Undistributed Income--Annuity Funds	1,150			
Cash		1,150		
6. Entry to record receipt of income on investments of life income funds (Cash Receipts Journal):				
Cash	4,000			
Undistributed Income--Life Income Funds		4,000		
7. Entry to record payment to beneficiaries of life income funds (Check Register):				
Undistributed Income--Life Income Funds	3,800			
Cash		3,800		
8. Entry to record termination of life income fund upon death of beneficiary. Fund is unrestricted as to use. Trustees transfer to Quasi-endowment Funds (Check Register):				
Annuity Funds Balances	3,000			
Cash		3,000		
In Subsidiary Annuity and Life Income Funds Ledger (Invoice):				
Principal Account			3,000	
(In Endowment and Similar Funds Group, debit Cash and credit Quasi-endowment Funds Balances.)				

C.   General Ledger--Annuity and Life Income Funds

Cash

		Beginning Balance	5,000	Entry	2	Purchase of Securities	6,000
Entry	1	Receipt of Annuity	5,000	Entry	5	Payment to Beneficiary	1,150
Entry	3	Receipt of Life Income		Entry	7	Payment to Beneficiary	3,800
		Fund	10,000	Entry	8	Transfer to Endowment	3,000
Entry	4	Receipt of Income	1,250				
Entry	6	Receipt of Income	4,000				
		(11,300)					

Investments--Securities

Entry	2	Beginning Balance Purchases	100,000 6,000				
		(106,000)					

Undistributed Income--Annuity Funds

Entry	5	Payment to Beneficiary	1,150	Entry	4	Beginning Balance Receipt of Income	1,000 1,250
						(1,100)	

Undistributed Income--Life Income Funds

Entry	7	Payment to Beneficiary	3,800	Entry	6	Beginning Balance Receipt of Income	2,000 4,000
						(2,200)	

Annuity Funds Balances

				Entry	1	Beginning Balance Receipt of Annuity	25,000 5,000
						(30,000)	

Life Income Funds Balances

Entry	8	Transfer to Endowment	3,000	Entry	3	Beginning Balance Receipt of Life Income Fund	77,000 10,000
						(84,000	

D. Balance Sheet at End of Period

BLANK COLLEGE

BALANCE SHEET
(End of Period)

ASSETS		LIABILITIES AND FUND BALANCES	
ANNUITY AND LIFE INCOME FUNDS:		ANNUITY AND LIFE INCOME FUNDS:	
Cash	11,300	Undistributed Income--Life Income Funds	2,200
Investments--Securities	106,000	Undistributed Income--Annuity Funds	1,100
		Life Income Funds Balances	84,000
		Annuity Funds Balances	30,000
Total Annuity and Life Income Funds	117,300	Total Annuity and Life Income Funds	117,300

E.   Statement of Changes in Fund Balances

BLANK COLLEGE

STATEMENT OF CHANGES IN FUND BALANCES
ANNUITY AND LIFE INCOME FUNDS
FOR THE YEAR ENDED 19__

	Total	Annuity Funds	Life Income Funds
Balances, Beginning of Year	102,000	25,000	77,000
Additions:			
Gifts	15,000	5,000	10,000
	117,000	30,000	87,000
Deductions:			
Transfers to Endowment upon Death of Annuitant	3,000		3,000
Balances, End of Year	114,000	30,000	84,000

CHAPTER XI

Accounting for Loan and Agency Funds

Loan Funds. Loan funds are those funds which are available for loans to students, faculty, and staff. Primarily, they are established for the purpose of aiding needy students.

Loan funds are provided by gifts and bequests, governmental grants, and, on occasion, by student contributions or fees. Loan funds arising from these sources generally are operated on a revolving fund basis, with repayments of loans and interest payments, if any, remaining in the Loan Funds group for lending to other students. Frequently, gifts to an institution are made under terms which provide that only the income from the investments of the original gift may be used as loan funds. In such cases, the income from the investments is classified in the Loan Funds group, the principal of the gift being accounted for in the Endowment and Similar Funds group. The identity of each loan fund must be shown clearly in the accounting records at all times.

If loan funds are temporarily invested, income from the investments should be credited to the principal of the funds so invested. Any realized gains and losses on the sale of the investments should be added to or deducted from the principal of the funds involved.

The ledgers used in accounting for loan funds are the general ledger, the subsidiary notes and interest receivable ledger (Form 11.1), and the subsidiary loan funds ledger (Form 11.2). In addition to the three ledgers, a vouchers payable register and a check register

BLANK COLLEGE

NOTES AND INTEREST RECEIVABLE LEDGER

Name_____

Address_____

Fund_____

Date of Note_____

Number of Note_____

Maturity of Note_____

Date	Reference	Interest		Notes Receivable		Balance	
		Debit	Credit	Debit	Credit	Interest	Note

BLANK COLLEGE

LOAN FUNDS LEDGER

Name of Fund_____

Date	Explanation	Cash			Notes Receivable			Principal		
		Debit	Credit	Balance	Debit	Credit	Balance	Debit	Credit	Balance

for the loan funds should be used. No separate cash receipts journal is needed for loan funds, as the cash receipts journal (Form 7.10) used for recording current and other funds receipts should be used for loan fund receipts. In this connection, it should be noted that many institutions handle the transactions of the loan funds through the current funds journals, registers, and ledgers, and the use of the Due To and Due From accounts in both the current funds and the loan funds groups.

The accounts usually found in the Loans Funds section of the general ledger include the following:

Asset Accounts
    Cash
    Due from Other Funds
    Notes Receivable
    Interest Receivable
    Temporary Investments
    Allowance for Doubtful Loans (Credit Balance Account)

Liability and Funds Balances Accounts
    Due to Other Funds
    National Defense Student Loan Fund—Repayable to Government
    National Defense Student Loan Fund—Institutional Share
    Loan Funds Balances

If an institution possesses more than one loan fund, the accounts should be maintained in a manner that will segregate between funds the information pertaining to cash, notes receivable, temporary investments, income and expenditures, and balances. Unless prohibited by the terms of the gifts or other instrument under which the loan funds arise, the assets of the funds may be pooled for lending purposes as well as for investment purposes. However, the principal of each loan fund must be identifiable in the accounting records.

The Notes Receivable account in the general ledger is the control account for the Notes Receivable columns in the subsidiary notes and interest receivable ledger. The Interest Receivable account in the general ledger is used only if interest is accrued on the notes receivable when it becomes due. If interest is not accrued, the Interest Receivable account will not be used.

Interest on loan fund notes receivable may be credited directly to the principal of the funds involved, to separate income and expense accounts for each fund, or to a single income and expense account for the Loan Funds group. Expenses for administration of the loan funds and other operating costs, also, may be charged directly to the principal of the funds involved, to separate income and expense accounts for the individual funds, or to a single income and expense account for the Loan Funds group. The degree of detailing in the accounts will be governed by the number and size of the funds in this group and the administrative needs with respect to day-by-day controls and periodic financial reporting. The income and expenditures of loan funds do not affect the current funds operations; therefore, the accounts for recording the former transactions should not be mingled with the revenue and expenditure accounts pertaining to current funds.

The accounting records should show separately the balances of governmental advances for loan funds, institutional contributions required to supplement such advances, other refundable loan funds, and funds available for loans to faculty and staff. In the event a governing board designates funds of other groups to function temporarily as loan funds, these should be identified separately, because the board may choose, at some future time, to transfer the funds to other fund groups or return them to the groups from which they were temporarily transferred.

Some institutions set aside out of loan funds income an allowance to cover possible losses from uncollectible loans. If this procedure is followed, the allowance should be shown as an account carrying a credit balance but reported as a deduction from the notes receivable account on the asset side of the Balance Sheet.

ILLUSTRATION

Following is an illustration of the accounting entries for loan funds. A beginning Balance Sheet, transactions during the fiscal year, closing entries, a final Balance Sheet, and a Statement of Changes in Fund Balances are presented.

A. Balance Sheet at Beginning of Period

BLANK COLLEGE

BALANCE SHEET
(Beginning of Period)

ASSETS		LIABILITIES AND FUND BALANCES	
LOAN FUNDS:		LOAN FUNDS:	
Cash	25,000	National Defense Student Loan	
Notes Receivable	700,000	Fund--Repayable to Federal	
Investments	30,000	Government	550,000
		National Defense Student Loan	
		Fund--Institutional Share	61,000
		Interest on National Defense	
		Student Loans	19,000
		Loan Funds Balances	125,000
Total Loan Funds	755,000	Total Loan Funds	755,000

B. Recording of Typical Transactions

	GENERAL LEDGER		SUBSIDIARY LEDGER	
	Dr.	Cr.	Dr.	Cr.
1. Entry to record receipt of gift to create new loan fund (Cash Receipts Journal):				
Cash	10,000			
Loan Funds Balances		10,000		
Loan Funds Ledger (Cash Receipts):				
Individual Loan Funds Account				10,000
2. Entry to record granting of loans other than N.D.S.L. loans (Check Register):				
Notes Receivable	10,000			
Cash		10,000		
In Notes and Interest Receivable Ledger (Vouchers):				
Individual Accounts			10,000	
3. Entry to record receipt of interest of temporary investments (Cash Receipts Journal):				
Cash	1,000			
Loan Funds Balances		1,000		
In Loan Funds Ledger (Cash Receipts):				
Individual Loan Funds Accounts				1,000
4. Entry to record collection of notes plus interest (Cash Receipts Journal):				
Cash	5,150			
Notes Receivable		5,000		
Loan Funds Balances		150		
In Loan Funds Ledger (Cash Receipts):				
Individual Loan Funds Accounts				150
In Notes and Interest Receivable Ledger (Cash Receipts):				
Individual Accounts				5,000

	GENERAL LEDGER		SUBSIDIARY LEDGER	
	Dr.	Cr.	Dr.	Cr.
5. Entry to record expenses of administration (Check Register):				
Loan Funds Balances	8,000			
Cash		8,000		
In Loan Funds Ledger (Vouchers):				
Individual Loan Funds Accounts			8,000	
6. Entry to record writing off uncollectible notes (Journal Voucher):				
Loan Funds Balances	1,000			
Notes Receivable		1,000		
In Loan Funds Ledger (Journal Voucher):				
Individual Loan Funds Accounts			1,000	
In Notes and Interest Receivable Ledger (Journal Voucher):				
Individual Accounts				1,000
7. Entry to record receipt of funds from U.S. government for N.D.S.L. loans (Cash Receipts):				
Cash	100,000			
National Defense Student Loan Funds--Repayable to U.S. government		100,000		
8. Entry to record transfer of institutional contribution to N.D.S.L. Funds (Cash Receipts):				
Cash	11,000			
National Defense Student Loan Funds--Institutional Share		11,000		
(In Unrestricted Current Funds, debit Transfers to Loan Funds and credit Cash.)				
9. Entry to record granting of N.D.S.L. Loans (Check Register):				
Notes Receivable	70,000			
Cash		70,000		
In Notes and Interest Receivable Ledger (Vouchers):				
Individual Accounts			70,000	
10. Entry to record repayments of N.D.S.L. loans (Cash Receipts):				
Cash	10,200			
Notes Receivable		10,000		
Interest of National Defense Student Loans		200		
In Notes and Interest Receivable Ledger (Cash Receipts):				
Individual Accounts				10,000

(Note: Interest received on National Defense Student loans is accumulated and is considered as Cash on Hand in subsequent funds applications to the U.S. government.)

11. Entry to write off National Defense Student Loan Receivable due to death of student borrower (Journal Voucher):

	GENERAL LEDGER		SUBSIDIARY LEDGER	
	Dr.	Cr.	Dr.	Cr.
National Defense Student Loans Funds-- Repayable to U.S. government	765			
National Defense Student Loans Funds-- Institutional Share	85			
Notes Receivable		850		
In Notes and Interest Receivable Ledger (Journal Voucher):				
Individual Account				850

C. General Ledger--Loan Funds Section

Cash

Entry	1	Beginning Balance	25,000	Entry	2	Granting of Loans	10,000
Entry	3	Gift	10,000	Entry	5	Expenses	8,000
Entry	4	Interest on Investments	1,000	Entry	9	Granting of Loans	70,000
Entry	7	Collection of Notes	5,150				
		Receipt of N.D.S.L. Funds	100,000				
Entry	8	Receipt of Institutional Share	11,000				
Entry	10	Collection of Notes	10,200				
		(74,350)					

Notes Receivable

		Beginning Balance	700,000	Entry	4	Collection of Notes	5,000
Entry	2	Granting of Loans	10,000	Entry	6	Notes Written Off	1,000
Entry	9	Granting of Loans	70,000	Entry	10	Collection of Notes	10,000
				Entry	11	Notes Written Off	850
		(763,150)					

Investments

Beginning Balance	30,000	
(30,000)		

National Defense Student Loan Fund--Repayable to Federal Government

Entry 11	Notes Written Off	765			Beginning Balance	550,000
			Entry	7	Receipt of Funds	100,000
					(649,235)	

National Defense Student Loan Fund--Institutional Share

Entry 11	Notes Written Off	85			Beginning Balance	61,000
			Entry	8	Transfer from Current Funds	11,000
					(71,915)	

Interest on National Defense Student Loan Funds

		Beginning Balance	19,000
Entry	10	Collection of Interest	200
		(19,200)	

Loan Funds Balances

					Beginning Balance	125,000
Entry	5	Expenses	8,000	Entry 1	Gift	10,000
Entry	6	Notes Written Off	1,000	Entry 3	Interest on Investments	1,000
				Entry 4	Interest on Loans	150
					(127,150)	

D.   Balance Sheet--End of Period

BLANK COLLEGE

BALANCE SHEET
(End of Period)

ASSETS		LIABILITIES AND FUND BALANCES	
LOAN FUNDS:		LOAN FUNDS:	
Cash	74,350	National Defense Student Loan	
Notes Receivable	763,150	Fund--Repayable to Federal	
Investments	30,000	Government	649,235
		National Defense Student Loan	
		Fund--Institutional Share	71,915
		Interest on National Defense	
		Student Loan Fund	19,200
		Loan Funds Balances	127,150
Total Loan Funds	867,500	Total Loan Funds	867,500

E.   Statement of Changes in Fund Balances

BLANK COLLEGE

STATEMENT OF CHANGES IN FUND BALANCES--LOAN FUNDS
(End of Period)

Balance, Beginning of Period		775,000
Additions:		
Federal Grant		100,000
Gifts		10,000
Interest Income		350
Investment Income		1,000
Transfers from Current Fund		11,000
		122,350
Deductions:		
Uncollectible Notes Charged Off		1,850
Expenses		8,000
		9,850
Balances, End of Period		
U.S. Government Grants, Refundable	649,235	
Interest on N.D.S.L. Loan Funds	19,200	
Institutional Loan Funds:		
Established by Donors	127,150	
Established by Governing Board	71,915	867,500

Agency Funds. Agency funds are those funds in the possession of an institution for which it is custodian but not owner. They are funds deposited with the institution for safekeeping, to be used or withdrawn by the depositor at will, the institution exercising no control over such withdrawals. The typical example of agency funds is deposits by students and student organizations, and various breakage deposits. Receipts and disbursements of agency funds should not be included in current funds operating statements, for they do not constitute current funds revenues and expenditures.

The ledgers used in accounting for agency funds are the general ledger and the subsidiary deposit ledger, which contains an individual account with each depositor. The journals employed include the vouchers payable register and the check register. Cash receipts are entered in the cash receipts journal used for current and other funds.

Accounting for these funds is not complicated. When funds are deposited, they are posted to the credit of the individual depositor. Form 11.3 is a type of deposit ledger card. When funds are withdrawn in accordance with specified rules and regulations, the individual withdrawing the fund is required to sign a withdrawal slip (Form 11.4). Later, this slip is used to charge the appropriate account in the deposit ledger. Many colleges employ mechanical cash registers which automatically post the deposit ledger and simul-

FORM 11.3

BLANK COLLEGE
AGENCY   FUNDS   DEPOSIT   LEDGER

Name_____

Address_____

Date	Description	Ref.	Charges	Credits	Balance

```
┌─────────────────────────────────────────────────────────────────┐
│                          BLANK COLLEGE          No. 1             │
│          A G E N C Y   F U N D S   W I T H D R A W A L   S L I P  │
│                                                                   │
│                                            Date_____  │
│ Charge Account of_____    │
│                                Name of Depositor                  │
│ _____  $_____   │
│ For Withdrawal of Funds                                           │
│                                                                   │
│                              _____ │
│                                      Signature of Depositor       │
└─────────────────────────────────────────────────────────────────┘
```

taneously produce a copy for the student or organization to use as a bank record.

An account in the general ledger, Agency Funds Balances, is the control account for all the accounts in the subsidiary deposit ledger. The subsidiary ledger should be balanced monthly with the general ledger control account.

The general ledger accounts needed to record agency fund transactions consist of the following:

ASSETS
  Cash
  Due From Other Funds
  Temporary Investments (if authorized by the depositor)

LIABILITIES AND FUNDS BALANCES
  Due to Other Funds
  Agency Funds Balances

ILLUSTRATION

The following is an illustration of the accounting for agency funds. A beginning Balance Sheet, transactions during the fiscal year, a final Balance Sheet, and a Statement of Changes in Fund Balances are shown.

A. Balance Sheet at Beginning of Period

BLANK COLLEGE

BALANCE SHEET
(Beginning of Period)

ASSETS		LIABILITIES AND FUNDS BALANCES	
AGENCY FUNDS:		AGENCY FUNDS:	
Cash	20,000	Agency Funds Balances	20,000
		Subsidiary Funds:	
		Student Deposits	15,000
		Organization Deposits	5,000
			20,000

B. Recording of Typical Transactions

	GENERAL LEDGER		SUBSIDIARY LEDGER	
	Dr.	Cr.	Dr.	Cr.
1. Entry to record receipt of deposits (Cash Receipts Journal):				
Cash	10,000			
Agency Funds Balances		10,000		
In Deposit Ledger (Cash Receipts):				
Student Deposits Accounts				9,000
Organization Deposits Accounts				1,000
2. Entry to record breakage deposits collected at beginning of year (Cash Receipts Journal):				
Cash	2,000			
Agency Funds Balances		2,000		
In Deposit Ledger (Cash Receipts):				
Breakage Deposit Accounts				2,000
3. Entry to record refund of breakage deposits at end of year (Check Register):				
Agency Funds Balances	1,800			
Cash		1,800		
In Deposit Ledger (Vouchers):				
Breakage Deposit Accounts			1,800	
4. Entry to record transfer of balances of breakage deposits, representing breakage charges, to general current funds (Check Register):				
Agency Funds Balances	200			
Cash		200		
In Deposit Ledger:				
Breakage Deposit Accounts			200	
(In Unrestricted Current Funds debit Cash and credit Miscellaneous Income or Appropriation Expenditures.)				
5. Entry to record withdrawal of deposits (Check Register):				
Agency Funds Balances	12,000			
Cash		12,000		
In Deposit Ledger (Withdrawal Slips)				
Student Deposits Accounts			10,000	
Organization Deposits Accounts			2,000	

C. General Ledger--Agency Funds Section

Cash

		Beginning Balance	20,000	Entry	3	Refund of Breakage	
Entry	1	Deposits	10,000			Deposits	1,800
Entry	2	Breakage Deposits	2,000	Entry	4	Transfer to General	
						Current Funds	200
		(18,000)		Entry	5	Withdrawal of Deposits	12,000

Agency Funds Balances

Entry	3	Refund of Breakage				Beginning Balance	20,000
		Deposits	1,800	Entry	1	Deposits	10,000
Entry	4	Transfer to General		Entry	2	Breakage Deposits	2,000
		Funds	200				
Entry	5	Withdrawal of Deposits	12,000				

D. Balance Sheet at End of Period

BLANK COLLEGE
BALANCE SHEET
(End of Period)

ASSETS		LIABILITIES AND FUND BALANCES	
AGENCY FUNDS:		AGENCY FUNDS:	
Cash	18,000	Agency Funds Balances	18,000

E. Statement of Changes in Fund Balances

BLANK COLLEGE

STATEMENT OF CHANGES IN FUND BALANCES--AGENCY FUNDS
(End of Period)

Balances, Beginning of Period	20,000
Additions	12,000
	32,000
Deductions	14,000
Balances, End of Period	18,000

CHAPTER XII

Accounting for Plant Funds

PLANT FUNDS CONSIST "of funds to be used for the construction, rehabilitation, and acquisition of physical properties for institutional purposes; funds already expended for plant properties; funds set aside for the renewal and replacement thereof; and funds accumulated for the retirement of indebtedness thereon." [1] The Plant Funds section of the Balance Sheet is divided into four subsections as follows:

Unexpended Plant Funds. Funds available for the acquisition or construction of physical plant to be used for institutional purposes.

Funds for Renewals and Replacements. Funds available for the renewal and replacement of institutional plant assets.

Funds for the Retirement of Indebtedness. Funds available for debt service charges and for the retirement of indebtedness on institutional plant.

Investment in Plant. Funds already invested in physical plant at book or carrying value.

An institution may, at its option, consolidate the Plant Funds group into two major subsections—Unexpended Plant Funds and Investment in Plant. In such cases, Retirement of Indebtedness and Renewals and Replacement funds are carried as equity accounts in the Unexpended Plant Funds subgroup.

---

[1] *College and University Business Administration,* 147.

The problems involved in accounting for the four types of plant funds are discussed in this chapter.

Unexpended Plant Funds. The routine of accounting for the transactions of unexpended plant funds is no different from that relating to current funds. The same requisition forms, purchase orders, and invoices are used, and documents are prepared in the same manner, except that they are identified as Unexpended Plant Funds or are coded appropriately. These documents are recorded in a separate set of journals, including a cash receipts journal, a voucher register, an orders placed and liquidated journal, a check register, and a general journal. In addition, a subsidiary ledger account is maintained for each unexpended plant fund. The regular allocations ledger form, with some adaptation, is suitable for this purpose.

Additions to Unexpended Plant Funds include gifts designated for plant use, governmental appropriations, proceeds from bond issues and other forms of financing, and income from and net realized gains on the sale of the temporary investments of funds belonging to this group. Deductions include disbursements for plant facilities and net realized losses on the sale of temporary investments.

Following are the accounts customarily used in accounting for Unexpended Plant Funds:

ASSET ACCOUNTS:
  Cash
  Temporary Investments
  Due from Other Funds
  State Appropriations Receivable
  Encumbrances (optional)
  Construction in Progress

LIABILITY AND FUNDS BALANCES ACCOUNTS:
  Vouchers Payable
  Due to Other Funds
  Bonds Payable
  Provision for Encumbrances (optional)
  Unexpended Plant Funds Balances

The State Appropriations Receivable account represents balances due to a college or university from capital outlay appropriations made by a state legislature. Accounting for the state appropriation varies in accordance with the fiscal system of the state. Funds for building purposes in some states are sent to the institution for deposit and disbursement. In other states, the funds remain in the state treasury to the credit of the institution and are subject to withdrawal upon submission of audited vouchers or warrants of the institution. The following entry is made on the institution's records in the Unexpended Plant Funds group to record the state appropriation for buildings or plant expansion:

State Appropriations Receivable
    Unexpended Plant Funds Balances

If funds are sent to the college for deposit, the following entry is made:

Cash
    State Appropriations Receivable

If funds are retained in the state treasury, the following entries are made when such funds are used:

1. Upon the approval of a voucher or warrant for the payment of expenditures related to a building project:

Construction in Progress
    State Appropriations Receivable

2. To transfer the value of the construction at the end of the fiscal period to the Investment in Plant section:

Unexpended Plant Funds Balances
    Construction in Progress

Unexpended Plant Funds Balances is a control account representing the sum of the individual funds being held for purposes of

financing plant additions. If an institution possesses only a few individual plant funds, separate accounts may be set up in the general
ledger for each fund. If separate funds for plant additions are numerous, however, a subsidiary ledger for unexpended plant funds
should be maintained. The regular allocations ledger form, illustrated on page 108, will serve in this connection. Because the budget
is not ordinarily posted to the accounts in the case of unexpended
plant funds, the column in the allocations ledger headed Allocations
and Other Credits is used to record receipts instead of departmental
budget allocations. The Free Balance column of the ledger form
shows the unencumbered cash balance of each fund. The Unexpended Plant Funds Balances account will control all columns in
the subsidiary ledger. Encumbering or charging purchase orders in
the records is optional. If purchase orders are recorded, the usual
procedure of encumbrance and liquidation is followed.

The entries to account for transactions pertaining to the expenditure of unexpended plant funds are as follows:

1. To record expenditure of funds for a building project in process of construction during the year:

Construction in Progress
    Cash

2. To transfer the value of the construction at the end of the year
to the Investment in Plant section:

Unexpended Plant Funds Balances
    Construction in Progress

3. To record the expenditure of funds for a plant asset item
through outright purchase, or other transaction, which is completed
within the fiscal period:

Unexpended Plant Funds Balances
    Cash

Funds for Renewals and Replacements. According to *College and University Business Administration*: "The necessity for providing for renewals and replacements of the physical plant facilities and other real properties of an institution depends on the class of property under consideration and the financial program of the institution." [2] Accounting for depreciation on property used for institutional purposes is not recommended. (See chapter 13 for further discussion of this subject.) However, it is frequently desirable periodically to set aside portions of unrestricted current funds revenues for the renewal, replacement, or expansion of physical properties. Bond issues on residence halls and other revenue-producing structures usually require that such reserves be created out of current revenues. The allocation of unrestricted current funds revenues for plant renewals on property used in the educational program is recorded as follows:

IN UNRESTRICTED CURRENT FUNDS
Transfer to Funds for Renewals and Replacements
   Cash

IN FUNDS FOR RENEWALS AND REPLACEMENTS
Cash
   Renewals and Replacements Funds Balances
   (Separate subsidiary accounts established as required)

In current funds, the allocation is reported in the transfers section of the Statement of Current Funds Revenues, Expenditures, and Transfers.

To set up replacement reserves for auxiliary enterprise plant, charges are made annually against the operations of the respective auxiliary enterprises and are entered as current expenses. In addition, there should be a transfer of cash from unrestricted current funds to funds for renewals and replacements. Actual replacements and renewals, as they occur, including equipment and major repairs, should be charged against the funds thus created.

The entries to account for transactions pertaining to funds for renewals and replacements on auxiliary enterprise plant are as follows:

---

[2] *Ibid.*, 148.

1. To record transfer of cash from unrestricted current funds to funds for renewals and replacements

   a. In Unrestricted Current Funds:
      Expenditures
        Cash
      In Subsidiary Allocations Ledger:
      Debit expenditure accounts of appropriate auxiliary enterprises.

   b. In Funds for Renewals and Replacements:
      Cash
        Renewals and Replacements Funds Balances

2. To record expenditures for renewals and replacements:

   In Funds for Renewals and Replacements:
   Renewals and Replacements Funds Balances
     Cash

The accounts of replacement funds should be kept in such a manner that the balance applicable to each enterprise or activity is shown or can be determined. This recommendation can be carried out either by coding entries in the Renewals and Replacements Funds Balances account or, preferably, by using subsidiary accounts for each activity, such as residence halls, cafeterias, and educational plant.

Costs of ordinary recurring repairs to buildings and equipment should be considered current expenses and paid out of current funds, but disbursements for extraordinary repairs, replacements, and renewals should not be reported as current expense. Disbursements of this nature should be made out of Funds for Renewals and Replacements and reported as part of the transactions of that fund group.

The following accounts are used in recording the transactions of Funds for Renewals and Replacements:

ASSET ACCOUNTS:
  Cash
  Due from Other Funds
  Temporary Investments

LIABILITY AND FUNDS BALANCES ACCOUNTS:
  Vouchers Payable
  Due to Other Funds
  Renewals and Replacements Funds Balances

Funds for Retirement of Indebtedness. This subdivision of Plant Funds is used to record transactions pertaining to the retirement of bonds, mortgages, or other forms of indebtedness on the plant assets used for institutional purposes. It does not apply to indebtedness on real estate properties which are the investment of Endowment and Similar Funds. The account Retirement of Indebtedness Funds Balances is credited with funds received for the appropriate purpose and is charged with disbursements resulting in the retirement of debts. Transfers from unrestricted current funds, income realized on the temporary investments of the retirement funds, governmental appropriations, and special student fees are the usual sources of funds for debt retirement. Even in the case of serial bonds, where it is not necessary to accumulate sinking funds, a transfer should be made from current funds to funds for retirement of indebtedness and the payment of all debt service expenses should be recorded in the latter fund group. Entries in the fund balances account should differentiate between principal repayments and interest charges, since payments on the principal of the indebtedness must be reflected as adjustments in the net investment in plant account.

Transfers from current funds to plant funds to cover debt service on bonds or mortgages acquired to finance construction of educational plant are recorded as follows:

IN UNRESTRICTED CURRENT FUNDS:
Transfers to Funds for Retirement of Indebtedness
  Cash

IN FUNDS FOR RETIREMENT OF INDEBTEDNESS:
Cash
  Retirement of Indebtedness Funds Balances
  (Separate subsidiary accounts established as required)

In the case of debt service on plant used for auxiliary enterprises, the charge in Unrestricted Current Funds is directly to the expenditures accounts of the auxiliary enterprises affected.

The following accounts are used in recording the transactions of funds for retirement of indebtedness:

ASSET ACCOUNTS:
  Cash
  Cash—Trustee Account
  Due from Other Funds
  Temporary Investments
  Receivables

LIABILITY AND FUNDS BALANCES ACCOUNTS:
  Vouchers Payable
  Due to Other Funds
  Retirement of Indebtedness Funds Balances

Investment in Plant. The Investment in Plant section of Plant Funds is used to account for fixed assets owned by the institution and used for institutional purposes, including land, buildings, improvements other than buildings, and equipment. Additions to plant may be acquired and financed directly through unexpended plant funds or through current funds. In addition, they may be financed indirectly through current funds by transfer from those funds to unexpended plant funds. All items of physical plant owned by the institution are reported in the Investment in Plant section of the Balance Sheet. Real property which is the investment of endowment and similar funds is not included here.

The following general ledger accounts are found in the Investment in Plant section of Plant Funds:

ASSET ACCOUNTS:
  Land
  Buildings
  Improvements other than Buildings
  Equipment
  Due from Other Funds
  Construction in Progress

LIABILITIES AND FUNDS BALANCES ACCOUNTS:
  Notes Payable
  Mortgages Payable
  Bonds Payable
  Due to Other Funds
  Net Investment in Plant

The Construction in Progress account is used to accumulate costs of construction while a project is under construction. As soon as construction is completed, this account is closed into a permanent property account, i.e., buildings, or improvements other than buildings.

The other asset accounts represent the permanent property of the institution. They are control accounts, each controlling a section of the subsidiary plant ledger, which contains a detailed record of individual items of plant such as parcels of land, individual buildings, and items of equipment. A complete discussion of the perpetual inventory system for fixed assets is found in chapter 13.

The Net Investment in Plant account represents the total equity of the institution in its physical plant assets. The assets should be valued at cost. If there are no bonds, mortgages, or notes outstanding, the total of the asset accounts for land, buildings, improvements, and equipment will equal the Net Investment in Plant account. However, if the college has outstanding bonds, mortgages payable, or notes, the Net Investment in Plant account will be less than the total of the assets by the amount of the outstanding debts. As the obligations are retired, the net investment in plant will increase to the point of equaling the value of the assets when all obligations have been liquidated. The Net Investment in Plant account should be set up so as to provide information concerning the source of the funds invested in plant—that is, from state appropriations, from current funds, or from gifts. This end may be accomplished through the use of code symbols.

As stated before, all fixed assets owned by the college, except those held as a part of endowment funds investments, should be included in the Investment in Plant section of Plant Funds, regardless of the source of the funds or the manner in which the assets were acquired.

Permanent property is acquired in the following ways: (1) direct purchase out of current funds, (2) transfer of funds from current to unexpended plant funds, (3) direct purchase out of unexpended plant funds, (4) issuance of bonds, (5) purchase out of funds for renewals and replacements, and (6) gift.

Equipment is usually purchased directly out of current funds. In making allocations to departments, equipment frequently is considered as a separate budget section coordinate with salaries, wages, and supplies and expense. Periodically, usually once a year, the expenditures for equipment made from current funds should be brought into the Investment in Plant section of Plant Funds. Illustrative entries to account for equipment purchases are as follows:

1. To record purchase of equipment out of current funds:

   IN UNRESTRICTED CURRENT FUNDS:
   Expenditures
     Cash
   In the subsidiary Allocations Ledger, debit departmental accounts.

2. To record capitalization of equipment expenditures:

   IN INVESTMENT IN PLANT FUNDS:
   Equipment
     Net Investment in Plant

When current funds are used to finance additions to plant other than equipment, the correct procedure is to transfer cash to Unexpended Plant Funds where the actual disbursement is made. The transfer of funds is recorded in Unrestricted Current Funds and appears in the Transfers section of the Statement of Current Funds Revenues, Expenditures, and Transfers. Expenditures for plant additions made from Unexpended Plant Funds are capitalized by entry in the Investment in Plant section. The entries to account for these transactions are as follows:

1. Entries to record transfer of funds from unrestricted current to unexpended plant funds:

   a. IN UNRESTRICTED CURRENT FUNDS:
   Transfers to Unexpended Plant Funds
     Cash

b. IN UNEXPENDED PLANT FUNDS:
   Cash
      Unexpended Plant Funds Balances

2. Entry to record the expenditure of funds for the construction of a building:

IN UNEXPENDED PLANT FUNDS:
   Construction in Progress
      Cash

3. Entries to record the transfer of the value of the building at the end of the fiscal period or upon completion of the project to the Investment in Plant section:

a. IN UNEXPENDED PLANT FUNDS:
   Unexpended Plant Funds Balances
      Construction in Progress

b. IN INVESTMENT IN PLANT FUNDS:
   Buildings
      Net Investment in Plant

If the expenditures were for the purchase of a building, or other plant asset, and all the financial matters were completed within the fiscal period, the entries would be:

a. IN UNEXPENDED PLANT FUNDS:
   Unexpended Plant Funds Balances
      Cash

b. IN INVESTMENT IN PLANT FUNDS:
   Buildings
      Net Investment in Plant

Bonds are sometimes issued to finance additions to plant. Frequently, so-called revenue bonds are sold to finance the purchase or construction of auxiliary plant, the bonds to be retired out of the earnings of the auxiliary enterprise. The proceeds of the bond issue are accounted for through Unexpended Plant Funds, as is the actual expenditure for the property being constructed or otherwise acquired. During the process of construction, the bond liability is carried temporarily in Unexpended Plant Funds, being transferred periodically to Investment in Plant as the construction proceeds.

The entries to show the acquisition of plant funds from a bond issue, the expenditure of such funds for the construction of a building, the capitalization of the value of the building, the recording of the indebtedness, and the retirement of bonds are as follows:

1. Entry to record the receipt of proceeds from a bond issue:

   In Unexpended Plant Funds:
      Cash
         Bonds Payable

2. Entry to record payments to contractors:

   In Unexpended Plant Funds:
      Construction in Progress
         Cash

3. Entries to record the capitalization of construction in process:

   a. In Unexpended Plant Funds:
      Bonds Payable (for amount of construction accomplished during the year)
         Construction in Progress

   b. In Investment in Plant Funds:
      Construction in Progress
         Bonds Payable

4. Entry to record completion of project:

   In Investment in Plant Funds:
   Buildings
      Construction in Progress

5. Entries to record retirement of the bonds:

   a. In Funds for Retirement of Indebtedness:
      Retirement of Indebtedness Funds Balances
         Cash

   b. In Investment in Plant Funds:
      Bonds Payable
         Net Investment in Plant

Gifts furnish a frequent source of funds for plant expansions. If the gift is in cash, it is handled through Unexpended Plant Funds, as already described. If the gift is in the form of property, it is entered in the Investment in Plant section as a debit to the appropriate asset account and a credit to Net Investment in Plant. The property representing the gift should be recorded at an appraised value, or if such is not obtainable, at a nominal value.

Following is an illustration of the accounting for the four subsections of Plant Funds. A beginning Balance Sheet, typical transactions during the fiscal year, closing entries, a final Balance Sheet, and a Statement of Changes in Fund Balances are presented.

A. Balance Sheet at Beginning of Period

BLANK COLLEGE

BALANCE SHEET
(Beginning of Period)

ASSETS		LIABILITIES AND FUND BALANCES	
UNEXPENDED PLANT FUNDS:		UNEXPENDED PLANT FUNDS:	
Cash	85,000	Notes Payable	10,000
Temporary Investments	75,000	Bonds Payable	100,000
Appropriations Receivable	100,000	Unexpended Plant Funds Balances[1]	200,000
Construction in Progress	50,000		
Total Unexpended Plant Funds	310,000	Total Unexpended Plant Funds	310,000

[1]Subsidiary Accounts:

Fund A--Green Hall	25,000
Fund B--Smith Hall	35,000
Fund C--Science Laboratory	140,000
	200,000

B. Recording of Typical Transactions

	GENERAL LEDGER		SUBSIDIARY LEDGER	
	Dr.	Cr.	Dr.	Cr.
1. Entry to record state appropriation for land ($5,500) and improvements ($11,000) (Journal Voucher):				
State Appropriations Receivable	16,500			
Unexpended Plant Funds Balances		16,500		
In Unexpended Plant Funds Ledger (Journal Voucher):				
Fund D--Land				5,500
Fund E--Improvements				11,000
2. Entry to record receipt of moneys from state for capital outlay appropriations granted in previous year (Cash Receipts Journal):				
Cash	100,000			
State Appropriations Receivable		100,000		

	GENERAL LEDGER		SUBSIDIARY LEDGER	
	Dr.	Cr.	Dr.	Cr.
3. Entry to record receipt of gift to equip Science Laboratory (Cash Receipts Journal):				
Cash	15,000			
Unexpended Plant Funds Balances		15,000		
In Unexpended Plant Funds Ledger (Cash Receipts):				
Fund C--Science Laboratory Equipment				15,000
4. Entry to record expenditures (Check Register):[3]				
Unexpended Plant Funds Balances	16,000			
Cash		16,000		
In Unexpended Plant Funds Ledger (Vouchers):				
Fund D--Land			5,000	
Fund E--Improvements			11,000	
(In Investment in Plant Funds, debit Land $5,000, Improvements Other Than Buildings $11,000, and credit Net Investment in Plant $16,000.)				
5. Entry to record receipt of funds for construction of dormitory made available through issuance of bonds (Cash Receipts Journal):				
Cash	100,000			
Bonds Payable		100,000		
6. Entry to record transfer of funds for the construction of Green Hall from current funds (Cash Receipts Journal):				
Cash	20,000			
Unexpended Plant Funds Balances		20,000		
In Unexpended Plant Funds Ledger (Cash Receipts):				
Fund A--Green Hall				20,000
(In Unrestricted Current Funds, debit Transfers to Unexpended Plant Funds and credit Cash.)				
7. Entry to record investment of surplus funds in securities (Check Register):				
Temporary Investments	10,000			
Cash		10,000		
8. Entry to record sale of worn-out equipment. Proceeds credited by trustees to Fund X--Undesignated (Cash Receipts Journal):				
Cash	1,000			
Unexpended Plant Funds Balances		1,000		
In Unexpended Plant Funds Ledger (Cash Receipts):				
Fund X--Unallocated				1,000
(In Investment in Plant Section of Plant Funds, debit Net Investment in Plant and credit Equipment.)				

[3] Entries involving vouchers payable omitted for simplicity.

		GENERAL LEDGER		SUBSIDIARY LEDGER	
		Dr.	Cr.	Dr.	Cr.
9. Entry to record return of unused state appropriation for land (Check Register):					
Unexpended Plant Funds Balances		500			
Cash			500		
In Unexpended Plant Funds Ledger (Voucher):					
Fund D--Farm Land					500
10. Entry to record progress payment on dormitory under construction (Check Register):					
Construction in Progress		50,000			
Cash			50,000		
11. Entry to record transfer of Construction in Progress to Investment in Plant (Journal Voucher):					
Bonds Payable		50,000			
Construction in Progress			50,000		

(In Investment in Plant Funds, debit
Construction in Progress and credit
Bonds Payable.)

C.   General Ledger--Unexpended Plant Funds Section

Cash

Entry	2	Beginning Balance	85,000	Entry	4	Plant Additions	16,000
Entry	2	State Appropriations	100,000	Entry	7	Temporary Investments	10,000
Entry	3	Gift	15,000	Entry	9	Return of State	
Entry	5	Issuance of Bonds	100,000			Appropriation	500
Entry	6	Transfer from Current		Entry	10	Construction	50,000
		Funds	20,000				
Entry	8	Sale of Used Equipment	1,000				
		(244,500)					

Temporary Investments

Entry	7	Beginning Balance	75,000				
		Investments	10,000				
		(85,000)					

State Appropriations Receivable

Entry	1	Beginning Balance	100,000	Entry	2	Cash Received	100,000
		Appropriation	16,500				
		(16,500)					

Construction in Progress

Entry 10	Beginning Balance	50,000	Entry 11	Transfer to Investment	
	Payments	50,000		in Plant	50,000
	(50,000)				

Notes Payable

		Beginning Balance	10,000
		(10,000)	

Bonds Payable

Entry 11	Transfer to Investment in Plant	50,000	Entry 5	Beginning Balance Issuance of Bonds	100,000 100,000
				(150,000)	

Unexpended Plant Funds Balances

Entry 4	Plant Additions	16,000		Beginning Balance	200,000
Entry 9	Return of State		Entry 1	State Appropriations	16,500
	Appropriation	500	Entry 3	Gift	15,000
			Entry 6	Transfer from Current Funds	20,000
			Entry 8	Sale of Used Equipment	1,000
				(236,000)	

D. Balance Sheet at End of Period

BLANK COLLEGE

BALANCE SHEET
(End of Period)

ASSETS		LIABILITIES AND FUND BALANCES	
PLANT FUNDS:		PLANT FUNDS:	
Unexpended Plant Funds:		Unexpended Plant Funds:	
Cash	244,500	Notes Payable	10,000
Temporary Investments	85,000	Bonds Payable	150,000
Appropriations Receivable	16,500	Unexpended Plant Funds	
Construction in Progress	50,000	Balances[1]	236,000
Total Unexpended Plant Funds	396,000	Total Unexpended Plant Funds	396,000

[1]Subsidiary Accounts:

Fund A--Green Hall	45,000
Fund B--Smith Hall	35,000
Fund C--Science Laboratory	155,000
Fund X--Undesignated	1,000
Total	236,000

E. Statement of Changes in Fund Balances

BLANK COLLEGE

STATEMENT OF CHANGES IN FUND BALANCES
UNEXPENDED PLANT FUNDS
FOR THE YEAR ENDED 19___

Balances, Beginning of Year	200,000
Additions:	
State Appropriations	16,500
Gifts	15,000
Transfers from Current Funds	20,000
Sale of Used Equipment	1,000
	52,500
Deductions:	
Expenditures for Plant Facilities	16,000
Return of Unused State Appropriation	500
	16,500
Balances, End of Year	236,000

A. Balance Sheet at Beginning of Period

BLANK COLLEGE

BALANCE SHEET
(Beginning of Period)

ASSETS		LIABILITIES AND FUND BALANCES	
PLANT FUNDS:		PLANT FUNDS:	
Funds for Renewals and Replacements:		Funds for Renewals and Replacements:	
Cash	10,000	Renewals and Replacement	
Temporary Investments	90,000	Funds Balances[1]	100,000
		Total Funds for Renewals and	
Total Assets	100,000	Replacements	100,000

[1]Subsidiary Accounts:

Fund A--Dormitory System	60,000	
Fund B--Food Services Equipment	10,000	
Fund C--Instructional Equipment	30,000	
Total	100,000	

B. Recording of Typical Transactions

	GENERAL LEDGER		SUBSIDIARY LEDGER	
	Dr.	Cr.	Dr.	Cr.
1. Entry to record annual transfer from Dormitory System and Food Services (Cash Receipts Journal):				
Cash	25,000			
Renewals and Replacements Funds Balances		25,000		
In Renewals and Replacements Funds Ledger:				
Fund A--Dormitory System				20,000
Fund B--Food Services Equipment				5,000
(In Unrestricted Current Funds, debit Expenditures and credit Cash. Also, charge operating accounts of respective Auxiliary Enterprises.)				
2. Entry to record transfer from Unrestricted Current Funds for Replacement of Instructional Equipment (Cash Receipts Journal):				
Cash	10,000			
Renewals and Replacements Funds Balances		10,000		
In Renewals and Replacements Funds Ledger:				
Fund C--Instructional Equipment				10,000
(In Unrestricted Current Funds, debit Transfers to Funds for Renewals and Replacements and credit Cash.)				
3. Entry to record disbursement of Funds for Renewals and Replacements (Check Register):				
Renewals and Replacements Funds Balances	10,000			
Cash		10,000		
In Renewals and Replacements Ledger:				
Fund A--Dormitory System			8,000	
Fund B--Food Services			1,000	
Fund C--Instructional Equipment			1,000	

	GENERAL LEDGER		SUBSIDIARY LEDGER	
	Dr.	Cr.	Dr.	Cr.
4. Entry to record receipt of income from Temporary Investments (Cash Receipts Journal):				
Cash	4,500			
Renewals and Replacements Funds Balances		4,500		
In Renewals and Replacements Funds Ledger:				
Fund A--Dormitory System				2,700
Fund B--Food Services				450
Func C--Instructional Equipment				1,350
5. Entry to record sale of Temporary Investments at profit (Cash Receipts Journal):				
Cash	3,000			
Temporary Investments		2,800		
Renewals and Replacements Funds Balances		200		
In Renewals and Replacements Funds Ledger:				
Fund A--Dormitory System				120
Fund B--Food Services				20
Fund C--Instructional Equipment				60

C. General Ledger--Renewals and Replacements Funds Section

Cash

	Beginning Balance	10,000	Entry	3	Payments	10,000
Entry 1	Transfer from Auxiliaries	25,000				
Entry 2	Transfer from Current Funds	10,000				
Entry 4	Investment Income	4,500				
Entry 5	Gain--Sale of Investments	3,000				
	(42,500)					

Temporary Investments

Beginning Balance	90,000	Entry	5	Sale of Investments	2,800
(87,200)					

Renewals and Replacements Funds Balances

Entry 3	Payments	10,000			Beginning Balance	100,000
			Entry	1	Transfer from Auxiliaries	25,000
			Entry	2	Transfer from Current Funds	10,000
			Entry	4	Investment Income	4,500
			Entry	5	Sale of Investments	200
					(129,700)	

D.   Balance Sheet at End of Period

BLANK COLLEGE

BALANCE SHEET
(End of Period)

ASSETS		LIABILITIES AND FUND BALANCES	

PLANT FUNDS:
  Funds for Renewals and Replacements:
		PLANT FUNDS:
		  Funds for Renewals and Replacements:	

Cash	42,500	Renewals and Replacements Funds	
Temporary Investments	87,200	Balances[1]	129,700
Total Funds for Renewals and Replacements	129,700	Total Funds for Renewals and Replacements	129,700

[1]Subsidiary Accounts:

Fund A--Dormitory System	74,820
Fund B--Food Services Equipment	14,470
Fund C--Instructional Equipment	40,410
Total	129,700

E.   Statement of Changes in Fund Balances

BLANK COLLEGE

STATEMENT OF CHANGES IN FUND BALANCES
FUNDS FOR RENEWALS AND REPLACEMENTS
FOR THE YEAR ENDED 19__

Balances, Beginning of Year	100,000
Additions: Transfers from Current Funds	10,000
Transfers from Auxiliary Enterprises	25,000
Investment Income	4,500
Net Gain--Sale of Investments	200
	139,700
Deductions: Expenditures	10,000
Balances, End of Year	129,700

A.   Balance Sheet at Beginning of Period

BLANK COLLEGE

BALANCE SHEET
(Beginning of Period)

ASSETS		LIABILITIES AND FUND BALANCES	

PLANT FUNDS:
  Funds for Retirement of Indebtedness:
		PLANT FUNDS:
		  Funds for Retirement of Indebtedness:	

Cash	50,000	Retirement of Indebtedness	
Temporary Investments	200,000	Funds Balances[1]	250,000
Total Funds for Retirement of Indebtedness	250,000	Total Funds for Retirement of Indebtedness	250,000

[1]Subsidiary Accounts:

Fund A--Dormitory System	150,000
Fund B--Science Center	100,000
Total	250,000

B. Recording of Typical Transactions

	GENERAL LEDGER		SUBSIDIARY LEDGER	
	Dr.	Cr.	Dr.	Cr.
1. Entry to record receipt of debt service payment covering Dormitory System bonds (Cash Receipts Journal):				
Cash	8,000			
Retirement of Indebtedness Funds Balances		8,000		
In Retirement of Indebtedness Funds Ledger (Cash Receipts):				
Fund A--Dormitory System				8,000
(In Unrestricted Current Funds, debit Expenditures and credit Cash. Also, debit Dormitory System operating accounts.)				
2. Entry to record receipt of debt service payment covering Science Center bonds (Cash Receipts Journal):				
Cash	6,000			
Retirement of Indebtedness Funds Balances		6,000		
In Retirement of Indebtedness Funds Ledger (Cash Receipts):				
Fund B--Science Center				6,000
(In Unrestricted Current Funds, debit Transfers to Funds for Retirement of Indebtedness and credit Cash.)				
3. Entry to record payment of debt service on bonds (Interest $2,000; principal $10,000) (Check Register):				
Retirement of Indebtedness Funds Balances	12,000			
Cash		12,000		
In Retirement of Indebtedness Funds Ledger (Vouchers):				
Fund A--Dormitory System			7,000	
Fund B--Science Center			5,000	
(In Investment in Plant Section, debit Bonds Payable and credit Net Investment in Plant $10,000.)				

C. General Ledger--Funds for Retirement of Indebtedness Section

Cash

	Beginning Balance	50,000	Entry	3	Payment of Debt Service	12,000
Entry	1	Transfer from Auxiliary Enterprises	8,000				
Entry	2	Transfer from Current Funds	6,000				
	(52,000)						

Temporary Investments

Beginning Balance	200,000	
(200,000)		

Retirement of Indebtedness Funds Balances

Entry 3 Payment of Debt Service	12,000	Beginning Balance	250,000
		Entry 1 Transfer from Auxiliary Enterprises	8,000
		Entry 2 Transfer from Current Funds	6,000
		(252,000)	

D. Balance Sheet at End of Period

BLANK COLLEGE

BALANCE SHEET
(End of Period)

ASSETS		LIABILITIES AND FUND BALANCES	
PLANT FUNDS:		PLANT FUNDS:	
Retirement of Indebtedness Funds:		Retirement of Indebtedness Funds:	
Cash	52,000	Retirement of Indebtedness Funds Balances[1]	252,000
Temporary Investments	200,000		
Total Retirement of Indebtedness Funds	252,000	Total Retirement of Indebtedness Funds	252,000

[1]Subsidiary Accounts:

Fund A--Dormitory System	151,000
Fund B--Science Center	101,000
Total	252,000

E. Statement of Changes in Fund Balances

BLANK COLLEGE

STATEMENT OF CHANGES IN FUND BALANCES
FUNDS FOR RETIREMENT OF INDEBTEDNESS
FOR THE YEAR ENDED 19__

Balances, Beginning of Year	250,000
Additions:	
Transfers from Current Funds	6,000
Transfers from Auxiliary Enterprises	8,000
	264,000
Deductions:	
Bonds Retired	10,000
Bond Interest Paid	2,000
	12,000
Balances, End of Year	252,000

A.   Balance Sheet at Beginning of Period

BLANK COLLEGE

BALANCE SHEET
(Beginning of Period)

ASSETS		LIABILITIES AND FUND BALANCES	
PLANT FUNDS: Investment in Plant:		PLANT FUNDS: Investment in Plant:	
Land	100,000	Net Investment in Plant:	
Buildings	1,500,000	From State Appropriations	1,700,000
Improvements other than		From Gifts	150,000
Buildings	150,000	From Current Funds	250,000
Equipment	350,000		
Total Invested in Plant	2,100,000	Total Invested in Plant	2,100,000

B.   Recording of Typical Transactions

	GENERAL LEDGER		SUBSIDIARY LEDGER	
	Dr.	Cr.	Dr.	Cr.
1. Entry to record receipt of parcel of land as a gift (Journal Voucher):				
Land (at appraised value)	1,000			
Net Investment in Plant		1,000		
In Plant Ledger (Journal Voucher):				
Individual Asset Account			1,000	
2. Entry to record receipt of used furniture as a gift (Journal Voucher):				
Equipment (at nominal value)	1			
Net Investment in Plant		1		
In Plant Ledger (Journal Voucher):				
Individual Asset Account			1	
3. Entry to record sale of bonds for construction of dormitory:				
(In Unexpended Plant Funds, debit Cash and credit Bonds Payable $100,000.)				
4. Entry to record transfer of construction in progress on building financed by bond issue:				
Construction in Progress	50,000			
Bonds Payable		50,000		
(In Unexpended Plant Funds, debit Bonds Payable and credit Construction in Progress $50,000.)				
5. Entry to record sale of truck costing $3,000 for $1,000 (Journal Voucher):				
Net Investment in Plant	3,000			
Equipment		3,000		
In Plant Ledger (Journal Voucher):				
Individual Asset Account				3,000
(In Unexpended Plant Funds, debit Cash and credit Unexpended Plant Funds Balances $1,000.)				

	GENERAL LEDGER		SUBSIDIARY LEDGER	
	Dr.	Cr.	Dr.	Cr.
6. Entry to record abandonment of old building (Journal Voucher):				
Net Investment in Plant	50,000			
Buildings		50,000		
In Plant Ledger (Journal Voucher):				
Individual Asset Account				50,000
7. Entry to record value of equipment reported by department heads as being lost, destroyed, or otherwise disposed of:				
Net Investment in Plant	10,000			
Equipment		10,000		
In Plant Ledger (Journal Voucher):				
Individual Asset Account				10,000
8. Entries to record capitalization of expenditures made out of Current Funds, Unexpended Plant Funds, and Funds for Renewals and Replacements (Journal Voucher):				
a. From Current Funds:				
Equipment	60,000			
Net Investment in Plant		60,000		
In Plant Ledger:				
Individual Asset Accounts			60,000	
(In Unrestricted Current Funds, debit Expenditures and credit Cash.)				
b. From Unexpended Plant Funds:				
Land	5,000			
Improvements Other Than Buildings	11,000			
Net Investment in Plant		16,000		
In Plant Ledger:				
Individual Asset Accounts			16,000	
(In Unexpended Plant Funds, debit Unexpended Plant Funds Balances and credit Cash.)				
c. Renewals and Replacements Funds:				
Equipment	10,000			
Net Investment in Plant		10,000		
In Plant Ledger:				
Individual Asset Accounts			10,000	
(In Renewals and Replacement Funds, debit Renewals and Replacements Funds Balances and credit Cash.)				
9. Entry to record retirement of some of the bonds (Journal Voucher):				
Bonds Payable	10,000			
Net Investment in Plant		10,000		
(In Retirement of Indebtedness Funds, debit Retirement of Indebtedness Funds Balances and credit Cash.)				

C. General Ledger--Investment in Plant Section

Land

Entry 1	Beginning Balance Gift (at appraised value)	100,000 1,000		
Entry 8b	Purchased from Plant Funds	5,000		
	(106,000)			

Buildings

Beginning Balance	1,500,000	Entry 6	Abandonment of Old Building	50,000
(1,450,000)				

Improvements Other Than Buildings

Entry 8b	Beginning Balance Purchased from Plant Funds	150,000 11,000	
	(161,000)		

Equipment

	Beginning Balance	350,000	Entry 5	Sale of truck	3,000
Entry 2	Gift (at nominal value)	1	Entry 7	Write Off	10,000
Entry 8a	Purchased from Current Funds	60,000			
Entry 8c	Purchased from Renewals and Replacements Funds	10,000			
	(407,001)				

Construction in Progress

Entry 4	Progress Payment	50,000	
	(50,000)		

Bonds Payable

Entry 9	Bonds Retired	10,000	Entry 4	Progress Payment	50,000
				(40,000)

Net Investment in Plant

Entry 5	Sale of Truck	3,000		Beginning Balance	2,100,000
Entry 6	Abandonment of Old Building	50,000	Entry 1	Gift of Land	1,000
			Entry 2	Gift of Furniture	1
Entry 7	Equipment Written Off	10,000	Entry 8a	Expenditures from Current Funds	60,000
			Entry 8b	Expenditures from Unexpended Plant Funds	16,000
			Entry 8c	Expenditures from Renewals and Replacement Funds	10,000
			Entry 9	Retirement of Bonds	10,000
				(2,134,001)	

D. Balance Sheet at End of Period

BLANK COLLEGE

BALANCE SHEET
(End of Period)

ASSETS		LIABILITIES AND FUND BALANCES	
PLANT FUNDS:		PLANT FUNDS:	
Investment in Plant:		Investment in Plant:	
Land	106,000	Bonds Payable	40,000
Buildings	1,450,000	Net Investment in Plant:	
Improvements Other Than		From State Appropriations	1,668,000
Buildings	161,000	From Current Funds	315,000
Equipment	407,001	From Gifts	151,001
Construction in Progress	50,000		
			(2,134,001)
Total Investment in Plant	2,174,001	Total Investment in Plant	2,174,001

E. Statement of Changes in Fund Balances

BLANK COLLEGE

STATEMENT OF CHANGES IN NET INVESTMENT IN PLANT
FOR THE YEAR ENDED 19___

Balances, Beginning of Year	2,100,000
Additions:	
Gifts of Plant Assets	1,001
Amounts Expended From:	
Unrestricted Current Funds	60,000
Unexpended Plant Funds	16,000
Funds For Renewals and Replacements	10,000
Funds For Retirement of Indebtedness	10,000
	2,197,001
Deductions:	
Disposal of Plant Assets	63,000
Balances, End of Year	2,134,001

CHAPTER XIII

Physical Plant Inventory

MANY COLLEGES AND universities which have up-to-date accounting systems do not have perpetual inventory systems for the fixed assets of their plant funds. This neglect seems to stem from a tendency on the part of institutional organizations to disregard values in the form of tangible assets. No question is raised as to the necessity of accounting accurately for receivables, payables, and cash, but frequently doubt is expressed as to the value of a systematic accounting for plant assets.

Several reasons are offered to explain the failure to include plant assets in the institutional record-keeping system. One is the rapid growth in the size of colleges and universities, accompanied by a corresponding expansion in physical plant. Because the staff of the business office does not grow proportionately, it is forced to leave some work undone, and so neglects the inventory of plant assets. Also, after a college or university becomes relatively large, time, effort, and the expenditure of funds are required to establish a plant inventory; therefore, it may be difficult to convince governing boards of the necessity of installing accounting controls over plant assets. Furthermore, the size and value of the physical plant have no immediate or direct bearing on the financing of the institution. Cash, receivables, and payables are current, and by nature demand a current accounting. Physical plant assets, representing funds already invested, are easily ignored.

Advantages of Plant Inventory Systems. The advantages of physical plant accounting and adequate inventories of plant assets are recognized by many institutions. Inventory control through the accounting system serves several practical purposes. A current record of investment in plant is justified on the grounds that one of the purposes of the accounting system is to accumulate all financial information concerning the institution. Without currently recording those transactions representing additions to or deductions from the physical plant, the financial history of the institution is incomplete. Also, the maintenance of a current account of plant investment obviates the necessity of taking a complete physical inventory of equipment each year and of having costly appraisals made of such items as land and buildings.

Another purpose of inventory control of plant assets is to fix responsibility for the custody and use of institutional property. In setting up the plant records by departments, the responsibility for the safekeeping of property is localized in department heads. With their aid and cooperation, physical checks can be made frequently to prove both the accuracy of the accounting records and the existence of the assets. When plant items, especially equipment, are purchased, even though charged to departmental budgets, they should be considered institutional property, not departmental property. If property is no longer needed by the department for which it was originally purchased, yet no provision has been made whereby this equipment can be transferred to other departments, a needless expenditure of institutional funds results in the purchase of more equipment of the same kind. The chief business officer should be given authority over the use and disposition of all institutional property regardless of its location. Classroom property, buildings, and other property of general usefulness should be placed under the custodianship of the director of physical plant.

An inventory system also provides information valuable for administrative purposes. As suggested, it enables the purchasing agent to utilize more efficiently existing property and avoid the purchase of duplicate equipment. Such a system assists the administration in determining the needs of an institution over a long period of time as regards maintenance and upkeep costs of plant assets, as well as replacement requirements of equipment and buildings. It helps the administration in reviewing the departmental requests for new equipment. It enables the purchasing agent to take advantage of savings resulting from quantity trade-ins of old equipment. Equipment and building inventory records are useful in determining the extent of losses in case of fire or theft and in establishing values for recovery. Finally, adequate records and inventories of plant assets are useful in the work of periodically adjusting insurance values in the light of major changes in price levels.

Classification of Plant Assets. The plant assets of educational institutions may be classified according to the following outline:

1. Land

2. Buildings
   a. Educational
   b. Organized activities relating to instruction
   c. Auxiliary enterprises
   d. Service activities

3. Improvements other than buildings
   a. Athletic field and recreational areas
   b. Gas system
   c. Gateways
   d. Lighting systems
   e. Heating and air conditioning systems
   f. Plantings and landscaping
   g. Roads, streets and sidewalks and parking facilities
   h. Sewer and storm drainage systems
   i. Water supply systems

4. Equipment
   a. Aircraft
   b. Athletic and recreational
   c. Automotive
   d. Building and general plant
   e. Cleaning and laundry
   f. Instructional and research
   g. Household
   h. Hospital
   i. Library books, slides and documents
   j. Library equipment
   k. Livestock
   l. Office furniture and equipment

Each of these subdivisions can be broken down further; for example, office furniture and equipment can be divided into desks, chairs, typewriters, adding machines, and filing equipment.

Valuation of Plant Assets. The basis for valuing plant assets for inventory purposes generally is either original cost (plus additions and minus abandonments at cost), or appraisals. Sometimes a combination of the two methods is used in which original valuations are established by appraisals, and subsequent additions are recorded at cost and deductions at either the appraised value or at cost. This last plan is resorted to when inventories must be determined long after the original acquisition of the property items. Property obtained through gift should be valued by the appraisal method. Whenever the appraisal method is used, this fact should be disclosed in all financial records and reports.

Ordinarily, original cost is the recommended basis for the valuation of educational property. Original cost is the outlay required to obtain plant fund items in condition ready for use. Thus, in ascertaining the cost of land, all the following items should be added to the invoice or contract price: assessments, taxes and fees, or commissions necessary to obtain the land; conveyances and notarial fees; and the cost of demolishing old buildings, grading or otherwise clearing the land. In case of buildings, cost includes all payments to contractors, taxes and fees, or commissions, as well as the cost of all permanent fixtures and appliances installed as a part of the buildings. If the building is constructed by the institution with borrowed funds, interest paid during the construction period should be included in determining cost. Similar elements of cost are included in the purchase or construction of improvements other than buildings.

Items of equipment also would be valued at total cost of acquisition. In the case of mechanical equipment, original cost includes cost necessary to install, test, or otherwise prepare the machine for operation.

In regard to equipment, it is necessary to establish more or less rigid rules as to which items will be added to the inventory records and which will be excluded. Many items, such as desks, typewriters, and automobiles clearly should be inventoried; but other items, such as laboratory slides and glassware, and minor replacement items may present problems. As a rule, the cost and probable serviceable life of equipment items are the two factors used in determining whether or not a specific piece of equipment should be taken into the equipment inventory records. Most institutions exclude items of small original cost value, e.g., those ranging in cost from $5 to $50 or even $100 and those having a probable useful life of less than two years. Elements of cost and length of life must be considered together in deciding whether or not items of equipment are to be inventoried. In any event, it is necessary to establish working rules, and it is desirable to make these rules known to department heads and all those concerned with the inventory of equipment and plant asset accounting.

In the case of certain types of equipment, such as furniture and linen for dormitory rooms, and china and glassware for dining halls, the practice sometimes is followed of inventorying the original equipment but charging replacements to current expense. This is justified on the grounds that average loss through breakage should be replaced each year as a charge to current operations, so that the original equipment inventory possesses a fixed value.

Library books create no particular problem from the accounting viewpoint, since they are recorded at cost. The same rule applies to microfilms and binding of periodicals. Where volumes and materials are removed, discarded, lost, or stolen, adjustments should be made in the library records. In most institutions, the details of the inventory are kept in the library, the business office maintaining only control accounts.

In the case of equipment manufactured on the campus, the approved procedure is to accumulate, through the cost system (see chapter 14), all costs of constructing the equipment and to bring it into inventory at such cost.

Depreciation of Fixed Assets. Closely related to the valuation of fixed assets is the question of depreciation. Authorities in the field of educational finance generally are agreed on the following points:[1]

1. The principles of depreciation accounting essential to proper accounting and financial reporting in commercial and business organizations do not apply to nonprofit educational institutions.

[1] *College and University Business Administration,* 285.

2. Some colleges and universities employ a procedure to which the term "depreciation accounting" is applied, but which is in reality the provision of funds for future renewal, replacement, or expansion of plant facilities. The distinction between "depreciation accounting" and providing for renewals, replacements, and the expansion of plant assets should be clearly recognized so that the practices employed by educational institutions and the ensuing transactions can be properly identified, classified, and reported.

3. If the financial program of an educational institution provides for the setting aside of funds for the renewal, replacement, and expansion of educational plant assets, the process should be recognized as such and should not be considered as "depreciation accounting."

4. "Depreciation accounting" as found in commercial and business organizations is not recommended for plant used by auxiliary enterprises. If the financial program of the institution provides for setting aside funds from the revenues of auxiliary enterprises for the replacement of plant facilities and assets, such provision may be based on equivalent depreciation computed in accordance with generally accepted practices, or it may be based on the anticipated replacement costs of the assets, adjusted in accordance with the recognized price index. Such provision should be identified as funds for renewals and replacements, not as depreciation. The annual additions to such funds should be shown in the Statement of Changes in Fund Balances—Funds for Renewals and Replacements. Cash or other liquid assets must be transferred from current to plant funds and reported in the Funds for Renewals and Replacements group.

5. Depreciation concepts and accounting should be followed in the case of real properties, except land, held as investments of endowment funds. Funded reserves for the accumulated depreciation charges should be established by the transfer of cash from the revenues of endowment properties and reported in the Endowment and Similar Funds portion of the Balance Sheet. The asset values of property should be reported net of the amount of such depreciation reserves.

Establishment of Inventory of Plant Assets. The initial step in establishing a perpetual inventory system for plant assets in an institution not having an inventory is to classify all properties in the manner described above and, with the assistance of department heads and the director of physical plant, to locate, count, and value all items of the physical plant. Various problems arise in inventorying each of the four classes of assets—land, buildings, improvements other than buildings, and equipment. Inventorying the land begins with obtaining and filing deeds to the land. Maps should be drawn showing the location and boundaries of each parcel of land owned. Other items of information necessary to establish the inventory of land are: original cost of the land, cost of subsequent additions or improvements, means of financing the original purchase, and date of acquisition. Form 13.1 is a suggested record for parcels of land owned. One card is prepared for each tract of land, each tract being indexed by number to the map.

In the case of buildings, some of the more important items of information to be gathered for each building are: the type of construction, the year of completion, the names of the architect and construction company, the gross and net square feet of floor space, the cubic footage, detailed floor plans showing the number and location of all utility outlets, the cost or appraisal value, and the source of funds used in acquiring the building. Photographs of the building, also showing adjoining structures or improvements, are a useful addition to the buildings section of the plant ledger. Similar information should be obtained for each improvement other than buildings. Form 13.1 will also serve as a perpetual inventory record for buildings and for improvements other than buildings.

Two points should be noted in connection with the establishment of inventories for plant assets. First, most of the responsibility for constructing the inventories should be placed in the business office. However, the director of physical plant can be of valuable assistance in this work. Second, in many cases the original cost method is not practicable because of lack of documentary information concerning costs. In such cases, the appraisal method must be employed to establish beginning inventory values.

The equipment inventory can be taken best with the assistance of department heads. Form 13.2 is a type of tabulation sheet used to accumulate the inventory data. It is filled in by the department head, then sent to the business office for a determination of values.

FORM 13.1

```
┌──────────────────────────────────────────────────────────────────┐
│                          BLANK COLLEGE                             │
│            R E A L    P R O P E R T Y    L E D G E R               │
│             (Land, Buildings, and Improvements)                    │
├──────────────────────────────────────────────────────────────────┤
│                                        Plant Book                  │
│ Description_____     Page No.       _____    │
│ _____     Land No.        _____    │
│ _____     Building No.    _____    │
│ _____     Improvement No._____    │
│ Location   _____                     _____    │
│ Size       _____                     _____    │
├──────────────────────────────────────────────────────────────────┤
│ Type of Deed _____ Date_____    If Gift, Exact Conditions    │
│                                        Donor_____ Date_____    │
│ Recorded _____ Vol._____ No.____    Purpose_____     │
├──────────────────────────────────────────────────────────────────┤
│      Cost     │  Valuation Data   │       Insurance                │
│ Date__ Amount__│ Date__ Amount____│ Date__ Amount____             │
│ Date__ Amount__│ Date__ Amount____│ Date__ Amount____             │
├──────────────────────────────────────────────────────────────────┤
│ Type of Construction _____     Completed Year_____            │
│ Name of Architect    _____     Square Feet _____             │
│ Construction Company _____     Cubic Feet  _____             │
├──────┬──────────────────┬────┬────────┬────────┬────────┤
│ Date │   Description    │Ref.│ Debits │ Credits│ Balance│
│      │                  │    │        │        │        │
└──────┴──────────────────┴────┴────────┴────────┴────────┘
```

The inventorying of equipment of a general nature, such as classroom furniture, can be assigned either to the departments adjoining the classrooms or to the physical plant department. The inventory of general plant equipment should be prepared by the director of

FORM 13.2

BLANK COLLEGE
MOVABLE EQUIPMENT INVENTORY

Department_____ Date Taken_____

Location_____ Inventory Date_____
    Room   Building

Estimated Life_____
Source of Funds_____ (Years)

College Serial Number	Description Including Name, Model, Size, Mfg. Serial No., and Number on Hand	Date Pur- chased	Condition (Good Fair Poor)	Cost or Ap- praised	Not Needed (Obso- lete)

Prepared By_____ Approved as Correct_____
    (Department Head)

FORM 13.3

BLANK COLLEGE
EQUIPMENT LEDGER CARD

No._____

Description_____
Department_____
Serial No._____ Make_____ Model_____
Date Received_____ P.O. No._____ Life_____

Transfer Record:
Date_____ Department_____ Place_____
Date_____ Department_____ Place_____

Date	Description	Ref.	Additions	Deductions	Balance

physical plant. For certain classes of equipment, check lists may be mimeographed and distributed to department heads for convenience in inventorying. For example, this method is feasible in inventorying the contents of dormitories where the same type of equipment is used in all rooms. Some of the more important information needed for each item of equipment includes the description and location of the article, serial number, make, model, its estimated life, and the source of funds from which purchased. Form 13.3 is an inventory record for movable equipment. For items that can be grouped together conveniently both by nature of the item and by location—such as chairs and tables of the same kind used in a given building—Form 13.4 may be used.

Marking or tagging each item of equipment with an identifying serial number is an important part of inventorying movable equipment. Some institutions employ elaborate systems of codes, one part of the code referring to the department using the equipment and the other part being a number for the equipment. Thus, a typewriter purchased for the business administration department would be marked BA-1. Marking or tagging equipment can be accom-

FORM 13.4

		BLANK COLLEGE					
		GROUP PROPERTY RECORD					

Article_____ Department_____

Description_____ Building_____ Room_____

Date	Ref.	Received		Dropped		Balance	
		Quantity	Value	Quantity	Value	Quantity	Value

plished through the use of one of several methods. Sometimes more than one method should be used because of the type, make, and form of the item. Small metal tags attached to the article are used probably more than any other marking device. Another method is the decalcomania transfer process. Its advantage is that it can be used on a great number of items, presents an attractive appearance, and can be affixed easily, yet it is relatively permanent, and, finally, can be replaced quickly and easily. Other methods of marking are stencils, glass acid, electric stylus, electric etchograph, laundry tags and India ink, and printing and engraving. Some institutions mark only those articles of equipment not identified by a serial number of the manufacturer. In marking equipment, an important rule to follow is that the marking should be accessible for inventory-checking purposes, yet should not interfere with normal use of the equipment. Also, it should not be placed in a position where constant usage of the article will cause deterioration in the tag.

Having established the inventory of plant assets and valued each item of each class through reference to purchase orders, invoices, and other original sources, or by appraisals, the next step is to set up the inventory on cards. The inventory cards for land, buildings, improvements other than buildings, and equipment constitute the plant ledger and are subsidiary to, and must be in agreement with, proper control accounts in the general ledger.

Operation of Perpetual Inventory System. Establishing a physical plant inventory in accordance with the procedure explained above involves considerable work. Its yearly repetition would be prohibitive. Therefore it is necessary to operate the inventory system on a perpetual basis. This may be accomplished through the following procedure under the direction of the purchasing agent. Requisitions, purchase orders, and invoices for plant assets are prepared and recorded the same as for other purchases, the documents flowing through the same channels. The invoices, however, are routed to an inventory clerk who, in small colleges, usually is assigned duties in addition to those of keeping inventory records. When the inventory clerk receives the invoice, he prepares an "addition to property" card (Form 13.5) in duplicate, one copy going to the department head who is to be custodian of the property, the other

FORM 13.5

```
┌─────────────────────────────────────────────────────────────────┐
│                          BLANK COLLEGE                            │
│           A D D I T I O N   T O   P R O P E R T Y                 │
│                                                                   │
│  Type of Property_____  Req. No._____    │
│  Date Purchased_____  P.O. No._____    │
│  Purchased From_____   │
│  Description_____   │
│               _____    │
│               _____    │
│                                                                   │
│  Cost:  Inv. Price        $_____  Department_____   │
│         Extras              _____  Location_____    │
│         Total             $_____  Manufacturer's No._____   │
│                                         College Serial No._____   │
│  Source of Funds_____  Disposed of_____    │
└─────────────────────────────────────────────────────────────────┘
```

being retained in the business office. The business office copy is used to record the purchase of the item in the plant journal (Form 13.6) and later is filed by departments. As the asset is recorded in the journal, it is given a serial number; later this number is attached to the article by one of the methods of marking described above. Deductions from fixed assets, as in the case of trade-ins or abandonments, may be entered in red in the plant journal. The purchase is then posted to the formal inventory cards (Forms 13.1 and 13.3). At

FORM 13.6

			How Acquired		
Date	From Whom Purchased and Type of Fixed Asset	College Serial Number	Current Funds	Plant Funds	Gift

the end of the month, the plant journal is summarized, the summary being posted to the Investment in Plant Section of the Plant Funds group. (See journal entry on page 279.)

The department head is held responsible for reporting to the business office any equipment which is worn out, broken, lost, transferred, or no longer needed by the department. Form 13.7, transfer of equipment, and Form 13.8, disposition of equipment, should be used in connection with adjustments to the perpetual inventory records.

The above procedure not only results in a correct inventory record of moveable equipment, but it also furnishes the business office with information regarding the location of the equipment, the number and value of each type of equipment owned by the institution, and a chronological record of equipment purchases. The additions to property cards, filed by departments, furnish information relative

FORM 13.7

	BLANK COLLEGE	No. 1

T R A N S F E R   O F   E Q U I P M E N T

Date_____

Transferred From_____

Transferred To_____

Item	College Serial Number	Remarks

The above items are no longer in my custody.	Transfer Approved:	I hereby accept the custody of the above items.
_____ Department Head	_____ Business Manager Entered_____ Inv. Clerk	_____ Department Head
Date_____		Date_____

FORM 13.8

BLANK COLLEGE

D I S P O S I T I O N   O F   E Q U I P M E N T

Date_____

The following equipment should be removed from the inventory of

the Department of_____

D e s c r i p t i o n	Inventory Number	Room and Building	Reason For Disposal

Posted:_____   _____
               Inventory Clerk   Head of Department

to the location of each item. The inventory cards, filed by types of fixed assets, afford information relative to the number and value of the articles in the inventory, and the plant journal provides a chronological and numerical listing of all additions to and deductions from investment in plant.

Institutions using electronic data processing equipment can place the entire inventory on tape or disc packs which can be updated as new items are acquired or removed. As a by-product of recording the data, printouts can be produced by departments, which provide all the details necessary to verify that the equipment is on hand.

At least once each year, physical inventories should be taken of all moveable equipment to prove the existence of the institutional equipment and to verify the accuracy of the perpetual inventory records. Another purpose of the physical inventory is to assist in bringing up to date the records regarding the present condition of the equipment. Some institutions require each department head to submit an inventory of equipment under his custody. This list is verified by the accounting office and reconciled with the equipment cards in the plant ledger. Under an EDP system, a hard copy print-out giving appropriate details about all equipment in each department can be produced routinely and sent to the department head for verification.

As an alternate proposal to the detailed inventory system previously discussed, some institutions have developed equipment inventory systems that are adequate and yet cost considerably less in terms of maintenance than the detailed system mentioned above. One technique employs the use of a wide-angle lens camera to photograph the entire contents of a room or equipment cabinet. The pictures can be used to identify each item in the room and in the entire building. Identification is achieved by including in each picture a sign showing the name of the building, the room number, and the date of the record. Pictures subsequently can be enlarged to ascertain details of the contents of the room. Costs are obtained from accounting records and these form an acceptable basis of insurance claims.

Where necessary for the computation of indirect cost rates, an institution can document equipment values by reference to lists of items originally purchased and to accounting documents for subsequent purchases. When these lists are accompanied by photographs of the equipment on hand, an audit can determine whether or not the values used in the computation are accurate.

CHAPTER XIV

Cost Accounting

COST ACCOUNTING FOR governmental agencies can be described as "that form of accounting activity which is designed to furnish information concerning the cost of units of services or goods produced. To a large extent, governmental expenditure accounting and statements have been confined to recording and reporting how much was spent; unit cost accounting, on the other hand, is an endeavor to record, measure, and report how much was accomplished and at what price." [1]

In this discussion of college and university accounting systems, attention has been focused primarily on expenditure accounting, not on cost accounting. Two basic considerations differentiate these two types of accounting. First, expenditure accounting is designed primarily to account for cash payments or the incurring of obligations, and cost accounting is concerned with that portion of materials or services which has been consumed. Second, expenditure accounting is concerned with funds paid out without specific reference to the work performed, whereas cost accounting attempts to relate cost to units of work. Moreover, expenditure accounting provides for a distribution of costs by departments but does not indicate what has been accomplished by incurring these costs.

It does not follow that expenditure accounting and cost account-

[1] R. M. Milesell and Leon E. Hay, *Governmental Accounting* (3rd ed.; Homewood, Ill.: Richard D. Irwin, Inc., 1961), 619.

ing are mutually exclusive in the college and university system, the differences between the two being a matter of emphasis and degree. Thus, expenditure accounting by departments or budgetary units is closely related to cost accounting in that all costs applicable to a given department are collected in the accounts. However, the emphasis in expenditure accounting is not so much on costs in terms of units of work as on gross expenditures in terms of the budget. An extension of expenditure accounting in the direction of cost accounting is in the allocation of salaries between departmental budgets, primarily to secure a correct determination of departmental costs. The accounting procedure in connection with central storerooms closely approximates cost accounting, in that the chief emphasis is not on the expenditure of funds to acquire supplies but on the consumption of those supplies as withdrawn for use.

Cost accounting developed slowly in governmental agencies in general and in particular in institutions of higher education. Cost accounting in educational institutions involves three definite phases: (1) cost accounting for certain service departments and auxiliary activities, (2) cost accounting for the physical plant department, and (3) cost accounting for instructional activities and programs in terms of the number of students taught.

Cost Accounting for Service Departments and Auxiliary Enterprises. Some of the usual service departments in which cost accounting methods are useful include printing shops, photographic and blueprinting studios, mimeographing and duplicating bureaus, and telephone exchanges. Each of these types of service enterprises has its own peculiar problems of cost analysis and record keeping. In the college printing shop, for example, the same type of job-order cost accounting records are kept as are found in commercial printing establishments. Many auxiliary activities, such as dormitories and dining halls, have the same need of cost records as comparable enterprises owned and operated by private capital. In these instances, reference should be made to the accepted principles of record keeping in the appropriate accounting fields, such as hotel accounting and restaurant accounting.

Cost Accounting for the Physical Plant Department. Several reasons exist for applying the principles of cost accounting to the physical plant department of educational institutions. First, an adequate system of cost accounting helps to prevent waste, theft, and inefficiency. Expenditures for salaries and materials to maintain the physical plant usually constitute a substantial percentage of the annual budget. The work performed in this connection is highly varied. Cost accounting makes possible close scrutiny of labor, materials, and equipment used by relating costs to the work performed. Second, cost accounting aids the administrative offices of educational institutions in the preparation of the budget. Without adequate cost records showing costs of the various jobs and other activities performed by the physical plant department over a period of years, the preparation of that part of the budget relating to plant operation and maintenance is a difficult task. Colleges having no cost records are forced to rely on records of past gross expenditures; this practice leads, in many instances, to continued excessive and uneconomical expenditures. With the aid of cost data, an intelligent program for the operation and maintenance of the physical plant can be established. Third, a cost system helps in the execution of the budget by serving as a guide in formulating policies regarding certain phases of the operation and maintenance of plant. Fourth, an adequate cost system assists in answering such questions as: (1) Should a given job be performed by the college force or by an outside agency? (2) When is it economical to abandon equipment and purchase new? (3) When should equipment be rented rather than purchased? Fifth, since the physical plant department services the entire plant and all departments, both educational and auxiliary, a cost accounting system is necessary if charges for work performed are to be assessed on a meaningful basis. Sixth, cost figures are useful in that they afford a comparison of costs of the various activities over a period of years, as well as comparisons with similar activities in other institutions.

Principles of Cost Accounting for Physical Plant. The physical plant department services auxiliary enterprises, such as dining halls, bookstores, and dormitories. All costs of operating auxiliary enterprises should be accumulated and charged against those agencies. This procedure is based on the assumption that auxiliary enterprises are quasi-business activities and should be operated as is private business, namely, by ascertaining profit or loss on operations. Although in some instances, auxiliary enterprises may not be expected to earn a profit as in private business, normally they should operate without loss to the institution. This requires the assessment of all proper charges against them. This reasoning does not apply to teaching and administrative departments; hence, costs of ordinary plant operation and maintenance, such as janitorial services, repairs to buildings, and utilities, are not charged to these departments. On the other hand, where work of an extraordinary and nonrecurring nature is performed by the physical plant department for instructional departments, the cost of such work is a proper charge against the budget of the departments affected. Thus, the cost of constructing desks, tables, and bookcases, which otherwise would have to be purchased in the open market, should be charged to the equipment budget of the department.

If the principles outlined above are followed, the cost system effects a complete separation between general overhead applicable to academic or instructional departments and that attributable to auxiliary or noninstructional departments. Thus, the net expenditures charged to the various activities of the physical plant department represent the costs of maintaining that portion of the physical plant devoted to instruction and to the administration of instruction. The budget for the various divisions of the physical plant department represents the outlays necessary to operate and maintain the buildings, grounds, and utilities used in the academic and instructional plant and excludes the costs necessary to maintain the auxiliary enterprises and activities.

Two different practices are followed by colleges and universities in keeping cost records. The cost records can be kept in the physical plant department, control accounts being maintained in the central accounting office; or, all cost records can be kept in the central accounting office. In normal circumstances, the former method is preferable and is the one described here.

Classification of Expenditures by Activities. The chart of expenditure accounts given in chapter 4 divides the physical plant department into thirteen subdepartments, each possessing a separate budget. For purposes of cost accounting, each of these subdepartments is classified according to the activities carried on by that department. The following outline is a suggested classification of physical plant expenditures by activities for purposes of cost accounting:

 1. Administration
 2. Janitorial Services
 3. Maintenance of Buildings
 4. Furniture and Equipment Repair
 5. Operation of Grounds
 6. Maintenance of Streets and Drives
 7. General Trucking
 8. Planning and Construction
 9. Fire Protection
10. Utilities
11. Electrical and Mechanical Services
12. Property Insurance
13. Police and Security (if supervised by the physical plant department)

Methods of Cost Accounting. In accounting for costs of the above activities, three different procedures are employed. First, job-order cost accounting is used for those activities whose costs are associated closely with specific jobs or orders. Thus the cost of repairing buildings or furniture, the cost of landscaping a particular part of the campus, or the cost of constructing minor equipment should be accumulated by specific jobs. Second, the cost of some activities, being recurring or continuous in nature, necessitates the employment of a form of cost accounting known as continuous-process costs. Under the continuous-process method, all costs applicable to a specific activity are collected for a given period of time. This method of cost accounting is employed in collecting the costs of operation and maintenance of each building on the campus. Third, certain costs of plant operation and maintenance must be allocated to specific jobs or to operating departments. Thus, in the operation of utilities, it is necessary to apportion costs of heat, electricity, gas, and water to the different buildings, as well as to auxiliary enterprises. General trucking and college automobiles, insurance, and administration of the operation and maintenance department are other examples of costs which must be apportioned.

The following chart lists each activity of the plant operation and maintenance department under the appropriate cost procedure. The discussion of cost accounting which follows is based on this outline.

1. Job-order cost accounting
   a. Special projects under care and maintenance of grounds
   b. Repairs to buildings
   c. Repairs to furniture and equipment
   d. Construction of minor equipment
2. Continuous-process cost accounting
   a. Campus upkeep
   b. Operation of buildings
3. Allocation of costs
   a. Supervision
   b. General overhead
   c. Heat
   d. Electricity
   e. Gas
   f. Water
   g. Sewage
   h. Trucks and automobiles
   i. Property insurance
   j. Police and security

1. *Job-Order Cost Accounting.* All jobs performed by the physical plant department for other departments originate with a formal requisition. This requisition, prepared by the department desiring to have work done, is sent to the purchasing agent. The regular purchase requisition (Form 3.1) may be used for work requests, or a special form may be used. The requisition follows the usual channels—going first to the purchasing agent, then to the accounting office, then back to the purchasing agent, where a work order is issued. In some institutions, certain types of work or jobs costing in excess of a stipulated amount may have to be approved by the chief business officer or other official. The requisitioning department may be required to obtain an estimate of the cost of the job from the physical plant department. If so, the request for estimate (Form 14.1) is prepared by the department head, in triplicate, all copies going to the physical plant department. The latter department estimates the total cost of the job and sends two copies of the estimate

back to the department head. The department head attaches one copy of the estimate to the purchase requisition and forwards it to the purchasing office. Upon receiving the purchase requisition together with attached request for estimate, the purchasing office

FORM 14.1

BLANK COLLEGE
REQUEST FOR ESTIMATE

Date_____

To Director of Physical Plant:

Please prepare an estimate of the cost of the following job:

Quantity	Description	Estimated Price

Work order will be issued for this project by the Purchasing Dept. following confirmation of requisition clearance by the Comptroller.

Please return this form to: ( ) Purchasing Department
        (check one)   ( ) Originating Department

Analysis of Estimated Cost:

Labor $_____

Materials   _____

Equipment   _____

Other   _____

Total $_____

Prepared by:_____
        Director of Physical Plant

Requested for
Department of:_____

Location:_____

Requested by:_____

Approved by:_____

Charge Account:_____

sends the document to the accounting office where it is checked for availability of funds. If funds are available, the purchasing office issues a work order (Form 14.2) to the physical plant department, authorizing the job to be placed in process.

FORM 14.2

BLANK COLLEGE

WORK ORDER

Date_____

Work Order Number

NO. 5485

R_____
Requisition No.

To ┌

This authorizes you to perform the work indicated below for:

────────────
Department

└   ┘

────────────
Building

────────────
Room

Charge Code

Estimated Cost

Partial Liquidations

Estimated Completion Date_____

To_____
        Foreman

Signed_____
            Purchasing Agent

Begin Work_____
        Department Head

Funds Available_____

One copy of the work order is sent to the director of physical plant, one copy to the accounting office, and one copy is retained by the purchasing agent. In some institutions, the department head only roughly estimates the cost of the job, leaving it to the purchasing office to obtain refined estimates from the physical plant department.

The above procedure is generally applicable, but there are two situations which call for deviation from the usual routine. First, many jobs are in the nature of recurring maintenance—such as replacing light bulbs and broken window panes—affecting only the budget of the physical plant department. In such cases, the director of physical plant is authorized to proceed without submitting a formal request to the purchasing agent. Second, many jobs are in the nature of emergencies. The director of physical plant has authority to originate such jobs. In such cases, an informal maintenance order is issued by the director or by one of his subordinate officers or foremen.

Accounting for job costs begins with the approval of the requisition and the work order by the accounting office. The work order is treated like any other order, being encumbered in the usual way.

Encumbrances
    Provision for Encumbrances

Detailed accounting for job costs in the physical plant department begins when the director of physical plant receives his copy of the work order. A job-cost sheet for that particular job is set up in the job-cost ledger (Form 14.3). The function of this ledger is to accumulate the costs of each job so that the efficiency of the job can be measured and the department benefiting from the job may be charged. As shown in the illustration of the job-cost ledger (Form 14.3), costs are accumulated for labor, materials, equipment use, and other (overhead). Some institutions, however, do not allocate overhead and equipment use to jobs.

Labor costs are ascertained from daily, weekly, biweekly, or semi-monthly time reports showing the number of hours of work per day devoted to each particular job and to the usual operation and maintenance activities for which specific jobs are not set up. Form 14.4 illustrates a type of daily time report. These daily time reports are accumulated onto weekly, biweekly, or semimonthly reports, such as the one illustrated in Form 14.5. The time reports are posted as charges against the appropriate jobs in the job-cost ledger. At the end of the payroll period, the physical plant department prepares the regular wage payroll vouchers for operation and maintenance labor. The time indicated on the wage vouchers is checked against the time allocated to various jobs and activities on the weekly, bi-weekly, or semimonthly time reports; if the two reports are in agreement, the payroll vouchers are sent to the accounting office, where checks are drawn in the usual manner. The accounting entry, in journal form, to record the issuance of the labor payroll checks, is:

FORM 14.3

	BLANK COLLEGE					
	J O B C O S T L E D G E R					
				Job No._____		
Department_____		Requisition No._____				
Account_____		Date Ordered_____				
Description of Job_____		To Be Completed_____ Int. Inv. No._____				
_____			Cost Summary			
_____				Estimated	Actual	
_____		Labor	$_____	$_____		
_____		Materials	_____	_____		
_____		Equipment	_____	_____		
		Other	_____	_____		
		Totals	$_____	$_____		
Date	Reference	Labor	Materials	Other		
				Description	Amount	
Totals						

FORM 14.4

```
┌─────────────────────────────────────────────────────────────────────┐
│                           BLANK COLLEGE                               │
│                  D A I L Y   T I M E   R E P O R T                    │
│                                                                       │
│   Group #                                         Date:               │
│                                                                       │
│                    Name                                               │
│                     of                                                │
│                  Employee                                             │
│                                                                       │
│  Description │ M.O. # │ Code │                                        │
│                                                                       │
│                                                                       │
│                                                                       │
│                                                                       │
│                                                                       │
│                                                                       │
│                                                                       │
│                                                                       │
│                                                                       │
│                                                                       │
│                                                                       │
│       I certify that this time report is correct and that the work was│
│   properly performed.                                                 │
│                                                                       │
│                        Supervisor_____        │
└─────────────────────────────────────────────────────────────────────┘
```

Expenditures (For labor chargeable against usual operation and maintenance accounts)
Work in Process (For labor chargeable against specific jobs)

  Cash

  The salaries of foremen and superintendents cannot be charged
directly against particular jobs, hence must be allocated. This allocation is made when the job is completed, as explained later in this
chapter.
  Materials for use on jobs are procured either through direct purchase or from institution storerooms. When acquired through direct

FORM 14.5

BLANK COLLEGE

T I M E   S H E E T

Name_____   Date_____

Employee No._____   Department_____

Day of Month															Total Time	Rate	Amount	Code No.	Description
1	2	3	4	5	6	7	8	9	10	11	12	13	14	15					
16	17	18	19	20	21	22	23	24	25	26	27	28	29	30	31				

Totals Forward

Totals

purchase, the individual job accounts in the job-cost ledger are posted directly from a copy of the invoice. In the central accounting office, the following entry is made:

Work in Process
    Vouchers Payable

When materials are issued to jobs from storerooms, the stores order (Form 14.6) serves as the record of materials used. Each day the storekeeper transmits the stores orders to the physical plant department office where they are checked and posted to the job-cost ledger. They are accumulated until the end of the month and then an interdepartmental invoice is prepared and sent to the accounting office where the following entry is made:

Work in Process
    Stores Inventory

When materials are returned, Form 14.7 is used. Appropriate adjustments are made to the inventory records and credit is given on the job-cost ledger. Stores return orders are accumulated until the end of the month and then forwarded to the accounting office, where the following entry is made:

Stores Inventory
    Work in Process

Materials used on jobs processed in the various maintenance shops, such as carpentry and electrical, are accounted for by the use of the shop material report (Form 14.8).

Overhead expenses, such as salaries of the foremen, charges for the use of institutionally owned equipment, costs of renting equipment (unless rented for specific jobs), and office expenses of the director's office, cannot be related directly to any job, hence must be prorated to jobs on some reasonable basis. As overhead costs are incurred, they are charged to expenditures accounts for administration of the physical plant department in the allocations ledger. As jobs are completed, overhead is allocated on the basis of a fixed per-

BLANK COLLEGE				No. SO 74111
	STORES ORDER			
			Date_____	

Item Number	Quantity	Description	Price		√
			Unit	Total	

Delivered by_____ | Maintenance Order Number | Charge Code_____
Date_____ | | Department_____
Posted by_____ | Work Order Number | Requested by_____
Date_____ | | Received by_____

BLANK COLLEGE				NO. SRO 1638
	STORES RETURN ORDER			
			Date_____	

Item Number	Quantity	√	Description	Price		√
				Unit	Total	

Delivered by_____ | Maintenance Order Number | Credit Code_____
Date_____ | | Department_____
Posted by_____ | Work Order Number | Returned by_____
Date_____ | |

BLANK COLLEGE — S H O P M A T E R I A L R E P O R T — No.			
For_____ Name or Description of Job	Work Order No._____ Maint. Order No._____ Charge No._____ Date_____		
Quantity	D e s c r i p t i o n	Unit	Total
Approved By:	Received By:		Voucher No.

centage of direct labor cost. The journal entry to record the charging of overhead to jobs is:

Work in Process
    Expenditures (Credit the administration budget of the physical plant department.)

As soon as a job is completed, the director of physical plant determines its cost from the job-cost ledger and prepares an interdepartmental invoice. The interdepartmental invoice (Form 14.9) is prepared in triplicate, one copy being retained in the physical plant department and two copies going to the department for which the work was performed. The department approves the invoice and transmits one copy of it to the accounting office. This copy serves as the basis for the following entry:

Expenditures (Charge appropriate departmental account in Allocations Ledger.)
    Work in Process

FORM 14.9

```
┌────────────────────────────────────────────────────────────────────────┐
│                          BLANK COLLEGE                                   │
│         I N T E R D E P A R T M E N T A L    I N V O I C E               │
│                                         Date_____             │
│  Credit Department of_____     │
│                         Rendering Service or Furnishing Material         │
│  Charge Department of_____     │
│                          Receiving Service or Material                   │
├──────────────────────────────────────────────────────────┬─────────────┤
│                    D e s c r i p t i o n                   │   Amount    │
│                                                            │             │
```

Charge: Account	Amount			Credit: Account	Amount
		Posted Charge_____			
		Posted Credit_____			
Service or Materials Received		Approved_____ Auditor		Service Rendered or Materials Delivered	
_____ Head of Dept.				_____ Head of Dept.	
FOR ACCOUNTING OFFICE			Voucher No.		

At this time, the entry encumbering the cost of the job is reversed as follows:

Provision for Encumbrances
    Encumbrances

Some institutions have found it useful to institute a different policy on work orders where the cost is small, say, less than $25, or some other amount fixed by agreement. This kind of order is shown as Form 14.10. A department may initiate a request for service or a repair job simply by calling the physical plant department. This procedure eliminates having to submit a request through the purchasing department and the accounting office prior to the time the work is performed. After the service has been delivered, the low-cost work order (Form 14.10) is completed by filling in the appro-

FORM 14.10

BLANK COLLEGE
Physical Plant Department

L O W - C O S T   W O R K   O R D E R

Charge To:_____   Date_____

Credit To: Physical Plant Dept - Work in Process   Account
                                                         Code_____

A charge is made against your budget for materials and/or services rendered by this department as authorized by telephone call from your department. Authorization for this charge and services requested are shown below.

Authorized by_____

Services Requested_____

_____

_____

_____

Cost:

Labor   _____

Materials_____

Equipment_____

Other   _____

Total Charge_____

Charge: Account	Amount		Credit: Account	Amount
		Posted Charge_____		
		Posted Credit_____		
Authorized by telephone conversation with:		Approved_____ Auditor		
			Director of Physical Plant	

Accounting Office - White
Physical Plant - Green
Department Requesting Service - Pink
Job Cost Accounts - Canary
Job Foreman - Goldenrod

Voucher No.

10401

priate cost information and is forwarded to the accounting office for recording as follows:

Expenditures (Charge appropriate departmental account in Allocations Ledger)
    Work in Process

Observe that for low-cost work, no encumbrance is made. It is assumed that the department will have funds to cover the small amounts involved.

At any time during the year, after all entries have been posted, the Work in Process account in the general ledger should agree with the sum of the individual job accounts in the subsidiary job-cost ledger. The Work in Process account appears in the Unrestricted Current Funds section of the Balance Sheet. Some institutions charge out all jobs, including those in process, at the end of the fiscal year. In such cases, the Work in Process account will show no balance after the entries are made and will not appear on the Balance Sheet.

The following illustration is presented for the purpose of supplementing the preceding discussion of job-cost accounting.

A. Transactions:

1. The department of art requests the physical plant department to construct a table at an estimated cost of $40. A work order (Job 63) is issued to the director of physical plant authorizing him to proceed with the work.

2. A work order (Job 69) is issued to the director of physical plant authorizing him to begin painting the dining hall. The job is estimated to cost $2,000.

3. Payrolls are received in the accounting office which include $20 charged to Job 63 and $1,000 to Job 69.

4. Interdepartmental invoices are received in the accounting office indicating material costs of $21 charged to Job 63 and $460 charged to Job 69.

5. Paint in the amount of $500 is purchased for exclusive use on Job 69.

6. Job 63 is completed. A job-cost voucher is prepared for $42, including $20 for labor, $21 for materials, and $1 for overhead.

B. Entries in Journal Form:

  1. Entry to record issuance of work order for Job Order 63 (Orders Placed and Liquidated Journal)
     Encumbrances   40
       Provision for Encumbrances   40
     In Allocations Ledger:
       Charge Equipment Budget of department of art

  2. Entry to record issuance of work order for Job Order 69 (Orders Placed and Liquidated Journal):
     Encumbrances   2000
       Provision for Encumbrances   2000
     In Allocations Ledger:
       Charge Supplies and Expenses Budget of Dining Hall

  3. Entry to record labor charges on Jobs 63 and 69 (Wage Payrolls):
     Work in Process   1020
       Cash   1020
     In Job-Cost Ledger:
       Charge Job 63 $20 and Job 69 $1000

  4. Entry to record materials from stores used on Jobs 63 and 69 (Interdepartmental Invoices):
     Work in Process   481
       Stores Inventory   481
     In Job-Cost Ledger:
       Charge Job 63 $21 and Job 69 $460

  5. Entry to record purchase of paint for Job 69 (Voucher):
     Work in Process   500
       Vouchers Payable   500
     In Job-Cost Ledger:
       Charge Job 69 $500

 6a. Entry to record allocation of overhead to Job 63 (Journal Voucher):
     Work in Process   1
       Expenditures   1
     In Job-Cost Ledger:
       Charge Job 63 $1

6b. Entry to record completion and invoicing of Job 63 (Journal Voucher):

Expenditures	42
Work in Process	42

In Job-Cost Ledger:
Credit Job 63 $42
In Allocations Ledger:
Charge Equipment Budget of department of art

6c. Entry to liquidate encumbrance on Job 63:

Provision for Encumbrances	40
Encumbrances	40

In Allocations Ledger:
Credit Equipment Budget of department of art

C. Ledger Accounts:

General Ledger

WORK IN PROCESS

(3)	1,020	(6b)	42
(4)	481		
(5)	500		
(6a)	1		
(Balance 1,960)			

STORES INVENTORY

	(4)	481

EXPENDITURES

(6b)	42	(6a)	1
(Balance 41)			

ENCUMBRANCES

(1)	40	(6c)	40
(2)	2,000		
(Balance 2,000)			

PROVISION FOR ENCUMBRANCES

(6c)	40	(1)	40
		(2)	2,000
		(Balance 2,000)	

CASH

	(3)	1,020

VOUCHERS PAYABLE

	(5)	500

Job-Cost Ledger
JOB NO. 63

(3)	20	(6b)	42
(4)	21		
(6a)	1		

JOB NO. 69

(3)	1,000		
(4)	460		
(5)	500		
(Balance 1,960)			

D. Reconciliation of General Ledger Control With Job-Cost Ledger:
   Control account in general ledger—Work in Process $1,960
   Sum of individual job accounts in Job-Cost Ledger $1,960

2. *Continuous-Process Cost Accounting.* Continuous-process cost accounting in educational institutions differs fundamentally in two respects from job-cost accounting. First, the activities for which costs are collected are continuous in nature, hence cannot be subdivided into specific jobs. Second, activities in this category are, for the most part, within the jurisdiction of the physical plant department, hence need not be initiated by means of requisitions to the purchasing agent. There are two important activities for which costs are accounted for in this manner: (1) the ordinary operation of buildings, including janitorial services and supplies, and repairs of a minor nature, and (2) the ordinary operation of grounds, such as cleaning and campus upkeep. Accounting for the costs of continuous activities is accomplished by opening a series of standing job accounts in which the cost of each activity is collected. In the case of buildings, a number of standing job accounts in which the cost of each activity is collected; and also, a number of standing job accounts are set up to collect cost data pertaining to the various types of supplies and activities involved in the operation and maintenance of buildings. To illustrate the extent of the detail that can

be furnished by the cost system, an excerpt from the chart of standing job accounts used by one university is given:

Standing Job Numbers
31. BUILDING OPERATION

31.01	Janitor Labor and Unclassified Supplies (suffix building number)
.0101	Toilet paper (round and oval)
.0102	Paper towels
.0103	Cloth towels (laundry)
.0104	Soap (liquid and bar for hand use)
.0105	Soap (scrubbing) and soap powders
.0106	Powdered cleansers (detergents)
.0107	Sani-flush, lye, etc.
.0108	Sweeping compound and sawdust
.0109	Push brooms, straw brooms, and counter brushes
.0110	Mop handles, mops (cotton, linen, dust)
.0111	Chalk and erasers
.0112	Door mats, sand, and salt
.0113	Roller towels
31.02	Window Washing and Venetian Blind Cleaning, labor and materials (suffix building number)
.0201	Window washing
.0202	Venetian blind cleaning
31.03	Departmental Moving
31.04	Floor Treatment (suffix building number)
.0401	Prepare, seal, and wax wood floors
.0402	Clean, re-treat, and wax sealed floors
.0403	Prepare and wax linoleum floors
.0404	Prepare and seal terrazzo floors
31.05	Operation of Sanitary Cabinets
.0501	Repairs on sanitary cabinets
.0502	Units used
.0503	Credits
31.06	Vacations
31.07	Sickness
31.08	Holidays
31.09	Foremen
31.10	Elevator Operation (suffix building number)
31.11	New Equipment (inventoried)

The chart of standing job accounts for this university, in addition to a section for Building Operation as illustrated above, includes sections for Building Maintenance, Grounds, General Maintenance, Trucks and Cars, Steam Generation, Power Generation, Auxiliary Equipment, Superintendence and Records, Gas, Water Station, Electrical and Mechanical Services, Fire Prevention and Safety, Police and Watchmen, and Administration. By suffixing a building number to each standing job number, cost information of the type described is available for each building on the campus. Ordinarily, this amount of detailing is possible only with the use of EDP systems.

In less elaborate systems, costs are collected by buildings for main items of expense, such as wages of janitors, cleaning and janitorial supplies, minor repairs, and allocation of utility costs and overhead.

At the end of the month, the standing job accounts are closed into the regular operation and maintenance budget accounts.

3. *Allocation of Costs*. Certain costs of the physical plant must be allocated on some reasonable basis to departments or to specific or standing jobs. A method of allocation of the physical plant overhead has been described above. Other costs to be allocated include utilities, trucks and automobiles, and insurance. The problem of utility allocation depends on whether or not the institution operates its own power plant. If so, it is necessary to design the cost system so as to accumulate the costs of the power plant, including overhead and supervision, then to allocate these costs to the various buildings and jobs. If the college does not operate a power plant, the problem is simply one of allocation. The unit to which utility costs are allocated is the building. The best way to determine the amount of the charge to each unit is to install in each building a meter which will show the amount of current used in that building. An alternative method is to prorate the costs on a reasonable basis. Electricity may be allocated on the basis of the relative number of kilowatt hours used in each building. This is determined by three factors: (1) the number of electrical outlets in each building, (2) the number of kilowatts used in each outlet, and (3) the number of hours the building is used. Gas, water, and heat, in the absence of meters, must be allocated on a more or less arbitrary basis, taking into account the number of outlets, the cubic feet of space in the building, and the number of hours the building is used a day or month.

Trucks and automobiles are used by many departments on the campus; thus it is necessary, first, to accumulate the costs of operating and maintaining the vehicles and, second, to allocate the costs to jobs and departments. The usual procedure is to charge all items of expense for operating and maintaining the equipment to a truck and automobile clearing account. These items include gasoline and oil, tires, repairs and replacements, insurance, registration and license plates, and the wages of the truck and car drivers. Theoretically, depreciation also should be included as an item of expense, but as a practical matter it should not be included unless the institution is able to fund the depreciation reserve. An individual equipment record (Form 14.11) is maintained for each piece of equipment. As trucks or automobiles are used, a record is kept of the exact nature of the operations, and summary reports are made daily on a truck report (Form 14.12). The truck report serves as the basis for charging a particular job or department for the use of the truck. The usual method is to allocate the expenses of operating the equipment by means of rental charges. The following entries, in journal form, illustrate the procedure:

1. To record payment of salary of truck driver:
   Expenditures (Charge General Trucking in the Allocations Ledger.)
       Cash

2. To record invoice for truck repairs:
   Expenditures (Charge General Trucking.)
       Vouchers Payable

3. To record withdrawal of gasoline from storeroom:
   Expenditures (Charge General Trucking.)
       Stores Inventory

4. To record use of truck on a specific job:
   Work in Process
       Expenditures (Credit General Trucking.)

5. To record use of truck by college department:
   Expenditures (Charge Departmental Budget.)
       Expenditures (Credit General Trucking).

FORM 14.11

BLANK COLLEGE

I N D I V I D U A L   E Q U I P M E N T   R E C O R D

FOR THE YEAR ENDED JUNE 30, 19____

Equipment No._____   Estimated Salvage Value_____

Motor No._____ Serial No._____   Estimated Life_____

Make_____   Deprec.--Current Year_____

Type_____   Estimated Miles or Hours This Year_____

Date Purchased_____   Rental Rates: Date_____ Rate_____ Per_____

Original Cost_____   Date_____ Rate_____ Per_____

Month	Gasoline		Oil		Repairs	Deprecia- tion	Total Cost	Miles Run	Hours Run	Cost per Mile or Hour	Miles per Gallon	Rental Credits Earned
	Gals.	Amt.	Qts.	Amt.								

FORM 14.12

BLANK COLLEGE			
D A I L Y T R U C K R E P O R T			
Physical Plant Department			
Truck No._____ Rental Rate Per Hour $_____ Date_____19____			
Name of Operator_____ Rate Per Hour $_____			

Description and Place of Work	Hours	Job No.

Entered By_____   _____Foreman

The General Trucking account is a clearing account and should be closed at the end of the year. Over- and under-absorptions of cost can be corrected by adjusting the rental rates.

Application of the accounting methods presented thus far in this chapter results in a complete separation of the cost of maintaining the educational plant and the cost of maintaining the auxiliary plant. As already explained, the physical plant budget is divided into several departments—administration, janitorial services, maintenance of buildings, furniture and equipment repair, operation of grounds, maintenance of streets and drives, general trucking, planning and construction, fire protection, utilities, and electrical and mechanical services, property insurance, and police and security. The budget for each of these departments provides only for the operation and maintenance of that part of the plant devoted to administration and instruction. The cost of maintaining the property used by auxiliary activities is included in the budgets of these activities.

Incomplete Cost Accounting System. The cost system described in the preceding sections of this chapter is complete and detailed and would require considerable personnel to operate it. Many colleges, particularly smaller ones, may be served better by a less elaborate cost system such as the one outlined below.

One of the essential purposes of an institutional cost accounting system is to effect a separation of costs between the maintenance of the academic and the auxiliary plant. In the complete cost system, this is accomplished primarily through job-cost accounting methods. The following procedures are designed to accomplish the same results less elaborately for the small institution:

1. Labor costs are charged to auxiliary enterprises from time sheets similar to the one illustrated in Form 14.5. No attempt is made to relate to particular jobs the work performed by the operation and maintenance department. The only concern is to charge the auxiliary activities for all labor costs involved in work performed in their behalf. This charge is made monthly on interdepartmental transfer vouchers through the following entry:

Expenditures (In Allocations Ledger, charge personal services account of respective auxiliary enterprises.)
    Expenditures (In Allocations Ledger, credit personal services account of the physical plant department.)

2. The cost of materials used by the physical plant department in performing services for auxiliary enterprises is charged directly to the enterprise concerned. This charge is made monthly from storeroom receipts indicating the cost of materials used for auxiliary activities. The following entry is made on an interdepartmental invoice:

Expenditures (In Allocations Ledger, charge individual auxiliary enterprises—supplies and expense accounts.)
    Stores Inventory

3. Utility costs, operation of trucks and automobiles, janitorial services, and insurance are allocated to auxiliary activities in a manner already described in the discussion beginning on page 320. The monthly entry, made on interdepartmental invoices, is as follows:

Expenditures (In Allocations Ledger, charge account of appropriate auxiliary activity.)
    Expenditures (In Allocations Ledger, credit appropriate account of the physical plant department.)

If the above procedure is followed, the costs of operation and maintenance of the physical plant used by the auxiliary enterprises will be clearly separated from the costs of the plant used for educational purposes. Although the cost system, as described, is incomplete, it is simple and achieves at least some of the purposes of a more complete cost accounting system.

Unit Costs of Educational Institutions. The expression of educational costs in terms of the number of students enrolled is the subject of much discussion. Here the advantages of unit costs, when properly determined and interpreted, will be explained, and a procedure for their calculation will be outlined and illustrated.

The determination of unit costs has both advantages and disadvantages. Unit costs, properly computed, are of value in managing educational institutions. Inasmuch as unit costs relate the expenditures of a given course, department, or curriculum to the number of students served in that division, it affords a more satisfactory index of financial performance than do gross expenditures. Various courses of study, departments, or colleges in an institution can be compared to other similar divisions through the use of per-student costs, so that the administration can determine which departments or courses of study are being developed or utilized and which ones need increased allocations. In this connection, unit costs render important assistance to the administration in preparing the annual budget.

Unit cost studies may be used as the basis of planning a reorganization of departments or colleges within an institution. Even more helpful is the use of unit costs in effecting satisfactory coordination between similar institutions within a state system of higher education. Unit costs have been used by accrediting agencies in determining whether a given college should be given an accredited standing. Finally, if used cautiously and judiciously, unit costs may be employed to make comparisons between institutions.

Certain qualifications in the use of unit costs should be noted. Unit costs, in themselves, do not solve financial and administrative problems, nor should they be used as the sole basis or guide for administrative action. Instead, unit costs are only a point of departure in any analysis and should be interpreted in view of all factors concerned. Furthermore, in comparing one department or curriculum with another department or curriculum, the inherent differences in the nature of the instruction in each division should be taken into account. Certain departments or curricula are basically more costly to operate than others; therefore the results reflected in the unit costs should be weighted to allow for such basic difference in costs. If one department has lower unit costs than another, it does not necessarily follow that it is operated more efficiently. The fact that a department has a high unit cost certainly does not in itself justify condemning that department as uneconomical.

One danger in the use of unit costs is that they may be employed without qualification and interpretation. Legislatures and state administrations sometimes attempt to justify a division of funds on the basis of per capita costs at the various state colleges and universities. Frequently, judgments are formed without taking into account the size of the institution or the type and grade of work it performs. A small institution may sometimes show a higher unit cost than a large one because of the relatively large amount of overhead in its budget, which is fixed without regard to enrollment. All attempts to determine per capita costs by general methods or use of totals without proper analysis and interpretation are strongly discouraged.

It should be obvious that all unit cost figures are open to question because of the many assumptions upon which they are necessarily based. It is also obvious that they will change with every shift of enrollment, registration, salary scale, and price level. For that reason, comparisons of unit cost figures, even when these figures have been computed in accordance with the same formulas, should be made only with great caution. Comparisons between institutions are particularly difficult. Comparisons between similar departments of the same institution and between different years for the same department will be of some service. No institution should be without figures of unit expense of instruction, but it should use them only with due regard for their uncertainty and complexity.

Two basic factors are involved in the determination of unit costs—the unit of measure and the expenditures by departments or colleges. The unit of measure most commonly used is the student-credit hour, which is defined as the measure of load represented by one student carrying a one-hour course. Other units that may be employed include the student-enrolled, the student-clock hour, and the semester-credit hour. For the calculation of the unit cost of the institution as a whole, the full-time student equivalent is generally recommended as the unit of measure. A full-time student equivalent is defined as one student taking a normal academic load.

Information on expenditures should be obtained, so far as possible, from the financial records of the institution. The expenditures of a department or a college for purposes of determining unit costs are classified according to the following outline:

1. Departmental or college expenditures, divided into
   a. Salaries
   b. Teaching supplies and expenses
   c. Departmental or college administration (including salaries, clerical help, and office supplies)
2. Overhead, divided into
   a. General administration, student services, staff benefits, and general institutional expense
   b. Library
   c. Physical plant

Unit costs can be determined for each instructor, course, curriculum, department, or college, and, in addition, for each level of student achievement—freshman, sophomore, junior, senior, graduate—and for the institution as a whole. Usually a separate calculation is made for extension courses and for the summer session. The study may cover a semester or an academic year. In any event, it is essential that the enrollment and financial data apply to the same period of time.

Procedure for Calculating Unit Costs. The procedure for calcu-

FORM 14.13

STATEMENT OF STUDENT-CREDIT HOURS			
College, Department, and Subject	1 Students Enrolled	2 Credit-Hour of Course	1 x 2 = 3 Student-Credit Hour
College I Department A Subject 1 Subject 2 Subject 3 Subject 4			
Total for Department			
Department B Subject 1 Subject 2 Subject 3 Subject 4 Subject 5			
Total for Department			
Total for the College			

lating unit costs by departments and colleges is outlined below.[2]

1. *Calculation of Student-Credit Hours by Department and College.* The number of students enrolled for each course offered in the department is listed on Form 14.13. In determining the number of students, two alternative methods may be employed. Under the first method, the number of students enrolled in each class at the end of the third or fourth week may be taken. Under the second method, the average number of students enrolled is calculated by adding the enrollment at the beginning and end of the semester and dividing by two.

Having ascertained the number of students enrolled in each course, the amount of credit which that course offers is obtained from the college catalogue and listed in the proper column on Form 14.13. The student-credit hours for each course are then obtained by multiplying the number of students enrolled by the credit hours. The student-credit hours for the department are obtained by adding the student-credit hours for each course listed under the depart-

[2] The procedures and methods discussed here are based on the most commonly accepted principles governing the computation of unit costs.

ment. The sum of the student-credit hours in the various departments within a college gives the total for the college.

2. *Calculation of the Direct Costs of Instruction in the Department and College.* As indicated, the direct costs for each department or college include teaching salaries, instructional supplies, and divisional administration. Inasmuch as the instructors of a given department devote only a part of their time to teaching, the first step in determining the costs of instruction is the allocation of teaching salaries between the various activities of the instructors, for example, teaching, research, departmental administration, institutional administration (committees, etc.), and public service. Form 14.14, prepared by each instructor, furnishes this information.

The departmental expenditures for salaries are obtained by list-

FORM 14.14

A L L O C A T I O N O F I N S T R U C T O R ' S T I M E		
Name_____ Date_____		
Department_____ College_____		
Record here the percentage distribution of your time to the various services you perform. If services are rendered in more than one department, indicate in the columns provided.		
T y p e o f S e r v i c e	% of Total Time	Other Departments
1. Instruction: Include preparation, lectures, recitations, conferences, laboratory work, and clerical work in connection with instruction.	%	
2. Departmental Administration: Include administrative and committee work for the department.	%	
3. Instructional Administration: Include administrative and committee work for the entire institution.	%	
4. Research: Include studies not connected with teaching work for which no compensation is received other than your regular annual salary.	%	
5. Public Services: Include extension, lectures, field services, professional, advisory and committee services, and editorial and journalistic activities rendered to the public to professional societies and agencies, for which no compensation is received other than your regular annual salary.	%	
	100%	

FORM 14.15

	1	2 3	4 5	6 7	8 9	10 11
			Depart-	Institu-		
Faculty	Salary	Instruction	mental	tional	Research	Public
Members			Adminis-	Adminis-		Services
			tration	tration		Etc.
		% | Amt.	% | Amt.	% | Amt.	% | Amt.	% | Amt.

(Table title: ALLOCATION OF INSTRUCTOR'S SALARIES)

ing each faculty member and prorating his salary on the basis indicated by the individual allocation sheet (Form 14.14). The total departmental expenditures for teaching salaries can be obtained from Column 3 of Form 14.15. If an instructor teaches in more than one department or college, his salary must be prorated accordingly. The departmental expenditure for teaching salaries is then expressed in student-credit hours for that department on Form 14.16.

Expenditures for teaching supplies and expenses may be added to teaching salaries as part of the above process or may be considered

FORM 14.16

TEACHING SALARIES PER STUDENT-CREDIT HOUR

Department and College	1 Amount of Teaching Salaries	2 Student-Credit Hours	1 ÷ 2 = 3 Teaching Salaries per Student-Credit Hour
College I Department A Department B Department C Department D			
Total for College			

as part of departmental administration. Other elements of departmental administration include the portion of instructors' salaries devoted to departmental administration (from Column 5, Form 14.17), stenographic and clerical help, and office supplies. In addition to these direct departmental costs, each department is charged with a share of the expense of administering the whole college. This allocation is made by averaging the results of two prorating factors. First, the ratio of the total of expenditures for college administration to the total of expenditures for the college is applied to the total expenditures for each department to secure the department's share of the college administration. Second, the total of expenditures for the administration of the college is divided by the number of student-credit hours to obtain the amount of administrative expenditures per student-credit hour. This same amount then is applied to each department by multiplying it by the number of student-credit hours in the department.

Form 14.17 shows the costs per student-credit hour of teaching supplies and expenses, departmental administration, and college administration. Combining Forms 14.16 and 14.17 gives the total costs of instruction for the department and the college.

3. *Calculation of overhead.* The procedure up to this point re-

FORM 14.17

	1 Teaching Supplies	2	3 Department Administration	4	5 College Administration	6	7 Total	8
Department and College	Amount	Unit Cost	Amount	Unit Cost	Amount	Unit Cost	Amount	Unit Cost
College I Department A Department B Department C Department D								
Total for College								

COST OF TEACHING SUPPLIES AND EXPENSES, DEPARTMENTAL ADMINISTRATION, AND COLLEGE ADMINISTRATION PER STUDENT-CREDIT HOUR

sults in a reasonably adequate index of departmental and college costs. Many unit cost studies go no further than the calculation of the direct costs of instruction per student-credit hour. If the unit cost analysis is to be complete, however, it is necessary to allocate the institutional overhead to the various departments. This overhead consists of libraries, student services, operation and maintenance of the physical plant, general administration, staff benefits, and general institutional expense. Skipping libraries and operation and maintenance for the moment, the other four functions may have costs allocated on Form 14.18. This form divides the expenditures of these functions into instruction, research, auxiliary enterprises, and other noneducational expenses. Student services includes such items as the office of the dean of men, office of the dean of women, registrar, and placement and are charged without allocation to instructional functions (Column 3, Form 14.18). General administration expenditures, such as the president's office and the business office, are distributed in accordance with their various functions, using the best judgment of each administrative officer as

FORM 14.18

Expenditure	1 Amount	2 3 Instructional Functions		4 5		6 7		8 9		10 11	
				Noninstructional Functions							
				Research		Public Services		Auxiliary Enterprises		Other Noneducational	
		%	Amt.	%	Amt.	%	Amt.	%	Amt.	%	Amt.
Board of Supervisors President's Office Business Manager Auditor Dean of Men Dean of Women Retirement Alumni Commencement											
Totals											

ALLOCATION OF GENERAL ADMINISTRATION, STUDENT SERVICES, STAFF BENEFITS, AND GENERAL INSTITUTIONAL EXPENSE

a guide. Staff benefits can best be allocated to the respective functions by the chief business officer. General institutional expense, such as alumni, commencement, lectures, memberships, and so on, must be allocated in an appropriate manner. The chief business officer should be able to guide the allocation of these expenses where direction is required.

The total sum expended for these four functional expenditures, determined from column 3 on Form 14.18, is allocated to the various departments on Form 14.19. The procedure in allocating these expenditures to departments is the same as the procedure already described for allocating college administration to departments—that is, an average of the budgetary expenditure and the student-credit hour prorating factors. To the four functional expenses allocated to each department is added the portion of salaries of instructors allocated to institutional administration (Column 7, Form 14.15).

Library expenditures are allocated first between instructional, noninstructional, and other activities, on Form 14.20. Then the amount allocated to instruction is distributed to departments on Form 14.21. Either one of two bases may be used for this distribution. The allocation may be proportionate to the extent to which

FORM 14.19

ALLOCATION OF GENERAL ADMINISTRATION, STUDENT SERVICES, STAFF BENEFITS, AND GENERAL INSTITUTIONAL EXPENSE TO DEPARTMENTS					
	1	2	3	4	3 + 4 ÷ 2 = 5
Department and College	Expenditures	Student Credit Hours	Amount Prorated on Basis of		Amount Allocated to Departments
			Expenditures	Student Credit Hours	
College I:					
Department A					
Department B					
Department C					
Department D					
Total for College					

the library facilities are used by students of each department or proportionate to the annual expenditures for books for each department.

FORM 14.20

PERCENTAGE DISTRIBUTION OF USE MADE OF LIBRARY BY VARIOUS SERVICES	
Estimate as accurately as possible the extent to which the library facilities are used by the functions listed below.	
T y p e o f S e r v i c e s	Percentage of Use
1. Instruction of Students	
2. Organized Research	
3. Noninstructional Extension	
4. Public Services	
5. Other	
6. Other	
	100%

FORM 14.21

ALLOCATION OF LIBRARY EXPENDITURES TO DEPARTMENTS		
Department and College	1 Percentage of Use of Library by Department	2 Amount Allocated to Department

College I
    Department A
    Department B
    Department C
    Department D		

Total for College		

Expenditures covering the operation and maintenance of physical plant[3] are allocated on the basis of a plant utilization study, in which two types of information are used—first, the number of hours per week which each classroom, laboratory, and office is used, and second, the number of square feet included in each. These two factors are combined to produce a square-foot hour of use unit. Operation and maintenance expenditures, then, are charged to each department in the proportion in which the square-foot hours of the department bear to the total square-foot hours in the educational plant. Form 14.22 is used to show the allocation of operation and maintenance expenditures to departments.

FORM 14.22

ALLOCATION OF OPERATION AND MAINTENANCE COSTS TO DEPARTMENTS					
Department and College	1 Square Feet	2 Hours Used	1 x 2 = 3 Square-Foot Hours	4 Percentage of Total	5 Amount Allocated
College I					
Department A					
Department B					
Department C					
Department D					
Total for College					

Form 14.23 shows the total allocation to departments of the expenditures for each type of overhead, also the cost for overhead in each department expressed in terms of student-credit hours.

3 If a cost system similar to the one outlined earlier in this chapter is in operation, the expenditures for operation and maintenance as shown by the records will represent the costs of maintaining the instructional and administrative offices and buildings and will exclude any noneducational costs, such as those for the auxiliary enterprises. If a cost system is not in operation, however, it will be necessary to divide the operation and maintenance costs between that portion of the plant devoted to education and that part devoted to auxiliary enterprises before proceeding with the allocation of plant costs to departments.

FORM 14.23

Department and College	COSTS FOR OVERHEAD PER STUDENT-CREDIT HOUR SUMMARY OF FORMS 14.19, 14.21, and 14.22							
	1 Institutional Administration Etc.	2	3 Library	4	5 Operation and Maintenance Plant	6	7 Total Overhead	8
	Amount	Unit Cost	Amount	Unit Cost	Amount	Unit Cost	Amount	Unit Cost
College I								
Department A								
Department B								
Department C								
Department D								
Total for College								

The total of departmental and college expenditures is obtained by adding the total expenditures for salaries (from Form 14.16), the total expenditures for teaching supplies, and (from Form 14.17) the total overhead expenditures allocated to the department (from Form 14.23). The unit cost of the department is determined on Form 14.24 by dividing the total expenditures of the department by the student-credit hours of the department (from Form 14.13).

FORM 14.24

Department and College	COST PER STUDENT-CREDIT HOUR BY DEPARTMENTS AND COLLEGES		
	1 Total Costs	2 Student-Credit Hours	1 ÷ 2 = 3 Cost per Student-Credit Hour
College I			
Department A			
Department B			
Department C			
Department D			
Total for College			

Unit cost for the institution as a whole is calculated by dividing the total departmental and college expenditures for teaching and overhead by the full number of full-time student equivalents. (A student equivalent is found by dividing the total student-credit hours by the normal academic load.) Form 14.25 is used to show unit costs for the entire institution. Cost for the entire institution is also expressed in terms of student-credit hours.

FORM 14.25

SUMMARY OF UNIT COSTS OF ENTIRE INSTITUTION			
College	Student-Credit Hours	Total Cost	Cost Per Student-Credit Hour
College I			
College II			
College III			
College IV			
College V			
College VI			
Total for Institution			
Cost per Full Time Student Equivalents*			

*Total Cost ÷ Full Time Student Equivalents $\dfrac{\text{Student-Credit Hours}}{\text{Normal Load}}$

CHAPTER XV

Internal Control and Audit

INTERNAL CONTROL and internal audit are important phases of the college and university accounting system. The accounting procedures which have been outlined in the preceding chapters are predicated upon an adequate system of internal control. In the chapters on purchasing, expenditures, and income, references were made to the techniques of internal auditing. It remains until now, however, to discuss completely the many aspects of this phase of the fiscal system.

Internal control is defined as the system of procedures, accounting records, methods, and details through which the work of each employee or group of employees is continually checked and verified by the work of some other employee or group of employees without duplication of effort and within the normal flow of operations. According to *College and University Business Administration*, internal control "comprises a plan of organization and the methods and procedures adopted by an institution to safeguard its assets, to check accuracy and reliability of its accounting data, to promote operational efficiency, and to encourage adherence to prescribed policies." [1] It implies that no one employee shall have complete or independent control over all phases of a business transaction; on the contrary, the work is so arranged and the responsibilities so assigned that the work and responsibility of one employee is comple-

1 *College and University Business Administration,* 215.

mentary to that of another and provides an automatic verification of the activities of each. Internal control is to be contrasted with external control which assumes that some outside person or organization provides the means of verifying the work of the staff. It should be emphasized that internal control is aimed not only at prevention of fraud but also at reduction of errors. If errors are made, a good system of internal control provides the means of their automatic and prompt discovery.

Internal audit is part of a complete system of internal control and consists of the deliberate and planned checking by one staff member of the work of other staff members. Internal auditing provides the same type of inquiry into the integrity and correctness of financial transactions as postauditing by an outsider. In larger colleges and universities there is generally found an internal auditing staff whose function it is to maintain a continuous audit on the operations of the business office and all outlying departments conducting affairs of a business nature. The internal auditor is responsible directly to the chief business officer and is as independent as possible of the other institutional business officers. He should have formal training in the principles and techniques of auditing and a thorough knowledge of accounting procedures and practices. He should be a person with considerable judgment and tact. Previous experience in auditing is desirable even though such institutions cannot utilize a full-time auditing department or even a full-time internal auditor. Some staff member from time to time assumes the role of internal auditor by conducting a planned review of the work of his associates or of the operations of outlying departments. Regardless of the completeness of the internal auditing facilities, however, the presence of such a system does not remove the desirability of the annual postaudit by an outside firm of reputable accountants or auditors.

Principles of Internal Control. The major principles or cardinal parts of a good system of internal control are as follows:

1. *Proper Organization for Business.* There should be a proper organization for the performance of the business and financial operations of a college or university, both in regard to the place of the business office in the institutional framework and to the internal

organization of that office. All institutional business operations should be the responsibility of a central business office headed by a single business officer responsible to the president. The business office should be solely responsible for the control and custody of cash, the entering of obligations against the institution, and the payment of claims. This concept does not preclude the possibility of some decentralization in the collection process or in the maintenance of accounting records. For example, some auxiliary enterprises may serve as collection agencies for the business office and may keep certain detailed operating records. The important concept is, however, that the ultimate responsibility and control for all business transactions should reside in the central business office. The practice of some institutions in setting up several autonomous, independent business offices on the same campus is not recommended.

As regards the internal organization of the business office, the primary purpose is to fix responsibilities and assignments so that the work of one employee or of one division serves constantly to check and verify that of another. The following chart depicts a satisfactory organization of the college business office from the point of view of internal control:

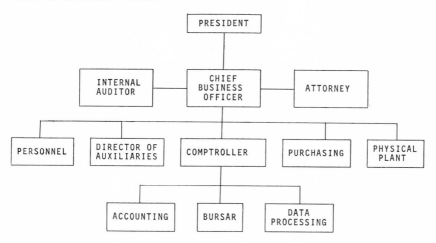

The merit of the above organization lies in the fact that the important functions of purchasing, receipt of cash, and record keeping are the responsibilities of coordinate divisions, independent of each other and each responsible directly or indirectly through the comptroller to the chief business officer. In addition, the internal auditor and hence the chief business officer have review responsibilities over all divisions. While the actual organization of college business offices will vary from the one portrayed above, nevertheless, the basic separation of functions, consistent with the size of the institution, is one of the prime requisites of internal control.

2. *Definite Fixing of Responsibilities.* Closely related to proper organization is the principle that there should be a definite fixing of responsibilities and a clear delineation of duties. This concept applies to the internal organization of the business office as well as to the relationship between that office and operating departments. Each employee of the business office should have a clear, unmistakable assignment of responsibility. If the organization is large, a procedural manual describing the duties of all positions will be helpful. As regards the external responsibilities of the business office, these should be clearly and completely set forth. It is especially important that the relative responsibilities of the business office and other departments conducting affairs of a business nature be definitely fixed. The governing board should establish overall procedures and assign responsibilities by setting down in its minutes a comprehensive manual of procedures, rules, and regulations relating to the business administration of the institution.

3. *Subdivision of Work.* There should be a subdivision of the work of the business office so that no one person has complete charge or control over a transaction. For example, no one employee should bill the student, collect the cash, and deposit it in the bank. Similarly, no one employee should hire the laborer, prepare the payroll, audit computations, and issue the check. In a large organization it is not difficult to subdivide the work so that no employee has complete control over one transaction or function. In even the small office, however, by judicious allocations of duties, the work of one employee in a given task can be made to serve as a check on the work of another employee. The business office should be organized in a manner to insure that every transaction is a valid one by having it authenticated by two or more responsible members of the staff.

4. *Use of Controlling Accounts and Subsidiary Ledgers.* When conventional mechanical accounting equipment is in use, detailed information should be segregated into subsidiary ledgers controlled by one or more accounts in the general ledger. Postings to the subsidiary ledger should be made by an employee other than the one who keeps the general ledger. In this way, the same information reaches the records through two different channels, thereby providing a means by which errors are discovered, the incidence of fraud is reduced, and the work of one employee serves as a check on that of another. The principle just expressed is best illustrated in connection with records of accounts receivable. If possible, different employees should take turns in reconciling subsidiary ledgers with the general ledger. If an electronic data processing system is in use, the detail accounts as well as the control accounts are likely to be posted by the EDP equipment. More will be said about the EDP internal controls later in this chapter.

5. *Use of Mechanical Equipment and Pre-Numbered Financial Documents.* The use of mechanical equipment enhances the efficiency of the system of internal control by providing additional checks and balances on the work of the staff and by reducing the possibility of error. Cash registers with locked-in counters and lists, accounting machines with automatic totaling devices, check-writing machines, and protectographs are important types of mechanical equipment used in colleges and universities. The proofs and checks built into the modern office machine reduce errors to a minimum and serve not only to produce better records but also to eliminate possibilities of fraud. Prenumbered financial documents, such as receipts, checks, and purchase orders, also are valuable aids in the system of internal control. The supply of prenumbered documents should be carefully controlled by employees other than those actually using the documents as part of the regular routine.

6. *Use of Electronic Data Processing Equipment.* Fundamental to the use of EDP equipment for institutional accounting is the establishment of the data processing center as a separately organized department or unit under the chief business officer. The center will operate as a separate service unit and as such will require special controls over its operation. The computer with its capabilities for

sorting, editing, proving, and processing data makes the control system for computer installations somewhat different from the conventional machine accounting system. This difference shows up primarily in controls that are exercised over the data sent to the computer and the controls that are built in, both in the program of instructions and in the equipment itself.

7. *Miscellaneous Factors Governing Personnel in the Business Office.* Personnel factors in the system of internal control include the bonding of employees, compulsory vacations, and rotation of employees. Every employee in the business office should be bonded for at least two reasons. First, a definite psychological effect is produced on the employee who is placed under bond which serves as a deterrent to fraudulent activity. Second, the institution is protected in the event of a loss due to defalcation. Employees in the business office should be required to take annual vacations. Not only does the institution benefit indirectly from the rest and relaxation thus afforded the employee, but the discovery of any fraud which a given employee may have successfully covered up during the year is facilitated. Rotation of employees in jobs, if practicable, is another successful method of turning up fraud which may have remained undiscovered for a long time. Rotation also has other advantages: it reduces the monotony of routine tasks and helps in training a well-rounded office staff.

8. *Internal Auditing.* There should be as much internal auditing as practicable, considering the size of the institution. The internal auditor should proceed in accordance with a planned audit program just as the outside auditor does. He should test check the preauditing of vouchers and cash receipts and should make careful investigations into the activities of branch offices and outside departments. He should be constantly vigilant concerning the adequacy of the system of internal control and should check to see whether the policies of the chief business officer, the president, and the governing board are being constructively obeyed. As a representative of the chief business officer, the internal auditor is in a position to conduct various special investigations. Included in the function of internal auditing is a review of business systems and procedures with suggestions for change and improvement. At the

conclusion of review, the internal auditor should prepare a formal report. This report should include a description of the activity examined, the period of time covered by the audit, exceptions noted, and recommendations for correction. The audit report should be addressed to the chief business officer who will determine what action, if any, is to be taken.

A formal, written program for internal auditing operations should be prepared. This program will define the extent and frequency of reviews and list the departments and activities subject to regular audit. The following outline indicates the scope of a well-rounded program of internal audit for the office of the chief accountant and the office of the bursar for a medium-sized university.[2]

I. *Office of the Chief Accountant*

Item   *Description*
1. Review payroll procedures to determine authority for payment of salaries and wages.
2. Determine propriety of deductions.
3. Determine that deductions are properly reported to the affected agencies.
4. Determine propriety of bank transfers.
5. Reconcile bank statements and check endorsements.
6. Preaudit vouchers in payment of claims presented for agreement in price, items, quantity, compliance with purchasing regulations.
7. Review cash receipt vouchers for source and disposition of receipts, bank deposit slips, and correctness of summary and total of receipts.
8. Review cash receipt forms and checks to verify the sequence of numbers.
9. Review registration cards for correctness of assessment of registration fees based on classification, curriculum, residence, housing, and correctness of distribution of fees.
10. Vouch distribution of undistributed endowment income to restricted income accounts.
11. Determine propriety of journal entries to general ledger and subsidiary accounts.
12. Vouch authority of miscellaneous wage payments.

2 The information is based on the internal auditing procedures of the University of Mississippi.

13. Determine (on preaudit) propriety of terminal pay.
14. Conduct general review to determine adequacy of the process of banking cash receipts.
15. Review internal control.

II. *Office of the Bursar*

    Item   *Description*
    1. Age accounts receivable to determine rapidity in collection of charges.
    2. Confirm all balances in excess of $25 and spot-confirm others in less amount that are in excess of 120 days.
    3. Investigate credit balances over 30 days old.
    4. Check to see that subsidiary accounts receivable records, security and room deposits, and other deposits agree with general ledger accounts.
    5. Count petty cash.
    6. Determine that cash receipts are being used numerically.
    7. Reconcile notes receivable to general ledger control accounts.
    8. Verify that notes receivable are properly supported by duly prepared and approved applications as required by University regulations.
    9. Verify safekeeping receipts.
    10. Investigate cash advances outstanding in excess of 30 days.
    11. Verify that proper approval has been obtained for cash advances.
    12. Review internal control.
    13. Check credits for collections against referenced cash receipts.

In the small institution, the functions of internal auditing cannot proceed to so great a degree of specialization as that indicated above. Even so, some internal auditing is necessary, particularly in connection with departments outside the business office.

9. *Internal Auditing of Records Maintained with Electronic Data Processing.* The above internal audit program is based on the use of conventional machine accounting equipment. If electronic data processing is used, major changes in internal auditing take place. The auditor, confronted with a review of electronic data records, finds the usual accounting journals and ledgers are no longer present. In place of the conventional records are magnetic tapes, punched cards, and printouts. The computer eliminates the customary audit trails and forces the auditor to rely more on a re-

view of other types of control procedures as well as to conduct portions of the audit with the computer itself.

The internal auditor, working with EDP systems, will be concerned with three major areas of control: control over input, built-in controls, and program controls.

In connection with control over input, it has already been suggested that the EDP unit be organized as a separate department. As such, it would have no authority to originate data, its responsibility being limited to that of processing data which it receives. Such data should be processed through the utilization of approved programs. A machine log should be made so that a record of all stops and interventions is recorded, thereby providing a check against operator manipulation of data. Further, control over input is enhanced if predetermined totals are recorded for batches of data being sent to the EDP unit. The auditor will want to be certain that tight controls over data being sent to the EDP unit are in existence and that such controls are working.

Built-in control refers to those controls designed into the machine itself to assure reliability. These controls help to insure that data are correctly received and processed and that appropriate results are produced. The auditor should be familiar with the built-in controls of the equipment such as double circuitry, double track, double arithmetic, and parity bits. He should be able either to test these controls or to require the equipment manufacturer to test them to assure proper functioning.

Program control can be exercised by requiring the EDP unit to use only programs which have been approved by proper officials. The auditor should be furnished an exact copy of each program. Changes in the programs should require the same official approval. Thus, at any time, the auditor can compare programs with the EDP units, or even rerun data to verify the use of approved programs. It should be observed that the EDP equipment cannot ignore the program of instructions but will operate exactly as instructed by such programs. Certain checks which will further assure accuracy of processing data can be built into the written programs. For example, in processing payrolls, all checks in excess of a certain amount can be determined by including a step in the program requiring a printout of such payments. These printouts may then be reviewed by proper officials.

The use of the computer as a tool of internal auditing has not been fully explored. As computer systems become more sophisticated, internal auditors will be forced to become more intimately acquainted with them and to make better use of them in auditing processes. Institutions using the total systems approach to business and administrative problems will have highly developed systems with a minimum of audit trails. Auditors will be required to develop written audit programs for use with the computer to make the required tests necessary to satisfy review requirements.

10. *External Auditing or Postauditing.* The external audit or postaudit by independent certified public accountants, while not a part of internal control in the usual sense, does constitute a type of internal control from the point of view of the president and the governing board. The independent auditor should be engaged by the governing board and should report directly to that body. The independent audit produces important results in addition to verification of the accuracy and integrity of the records. It brings into the college business office a fresh point of view as regards possible improvements in the accounting system, and it affords expert advice and assistance to the staff on accounting and fiscal problems.

Detailed Requirements of Internal Control. The detailed requirements of a satisfactory system of internal control will be discussed under the following three headings: control over cash receipts, control over disbursements, and control over inventories.

1. *Control Over Cash Receipts.* A proper subdivision of duties is a principal requirement of internal control as regards the safekeeping of cash. The individual or division responsible for the receiving, handling, and depositing of cash should be separated from the individual or division which keeps the records. The cashier's division is responsible for (a) receiving cash, (b) preparing receipts for all cash received, and (c) depositing cash daily and intact. The accounting division, insofar as cash is concerned, is responsible for (a) keeping all records of cash received, including bank accounts, student accounts, and detailed revenue accounts, (b) auditing daily cash re-

ceipts by comparing the receipts with bank deposits tickets, and (c) verifying accuracy of cash accounts by reconciling all bank accounts. By a proper subdivision of responsibilities between the cashier's division, the accounting division, and the auditing division, as outlined above, errors are disclosed and traced automatically, and misuse of funds is discouraged.

The use of control devices such as prenumbered receipts and mechanical equipment is another phase of the internal control of cash. In the absence of mechanical cash registers, at least three copies of a receipt should be written for every item of cash received. The original copy is given to the payer, the duplicate is routed to the accounting department, and the triplicate is retained by the cashier. Receipt forms should be numbered by the printer and controlled by an employee of the accounting or auditing division—that is, a record of the numbers received and issued to cashiers should be maintained. Spoiled receipts should be marked "void" by the cashier and should be retained by someone other than the cashiers. Far more satisfactory than manual receipting in most cases is receipting through mechanical cash registers. These machines can be obtained in all sizes and are equipped with a varying number of control registers. The more complicated cash registers provide for a distribution of cash receipts by depressing various marked keys. This device assists the accounting department in breaking down cash receipts for entry in the records and also in the daily audit of cash. Most cash registers provide a method of locking in totals, either in registers or on tapes; these totals can be read and registers reset only by employees who do not have access to cash or to the operation of the registers.

Cash received through the mails should be listed by an employee other than the cashier before it is turned over to the latter. One copy of this list should be sent to the accounting or auditing department where it will be checked against the cashier's daily report of cash received.

The institution should require that all checks be made payable to the institution rather than to individuals, departments, or cash. Checks improperly prepared should be returned for correction.

Control over billings and assessments of student fees and charges is another important aspect of internal control over cash and revenues. Whenever practicable, assessments should be initiated in an office other than the business office. For example, all assessments of fees and charges at registration time should be made by representatives of the registrar's office. The business office's duty should be to collect and deposit fees and audit documents. The assessment records of the registrar's office thus serve as a check on the collection records of the business office, and the procedure provides an excellent method of internal control on the revenues from registration and on the cashiers who handle large sums of money during the registration period. In the case of deferred payments for fees and room and board, the amount deferred is set up as accounts receivable, with a subsidiary student ledger card established for each debtor. The student ledger is kept by an employee of the accounting office and is not accessible to the cashiers.

Monthly statements are sometimes prepared by an employee other than the one who regularly maintains the student ledger in order to prevent collusion between the cashier and the student ledger bookkeeper. In machine accounting systems, the monthly statements usually are prepared as duplicates of the ledger card. In such cases, follow-up notices of delinquent accounts should be prepared and mailed by an employee other than one regularly engaged in posting the student ledger. No abatements, refunds, or write-offs of amounts set up as accounts receivable should be allowed without the proper authorization of a designated officer. After the registration period is over, supplementary fees, such as those for diplomas, transcripts, and special examinations should be assessed in the registrar's office and collected in the business office. Periodically, test checks should be made of the student ledger by comparing fees listed thereon with academic records kept in the registrar's office to see that fees have been collected for all students. Room, board, laboratory, and other charges can be verified by checking against records of appropriate auxiliary enterprises or academic departments. Periodic audit of the resident or nonresident classification of students should be conducted by the internal auditor. Institutions using advance billing procedures will have to adapt internal control procedures to accommodate this kind of system.

The cashing of checks for students is usually a service which most institutions provide. In such cases, the cashier should be given a separate fund for cashing checks. All checks cashed should be deposited separately to the credit of the institution and a reimbursement check issued to the cashier to replenish his fund. The reimbursement check may be cashed out of regular receipts or out of the petty cash fund. In order that receipts may be deposited intact each day, a special change fund should also be issued to the cashier.

Cash should be deposited daily and intact. The following are advantages of this procedure: (a) the auditing of receipts and bank deposits is facilitated; (b) the possibility of recovery on checks returned by the bank because of insufficiency of funds and for other reasons is enhanced; (c) cashiers are given daily clearance; (d) the possibility of manipulation of undeposited receipts is reduced; (e) the process of balancing cash on hand at the end of the day with actual receipts results in greater accuracy in record keeping than is possible if a partial amount of receipts on hand is deposited; and (f) prompt banking of cash results in increased earnings if funds are temporarily invested. Deposit slips should be prepared by the cashier's division in quadruplicate—the original and duplicate go to the bank, the triplicate is routed to the accounting department, and the fourth copy is retained in the cashier's division. The duplicate is signed by the bank teller and returned to the accounting office, while the triplicate is used by the accounting division to verify the cashier's daily report of cash received. All legal and statutory requirements should be adhered to as regards the selection of the depository for institutional funds. State laws usually designate certain banks as eligible depositories for state funds and set forth qualifying requirements, such as the amount and type of collateral needed to support deposits.

Bank statements should be reconciled by a representative of the accounting or auditing staff, not by an employee of the cashier's division or by one engaged in the disbursement process. Bank reconciliations should be made monthly. All endorsements on canceled checks should be carefully examined. Checks which have been outstanding for more than two or three months should be investigated through correspondence with payees. Some institutions have the notation "Not negotiable after 60 days" printed on checks to encourage prompt cashing or depositing of checks by payees. Reconciliation through the use of unit record or computer equipment becomes a simple routine procedure, with lists of outstanding checks automatically produced as a by-product of the run.

The business office should maintain as complete control as possible over cash collected in outside departments. Auxiliary departments, such as cafeterias, dining halls, athletic departments, and bookstores, which ordinarily must serve as collecting agencies, should be required to follow the detailed rules and regulations of the business office as regards the receipts of cash. All possible safeguards should be established to insure proper handling of receipts. All cash received should be deposited daily and intact with the cashiers in the business office, supported by sales tickets or cash receipts. All receipt forms used by outside departments should be prenumbered and controlled by the business office. Where feasible, cash registers should be used and departments required to submit adding machine tapes in support of receipts. Normally, bank deposits should not be made directly by the outside collecting departments. The business office should institute and supervise an appropriate system of internal check and control in each outside agency or department which collects cash. One of the important functions of the internal auditor is to maintain continuous audits of outlying departments such as those just described.

2. *Control Over Disbursements.* The importance of subdividing responsibilities and duties in the business office as a prime requisite of the system of internal check has already been discussed both generally and with special reference to the control of cash. This concept is equally important in the internal control system for disbursements. The preparation of disbursement vouchers, maintenance of the voucher register, auditing of claims, signing of checks, and handling of the general ledger should be the responsibility of different individuals. In the small business office, of course, such specialization is not possible, however, the processes involved in disbursing can be allocated in such a way as to provide adequate internal control. Under an integrated EDP system, such subdivision of responsibilities is impossible, and reliance must be placed in

the controls over input, built-in machine controls, and program controls.

All disbursements, except those insignificant in amount, should be made by check. Small items may be paid out of a properly controlled petty cash fund. Petty cash should be handled in accordance with the so-called imprest method.[3] Other important concepts concerning the proper handling of petty cash disbursements are:

(a) The amount of the fund should be limited to the absolute minimum necessary to carry on the work. The fund should be made the definite responsibility of one employee.

(b) A definite set of rules governing the use of the fund, and the items and amounts payable out of it, should be established. Payments from petty cash should be limited to small amounts.

(c) Vouchers for disbursing petty cash funds should bear the approval of a responsible person before cash is paid out.

(d) The petty cash cashier should not have access to the file of cancelled petty cash vouchers. Such vouchers should be marked in order to prevent their being used to support fraudulent disbursements.

(e) Refunds of student fees or charges should be initiated in a department outside the business office. If fees are to be refunded, the registrar's office should issue the refund order. If charges for room and board are to be refunded, the manager of the dormitory or dining hall should issue the order calling for the refund.

(f) There should be a thorough audit of petty cash vouchers by the accounting or auditing division before reimbursement is made. Occasionally a surprise count of cash on hand and an analysis of the petty cash vouchers on hand should be made. Petty cash funds issued to departments outside the business office should receive particularly careful attention.

Centralized purchasing and departmental requisitioning are essential to a good system of internal control. All purchases should originate in departments, which make their needs known by addressing requisitions to the central purchasing authority. No purchase should be made without a requisition checked and approved by proper budgetary officers. Based on the approved requisition, a

[3] See chapter 6 for a complete discussion of accounting for petty cash.

written purchase order showing actual or estimated cost is prepared and sent to the accounting office to determine availability of funds prior to release to vendor. The accounting office should also satisfy itself that all statutory requirements with respect to bids and quotations have been adhered to fully. The purchase order should be prenumbered and controlled by number in the accounting office or auditing division.

When the invoice is received, it should be checked by the purchasing office as to price and quantity, then subjected to complete audit by the accounting office. This audit should consist of (a) certification by the department receiving goods or service that the articles ordered have been received in good condition and that an invoice based on the order is properly payable; (b) comparison of vendor's invoice with purchase order and requisition; and (c) verification of computations and footings on vendor's invoice. Under this procedure, duplicate payments of vendor's claims are rendered virtually impossible because, for a double payment to occur, it would be necessary to duplicate not only the vendor's invoice, but also the requisition, purchase order, and receiving report.

As stated previously, all disbursements should be made by check and supported by properly audited vouchers. As to the number of signatures needed on the check, the facts of the individual situation will govern. In small colleges, the president and the business manager frequently sign checks. In the larger institutions, the treasurer and comptroller, auditor and comptroller, or bursar and comptroller are the usual combinations of signatures. If the countersignature on the check is not considered a formality, and if the countersigner actually scrutinizes the supporting vouchers, the two-signature method has definite advantages with respect to internal control. On the other hand, if the countersignature is done in a perfunctory manner, it serves no real purpose and simply slows down the disbursement process. A check-signing machine is satisfactory from the point of view of internal control and is essential in the large institution. When the machine is not in use, care should be taken to keep it properly locked and the signature plate removed. Institutional checks should be prenumbered, with all numbers accounted for. Signed checks should be mailed direct to the payee by the division in which the checks are signed. Checks should never be mailed by the purchasing division.

Prompt recording of disbursements is an aid to the system of internal control. A useful device in recording charges to departmental budget accounts is the provision of a duplicate copy for the department head. This procedure enables him to bring errors to the attention of the accounting office and assists in exposing incorrect or dishonest postings.

Payroll procedure is an important phase of the disbursement process. The responsibility for the various phases in the preparation of the payroll should be allocated so as to separate as much as possible the functions of employing, timekeeping, computing and checking payrolls from the paying process. No person should be listed on a payroll whose name has not been certified officially by an authority outside the business office. Salaried personnel are generally approved by the governing board at the time the institutional budget is adopted. Changes in salaried personnel after that date should be made in strict conformance with procedures laid down by the board. Nonsalaried or wage personnel are paid on the basis of payrolls prepared by individual departments. No name on a wage payroll should be honored unless proper authorization has been received from the employment division of the institution. Payment to all types of personnel should be made by check.

Checks are distributed either directly by the payroll department or may be given to department heads who in turn distribute them to the individual employees. The internal auditor or other representative of the business office at irregular and unannounced intervals should distribute the checks directly to the individual employees. This procedure assists in exposing padded payrolls. In the event payments are made in cash, a signed receipt should be obtained from each employee. Checks may also be distributed by mailing to banks as directed by the employees. Separate payroll bank accounts, operated on the imprest method, are frequently employed.

An earnings record on each employee has the following advantages with respect to the system of internal control. (a) It serves as a check on duplicate salary payments, since an individual record is set up for authorized employees only. (b) It calls attention to changes in earnings from prior periods, thus assisting the auditor in verifying the authenticity of salary increases. (c) It serves as a valuable aid in checking and verifying deduction accounts, since it records all deductions made from the employee's salary. Under EDP systems, the employee's earning record will be on tape or in other memory devices. Information needed for audit purposes can be acquired by the auditor through the use of a written program of instructions to the computer.

3. *Control Over Inventories.* There are several types of inventories in colleges and universities; namely, consummable supplies, merchandise for resale, food supplies, and movable property. The system of internal control is concerned with safeguarding these inventories. Control over all inventories, with the possible exception of merchandise for resale, can be obtained by establishing perpetual inventory systems, with control accounts in the business office. Withdrawal of supplies from storerooms should be made only upon properly signed and approved requisitions and should be made by departments in reasonable quantities. Periodically, the business office should make a physical count of the inventories and investigate differences between physical and book inventories. It is generally not practicable to maintain perpetual inventories over merchandise for resale, as, for example, in the bookstore. In such cases, the business office should require frequent physical inventories and should carefully test and analyze operating results. In regard to movable property or equipment, the responsibility for the safekeeping of institutional property should be allocated to the department head in whose custody the property is placed. The business office should establish and maintain accounting records of movable property and, with the cooperation of department heads, should make periodic physical checks in order to verify the accuracy of the perpetual inventory of equipment maintained in the business office.

CHAPTER XVI

Financial Reports and Statements

FINANCIAL REPORTING is a logical extension of the accounting system. If the accounting records are adequate, the preparation of financial reports and statements is primarily a matter of regrouping and classifying the information supplied by the books of account. Financial support for higher education is provided by many segments of society: by governments, private philanthropy, business and industry, and by parents of students. For this reason, the financial information pertaining to the operations of a college or university is of considerable interest to many people. Those who administer educational institutions are obligated to report on the results of their financial operations.

The publicly supported institution is financed by taxpayers who have a right to expect an accounting of the use of their contributions. The privately supported institution is financed by gifts and endowments, the donors of which have a right to know how their donations are being expended.

The annual published report of a college serves not only to inform the supporters of the institution about the results of the period's operations, but it also conveys important facts about the institution to legislators, alumni, parents of students, donors, and the public at large. Well-prepared financial reports do much to inspire the public with confidence in the work of educational institutions and of their leaders.

One of the important responsibilities of the chief business officer is to decide to what extent the publication of financial data about the institution will justify the cost of preparing, printing, and distributing the report.

In addition to the published report, other forms of financial statements serve important purposes in colleges and universities. Reports to administrative officers and governing boards furnish current information concerning the operations of the institution, without which intelligent administration is impossible. Reports to division heads and deans concerning the status of budgets are an essential part of the system of budgetary control. Reports to heads of auxiliary enterprises and other organized activities, such as bookstores and dining halls, render important assistance to the managers of those enterprises.

Financial reports for the institution as a whole serve also to provide a permanent record of financial transactions as well as data for budgets and programs of subsequent periods. Especially valuable is that type of report which makes the financial statements of one institution reasonably comparable to reports of other similar institutions. The codification of the principles of accounting and reporting as it appears in *College and University Business Administration* has been the greatest single influence making for the establishment of uniform financial reports and statements for educational institutions.

As indicated above, there are four types of financial reports:

1. The budget report to department heads
2. The internal report to the president and governing board
3. Interim reports for management
4. The annual financial report

Each of these types of reports is discussed in the subsequent sections of this chapter.

The Budget Report to Department Heads. The ideal form of departmental budgetary statement, as discussed in chapter 5, is an allocations ledger so devised as to provide a duplicate copy for the head of the budget unit. This type of statement has three advantages. First, it provides the department head with a complete budget statement showing budget allocations, outstanding orders, expenditures, and free balances. Second, by furnishing the department head with a complete transcript of the formal accounting record, the accounting department is assisted in locating errors. Third, because this type of report is produced automatically as the by-product of posting the account, no additional effort or work is required in its preparation. A departmental statement of this kind is feasible only where records are kept on bookkeeping machines or tabulating or computing equipment. If mechanical posting devices are not employed, the statement illustrated in Form 16.1 serves as an adequate report to department heads.

FORM 16.1

BLANK COLLEGE
M O N T H L Y   B U D G E T   R E P O R T

For the Department of _____ Art _____

Month of _____ May, 19-- _____

Budget	Budget Appropriation	Less: Expenditures	Less: Encumbrances	Free Balance
Salaries	$ 25,000.	$ 23,000	$ -0-	$ 2,000
Wages	500	400	-0-	100
Supplies & Expense	4,000	3,900	50	50
Equipment	1,000	500	500	-0-
Totals	$ 30,500	$ 27,800	$ 550	$ 2,150

The Internal Report for the President and Governing Board. Reports for internal use should be made monthly or at such other intervals as are considered necessary. The statements illustrated below are essential components of the internal report to the administrators of the institution. Other types of reports should be included as the individual situation requires:

1. Balance Sheet (Form 16.2)
2. Summary Budget Report (Form 16.3)

3. Summary of Expenditures Compared to Budget (Form 16.4)
4. Detailed Statement of Allocations and Expenditures (Form 16.5)
5. Statement of Realization of Revenues (Form 16.6)
6. Operating reports for auxiliary enterprises (Forms 16.28–16.33)

The Balance Sheet is illustrated in Form 16.2. It differs in few respects from the Balance Sheet included as part of the annual report. The primary difference is that the interim Balance Sheet includes among the current funds accounts certain budgetary and nominal accounts reflecting the progress of the institutional budget which will be closed into Current Fund Balances at the end of the fiscal year. The summary budget report shows increases and decreases in estimated revenues and anticipated expenditures since the original approval of the annual budget. Expenditures to date are compared in summary and in detail with the original budget allocations to each department (adjusted by any recorded amendments). These statements serve to inform the administration of the progress of the entire institutional budget. The statement of realization of revenues informs the administration of the progress of the revenue phases of the budget by showing the original estimate of revenue, the amount realized to date, and the balance expected to be realized.

Operating statements for auxiliary activities are essential components of the system of interim financial reporting. Not only is the information in these reports of vital significance to the managers of the auxiliary enterprises, the statements are also an important source of information to the chief business officer, the president, and the governing board.

Interim Reports for Management. Other types of interim reports include reports concerning the operations of restricted current funds, sponsored research projects, gifts received, inventories, and cash flow. It is useful also to prepare periodic reports, usually monthly, on the performance of the investments of endowment funds, as well as periodic reports of gifts received, classified by types of donors and by the purposes for which the gifts were made.

The number, frequency, and general content of internal reports will vary according to the needs of the institution. Small institu-

FORM 16.2

BLANK COLLEGE

BALANCE SHEET
(Before Closing)

ASSETS

CURRENT FUNDS:
Unrestricted -
Cash ... $ 168,620
Temporary investments, at cost (approximate market $225,000) ... 196,000
Accounts receivable--students, less allowance for doubtful accounts of $5,620
Accounts receivable--others, less allowance for doubtful accounts of $2,000 ... 6,080
State appropriations receivable ... 1,000
Inventories, at cost ... 300,000
Prepaid expenses and deferred charges ... 91,800
Due from other funds: ... 5,400
  Loan funds $ 6,000
  Unexpended plant funds 3,000
Transfers to other funds:
  Quasi-endowment funds $ 75,000
  Plant funds for -
    Additions 69,000
    Renewals and replacements 30,000
    Retirement of indebtedness 26,000 ... 9,000
... 200,000
Unrealized revenues $3,102,000
Less realized revenues 3,007,550 ... 94,450 $1,072,350

Restricted -
Cash ... $ 12,500
Temporary investments, at cost (approximate market $55,000) ... 52,000
Accounts receivable--principally agencies of the U.S. government ... 145,000   209,500

TOTAL CURRENT FUNDS $1,281,850

LOAN FUNDS:
Cash ... $ 37,640
Notes receivable, less allowance for doubtful accounts of $1,200 ... 187,500

TOTAL LOAN FUNDS $ 225,140

LIABILITIES AND FUND BALANCES

CURRENT FUNDS:
Unrestricted -
Accounts payable ... $ 553,000
Due to Teacher Retirement System ... 9,600
Deferred revenues ... 90,000
Provision for encumbrances ... 5,000
Departmental allocations $2,820,000
Less:
  Expenditures $2,754,265
  Encumbrances 22,000 2,776,265
Unallocated revenues ... 43,735
Fund balances ... 282,000
... 89,015 $1,072,350

Restricted -
Accounts Payable ... $ 6,000
Provision for endowment income stabilization ... 14,000
Fund balances ... 189,500   209,500

TOTAL CURRENT FUNDS $1,281,850

LOAN FUNDS:
Due to Unrestricted Current Funds ... $ 6,000
Fund balances ... 219,140

TOTAL LOAN FUNDS $ 225,140

ASSETS

ENDOWMENT AND SIMILAR FUNDS:		
Cash		$ 12,200
Investments, at cost (approximate market $2,902,000)		2,170,850
(Funds held in trust by others, approximate market value of $49,900, earnings thereon to benefit the college)		–
TOTAL ENDOWMENT AND SIMILAR FUNDS		**$2,183,050**

PLANT FUNDS:			
Unexpended Plant Funds –			
Cash		$ 112,000	
Temporary investments, at cost (approximate market $295,000)		290,000	
Appropriations receivable		33,500	$ 435,500
Funds for Renewals and Replacements –			
Cash		$ 11,000	
Temporary investments, at cost (approximate market $50,000)		47,500	58,500
Funds for Retirement of Indebtedness –			
Cash		$ 37,000	
Temporary investments, at cost (approximate market $100,000)		97,000	134,000
Investment in plant, at cost –			
Land		$ 810,000	
Buildings		7,361,000	
Improvements other than buildings		340,000	
Equipment		2,780,000	
Construction in progress		650,000	11,941,000
TOTAL PLANT FUNDS			**$12,569,000**

ANNUITY AND LIFE INCOME FUNDS:		
Cash		$ 3,790
Investment, at cost (approximate market $422,000)		381,000
TOTAL ANNUITY AND LIFE INCOME FUNDS		**$ 384,790**

AGENCY FUNDS:		
Cash		$ 12,250
Temporary investments, at cost (approximate market $50,000)		49,200
TOTAL AGENCY FUNDS		**$ 61,450**

LIABILITIES AND FUND BALANCES

ENDOWMENT AND SIMILAR FUNDS:		
Mortgages payable		$ 17,500
Fund balances:		
Endowment funds	$1,917,550	
Term endowment funds	146,000	
Quasi-endowment funds	90,000	
Net adjusted gains or losses	12,000	2,165,550
TOTAL ENDOWMENT AND SIMILAR FUNDS		**$2,183,050**

PLANT FUNDS:			
Unexpended Plant Funds –			
Accounts payable		$ 12,500	
Temporary notes payable to banks		10,000	
Bonds payable		100,000	
Due to Unrestricted Current Funds		3,000	
Fund balances		310,000	$ 435,500
Funds for Renewals and Replacements –			
Accounts payable		$ 2,500	
Fund balances		56,000	58,500
Funds for Retirement of Indebtedness –			
Fund balances			134,000
Investment in Plant –			
Notes		$ 130,000	
Bonds payable		2,100,000	
Net investment in plant		9,711,000	11,941,000
TOTAL PLANT FUNDS			**$12,569,000**

ANNUITY AND LIFE INCOME FUNDS:		
Fund balances		$ 384,790
TOTAL ANNUITY AND LIFE INCOME FUNDS		**$ 384,790**

AGENCY FUNDS:		
Accounts payable		$ 470
Fund balances		60,980
TOTAL AGENCY FUNDS		**$ 61,450**

FORM 16.3

BLANK COLLEGE

SUMMARY BUDGET REPORT
(End of Month)

	Budget July 1, 19--	Increases to date	Decreases to date	Adjusted budget
REVENUES:				
I. Educational and General:				
Tuition and Fees	246,000	6,000		252,000
Governmental Appropriations	1,800,000			1,800,000
Endowment Income	56,000			56,000
Gifts	100,000	8,000	2,000	106,000
Sponsored Research	232,700	12,000		244,700
Other Separately Budgeted Research	18,000		500	17,500
Other Sponsored Programs	14,000	1,000		15,000
Recovery of Indirect Costs - Sponsored Programs	20,500	1,200		21,700
Sales and Services of Educational Departments	32,000	3,000		35,000
Organized Activities Relating to Educational Departments	12,800			12,800
Other Sources	48,000	4,000		52,000
Total Educational and General	2,580,000	35,200	2,500	2,612,700
II. Student Aid	20,000			20,000
III. Auxiliary Enterprises	1,000,000	11,000	7,000	1,004,000
TOTAL REVENUES	3,600,000	46,200	9,500	3,636,700
EXPENDITURES:				
I. Educational and General:				
Instruction and Departmental Research	1,200,000	6,000		1,206,000
Organized Activities Relating to Educational Departments	24,000			24,000
Sponsored Research	232,700	12,000		244,700
Other Separately Budgeted Research	18,000		500	17,500
Other Sponsored Programs	14,000	1,000		15,000
Extension and Public Services	17,000			17,000
Libraries	200,000	3,300		203,300
Student Services	10,000	100		10,100
Operation and Maintenance of Physical Plant	750,000	4,100		754,100
General Administration	51,300			51,300
Staff Benefits	32,000	700		32,700
General Institutional Expense	12,000	500		12,500
Total Educational and General	2,561,000	27,700	500	2,588,200
II. Student Aid	25,000			25,000
III. Auxiliary Enterprises	900,000	2,000	1,000	901,000
TOTAL EXPENDITURES	3,486,000	29,700	1,500	3,514,200
Unallocated Revenues	114,000			122,500

tions usually require less formal reports. The large, complex university generally requires a variety of interim reports dealing with different phases of business and fiscal administration.

The Annual Financial Report. Every institution, regardless of size, should have an annual financial report prepared by the staff of the institution. In many cases, annual financial reports are printed or reproduced in some manner and made available to governing boards, faculty members, members of the state legislature, alumni, donors, and other interested parties. The annual financial

FORM 16.4

BLANK COLLEGE

SUMMARY STATEMENT OF EXPENDITURES
COMPARED TO BUDGET
(End of Month)

	Budget allo- cations	Expendi- tures to date	Out- standing encum- brances	Free balance
I. Educational and General:				
Instruction and Departmental Research:				
College of Liberal Arts	380,000	330,000	22,000	28,000
College of Business and Government	120,000	102,000	7,500	10,500
College of Education	92,000	80,000	2,000	10,000
College of Engineering	240,000	209,000	4,800	26,200
School of Law	125,000	101,500	3,400	20,100
School of Pharmacy	74,000	60,000	2,250	11,750
Graduate School	122,000	87,000	17,300	17,700
Summer Session	47,000	41,300	2,150	3,550
Other Instructional Expenses	6,000	5,200	200	600
Total Instruction and Departmental Research	1,206,000	1,016,000	61,600	128,400
Organized Activities Relating to Eduational Departments	24,000	21,000	300	2,700
Sponsored Research	244,700	227,300	12,600	4,800
Other Separately Budgeted Research	17,500	13,200	1,000	3,300
Other Sponsored Programs	15,000	12,000	150	2,850
Extension and Public Services	17,000	14,100	200	2,700
Libraries	203,300	191,300	5,000	7,000
Student Services	10,100	8,900	200	1,000
Operation and Maintenance of Physical Plant	754,100	691,700	11,000	51,400
General Administration	51,300	42,000	1,100	8,200
Staff Benefits	32,700	29,000		3,700
General Institutional Expense	12,500	10,000	50	2,450
Total Educational and General	2,588,200	2,276,500	93,200	218,500
II. Student Aid	25,000	22,000		3,000
III. Auxiliary Enterprises:				
Bookstore	275,000	250,000	8,000	17,000
Cafeteria	160,000	147,500	4,300	8,200
Residence Halls--Single	95,000	84,000	4,200	6,800
Residence Halls--Married	47,000	37,000	3,800	6,200
Intercollegiate Athletics	274,000	242,500	11,000	20,500
College Union	40,000	33,000	2,000	5,000
Airport	10,000	9,200		800
Total Auxiliary Enterprises	901,000	803,200	33,300	64,500
Total	3,514,200	3,101,700	126,500	286,000

report is divided into three sections: (1) general information; (2) primary statements; (3) supporting schedules.

The first section on general information has as its primary purpose the presentation of summary data describing the financial operations of the institution for the fiscal year covered by the report. It is designed to give the casual reader, particularly the layman, a condensed picture of the financial operations for the period. This section may be informal in nature and may include, in addition to financial summaries, discussions, analyses, and interpretations by the chief business officer. Frequently, graphs and flow charts are provided along with the summary information. Letters of trans-

FORM 16.5

BLANK COLLEGE

DETAILED STATEMENT OF ALLOCATIONS AND EXPENDITURES
(End of Month)

	Budget allo-cations	Expenditures to date	Outstanding encumbrances	Free balance
I. Educational and General:				
Instruction and Departmental Research:				
College of Liberal Arts:				
Office of the Dean:				
Salaries and Wages	26,500	25,000		1,500
Supplies and Expense	3,000	1,000	1,800	200
Equipment	500	200	200	100
Total	30,000	26,200	2,000	1,800
Aerospace Studies:				
Salaries and Wages	13,000	12,100		900
Supplies and Expense	1,800	1,200	400	200
Equipment	200	100	100	
Total	15,000	13,400	500	1,100
Art:				
Salaries and Wages	12,100	11,000		1,100
Supplies and Expense	2,100	1,850	150	100
Equipment	800	650	150	
Total	15,000	13,500	300	1,200
Biology:				
Salaries and Wages	32,200	29,000		3,200
Supplies and Expense	5,500	2,000	3,200	300
Equipment	2,300	2,000	300	
Total	40,000	33,000	3,500	3,500
Chemistry:				
Salaries and Wages	30,000	28,200		1,800
Supplies and Expense	6,700	1,200	5,000	500
Equipment	2,600	2,000	400	200
Total	39,300	31,400	5,400	2,500
Classics:				
Salaries and Wages	11,000	10,000		1,000
Supplies and Expense	1,000	500	400	100
Total	12,000	10,500	400	1,100
English:				
Salaries and Wages	20,000	18,000		2,000
Supplies and Expense	2,000	1,600	200	200
Total	22,000	19,600	200	2,200
History:				
Salaries and Wages	16,100	15,100		1,000
Supplies and Expense	900	700	100	100
Total	17,000	15,800	100	1,100
Home Economics:				
Salaries and Wages	14,155	13,400		755
Supplies and Expense	845	300	470	75
Total	15,000	13,700	470	830
Mathematics:				
Salaries and Wages	34,000	32,000		2,000
Supplies and Expense	6,000	2,000	2,900	1,100
Equipment	1,000	300	700	
Total	41,000	34,300	3,600	3,100
Military Science:				
Supplies and Expense	1,200	1,100	50	50
Equipment	300	300		
Total	1,500	1,400	50	50

	Budget allo-cations	Expendi-tures to date	Out-standing encum-brances	Free balance
Business Education and Office Administration:				
Salaries and Wages	14,500	13,850		650
Supplies and Expense	2,300	1,700	400	200
Equipment	1,700	750	200	750
Total	18,500	16,300	600	1,600
Political Science:				
Salaries and Wages	14,600	13,120		1,480
Supplies and Expense	2,200	380	1,620	200
Equipment	200		200	
Total	17,000	13,500	1,820	1,680
Total College of Business and Government	120,000	102,000	7,500	10,500
College of Education:				
Office of the Dean:				
Salaries and Wages	26,000	23,900		2,100
Supplies and Expense	6,000	5,200	500	300
Equipment	1,200	900	250	50
Total	33,200	30,000	750	2,450
Health, Physical Education, and Recreation:				
Salaries and Wages	24,000	21,200		2,800
Supplies and Expense	4,500	3,700	400	400
Equipment	1,500	1,100	200	200
Total	30,000	26,000	600	3,400
Library Science:				
Salaries and Wages	14,000	13,100		900
Supplies and Expense	2,000	1,300	100	600
Equipment	600	600		
Total	16,600	15,000	100	1,500
Reading Clinic:				
Salaries and Wages	10,000	8,200		1,800
Supplies and Expense	1,500	400	350	750
Equipment	700	400	200	100
Total	12,200	9,000	550	2,650
Total College of Education	92,000	80,000	2,000	10,000
College of Engineering:				
Office of the Dean:				
Salaries and Wages	29,000	25,700		3,300
Supplies and Expense	4,300	3,550	200	550
Equipment	700	450	200	50
Total	34,000	29,700	400	3,900
Chemical Engineering:				
Salaries and Wages	30,750	28,400		2,350
Supplies and Expense	8,200	6,180	440	1,580
Equipment	1,250	720	260	270
Total	40,200	35,300	700	4,200
Civil Engineering:				
Salaries and Wages	30,400	27,150		3,250
Supplies and Expense	6,200	4,050	1,000	1,150
Equipment	900	900		
Total	37,500	32,100	1,000	4,400
Electrical Engineering:				
Salaries and Wages	30,600	28,900		1,700
Supplies and Expense	5,150	4,350	300	500
Equipment	1,350	1,000	150	200
Total	37,100	34,250	450	2,400
Geology and Geological Engineering:				
Salaries and Wages	22,150	20,350		1,800
Supplies and Expense	5,850	5,100	650	100
Equipment	1,000	450	450	100
Total	29,000	25,900	1,100	2,000

	Budget allocations	Expenditures to date	Outstanding encumbrances	Free balance
Modern Languages:				
Salaries and Wages	13,200	12,100		1,100
Supplies and Expense	800	630	70	100
Total	14,000	12,730	70	1,200
Music:				
Salaries and Wages	13,800	13,000		800
Supplies and Expense	1,100	650	390	60
Equipment	1,100	1,000	100	
Total	16,000	14,650	490	860
Naval Science:				
Supplies and Expense	1,700	1,200	300	200
Equipment	500	400	100	
Total	2,200	1,600	400	200
Philosophy:				
Salaries and Wages	13,000	12,000		1,000
Supplies and Expense	1,500	1,000	400	100
Equipment	500	100	350	50
Total	15,000	13,100	750	1,150
Physics and Astronomy:				
Salaries and Wages	24,700	23,100		1,600
Supplies and Expense	4,200	3,000	1,100	100
Equipment	1,100	200	870	30
Total	30,000	26,300	1,970	1,730
Psychology:				
Salaries and Wages	20,500	19,200		1,300
Supplies and Expense	1,000	800	50	150
Total	21,500	20,000	50	1,450
Sociology and Anthropology:				
Salaries and Wages	16,000	14,800		1,200
Supplies and Expense	2,000	600	1,100	300
Equipment	500	420		80
Total	18,500	15,820	1,100	1,580
Speech and Theater:				
Salaries and Wages	13,100	12,000		1,100
Supplies and Expense	1,200	350	600	250
Equipment	700	650	50	
Total	15,000	13,000	650	1,350
Total College of Liberal Arts	380,000	330,000	22,000	28,000
College of Business and Government:				
Office of the Dean:				
Salaries and Wages	20,000	18,000		2,000
Supplies and Expense	2,800	1,200	1,500	100
Equipment	700		700	
Total	23,500	19,200	2,200	2,100
Accounting:				
Salaries and Wages	23,700	21,900		1,800
Supplies and Expense	1,700	200	1,400	100
Equipment	600	100	350	150
Total	26,000	22,200	1,750	2,050
Economics and Business Administration:				
Salaries and Wages	19,000	17,355		1,645
Supplies and Expense	2,500	1,320	980	200
Equipment	500	425		75
Total	22,000	19,100	980	1,920
Journalism:				
Salaries and Wages	11,000	10,000		1,000
Supplies and Expense	2,000	1,700	150	150
Total	13,000	11,700	150	1,150

	Budget allocations	Expenditures to date	Outstanding encumbrances	Free balance
Mechanical Engineering:				
Salaries and Wages	28,700	25,475		3,225
Supplies and Expense	5,100	3,595	355	1,150
Equipment	1,200	630	245	325
Total	35,000	29,700	600	4,700
Seismological Laboratory:				
Salaries and Wages	20,200	18,700		1,500
Supplies and Expense	4,900	3,130	120	1,650
Equipment	2,100	220	430	1,450
Total	27,200	22,050	550	4,600
Total College of Engineering	240,000	209,000	4,800	26,200
School of Law:				
Office of the Dean:				
Salaries and Wages	39,200	37,600		1,600
Supplies and Expense	6,400	1,900	360	4,140
Equipment	600	600		
Total	46,200	40,100	360	5,740
Law Extension:				
Salaries and Wages	43,700	39,350		4,350
Supplies and Expense	7,290	1,650	2,140	3,500
Equipment	400	250	150	
Total	51,390	41,250	2,290	7,850
Legal Institute for Agriculture and Resource Development:				
Salaries and Wages	21,500	18,120		3,380
Supplies and Expense	5,040	1,560	525	2,955
Equipment	870	470	225	175
Total	27,410	20,150	750	6,510
Total School of Law	125,000	101,500	3,400	20,100
School of Pharmacy:				
Office of the Dean:				
Salaries and Wages	43,600	37,100	300	6,500
Supplies and Expense	21,200	17,900	1,950	3,000
Equipment	9,200	5,000	2,250	2,250
Total	74,000	60,000	2,250	11,750
Total School of Pharmacy	74,000	60,000	2,250	11,750
Graduate School:				
Office of the Dean:				
Salaries and Wages	68,200	58,450		9,750
Supplies and Expense	21,400	9,175	6,075	6,150
Equipment	4,400	2,200	1,900	300
Total	94,000	69,825	7,975	16,200
City Planning:				
Supplies and Expense	23,900	16,700	6,025	1,175
Equipment	4,100	475	3,300	325
Total	28,000	17,175	9,325	1,500
Total Graduate School	122,000	87,000	17,300	17,700
Summer Session:				
Office of the Director:				
Salaries and Wages	13,600	12,200		1,400
Supplies and Expense	1,200	550	600	50
Equipment	300	300		
Total	15,100	13,050	600	1,450
University:				
Salaries and Wages	11,900	11,100		800
Supplies and Expense	1,850	1,070	450	330
Equipment	250	100	150	
Total	14,000	12,270	600	1,130

FORM 16.6

BLANK COLLEGE

STATEMENT OF REALIZATION OF REVENUES
(End of Month)

	Estimated revenues	Realized to date	Balance to be realized
I. Educational and General:			
Tuition and Fees	252,000	240,000	12,000
Governmental Appropriations			
State--General Support	1,600,000	1,600,000	
Research Institute of Pharmaceutical Sciences	200,000	100,000	100,000
Endowment Income			
Unrestricted	46,000	32,000	14,000
Restricted	10,000	5,000	5,000
Gifts	106,000	92,000	14,000
Sponsored Research	244,700	200,000	44,700
Other Separately Budgeted Research	17,500	16,000	1,500
Other Sponsored Programs	15,000	15,000	
Recovery of Indirect Costs - Sponsored Programs	21,700	21,900	200*
Sales and Services of Educational Departments	35,000	34,000	1,000
Organized Activities Relating to Educational Departments	12,800	13,500	700*
Other Sources			
Library Fines	3,000	2,500	500
Interest on Temporary Investments of Current Funds	40,000	41,200	1,200*
University News Service	1,500	1,000	500
Swimming Pool	7,500	6,000	1,500
Total Educational and General	2,612,700	2,420,100	192,600
II. Student Aid:			
Gifts	15,000	16,000	1,000*
Endowment Income	5,000	3,500	1,500
Total Student Aid	20,000	19,500	500
III. Auxiliary Enterprises:			
Bookstore	229,000	205,000	24,000
Cafeteria	150,000	130,000	20,000
Residence Halls	220,000	221,000	1,000*
Intercollegiate Athletics	350,000	357,000	7,000*
College Union	30,000	22,500	7,500
Airport	15,000	13,000	2,000
Motor Pool	10,000	8,700	1,300
Total Auxiliary Enterprises	1,004,000	957,200	46,800
Total Revenues	3,636,700	3,396,800	239,900

* Indicates excess of revenues over budget estimates.

mittal and the certificate of the auditor usually precede the discussion of the financial operations. Increasing numbers of institutions are following the practice of printing and distributing a summary financial report, with the details of the financial transactions for the year duplicated but retained primarily for the use of the governing board and the college administration.

The second section of the annual report, the primary statements, presents the financial data for the year's operations. *College and University Business Administration* indicates that this part of the report must include three primary statements—the Balance Sheet, the Statement of Changes in Fund Balances, and the Statement of Current Funds Revenues, Expenditures, and Transfers. The purpose of the Balance Sheet is to report the financial condition of the institution at the end of the fiscal year. It shows what assets the institution possesses at the close of the year and what obligations exist against these assets. Following the pattern of the accounting system, the Balance Sheet is divided into fund groups. Usually it is presented as illustrated in this chapter; however, it may be arranged in a multicolumnar form, using a separate column for each fund group and major subgroup. If the alternate form is used, there should be no "total" column in which like assets and liabilities and fund balances of all fund groups are combined.

In support of the Balance Sheet, the Statement of Changes in Fund Balances shows the beginning balance in each fund group, the additions and deductions during the year, and the final balance, which is reflected on the Balance Sheet. In describing the significance of the Statement of Changes in Fund Balances, *College and University Business Administration* asserts that it is a primary statement, equal in importance to the Balance Sheet and the Statement of Current Funds Revenues, Expenditures, and Transfers.

The Statement of Current Funds Revenues, Expenditures, and Transfers is the operating statement showing in summary form the results of the current operations of the institution during the fiscal period. In addition to revealing revenues by sources and expenditures by function, it also shows transfers made from the current funds group to other funds.

The third section of the financial report is composed of supporting schedules which supply detailed information already summarized in the preceding section. The most important schedule is the detailed Statement of Current Funds Revenues, Expenditures, and Transfers. Other schedules include an operating statement for each auxiliary enterprise and detailed reports on the operation of loan, endowment, annuity and life income, plant and agency funds.

A study of a large number of published reports shows that many other types of financial statements are included in annual reports of colleges and universities. Many of these statements present comparisons with previous years, which are useful sources of information to the reader. Whether additional statements should be included in the annual report depends upon the circumstances in the individual institution.

It is desirable that the financial reports of separately incorporated agencies, such as research foundations, university presses, and athletic associations, be at least appended to the institutional financial report.

A suggested outline for the annual published report is given below. The tables, exhibits, and schedules listed are illustrated on pages 372 to 407.

I. General
   A. Letter of transmittal from the chief business officer to the president (page 372)
   B. Accountant's Opinion (pages 372–73)
   C. General condensed summary (pages 373–76)

II. Primary Statements
   A. Balance Sheet (Form 16.7)
   B. Statement of Current Funds Revenues, Expenditures, and Transfers (Form 16.8)
   C. Statement of Changes in Fund Balances
      1. Statement of Changes in Fund Balances— Unrestricted Current Funds (Form 16.9)
      2. Statement of Changes in Fund Balances— Restricted Current Funds (Form 16.10)
      3. Statement of Changes in Fund Balances— Loan Funds (Form 16.11)
      4. Statement of Changes in Fund Balances— Endowment and Similar Funds (Form 16.12)
      5. Statement of Changes in Fund Balances— Annuity and Life Income Funds (Form 16.13)
      6. Statement of Changes in Fund Balances— Plant Funds
         a. Unexpended Plant Funds (Form 16.14)
         b. Funds for Renewals and Replacements (Form 16.15)
         c. Funds for Retirement of Indebtedness (Form 16.16)
         d. Investment in Plant (Form 16.17)
      7. Statement of Changes in Fund Balances— Agency Funds (Form 16.18)

III. Supporting Schedules:
      1. Schedule of Current Funds Revenues (Form 16.19)
      2. Schedule of Current Funds Expenditures (Form 16.20)
      3. Schedule of Changes in Fund Balances— Loan Funds (Form 16.21)
      4. Schedule of Changes in Fund Balances—

Endowment and Similar Funds (Form 16.22)
5. Schedule of Changes in Fund Balances—
   Annuity and Life Income Funds (Form 16.23)
6. Schedule of Changes in Fund Balances—
   Unexpended Plant Funds (Form 16.24)
7. Schedule of Changes in Fund Balances—
   Funds for Renewals and Replacements (Form 16.25)
8. Schedule of Changes in Fund Balances—
   Funds for Retirement of Indebtedness (Form 16.26)
9. Schedule of Changes in Investment in Plant (Form 16.27)
10. Revenues and Expenditures of Auxiliary Enterprises
    a. Intercollegiate athletics (Form 16.28)
    b. Residence halls—single students (Form 16.29)
    c. Residence halls—married students (Form 16.30)
    d. Bookstore (Form 16.31)
    e. Cafeteria (Form 16.32)
    f. College union (Form 16.33)
11. Schedule of investments by fund groups (Form 16.34)
12. Schedule of long-term notes and bonds payable (Form 16.35)
13. Balance sheet (applied method of reporting unrestricted gifts) (Form 16.36)
14. Statement of Current Funds Revenues, Expenditures and Transfers (applied method of reporting unrestricted gifts) (Form 16.37)
15. Statement of Changes in Fund Balances—
    Unrestricted Gifts (applied method of reporting unrestricted gifts) (Form 16.38)
16. Statement of Changes in Fund Balances—
    Unrestricted Current Funds—Other (Form 16.39)

The foregoing outline contains the necessary minimum of financial statements and schedules. Other information frequently found in published reports of colleges and universities includes:

1. Comparative statements for a period of years showing
   a. Expenditures
   b. Revenues
   c. Operation and maintenance costs
   d. Enrollments
   e. Per student costs
2. Description and map of college

3. Expenditures by programs, projects, and other similar objectives
4. Various charts and diagrams
5. Statements of endowment and other investments

The remaining portion of this chapter is devoted to presenting a model annual report. Included are letters of transmittal, comments and summaries by the chief business officer, and the statements considered to be essential in most college and university annual reports.

MODEL ANNUAL REPORT

LETTER OF TRANSMITTAL

BLANK COLLEGE
Blank, State

Office of the
Vice-President and Comptroller

September 30, 19___

President John Doe

Dear President Doe:

I am submitting herewith the annual financial report of the College for the fiscal year ended June 30, 19___. This report contains summaries of important financial data as well as more detailed tables, statements, and schedules designed to present a complete financial picture of all phases and all funds of the College.

Accounts of the College have been examined by Rohn and Company, Certified Public Accountants, and their opinion is made a part of this record.

Respectfully submitted,

David Smith
Vice-President and Comptroller

Rohn and Company
Certified Public Accounts

Manson Building
Blank, State

ACCOUNTANT'S OPINION

Board of Trustees
Blank College

We have examined the Balance Sheet of Blank College as of June 30, 19___ and the Statement of Current Funds Revenues, Expenditures, and Transfers, the Statement of Changes in Unrestricted Current Funds Balances, and all other statements of changes in fund balances for the year then ended. Our examination was made in accordance with generally accepted auditing standards, and accordingly included such tests of the accounting records and such other auditing procedures as we considered necessary in the circumstances.

In our opinion, the Balance Sheet, Statement of Current Funds Revenues, Expenditures, and Transfers, the Statement of Changes in Unrestricted Current Funds Balances, and all other statements of changes in fund balances present fairly the financial position of the College at June 30, 19__ and the results of its operations for the year then ended, in conformity with generally accepted accounting principles applied on a basis consistent with that of the preceding year.

ROHN AND COMPANY

September 20, 19__

CONDENSED GENERAL SUMMARY

CURRENT REVENUES FOR THE YEAR

Current revenues for the year, including restricted research and other sponsored projects and auxiliary enterprises, total $4,010,750. This compares to $3,840,000 in the previous year.

Revenues increased principally from restricted research and other sponsored projects, student tuition and fees, and unrestricted gifts and grants.

The following table shows in summary the revenues for the year:

	Amount	Percent of total revenues	Percent of educational and general revenues
Student tuition and fees	$ 251,000	6.2%	8.5%
Governmental appropriations	1,800,000	44.7%	60.1%
Income from endowment investments	116,000	3.0%	3.9%
Gifts	123,400	3.1%	4.2%
Research and other sponsored projects	579,850	14.4%	19.6%
Sales and services of educational departments	46,300	1.2%	1.6%
Organized activities relating to educational departments	29,450	.8%	1.0%
Other sources	32,900	.8%	1.1%
Total Educational and General	$2,979,000	74.2%	100.0%
Student Aid	36,400	.9%	
Auxiliary enterprises	995,350	24.9%	
Total Current Revenues	$4,010,750	100.0%	

A detailed report of current funds revenues will be found in Schedule 1, pages 386–87.

CURRENT EXPENDITURES FOR THE YEAR

Current expenditures for the year, including restricted funds and auxiliary enterprises, total $3,779,465, which compares to $3,720,500 in the previous year. Expenditures and transfers to other funds totaled $3,979,465, and resulted in a total addition of $31,285 to the balance of unrestricted current funds. The following table shows in summary the expenditures for the year:

	Amount	Percent of total expenditures	Percent of educational and general expenditures
Instruction and departmental research	$1,232,640	32.6%	43.5%
Organized activities relating to educational departments	26,000	.7%	.9%
Research and other sponsored projects	605,675	16.0%	21.3%
Extension and public services	19,250	.5%	.7%
Libraries	92,000	2.4%	3.2%
Student services	89,500	2.3%	3.1%
Operation and maintenance of physical plant	479,900	12.7%	16.9%
General administration	115,230	3.1%	4.2%
Staff benefits	137,600	3.6%	4.8%
General institutional expense	38,370	1.0%	1.4%
Total Educational and General	$2,836,165	74.9%	100.0%
Student aid	40,650	1.1%	
Auxiliary enterprises	902,650	24.0%	
Total Current Expenditures	$3,779,465	100.0%	

A detailed statement of current funds expenditures will be found in Schedule 2, pages 388–90.

LOAN FUNDS

Loan funds totaled $219,140 at the end of the fiscal year, an increase of $31,680 during the year. Primarily, the increase resulted from gifts and a transfer of $10,000 from current funds. At June 30, 19___, a total of $188,700 loans had been issued to needy students. Detailed statements of loan funds will be found on pages 382 and 391.

ENDOWMENT AND SIMILAR FUNDS

The College's endowment fund and the income it produces are vital sources of support for current operations. During the year, endowment investments earned $116,000, of which $103,350 was designated for current operations of the College and certain specific schools and departments.

Endowment and similar funds increased during the year in the amount of $202,200, largely from capital gains of $103,400 and a transfer of $75,000 from current funds. The assets of the various funds are pooled for investment purposes, and each fund shares proportionately in income and capital gains generated by the pool. To date, the College has advanced a total of $90,000 from current funds to serve temporarily as endowment.

Detailed statements of endowment and similar funds are presented on pages 383 and 392.

PLANT FUNDS

The total investment in plant at June 30, 19___, valued at cost, is as follows:

Land	$ 810,000
Buildings	7,361,000
Improvements other than buildings (fencing, parking lot, roadways, and underground piping)	340,000
Equipment	2,780,000
Construction in progress	650,000
	$11,941,000

Additions to the physical plant increased during the year in the amount of $332,020, representing an addition of $72,000 expended on the Arts and Crafts building, a net increase in movable equipment in the amount of $91,020, and an increase of $169,000 on new construction in progress.

Unexpended plant funds increased during the year in the amount of $377,900, primarily from governmental appropriations, gifts and grants, and the transfer of $69,000 from current funds. During the year, $245,000 was expended for additions to plant facilities.

During the year, funds for renewals and replacements were expended in the amount of $50,700 for equipment. At June 30, 19___, funds for renewals and replacements had a balance of $56,000.

The College liquidated $109,000 of outstanding bonds during the year through funds for retirement of indebtedness, reducing bonds and notes payable of the plant funds to $2,330,000 at June 30, 19___.

Detailed statements of investment in plant, unexpended plant funds, funds for renewals and replacements, and funds for retirement of indebtedness are presented on pages 384–85 and 394–97.

AGENCY FUNDS

Agency funds consist primarily of deposits of students and organizations held in trust by the College, and for which the College acts only as a fiscal agent. A brief statement of Agency Funds Balances appears on page 385.

FORM 16.7

BLANK COLLEGE

BALANCE SHEET

JUNE 30, 19___

ASSETS

CURRENT FUNDS:
Unrestricted -
Cash $ 177,620
Temporary investments, at cost (approximate market $225,000) 196,000
Accounts receivable--students, less allowance for doubtful accounts of $5,620
Accounts receivable--others, less allowance for doubtful accounts of $2,000 6,080
State appropriations receivable 1,000
Inventories, at cost 300,000
Prepaid Expenses and deferred charges 91,800
5,400
$ 777,900

Restricted -
Cash $ 12,500
Temporary investments, at cost (approximate market $55,000) 52,000
Accounts receivable, principally agencies of the U.S. government 145,000
209,500

TOTAL CURRENT FUNDS $ 987,400

LOAN FUNDS:
Cash $ 31,640
Notes receivable, less allowance for doubtful accounts of $1,200 187,500

TOTAL LOAN FUNDS $ 219,140

ENDOWMENT AND SIMILAR FUNDS:
Cash $ 12,200
Investments at cost, adjusted for premiums and discounts on bonds (approximate market $2,902,000) 2,170,850
(Funds held in trust by others; approximate market value of $49,000, earnings thereon to benefit the college) -

TOTAL ENDOWMENT AND SIMILAR FUNDS $2,183,050

ANNUITY AND LIFE INCOME FUNDS:
Cash $ 3,790
Investments, at cost (approximate market $422,000) 381,000

TOTAL ANNUITY AND LIFE INCOME FUNDS $ 384,790

LIABILITIES AND FUND BALANCES

CURRENT FUNDS:
Unrestricted -
Accounts payable $ 553,000
Due to Teacher Retirement System 9,600
Deferred revenues 90,000
Provision for encumbrances 5,000
Fund balances 120,300
$ 777,900

Restricted -
Accounts payable $ 6,000
Provision for endowment income stabilization 140,000
Fund balances 189,500
209,500

TOTAL CURRENT FUNDS $ 987,400

LOAN FUNDS:
Fund balances $ 219,140

TOTAL LOAN FUNDS $ 219,140

ENDOWMENT AND SIMILAR FUNDS:
Mortgages payable $ 17,500
Fund balances -
Endowment funds $1,917,550
Term endowment funds 146,000
Quasi-endowment funds 90,000
Net adjusted gains and losses 12,000
2,165,550

TOTAL ENDOWMENT AND SIMILAR FUNDS $2,183,050

ANNUITY AND LIFE INCOME FUNDS:
Fund balances $ 384,790

TOTAL ANNUITY AND LIFE INCOME FUNDS $ 384,790

ASSETS

PLANT FUNDS:
Unexpended Plant Funds -
Cash $ 109,000
Temporary investments, at cost (approximate market $295,000) 290,000
Appropriations receivable 33,500 $ 432,500

Funds for Renewals and Replacements -
Cash $ 11,000
Temporary investments, at cost (approximate market $50,000) 47,500 58,500

Funds for Retirement of Indebtedness -
Cash $ 37,000
Temporary investments, at cost, (approximate market $100,000) 97,000 134,000

Investment in plant, at cost -
Land $ 810,000
Buildings 7,361,000
Improvements other than buildings 340,000
Equipment 2,780,000
Construction in progress 650,000 11,941,000

TOTAL PLANT FUNDS $12,566,000

AGENCY FUNDS:
Cash $ 12,250
Temporary investments, at cost (approximate market $50,000) 49,200

TOTAL AGENCY FUNDS $ 61,450

LIABILITIES AND FUND BALANCES

PLANT FUNDS:
Unexpended Plant Funds -
Accounts payable $ 12,500
Temporary notes payable to banks 10,000
Bonds payable 100,000
Fund balances 310,000 $ 432,500

Funds for Renewals and Replacements -
Accounts payable 2,500
Fund balances 56,000 58,500

Funds for Retirement of Indebtedness -
Fund balances 134,000

Investment in Plant -
Notes payable $ 130,000
Bonds payable 2,100,000
Net investment in plant 9,711,000 11,941,000

TOTAL PLANT FUNDS $12,566,000

AGENCY FUNDS:
Accounts payable $ 470
Fund balances 60,980

TOTAL AGENCY FUNDS $ 61,450

FORM 16.8

BLANK COLLEGE

STATEMENT OF CURRENT FUNDS REVENUES, EXPENDITURES, AND TRANSFERS
FOR THE YEAR ENDING JUNE 30, 19___

	Total	Unrestricted	Restricted
Revenues:			
Educational and General -			
Student Tuition and Fees	$ 251,000	$ 251,000	$
Governmental Appropriations	1,800,000	1,426,500	373,500
Endowment Income (including $1,900 received from funds held in trust by others)	116,100	103,350	12,750
Gifts	123,400	87,500	35,900
Sponsored Research -			
Governmental	396,000		396,000
Nongovernmental	81,700		81,700
Other Separately Budgeted Research	36,800	36,800	
Other Sponsored Programs -			
Governmental	44,350		44,350
Nongovernmental	21,000		21,000
Recovery of Indirect Costs--Sponsored Programs	20,000	20,000	
Sales and Services of Educational Departments	46,300	46,300	
Organized Activities Relating to Educational Departments	29,450	29,450	
Other Sources	12,900	11,300	1,600
TOTAL EDUCATIONAL AND GENERAL	$2,979,000	$2,012,200	$ 966,800
Student Aid	36,400		36,400
Auxiliary Enterprises	995,350	995,350	
TOTAL REVENUES	$4,010,750	$3,007,550	$1,003,200
Expenditures:			
Educational and General -			
Instruction and Departmental Research	$1,232,640	$ 838,040	$ 394,600
Organized Activities Relating to Educational Departments	26,000	26,000	
Sponsored Research	491,025		491,025
Other Separately Budgeted Research	49,300	49,300	
Other Sponsored Programs	65,350		65,350
Extension and Public Services	19,250	14,875	4,375
Libraries	92,000	80,550	11,450
Student Services	89,500	89,500	
Operation and Maintenance of Physical Plant	479,900	479,900	
General Administration	115,230	115,230	
Staff Benefits	137,600	137,600	
General Institutional Expense	38,370	38,370	
TOTAL EDUCATIONAL AND GENERAL	$2,836,165	$1,869,365	$ 966,800
Student Aid	40,650	4,250	36,400
Auxiliary Enterprises (including debt service of $14,400)	902,650	902,650	
	$3,779,465	$2,776,265	$1,003,200
Transfers:			
To -			
Quasi-endowment funds	$ 75,000	$ 75,000	
Plant funds for -			
Additions	69,000	69,000	
Renewals and replacements	30,000	30,000	
Retirement of indebtedness	26,000	26,000	
TOTAL TRANSFERS	$ 200,000	$ 200,000	
EXCESS OF REVENUES OVER EXPENDITURES AND TRANSFERS	$ 31,285	$ 31,285	

FORM 16.9

BLANK COLLEGE

STATEMENT OF CHANGES IN FUND BALANCES
UNRESTRICTED CURRENT FUNDS
FOR THE YEAR ENDED JUNE 30, 19____

	Total	Unallocated	Allocated
Balances, July 1, 19____	$ 95,915	$ 85,915	$ 10,000
Additions -			
Excess of revenues over expenditures and transfers	$ 31,285	$ 31,285	
Release of prior year encumbrances	3,100	3,100	
	$ 34,385	$ 34,385	
Deductions -			
Transfers to loan funds	$ 10,000	$ 10,000	
Transfers between unallocated and allocated -			
Amounts included in current expenditures on projects for which funds had previously been allocated - student activities		$ 4,000	$ (4,000)
Allocations for specific future operating purposes - student activities		(5,000)	5,000
		$ (1,000)	$ 1,000
Balances, June 30, 19____	$ 120,300	$ 109,300	$ 11,000

FORM 16.10

BLANK COLLEGE

STATEMENT OF CHANGES IN FUND BALANCES
RESTRICTED CURRENT FUNDS
FOR THE YEAR ENDED JUNE 30, 19___

	Total	Educational and General	Student Aid	Auxiliary Enterprises
Balances, July 1, 19___	$ 133,700	$ 109,800	$ 17,650	$ 6,250
Additions -				
Governmental appropriations	$ 290,000	$ 290,000		
Endowment income	31,000	29,000	$ 2,000	
Gifts	122,500	85,750	35,750	$ 1,000
Sponsored research	571,400	571,400		
Other sponsored programs	71,700	71,700		
Transfers within restricted current funds	14,500	14,500		
	$1,101,100	$1,062,350	$ 37,750	$ 1,000
Deductions -				
Expenditures	$1,003,200	$ 966,800	$ 36,400	
Indirect cost recoveries on sponsored programs transferred to unrestricted current funds	20,000	20,000		
Refunds to grantors	7,600	7,600		
Transfers within restricted current funds	14,500	14,500		
	$1,045,300	$1,008,900	$ 36,400	$ -
Balances, June 30, 19___	$ 189,500	$ 163,250	$ 19,000	$ 7,250

FORM 16.11

BLANK COLLEGE

STATEMENT OF CHANGES IN FUND BALANCES
LOAN FUNDS
FOR THE YEAR ENDED JUNE 30, 19___

Balances, July 1, 19___		$ 187,460
Additions -		
Gifts		$ 18,460
Endowment income		350
Interest and investment income		3,900
Transfers from current funds		10,000
		32,710
Deductions -		
Uncollectible notes charged off		$ 110
Death and teachers' cancellations		920
		1,030
Balances, June 30, 19___		$ 219,140
U.S. government grants, refundable	$ 130,000	
University loan funds -		
Established by donors	74,140	
Established by Governing Board	15,000	

FORM 16.12

BLANK COLLEGE

STATEMENT OF CHANGES IN FUND BALANCES
ENDOWMENT AND SIMILAR FUNDS
FOR THE YEAR ENDED JUNE 30, 19___

	Total	Endowment funds	Term endowment funds	Quasi-endowment funds	Net adjusted gains and losses
Balances, July 1, 19___	$1,963,350	$1,814,550	$127,200	$21,600	
Additions -					
Gifts	27,800	17,000	10,800		
Income added to principal	1,000	1,000			
Annuity funds upon death of annuitant	4,600	4,600			
Net gains on investments sold or exchanged	103,400	80,400	8,000	3,000	12,000
Transfers from current funds	75,000			75,000	
Transfers within endowment and similar funds	7,000			7,000	
	218,800	103,000	18,800	85,000	12,000
Deductions -					
Transfers to unexpended plant funds	9,600			9,600	
Transfers within endowment and similar funds	7,000			7,000	
	16,600			16,600	
Balances, June 30, 19___	$2,165,550	$1,917,550	$146,000	$90,000	$12,000

FORM 16.13

BLANK COLLEGE

STATEMENT OF CHANGES IN FUND BALANCES
ANNUITY AND LIFE INCOME FUNDS
FOR THE YEAR ENDED JUNE 30, 19___

	Total	Annuity funds	Life income funds
Balances, July 1, 19___	$368,889	$96,500	$272,389
Additions -			
Gifts	21,800		21,800
Investment income	8,700	3,100	5,600
	30,500	3,100	27,400
Deductions -			
Payments to annuitants	8,750	3,150	5,600
Net losses on investments sold or exchanged	1,249	100	1,149
Transfer to endowment funds on death of annuitant	4,600		4,600
	14,599	3,250	11,349
Balances, June 30, 19___	$384,790	$96,350	$288,440

FORM 16.14

BLANK COLLEGE

STATEMENT OF CHANGES IN FUND BALANCES
UNEXPENDED PLANT FUNDS
FOR THE YEAR ENDED JUNE 30, 19__

Balances, July 1, 19__	$ 177,100
Additions -	
Governmental appropriations	$ 250,000
Investment income	11,800
Gifts and grants	37,500
Transfers from current funds	69,000
Transfers from endowment and similar funds	9,600
	$ 377,900
Deductions -	
Expenditures for plant facilities	$ 245,000
Balances, June 30, 19__	$ 310,000

FORM 16.15

BLANK COLLEGE

STATEMENT OF CHANGES IN FUND BALANCES
FUNDS FOR RENEWALS AND REPLACEMENTS
FOR THE YEAR ENDED JUNE 30, 19__

Balances, July 1, 19__	$ 47,700
Additions -	
Investment income	$ 1,500
Transfers from current funds	30,000
Transfers from auxiliary enterprises	27,500
	$ 59,000
Deductions -	
Expenditures	$ 50,700
Balances, June 30, 19__	$ 56,000

FORM 16.16

BLANK COLLEGE

STATEMENT OF CHANGES IN FUND BALANCES
FUNDS FOR RETIREMENT OF INDEBTEDNESS
FOR THE YEAR ENDED JUNE 30, 19__

Balances, July 1, 19__	$ 133,300
Additions -	
Investment income	$ 4,000
Transfers from current funds	26,000
Transfers from auxiliary enterprises	115,900
Accrued interest on sale of bonds	700
	$ 146,600
Deductions -	
Bonds retired	$ 96,000
Bond interest paid	35,000
Principal repayment on notes payable to banks	13,000
Bank charges	1,900
	$ 145,900
Balances, June 30, 19__	$ 134,000

FORM 16.17

BLANK COLLEGE

STATEMENT OF CHANGES IN NET INVESTMENT IN PLANT
FOR THE YEAR ENDED JUNE 30, 19__

Balances, July 1, 19__	$9,329,700
Additions -	
Amounts expended from -	
Unrestricted current funds	$ 21,500
Unexpended plant funds	245,000
Funds for retirement of indebtedness	109,000
Funds for renewals and replacements	12,000
	$ 387,500
Deductions -	
Disposals of plant facilities	$ 6,200
Balances, June 30, 19__	$9,711,000

FORM 16.18

BLANK COLLEGE

STATEMENT OF CHANGES IN FUND BALANCES
AGENCY FUNDS
FOR THE YEAR ENDED JUNE 30, 19__

Balances, July 1, 19__	$ 50,330
Additions	$ 72,350
Deductions	$ 61,700
Balances, June 30, 19__	$ 60,980

Form 10.19

BLANK COLLEGE

SCHEDULE OF CURRENT FUNDS REVENUES
FOR THE YEAR ENDED JUNE 30, 19___

	Total	Unrestricted	Restricted
Educational and General:			
Student Tuition and Fees -			
Tuition and Fees	$ 232,700	$ 232,700	
Test and examination fees	3,700	3,700	
Incidental fees	6,000	6,000	
University extension	8,600	8,600	
	$ 251,000	$ 251,000	
Governmental Appropriations -			
State government	$1,500,000	$1,375,000	$ 125,000
Federal government	300,000	51,500	248,500
	$1,800,000	$1,426,500	$ 373,500
Endowment Income	$ 116,100	$ 103,350	$ 12,750
Gifts -			
Alumni	$ 36,400	$ 33,000	$ 3,400
Foundations	62,000	47,000	15,000
Industrial	25,000	7,500	17,500
	$ 123,400	$ 87,500	$ 35,900
Sponsored Research -			
Federal government	$ 396,000		$ 396,000
Foundations	40,000		40,000
Industrial	41,700		41,700
	$ 477,700		$ 477,700
Other Separately Budgeted Research	$ 36,800	$ 36,800	
Other Sponsored Programs -			
Governmental	$ 44,350		$ 44,350
Nongovernmental	21,000		21,000
	$ 65,350		$ 65,350
Recovery of Indirect Costs--Sponsored Programs -			
Federal government	$ 18,300	$ 18,300	
Nonfederal government	1,700	1,700	
	$ 20,000	$ 20,000	
Sales and Services of Educational Departments -			
Engineering Testing	$ 39,700	$ 39,700	
Home economics	6,600	6,600	
	$ 46,300	$ 46,300	
Organized Activities Relating to Educational Departments -			
Computer Center	$ 12,400	$ 12,400	
Home Economics Cafeteria	11,200	11,200	
Farm	5,850	5,850	
	$ 29,450	$ 29,450	

	Total	Unrestricted	Restricted
Other Sources -			
Library fines	$ 200	$ 200	
Interest on temporary investment of current funds	2,000	400	$ 1,600
Cost of educational allowances	8,000	8,000	
Transcripts	650	650	
University news service	550	550	
Swimming pool	1,500	1,500	
	$ 12,900	$ 11,300	$ 1,600
TOTAL EDUCATIONAL AND GENERAL	$2,979,000	$2,012,200	$ 966,800
Student Aid:			
Gifts	$ 24,900		$ 24,900
Endowment income	11,500		11,500
	$ 36,400		$ 36,400
Auxiliary Enterprises:			
Bookstore	$ 200,950	$ 200,950	
Cafeteria	326,200	326,200	
Residence halls--single students	278,900	278,900	
Residence halls--married students	63,500	63,500	
Intercollegiate athletics	91,400	91,400	
College union	34,400	34,400	
	$ 995,350	$ 995,350	
TOTAL REVENUES	$4,010,750	$3,007,550	$1,003,200

FORM 16.20

BLANK COLLEGE

SCHEDULE OF CURRENT FUNDS EXPENDITURES
FOR THE YEAR ENDED JUNE 30, 19____

	Total	Unrestricted	Restricted
Educational and General:			
Instruction and Departmental Research -			
College of Liberal Arts	$ 384,000	$ 292,600	$ 91,400
College of Business and Government	122,000	85,000	37,000
College of Education	94,000	74,000	20,000
College of Engineering	249,000	176,650	72,350
School of Law	126,100	82,500	43,600
School of Pharmacy	78,300	13,300	65,000
Graduate School	126,400	84,600	41,800
Summer Session	51,200	27,750	23,450
Other instructional expenses	1,640	1,640	
	$1,232,640	$ 838,040	$ 394,600
Organized Activities Relating to Educational Departments -			
Computer Center	$ 16,500	$ 16,500	
Home Economics Cafeteria	4,200	4,200	
Farm	5,300	5,300	
	$ 26,000	$ 26,000	
Sponsored Research -			
College of Liberal Arts	$ 131,700		$ 131,700
College of Business and Government	37,500		37,500
College of Education	22,000		22,000
College of Engineering	217,600		217,600
School of Law	17,000		17,000
School of Pharmacy	51,000		51,000
Graduate School	14,225		14,225
	$ 491,025		$ 491,025
Other Separately Budgeted Research -			
Bureau of Business and Economic Research	$ 16,400	$ 16,400	
Bureau of Education Research	7,250	7,250	
Engineering Experiment Station	12,000	12,000	
Institute of Urban Research	8,000	8,000	
Bureau of Governmental Research	4,300	4,300	
Bureau of School Services	1,350	1,350	
	$ 49,300	$ 49,300	
Other Sponsored Programs -			
College of Liberal Arts	$ 32,650		$ 32,650
College of Education	23,800		23,800
School of Pharmacy	8,900		8,900
	$ 65,350		$ 65,350
Extension and Public Services -			
Office of the Director	$ 10,750	$ 8,750	$ 2,000
Extension classes and testing service	2,300	1,200	1,100
Conferences, institutes, and short courses	1,900	1,900	
Program planning and library service	1,175	675	500
Educational film production	1,100	325	775
Correspondence study	2,025	2,025	
	$ 19,250	$ 14,875	$ 4,375

	Total	Unrestricted	Restricted
Libraries -			
General	$ 55,500	$ 51,550	$ 3,950
Law	24,300	21,800	2,500
Pharmacy	12,200	7,200	5,000
	$ 92,000	$ 80,550	$ 11,450
Student Services -			
Division of student personnel	$ 9,500	$ 9,500	
Dean of women's office	12,700	12,700	
Registrar's office	12,600	12,600	
Student counselling center	4,000	4,000	
Religious life	4,800	4,800	
Placement office	9,200	9,200	
Student financial aid office	9,300	9,300	
Student activities	3,800	3,800	
Health services	23,600	23,600	
	$ 89,500	$ 89,500	
Operation and Maintenance of Physical Plant -			
Administration	$ 41,500	$ 41,500	
Janitorial services	51,200	51,200	
Maintenance and buildings	189,800	189,800	
Furniture and equipment repair	7,050	7,050	
Operation of grounds	23,400	23,400	
Maintenance of streets and drives	12,200	12,200	
General trucking	8,170	8,170	
Property insurance	10,000	10,000	
Planning and construction	11,400	11,400	
Fire protection	27,700	27,700	
Utilities	70,550	70,550	
Electrical and mechanical services	17,480	17,480	
Other maintenance renovations, and alterations of physical plant	9,450	9,450	
	$ 479,900	$ 479,900	
General Administration -			
President	$ 21,900	$ 21,900	
Executive Vice-President	17,750	17,750	
Vice-President for Academic Affairs	16,650	16,650	
Business Manager	12,100	12,100	
Accounting Office	16,300	16,300	
Bursar	12,780	12,780	
Internal Auditor	6,300	6,300	
Purchasing	11,450	11,450	
	$ 115,230	$ 115,230	
Staff Benefits -			
Employer's contribution to retirement system	$ 33,000	$ 33,000	
Employer's contribution to social security	41,100	41,100	
Group insurance	27,900	27,900	
Health, medical, and surgical insurance	11,400	11,400	
Workmen's compensation insurance	24,200	24,200	
	$ 137,600	$ 137,600	

	Total	Unrestricted	Restricted
General Institutional Expense -			
Alumni activities	$ 12,300	$ 12,300	
Nonacademic personnel	1,600	1,600	
University development	12,500	12,500	
Mail service	7,000	7,000	
Catalogues, bulletins, and directories	1,250	1,250	
Commencement	600	600	
Convocations, conferences, and institutes	2,000	2,000	
Official entertainment	600	600	
Memberships in organizations	400	400	
Other general institutional expense	120	120	
	$ 38,370	$ 38,370	
TOTAL EDUCATIONAL AND GENERAL	$2,836,165	$1,869,365	$ 966,800
Student Aid:			
Scholarships and fellowships	$ 40,250	$ 4,050	$ 36,200
Prizes and awards	400	200	200
	$ 40,650	$ 4,250	$ 36,400
Auxiliary Enterprises:			
Bookstore (including debt service of $2,500)	$ 194,620	$ 194,620	
Cafeteria (including debt service of $13,000)	297,400	297,400	
Residence halls--single (including debt service of $74,870)	244,800	244,800	
Residence halls--married (including debt service of $20,970)	56,300	56,300	
Intercollegiate athletics (including debt service of $24,000)	87,320	87,320	
College union (including debt service of $8,060)	22,210	22,210	
	$ 902,650	$ 902,650	
TOTAL EXPENDITURES	$3,779,465	$2,776,265	$1,003,200

FORM 16.21

BLANK COLLEGE

SCHEDULE OF CHANGES IN FUND BALANCES
LOAN FUNDS
FOR THE YEAR ENDED JUNE 30, 19___

	Balances July 1, 19___	Additions				Deductions		Balances June 30, 19___	Cash available for loans
		Gifts	Endowment income	Interest and invest-ment income	Transfers from current funds	Uncollec-tible notes charged off	Death and teachers' cancel-lations		
University loan funds -									
John Armstrong loan fund	$ 1,000	$ 100						$ 1,100	$ 200
(List remaining funds alphabetically)	58,133	18,360	$ 350	$ 1,300	$ 10,000	$ 11	$ 92	88,040	10,840
	$ 59,133	$18,460	$ 350	$ 1,300	$ 10,000	$ 11	$ 92	$ 89,140	$ 11,040
U.S. government participation loan funds -									
Health professions student loan fund	$ 36,500			$ 1,040			$540	$ 37,000	$ 3,280
Loan program for Cuban students	9,790			210				10,000	1,030
National defense student loan fund	82,037			1,350		$ 99	288	83,000	16,290
	$128,327			$ 2,600		$ 99	$828	$130,000	$ 20,600
TOTAL	$187,460	$18,460	$ 350	$ 3,900	$ 10,000	$110	$920	$219,140	$ 31,640

FORM 16.22

BLANK COLLEGE
SCHEDULE OF CHANGES IN FUND BALANCES
ENDOWMENT AND SIMILAR FUNDS
FOR THE YEAR ENDED JUNE 30, 19___

	Balances July 1, 19___	Additions						Deductions		Balances June 30, 19___
		Gifts	Income added to principal	Annuity funds upon death of annuitant	Net gains on investments sold or exchanged	Transfers from current funds	Transfers within endowment and similar funds	Transfers to unexpended plant funds	Transfers within endowment and similar funds	
Endowment Funds:										
Educational and general –										
Instruction and departmental research –										
Josiah Abramson	$ 198,000				$ 10,000					$ 208,000
Endowment Fund (List remaining funds alphabetically)	1,271,150				55,900					1,327,050
Libraries – (List remaining funds alphabetically)	20,500	$10,000			1,000					31,500
Student aid –										
Scholarships and fellowships (List individual funds alphabetically)	289,900		4,500	$ 1,000	12,000					312,000
Prizes and awards – (List individual funds alphabetically)	19,300		2,500		800					22,600
Loans – (List individual funds alphabetically)	15,700				700					16,400
	$1,814,550	$17,000	$1,000	$ 4,600	$ 80,400					$1,917,550
Term Endowment Funds:										
Educational and general –										
Instruction and departmental research – (List individual funds alphabetically)	$ 127,200	$10,800			$ 8,000					$ 146,000
	$ 127,200	$10,800			$ 8,000					$ 146,000
Quasi-endowment Funds:										
Educational and general –										
Instruction and departmental research – (List individual funds alphabetically)	$ 11,600				$ 2,000	$ 25,000	$ 7,000	$ 9,600	$ 7,000	$ 29,000
Student aid –										
Scholarships and fellowships (List individual funds alphabetically)	10,000				1,000	50,000				61,000
	$ 21,600				$ 3,000	$ 75,000	$ 7,000	$ 9,600	$ 7,000	$ 90,000
Net adjusted gains and losses					12,000					12,000
TOTAL	$1,963,350	$27,800	$1,000	$ 4,600	$103,400	$ 75,000	$ 7,000	$ 9,600	$ 7,000	$2,165,550

FORM 16.23

BLANK COLLEGE

SCHEDULE OF CHANGES IN FUND BALANCES
ANNUITY AND LIFE INCOME FUNDS
FOR THE YEAR ENDED JUNE 30, 19___

	Balances July 1, 19	Additions			Deductions		Balances June 30, 19
		Gifts	Investment income	Payments to annuitants	Net losses on investments sold or exchanged	Transfer on death of annuitant	
Annuity funds:							
Joseph Adams	$ 17,000		$ 600	$ 600			$ 17,000
Mary Parker Battle	6,900		320	300			6,920
James H. Higgins	21,500		930	600			21,730
Sherman Kohlmeyer	40,000		1,000	1,500			39,500
Meyer Wattingly	11,100		250	150	$ 100		11,200
	$ 96,500		$ 3,100	$ 3,150	$ 100		$ 96,350
Life income funds:							
A. Stanley Bartwell	$102,000		$ 1,900	$ 1,900	$ 1,149		$100,851
Candice C. Loman	4,600		120	120		$ 4,600	
Maybelle Parker Manning	34,200	$ 15,000	620	620			49,200
Crawford J. Powell	39,000		1,100	1,100			39,000
Janet R. Shannon	46,000		1,200	1,200			46,000
Stella Zellinger	46,589	6,800	660	660			53,389
	$272,389	$ 21,800	$ 5,600	$ 5,600	$ 1,149	$ 4,600	$288,440
TOTAL	$368,889	$ 21,800	$ 8,700	$ 8,750	$ 1,249	$ 4,600	$384,790

FORM 16.24

BLANK COLLEGE

SCHEDULE OF CHANGES IN FUND BALANCES
UNEXPENDED PLANT FUNDS
FOR THE YEAR ENDED JUNE 30, 19___

	Balances July 1, 19___	Additions					Deductions	Balances June 30, 19___
		Governmental appropriations	Gifts and grants	Investment income	Transfers from current funds	Transfers from endowment and similar funds	Expenditures for plant facilities	
Arts and crafts building	$ 11,000	$ 80,000		$ 3,500	$12,000	$9,600	$ 94,550	$ 21,550
Bell chapel fund	7,500		$10,000				6,000	11,500
Howard Hall construction	33,700						12,700	21,000
Law School building fund	28,900		17,000	1,000				46,900
Law School construction	3,940							3,940
Library building fund	28,000	$ 70,000	10,500	7,300	25,000			140,800
Library construction	16,320						14,250	2,070
Richardson Hall building fund	19,000				20,000			39,000
Rivergate landing field		15,000						15,000
Wesley science center construction	28,740	85,000			12,000		117,500	8,240
TOTAL	$177,100	$250,000	$37,500	$11,800	$69,000	$9,600	$245,000	$310,000

FORM 16.25

BLANK COLLEGE

SCHEDULE OF CHANGES IN FUND BALANCES
FUNDS FOR RENEWALS AND REPLACEMENTS
FOR THE YEAR ENDED JUNE 30, 19___

	Balances July 1, 19___	Additions			Deductions	Balances June 30, 19___
		Investment income	Transfers from current funds	Transfers from auxiliary enterprises	Expenditures	
Intercollegiate athletics	$ 2,300			$ 4,000	$ 900	$ 5,400
Bookstore	3,500			2,500	3,000	3,000
Cafeteria	2,500			3,000	5,000	500
Residence halls--single	18,500	$ 790		11,000	14,370	15,920
Residence halls--married	17,800	710		7,000	12,400	13,110
College union	2,000				1,400	600
Science laboratory	300		$20,000		11,000	9,300
Wellington observatory	600		7,000		2,630	4,970
Young recreation center	200		3,000			3,200
TOTAL	$47,700	$1,500	$30,000	$ 27,500	$50,700	$56,000

FORM 16.26

BLANK COLLEGE

SCHEDULE OF CHANGES IN FUND BALANCES
FUNDS FOR RETIREMENT OF INDEBTEDNESS
FOR THE YEAR ENDED JUNE 30, 19___

	Balances July 1, 19___	Invest- ment income	Additions			Deductions				Balances June 30, 19___
			Transfers from current funds	Transfers from auxiliary enterprises	Accrued interest on sale of bonds	Bonds Retired	Bond interest paid	Principal repayment on notes payable to banks	Bank charges	
First mortgage dormitory bonds of 1957	$ 53,520	$ 700		$ 63,870		$58,000	$ 12,240		$ 550	$ 47,300
Student apartment housing bonds of 1961	34,000	1,900		33,970		24,000	14,400		470	31,000
First mortgage dormitory bonds of 1962	29,000	1,400		18,060		8,000	4,900		560	35,000
Student infirmary bonds of 1958	6,780		$ 13,000		$ 700	6,000	3,460		320	10,700
Notes payable to banks	10,000		13,000					$13,000		10,000
TOTAL	$133,300	$ 4,000	$ 26,000	$ 115,900	$ 700	$96,000	$ 35,000	$13,000	$ 1,900	$134,000

FORM 16.27

BLANK COLLEGE

SCHEDULE OF CHANGES IN INVESTMENT IN PLANT
FOR THE YEAR ENDED JUNE 30, 19___

	Book value June 30, 19	Additions Current funds	Gifts	Deductions Disposals	Book value June 30, 19
Land:					
Campus grounds	$ 700,000				$ 700,000
Halsey field	110,000				110,000
	$ 810,000				$ 810,000
Buildings:					
Arts and crafts building	$1,128,000	$ 12,000	$ 60,000		$1,200,000
Central building	462,000				462,000
Bookstore building	670,000				670,000
Cafeteria building	491,500				491,500
College union	724,900				724,900
Halsey Hall	753,000				753,000
Power plant	1,480,000				1,480,000
Rosen House	980,600				980,600
Wellington observatory	260,000				260,000
Young recreation center	339,000				339,000
	$7,289,000	$ 12,000	$ 60,000		$7,361,000
Improvements other than buildings:					
Fencing	$ 6,250				$ 6,250
Howard mall	3,400				3,400
Parking lot	20,000				20,000
Roadways	14,350				14,350
Underground piping	296,000				296,000
	$ 340,000				$ 340,000
Equipment:					
Arts and crafts building	$ 868,200	$ 4,000	$ 2,200	$ 700	$ 873,700
Central building	381,250	41,700		3,450	419,500
Bookstore building	37,900	8,900		2,400	44,400
Cafeteria building	42,900	6,300			49,200
College union	54,650	6,350			61,000
Halsey Hall	79,110	8,240		1,050	86,300
Power plant	1,057,450	13,250		8,900	1,061,800
Rosen House	61,600	12,400			74,000
Wellington observatory	86,520	2,630	850		90,000
Young recreation center	19,400	700	400	400	20,100
	$2,688,980	$104,470	$ 3,450	$ 16,900	$2,780,000
Construction in progress	$ 481,000	$ 53,000	$116,000		$ 650,000
TOTAL INVESTMENT IN PLANT	$11,608,980	$169,470	$179,450	$ 16,900	$11,941,000

FORM 16.28

BLANK COLLEGE

SCHEDULE OF REVENUES AND EXPENDITURES
INTERCOLLEGIATE ATHLETICS
FOR THE YEAR ENDED JUNE 30, 19__

Revenues:		
Sports -		
Basketball		$ 8,940
Football		76,510
Spring sports		970
		$86,420
Other -		
Radio rights		$ 4,000
Concessions		980
		$ 4,980
	TOTAL REVENUES	$91,400
Expenditures:		
General administration -		
Salaries and wages		$15,800
Office supplies		1,880
Postage and freight		950
Telephone and telegraph		800
Travel		990
Heat, light, and water		4,000
		$24,420
Sports -		
Salaries and wages		$23,590
Publicity		3,100
Travel		6,980
Office supplies		1,940
Telephone and telegraph		3,290
		$38,900
Transfers to plant funds for -		
Retirement of indebtedness		$20,000
Renewals and replacements		4,000
		$24,000
	TOTAL EXPENDITURES	$87,320
EXCESS OF REVENUES OVER EXPENDITURES AND		
TRANSFERS		$ 4,080

FORM 16.29

BLANK COLLEGE

SCHEDULE OF REVENUES AND EXPENDITURES
RESIDENCE HALLS--SINGLE STUDENTS
FOR THE YEAR ENDED JUNE 30, 19__

Revenues:	
Room rentals--regular	$268,320
Room rentals--summer session	8,400
Guest rooms	1,200
Miscellaneous	980
TOTAL REVENUES	$278,900
Expenditures:	
Salaries and wages	$ 64,700
Office supplies	1,970
Travel	3,940
Telephone and telegraph	6,980
Janitorial, cleaning, and laundry supplies	17,350
Heat, light, and water	56,900
Insurance	9,100
Repairing and servicing to equipment	2,470
Other	6,520
	$169,930
Transfers to plant funds for -	
Retirement of indebtedness	$ 63,870
Renewals and replacements	11,000
	$ 74,870
TOTAL EXPENDITURES	$244,800
EXCESS OF REVENUES OVER EXPENDITURES AND TRANSFERS	$ 34,100

FORM 16.30

BLANK COLLEGE

SCHEDULE OF REVENUES AND EXPENDITURES
RESIDENCE HALLS--MARRIED STUDENTS
FOR THE YEAR ENDED JUNE 30, 19__

Revenues:	
Apartment rentals	$62,530
Guest rooms	600
Miscellaneous	370
TOTAL REVENUES	$63,500
Expenditures:	
Salaries and wages	$12,000
Office supplies	490
Telephone and telegraph	2,100
Janitorial, cleaning, and laundry supplies	5,200
Heat, light, and water	10,400
Insurance	3,300
Repairing and servicing to equipment	390
Equipment	1,080
Other	370
	$35,330
Transfers to plant funds for -	
Retirement of indebtedness	$13,970
Renewals and replacements	7,000
	$20,970
TOTAL EXPENDITURES	$56,300
EXCESS OF REVENUES OVER EXPENDITURES AND TRANSFERS	$ 7,200

FORM 16.31

BLANK COLLEGE

SCHEDULE OF REVENUES AND EXPENDITURES
BOOKSTORE
FOR THE YEAR ENDED JUNE 30, 19___

Revenues:
Sales of books	$154,900
Sales of supplies	37,400
Miscellaneous sales	8,650
TOTAL REVENUES	$200,950

Expenditures:
Cost of sales	$141,280
Gross Profit on Sales	$.59,670
Administrative salaries	$ 21,700
Salaries and wages--selling	22,360
Office supplies	270
Janitorial supplies	400
Postage and freight	920
Telephone and telegraph	670
Travel	250
Pricing supplies	110
Heat, light, and water	3,600
Equipment	560
	$ 50,840
Transfers to plant funds for renewals and replacements	$ 2,500
TOTAL EXPENDITURES	$ 53,340
EXCESS OF REVENUES OVER EXPENDITURES AND TRANSFERS	$ 6,330

FORM 16.32

BLANK COLLEGE

SCHEDULE OF REVENUES AND EXPENDITURES
CAFETERIA
FOR THE YEAR ENDED JUNE 30, 19__

Revenues:
Cafeteria sales	$267,810
Snack bar sales	41,900
Faculty dining room sales	16,490
TOTAL REVENUES	$326,200

Expenditures:
Food purchased	$159,560
Administrative salaries	$ 32,600
Salaries and wages--other	53,750
Office supplies	930
Janitorial and cleaning supplies	4,800
Laundering and uniforms	4,950
Tableware and linens	7,340
Telephone and telegraph	620
Heat, light, and water	9,100
Insurance	2,150
Repairing and servicing equipment	4,020
Equipment	3,900
Other	680
	$124,840
Transfers to plant funds for -	
Retirement of indebtedness	$ 10,000
Renewals and replacements	3,000
	$ 13,000
TOTAL EXPENDITURES	$297,400
EXCESS OF REVENUES OVER EXPENDITURES AND TRANSFERS	$ 28,800

FORM 16.33

BLANK COLLEGE

SCHEDULE OF REVENUES AND EXPENDITURES
COLLEGE UNION
FOR THE YEAR ENDED JUNE 30, 19__

Revenues:
Room rentals	$15,120
Games rooms	14,980
Barber shop	1,100
Vending machines	3,200
TOTAL REVENUES	$34,400

Expenditures:
Administrative salaries	$ 5,600
Recreational salaries and wages	5,060
Office supplies	460
Recreational supplies	270
Heat, light, and water	1,050
Janitorial and cleaning supplies	780
Repairing and servicing of equipment	290
Equipment	640
	$14,150
Transfers to plant funds for -	
Retirement of indebtedness	$ 8,060
TOTAL EXPENDITURES	$22,210
EXCESS OF REVENUES OVER EXPENDITURES AND TRANSFERS	$12,190

FORM 16.34

BLANK COLLEGE

SCHEDULE OF INVESTMENTS BY FUND GROUPS
JUNE 30, 19___

	Current Funds		Endowment and Similar Funds	Annuity and Life Income Funds	Plant Funds			Agency Funds
	Un-restricted	Restricted			Unexpended	Renewals and Replacements	Retirement of Indebtedness	
U.S. Treasury bills	$100,000	$52,000	$ 180,000	$ 33,980	$290,000	$ 47,500	$ 40,000	$ 49,200
U.S. Treasury notes			107,550	125,910			57,000	
Corporate bonds			237,600	107,900				
Preferred stocks			295,700	70,600				
Common stocks			959,700					
Mortgage notes								
Certificates of deposit			50,000	12,000				
Real estate, less accumulated depreciation of $29,700 and $4,200, respectively	96,000		340,300	30,610				
TOTAL	$196,000	$52,000	$2,170,850	$ 381,000	$290,000	$ 47,500	$ 97,000	$ 49,200

FORM 16.35

BLANK COLLEGE

SCHEDULE OF LONG-TERM NOTES AND BONDS PAYABLE
FOR THE YEAR ENDED JUNE 30, 19___

	First mortgage dormitory bonds of 1957	Student apartment housing bonds of 1961	First mortgage dormitory bonds of 1962	Student infirmary bonds of 1968	Notes payable to banks	Total
Balances, July 1, 19___	$1,036,000	$ 760,000	$ 300,000	$ 200,000	$ 143,000	$2,439,000
Deductions - Bonds retired and note payments	58,000	24,000	8,000	6,000	13,000	109,000
Balances, June 30, 19___	$ 978,000	$ 736,000	$ 292,000	$ 194,000	$ 130,000	$2,330,000
Unexpended plant funds - Bonds payable						$ 100,000
Investment in plant - Notes payable						130,000
Bonds payable						2,100,000
						$2,330,000

FORM 16.36

BLANK COLLEGE

BALANCE SHEET
JUNE 30, 19___

ASSETS

CURRENT FUNDS:
Unrestricted -
Cash .... $ 177,620
Temporary investments, at cost
(approximate market $225,000) 196,000
Accounts receivable--students, less
allowance for doubtful accounts
of $5,620
Accounts receivable--other, less
allowance for doubtful accounts
of $2,000 6,080
State appropriations receivable 1,000
Inventories, at cost 300,000
Prepaid expenses and deferred charges 91,800
    5,400 $ 777,900

Restricted -
Cash .... $ 12,500
Temporary investments, at cost
(approximate market $55,000) 52,000
Accounts receivable, principally
agencies of the U.S. government 145,000   209,500

    TOTAL CURRENT FUNDS $ 987,400

LIABILITIES AND FUND BALANCES

CURRENT FUNDS:
Unrestricted -
Accounts payable .... $ 553,000
Due to Teacher Retirement System 9,600
Deferred revenues 90,000
Provision for encumbrances 5,000
Fund balances from -
Gifts $68,940
Other .... 51,360 120,300 $ 777,900

Restricted -
Accounts payable .... $ 6,000
Provision for endowment income
stabilization 14,000
Fund balances 189,500   209,500

    TOTAL CURRENT FUNDS $ 987,400

Note: Forms 36, 37, 38, and 39 illustrate the applied method of reporting unrestricted gifts in the current funds group of accounts. Statements for reporting the transactions of the other fund groups would remain the same as illustrated.

FORM 16.37

BLANK COLLEGE

STATEMENT OF CURRENT FUNDS REVENUES, EXPENDITURES, AND TRANSFERS
FOR THE YEAR ENDED JUNE 30, 19___

	Total	Unrestricted	Restricted
Revenues:			
Educational and General -			
Student Tuition and Fees	$ 251,000	$ 251,000	
Governmental Appropriations	1,800,000	1,426,500	$ 373,500
Endowment Income (including $1,900 received from funds held in trust by others)	116,100	103,350	12,750
Gifts Applied	92,115	56,215	35,900
Sponsored Research -			
Governmental	396,000		396,000
Nongovernmental	81,700		81,700
Other Separately Budgeted Research	36,800	36,800	
Other Sponsored Programs -			
Governmental	44,350		44,350
Nongovernmental	21,000		21,000
Recovery of Indirect Costs--Sponsored Programs	20,000	20,000	
Sales and Services of Educational Departments	46,300	46,300	
Organized Activities Relating to Educational Departments	29,450	29,450	
Other Sources	12,900	11,300	1,600
TOTAL EDUCATIONAL AND GENERAL	$2,947,715	$1,980,915	$ 966,800
Student Aid	36,400		36,400
Auxiliary Enterprises	995,350	995,350	
TOTAL REVENUES	$3,979,465	$2,976,265	$1,003,200

	Total	Unrestricted	Restricted
Expenditures:			
Educational and General -			
Instruction and Departmental Research	$1,232,640	$ 838,040	$ 394,600
Organized Activities Relating to Educational Departments	26,000	26,000	
Sponsored Research	491,025		491,025
Other Separately Budgeted Research	49,300	49,300	
Other Sponsored Programs	65,350		65,350
Extension and Public Services	19,250	14,875	4,375
Libraries	92,000	80,550	11,450
Student Services	89,500	89,500	
Operation and Maintenance of Physical Plant	479,900	479,900	
General Administration	115,230	115,230	
Staff Benefits	137,600	137,600	
General Institutional Expense	38,370	38,370	
TOTAL EDUCATIONAL AND GENERAL	$2,836,165	$1,869,365	$ 966,800
Student Aid	40,650	4,250	36,400
Auxiliary Enterprises (including debt service of $143,400)	902,650	902,650	
TOTAL EXPENDITURES	$3,779,465	$2,776,265	$1,003,200
Transfers:			
To -			
Quasi-endowment funds	$ 75,000	$ 75,000	
Plant funds for -			
Additions	69,000	69,000	
Renewals and replacements	30,000	30,000	
Retirement of indebtedness	26,000	26,000	
TOTAL TRANSFERS	$ 200,000	$ 200,000	
EXCESS OF REVENUES OVER EXPENDITURES AND TRANSFERS	$ -	$ -	$ -

FORM 16.38

BLANK COLLEGE

STATEMENT OF CHANGES IN FUND BALANCES
UNRESTRICTED CURRENT FUNDS--GIFTS
FOR THE YEAR ENDED JUNE 30, 19__

Balances, July 1, 19__	$37,655
Additions -	
Gifts received from -	
Alumni	$13,700
Corporations	41,000
Foundations	28,000
Other	4,800
	$87,500
Deductions -	
Gifts applied as current fund revenues	$56,215
Balances, June 30, 19__	$68,940

FORM 16.39

BLANK COLLEGE

STATEMENT OF CHANGES IN FUND BALANCES
UNRESTRICTED CURRENT FUNDS--OTHER
FOR THE YEAR ENDED JUNE 30, 19___

	Total	Unallocated	Allocated
Balances, July 1, 19___	$ 58,260	$ 48,260	$ 10,000
Additions -			
Excess of revenues over expenditures and transfers	$ -	$ -	
Release of prior year encumbrances	3,100	3,100	
	$ 3,100	$ 3,100	
Deductions -			
Transfers to loan funds	$ 10,000	$ 10,000	
Transfers between unallocated and allocated -			
Amounts included in current expenditures on projects for which			
funds had previously been allocated--student activities		$ 4,000	$ (4,000)
Allocations for specific future operating purposes--			
student activities		$ (5,000)	$ 5,000
		(1,000)	1,000
Balances, June 30, 19___	$ 51,360	$ 40,360	$ 11,000

Index